MW00575187

Remembering Peasants

A Personal History of a Vanished World

PATRICK JOYCE

SCRIBNER

New York London Toronto Sydney New Delhi

Scribner
An Imprint of Simon & Schuster, LLC
1230 Avenue of the Americas
New York, NY 10020

First Scribner hardcover edition February 2024

Manufactured in the United States of America

10 9 8 7 6 5 4 3 2 1

Library of Congress Cataloging-in-Publication Data

Names: Joyce, Patrick, 1945– author.
Title: Remembering peasants : a personal history of a vanished world / Patrick Joyce.
Description: First Scribner hardcover edition. | New York, NY : Scribner, 2024. | Includes bibliographical references. | Identifiers: LCCN 2023046380
Subjects: LCSH: Peasants—Europe—History. | Peasants—Europe—Social conditions. | Peasants—Europe—Social life and customs.
Classification: LCC HD1531.5 .J69 2024 | DDC 305.5/633094--dc23/eng/20231005
LC record available at https://lccn.loc.gov/2023046380

ISBN 978-1-6680-3108-7
ISBN 978-1-6680-3110-0 (ebook)

For the peasants, and in memory of Seán Seoighe, 1941–2002

Contents

Stone upon stone
On stone a stone
And on that a stone
Another stone

From a Polish folk song, after Wiesław Myśliwski

Prologue

We do not easily remember peasants. The realities of their lives are a dim presence in the historical record. We catch only glimpses. These are two glimpses into the great obscurity that is the centuries-old peasant past of Europe. The first is from the Poland of a century ago:

> Every field knows its owner, the Earth is indignant at every crime committed on its face. The moon watches and prayers are still said to it. The stars answer a woman or man who knows the right way to ask them. Nothing bad should be said near water. The wind listens and talks . . . While animals do not know as much as man they know things he does not, the properties of plants and substances for instance, which are shown to men by animals. Some animals understand and condemn the immoral acts of man, the bee will never stay with the thief, the stork and the swallow leave a farm when an evil deed has been committed there . . . The lark, which soars so high, is the favourite bird of the Angels; during a storm they hold it in their hands, and when, with every lightning flash the heaven opens, it is allowed to look in.[1]

This way of understanding the Earth and the heavens is part of a past we have now lost, lost in less than a single lifetime, lost with barely a sign of its loss in a present that is obsessed with itself. The second glimpse is from the mid-1990s. The place is the Bluestack Mountains in Ireland's far north-west Donegal. A man who had come from the outside in search of the eternal peasant walks and talks with a man called Jimmy as they pass along one of the old roads. It is very late at night. The night is that of the long past of peasant Europe:

> 'Not a light,' [Jimmy] said. 'Not a light.' I was puzzled by the remark and didn't answer. We walked on. 'They're all asleep,' he went on. 'Not a man up. And you see the way we haven't met a one on the road? Not a one.' I wondered who Jimmy expected to meet on the road at 3 a.m., but I grunted a soft assent. We walked on along the ascending road, once more in silence. 'Not a one,' Jimmy repeated after a while. And then, as though he sensed my perplexity, he added, 'I remember the time there be ones up and down this road all night, until dawn, until morning they be comin' and goin'. Comin' and goin', you see, ramblin', to the cards and music and dancin' and all. Piles of them. Always.' 'All night?' 'All night.'[2]

Agriculture in Europe first appeared around 8,500 years ago in what is now modern-day Turkey, spreading west and north thereafter and appearing in Britain, Ireland and northern Europe approximately 6,000 years ago. At one time, not so long ago in the greater scheme of things, the vast majority of people on the globe were workers on the land, so that it can be said that almost all of us are in one way or another the children of peasants. Now it is all ending, vanishing before our inattentive eyes. These thousands of years of history are coming to an end.

In the Introduction to his remarkable work on late twentieth-century peasant experience, *Into Their Labours*, John Berger wrote that peasants are, in their essential nature, survivors.[3] He went on to say, 'For the first time ever it is possible that the class of survivors may not survive. Within a century there may be no more peasants. In western Europe, if the plans work out as the economic planners have foreseen, there will be no more peasants within twenty-five years.' He wrote these words over a quarter of a century ago, and got it very nearly right. The planners won. Already, by the time he was writing *Into Their Labours*, he knew that, after millennia, 'The remarkable continuity of peasant experience and the peasant view of the world acquires, as it is threatened with extinction, an unprecedented and unexpected urgency.'[4]

This vanishing has since 1950 been worldwide, as the majority of the world's population has come to live an urban life. As the great social historian Eric Hobsbawm recognized, this change is perhaps the most fundamental one the contemporary world has seen, all the other vast changes notwithstanding: 'The most dramatic and far-reaching social change of the second half of this [the twentieth] century, and the one which cuts us off for ever from the world of the past, is the death of the peasantry. For since the neolithic era most human beings had lived off the land and its livestock or harvested the sea as fishers. With the exception of Britain, peasants and farmers remained a massive part of the occupied population even in industrialized countries until well into the twentieth century.'[5]

If we are cut off from the past, we are also cut off from ourselves. The epigraph to Berger's *Into Their Labours* is taken from St John 4:38: 'Others have laboured and ye are entered into their labours.' We are indeed entered into the labour of peasants and so have a debt to them, a debt which is also one we have to ourselves. Debts should be redeemed. If we are in a sense ultimately the children of peasants, then a kind of redemption may lie in honouring our forebears, for surely children should pay respect to their parents, which is to say, their ancestors.

Perhaps more than respect is due, namely homage, which is simply a public show of respect. This book is an attempt to pay that homage, to remember the goodness of peasants, to respect their dignity, to reflect on the delicacy and grace of those who have so often been called ignorant, boorish, a thousand insults theirs to be borne, the victims of history as they so often were, and are. Theirs was a culture of richness and complexity, made all the more rich and complex in the teeth of the privations they so often had to endure. So, theirs is a history of abjection and subjection too. Respect must include this, must acknowledge the forces tearing them apart as well as welding them together, forces from within as well as without.

Many in our time take great interest in the destruction of the planet. While we may all in the end pay a common price for this destruction, peasants have already paid theirs. Not just with environmental destruction and agribusiness in recent decades but over centuries, for the great victims of modernity and progress have been peasants. Large numbers of those who today are concerned with and knowledgeable about the destruction of the natural world have hardly any idea of what peasants are or were. Peasants are among the closest of humankind to nature, knowing intimately and with great depth what nature is, even though their idea of nature is assuredly not ours. Perhaps we might even learn something from them, something about the 'nature' we think we know, and something about what we call progress has done to nature.

Peasants were, after all, right to distrust progress. We may all have to learn before too long how to be survivors, and peasants, the class of survivors, have things to teach us. They face extinction just as we may do. Peasants come from a world that in essence is not capitalist, although they have coexisted with capitalism for centuries. They do not conceive of a world of unlimited increase, the world of progress that is, for they know things are finite. Capitalism lives for unlimited increase, which it sees only by looking to the future, upon which it depends (*credit* always refers to future possibility). In its nature capitalism must erase the past to realize this future. Peasants hope for the future but do not forget the past.

Peasants have been, and in some respects still are, the foundation that holds the whole edifice of society up, though this too is forgotten. For most of history, people have lived their lives as peasants. Empires have survived for centuries, sat upon the backs of peasants. Landlords have received money for which they do not have to labour and enforced order upon peasants on behalf of the state. The state has depended on the taxes of peasants. Peasants have fought their wars: the decimated youth of France in 1918 was a peasant youth, for peasants historically were always the first to be put in the front lines. 'What the skeleton is to anatomy, the peasant is to history, its essential, hidden support.'[6] And so culture is made possible, the culture that gets put in the great museums, not the age-old culture of peasants. Their fate is at best to be of the ethnos, of the folk, that of the ethnographic museum.

The past is never over. It still belongs to us even when we are cut off from it. And we constantly betray what is ours. Seamus Deane, in reflecting on the Irish famine, wrote these words: 'None of us is beyond betrayal, a betrayal that will always make us foreign, especially to ourselves and to a past that is ours but to which we only weakly belong, since it asks more questions of us than we do of it.'[7] We owe it to both those who survived and those who did not that we remember whatever they had to endure. If we are to be less foreign to ourselves then we should recognize that peasants belong to us.

This book's title is *Remembering Peasants*: its plan is simple: in the first chapter I give an account of the losing of peasant worlds, what I call 'The Vanishing', for after 1945 the demise of this way of being was rapid, more rapid in western than in eastern Europe. My next concern is the question of what a peasant is. The answer to the question is not a simple one: it demands a two-fold answer, the first a matter of definition, the second to do with how the name carries a curse. The peasant is almost invariably the most cursed human being, since they exist at the bottom of the edifice of society while holding the whole thing up.

The variety and complexity of peasant society are then treated in the first chapter in the second section of the book. In this section I consider worlds that are now lost, and here I bring forward for the reader the homes, the labour, the beliefs, the religion, the suffering and the creativity of the people I consider. Also, their own fightback against power. In the last section my subject is twofold, first how peasants at the waning of the old order remember themselves, and then how we remember them (or, more often, have forgotten them, or have never had them in mind in the first place). The means of this remembrance are considered, particularly the museum, which these days has become perhaps the primary institution of contemporary remembrance.

While I will explore Europe as a whole in what follows, I concentrate on Ireland, Poland and to a lesser degree Italy. And within these nations I focus on particular parts, the Irish West, the Polish

South, the Italian South, places where peasant culture has endured longer than elsewhere. All three are also places to which many others have been drawn, for each represents a sort of dream, a locus of imagined peasant worlds that are in varying guises held to be elemental, nearer to the origin and meaning of things than the modern world is felt to be. The Irish West, where the playwright J. M. Synge collected peasant stories along the roads of Mayo; the Lucania (now Basilicata) of Carlo Levi where 'Christ stopped at Eboli', beyond which point the ancient elemental reigns; and Galicia, so called in Austrian imperial days, the land of the border, of the deep peasant, but also of the deep Jew, for who can write about European peasants without considering European Jews.[8] The dream as well as the reality of peasants is important.

John Berger wrote in 1987 that 'very few peasants become artists – occasionally perhaps the son or daughter of peasants has done so.' He writes about the lack of records of peasant experience – some songs, a few autobiographies, very little: 'This lack means that the peasant's soul is as unfamiliar or unknown to most urban people as are his physical inventories and the material conditions of his labour.'[9] This is so. But while Berger is right, it is only in part, for if the peasant's own speaking voice is absent (there are in truth only a tiny few memoirs, given the peasant millions who have lived and died) there are many more than a few songs. And through ethnographic study we now know a great deal of much else. Yet this is almost always mediated knowledge – vastly illuminating, but often historically about things called the 'folk' and their 'lore', these terms meaning nothing to peasants themselves. Knowledge from the outside, in other words. There is also the knowledge as well of tax collectors, policemen, lawyers, recruiting sergeants, land surveyors and many others of the 'official' world. So we interpret, hearing only the echoes of the soul.

However, I hear the echoes of the body as well as the soul, for, like some of my interlocutors in the book, I am the son of peasants, although that word is mostly not used in Ireland. Perhaps between us we have something to say that is different from the academic literature on peasants. As the London-born child of Irish rural immigrant parents, now a man of seventy-eight years of age, I am a sort of relict of what we have lost. A relict that will in turn pretty soon be gone. I had some immediate experience of the old world, and this is the reason I write this book as I do. It is a homage to my own.

PART ONE

Endings

I.

The Vanishing

You travel north from my father's house on the Galway–Mayo border in Ireland's far West. North and west of you and never far away lies the Atlantic Ocean. Belderrig is reached after a long drive, for the county of Mayo is big, and the narrow country roads take long to travel. Though not as long as in the days of J. M. Synge, that great theatrical fabulist of peasants, who over a century ago took the same roads as me as he went north into Mayo in search of rural Ireland.[1] Along the way the land is thinly populated, less than 10 per cent of the population density of England, less than a third that of Ireland as a whole. Once, before the Great Famine of the 1840s, the county teemed with people, so many that the famine could not take them all. Despite its catastrophic failure in the 1840s, the potato crop kept them alive after that time just as it had done so before. In Mayo the ridges on which the potato was grown centuries ago are still visible in the landscape, still there, but now grown over.[2] There is an old Irish proverb about potato ridges: three times the life of a whale is the lifespan of a ridge, and three times the life of a ridge is the lifespan of the world.

Belderrig (Béal Deirg) is a tiny and remote settlement at Mayo's northern Atlantic margin. It lies 4 miles to the west of Céide Fields, a prehistoric landscape of field systems and domestic and ritual structures created by Neolithic farmers and said to date back 5,700 years. Céide Fields is recognized by UNESCO as the most extensive Stone Age monument in the world and the oldest enclosed landscape in Europe. The low straight piles of stones are an indication of land cleared for pastures, and perhaps for crops too. Certainly, later on, there are clear indications of the arable 'Celtic field' type common in north-western Europe and lasting from the later Bronze

Age (two and a half millennia ago) for almost 2,000 years. The blanket bog under which the 5 square miles of the Céide Fields lie is up to 16 feet deep in places, as it slopes down in a great horizontal arc to the North Atlantic below.

In 1974, Seamus Heaney composed a poem called 'Belderg'. Here are two stanzas from it:

> A landscape fossilized,
> Its stone-wall patternings
> Repeated before our eyes
> In the stone walls of Mayo.
> Before I turned to go
> He talked about persistence,
> A congruence of lives,
> How, stubbed and cleared of stones,
> His home accrued growth rings
> Of iron, flint and bronze.[3]

Iron, flint and bronze: the ages of human culture, going back 3,000 years and more before Christ, the rings accruing around a home that is, however now, in the present. The words speak of recurrence, of persistence and of a congruence of lives over great stretches of historical time, the ghosts of the past not deserting us. The potato ridges speak about a time that is shorter, but it is the same things that are spoken of. For the potato is still sown here around Céide Fields just as stone walls are still built.

The site was discovered in the 1930s by the local schoolmaster Patrick Caulfield when out cutting his own turf (turf is peat, cut then in Ireland by all for fuel, but these days by fewer and fewer). His son Seamus, an archaeologist, went on to excavate the site and so to end this long vanishing, even though the bog remains relentless in its annual growth, fed as it is by the immense wetness of the place. The houses are built to withstand the Atlantic winds, which are as constant as the Atlantic rains. It is Seamus the son who talks in the poem, it is his home that is mentioned. And it is Seamus the poet who listens, the poet who was the son of a small farmer like those around here, a man who had a deep affinity with this agricultural landscape. Heaney's father farmed further north, although Mayo's north is well on the way to Heaney's, and Belderrig's churchyard is full of the 'Macs' who proliferate in the North.

My father came from the same kind of people as live and lived here and, 50 miles to the south, in Galway's north, in Rosshill graveyard beside the village of Clonbur, lie many Joyces. For this part of Ireland has of old been called the Joyce Country, Dúiche Seoighe in Irish. Dúiche is derived from *Dúchas*, which is a term akin to 'patrimony' in French. It is an Irish language noun that fuses the sense of the innate quality of a person or a way of life with the idea of these being located in a particular place. The idea of an inheritance handed down is also present, one that makes one truly a native of a place. The word conveys much more than 'country' in its English translation ('duchy' is also there, in the English word), more than the sense of 'home' also, which it nonetheless embraces.

Dúiche Seoighe is essentially the northern part of Connemara, and so, like Belderrig, Irish-speaking. The last remnant of the little that is left of the old Gaelic culture. The Joyces lie with ample numbers of Coynes, Flynns, Lydons and others, the family name in Ireland still a great marker of place. The Bowes of my mother's side of the family lie with the Kents, Corishes, Englishes and Sherlocks in a different Ireland, that of Wexford in the island's south-east corner. But, in one sense, that Ireland is pretty much the same as Joyce Country – it too is the land of the small farmer, though there the farms are bigger if not greatly prosperous, at least around the 50-acre mark of my mother's place, the 'home place' as the house and farm are called in Ireland.[4]

Unlike Heaney's parents, mine were forced to leave Ireland in the 1930s. My father first went to England in 1929, then back and forth for a while working, as they all did, on 'the buildings' (construction). Then finally he settled in London, marrying my mother, Kitty Bowe, in 1944. Three years younger than my father, she first went to England in 1932. Kitty was the daughter of a farmer better off than some around him, though what advantage the family had in terms of good land, and more of it than in the West, was whittled away by the ten mouths that had to be fed (those being the mouths that survived, four children dying very young), and by a father, a spoiled only child by all accounts, who is said to have drunk away the equivalent of three farms of land.

Four out of five of my father's siblings emigrated, three to the USA, for long the favoured destination of the western parts of Ireland. On the somewhat more benign, eastern side of my mother's Wexford, three out of the ten who survived left for England, and most of the girls who did not go to England were spread around Ireland and far from home. Born to leave, as they say, at least then, emigration having been the pattern for centuries, especially in the post-famine West.

This is the face of one of those who stayed, a face I loved. The photograph above is of my cousin Seán Joyce (1941–2002), Seán Seoighe, a small farmer-cum-peasant. A man of whom it was always said that he was of the old school, even by the old schoolers themselves. He was the youngest child, and the only son, and thus the one who inherited. A 'peasant proprietor', in fact, a figure that in the Ireland of his childhood and youth was the ideal of the newly independent state, a nation only nineteen years old when he was born. This state, made in the image of the imagined peasant, was conservative and clerical. It is an image many of the Irish now prefer to forget. This forgetting, understandable in part, is in larger part a loss of the greatest magnitude.

There is a certain distance to Seán's outward gaze: the photograph was taken by a holidaying American 'stranger' (with no Irish connections but those in the head). It seems to me the sitter would have found it awkward to present himself to the camera, unlike the posing of the holiday 'snap', for which he would have tidied himself up (the Sweet Afton cigarettes bulge from the pocket of his none-too-tidy shirt).[5] His hands, just visible here, tell of the peasant, for they are big, made big by toil. Seán was a big man, 6 feet and 5 inches. At work early, as the children were then, he left school early too, a farmer at thirteen years old, his father Stephen dead before his time, just like Stephen's brother, my father Johnny. Seán sits in the kitchen of my father's house, the house he had to leave, the new house of 1905, nearer the road (but still a long way up Kilbride Mountain) than the old one before it. The mountains took Seán's life, for he worked all hours, in all weathers, until his legs gave way and he could walk no longer. He lived his life alone, a bachelor, well cared for by his kin, who managed his obduracy as best they could. Seán was a hill bachelor, as such men are called in William Trevor's literary account.[6] The ending that was the vanished world of the isolated hill bachelors is only one vanishing in this place of many vanishings, vanishings past and present, those of famine and massive migration.

The Joyce Country is a small block of land to the east of which are two wide lakes, Corrib, and Mask, to Corrib's north. On the other, western, side lies the Atlantic Ocean. Hemmed in and separated by water as it is, it is a remote and difficult region to access. The area straddles the county of Galway in the south and Mayo in the north. Immediately to the south of it once lay the single biggest landed estate in Ireland, the almost 200,000 acres known at the time of the famine as the Martin Estate. The late Tim Robinson was a renowned chronicler of Connemara and its vanishings. In 1995, Robinson edited the journal of a survey of the Martin Estate made in

1853, the aim of the survey having been to present to potential buyers an investment opportunity of unrivalled possibility, now that the estate was free of the encumbrance of living souls. This is a passage from the journal:

> The very dogs which had lost their masters or were driven from their homes became roving denizens of this district and lived on the unburied or partially buried corpses of their late owners & others, and there was no help for it, as all were prostrate alike, the territory so extensive, and the people so secluded and unknown.[7]

This next image is a different sort of photograph. An 'art' photograph, one might say. It is titled 'Irlande 1972'. It is from a collection of the great Czech photographer Josef Koudelka entitled *Exiles*. The three men kneel at the summit of Croagh Patrick in the far West of Ireland, the Atlantic Ocean immediately below. Croagh Patrick has been a site of pilgrimage for over a millennium and a half. In the background is Clew Bay, and the town of Westport lies only a few miles east of here. There is no mistaking Koudelka's employment of the imagery of the Crucifixion in the photograph.

The man on the right of the image is my cousin Seán Joyce, then only twenty-eight years old. Again, as in the first image, he looks out at the camera and the man who holds it with some suspicion. On the left of the central figure is Paddy Kenny (Pádraig Ó Cionnaith), who was married to Seán's sister Sally. In the middle is a close friend and neighbour, Martin Mangan (Máirtín Maingín). Again, the size of their hands is apparent, the sign of those who work the land. They lean on blackthorn sticks, which they will have fashioned with these hands. I do not know for sure if that year they had walked the twenty and more miles over the hills from the Joyce Country, but they did this often, as was the custom (there were precious few cars around locally in 1972 anyway). Many did and still do make part of the ascent of Croagh Patrick on their knees.

The men seem separated from the others around them, not only by distance but by the gravity of their demeanour; the other figures seem to be admiring the view, the three men are aware of this holy place, where St Patrick is held to have appeared. The dark hair of the three men is striking, like so many from the West. They wear suits, to us perhaps a strange garb for such a journey as theirs, but this is a sign of their respect, of gravity realized. My kin have somehow become epic, monumental. Such is the power of the photograph. They have become as monuments to the vanishing of peasant Europe.

My eyes look up from these photographs of Seán Seoighe, and I see that the span of his lifetime is essentially the same as that of the end of peasant Europe.

The urban-dwelling proportion of the world's population has increased from just over 20 per cent of the total in 1950 to approaching 60 per cent today. Most of these people live in the cities of the Global South, once the locations of little but the vast peasant millions. The pace quickens: between 1991 and 2019 the proportion of the world's population engaged in agriculture fell from 44 per cent to 27 per cent. And yet not so long ago the world looked very different. Within my own span of years, as an adolescent I saw the Spanish peasantry labouring in the fields in the poverty-disfigured Spain of the early 1960s, riding for days and nights the fourth-class wooden railway carriages of the time, the people of the land I passed through constantly getting on and off the train, something easy to do, given the slowness of the passage through the great open spaces of Castile and Andalucía. And I remember the delight and kindness shown us by these peasant fellow travellers as they came and went in the darkness of the night, ever ready as they were to share their food with us, and pass their goatskin-covered wine casks to those reciprocally delighted working-class Irish London boys, visitors from another world now united in the comradeship of the fourth-class carriage.

Between 1950 and 1970 the Spanish peasantry almost halved in number. Yet this still seemed to be a world that had changed little over centuries and would continue to survive into the future. We did not know then that it would end so abruptly. In Spain agricultural workers formed just under half the population in 1950. This was reduced to 14.5 per cent by 1980 (to 17.6 per cent from a similar earlier number in Portugal), and to less than 5 per cent of the workforce by 2020.[8] The Andalucíans had gone to neighbouring Catalonia, Barcelona especially, and spread out across Europe; the Portuguese to France and beyond. In the Ireland of the 1950s perhaps as much as a fifth of the population left for the British cities. This was the story everywhere in Europe, even in the Communist East, where the decay of the peasantry was not so marked. Italy, too, was transformed very early after the war by the vast movement of people from the rural South, the Mezzogiorno, to the rapidly industrializing North.

In fact, Germany, France and other supposedly industrial nations were still substantially peasant countries up to the Second World War.[9] And even afterwards peasants were, for a time, a national force. In Britain the extinction of the small farmer and rural labourer was slower than supposed, though it is true Britain was the most industrial and urban country in Europe, and for some time the world. I look out from the room in which I write these words at the hills of the Derbyshire Peak District. On these hills I see sheep grazing. It is July and the hay has been cut, leaving the fields the most subtly and beautifully different shades of green. There are around 2,000 farms in the Peak District, hill farms with sheep and some cattle. Hill farms in Britain do not make a fortune, and these farmers are miles distant economically and geographically from the agribusiness farms of the South. They are not, however, peasants, but rather what may be called medium-size farmers – economically minded and set up to function in ways and with resources beyond the wildest dreams of people we would usually call peasants. Big sheds, big tractors, big stone houses built centuries ago. Nonetheless, as we shall see later, in defining 'peasant', conditions are not fixed limits but rather signify gradations.

Ronald Blythe's sad and beautiful *Akenfield*, published in 1969, recorded the days of a rural England even by then almost completely over with. Thirty-seven years after its publication, Craig Taylor wrote *Return to Akenfield*: the last of the horsemen and ploughmen had been replaced by the internet entrepreneur selling 'locally sourced' produce online at high prices to the better-off people who have come in from outside in search of the good life, people seeking to reinvent the dying local pub as a 'community venture'.[10] There were, however, some Polish immigrant workers, people now more likely to have been peasants than anyone else in the place.

In Taylor's account, Akenfield is a quiet place, near-silent, unlike the days when people worked and talked in the fields, to which they walked or cycled, the days when children were to be heard as they went to school. This falling silent of the countryside is remarked upon everywhere; in the Breton villages of the 1960s and 70s, for instance, just as here by Blythe in the 1960s.[11] People have moved to the new Akenfield after Blythe's time, but the silence has only deepened. Blythe had been keenly alert to the poverty and the limited lives of former times, but also recaptured the reality of a distinct way of life going out of living memory. In comments on the publication of *Return to Akenfield*, the then-octogenarian Blythe said of this life, 'Some of it will be missed; the part that cannot be put into words.'

While the last days of an ancient Akenfield, the least peasant area of Europe, were being played out in England, the part that has for centuries been the most peasant-occupied, the centre and East, lagged behind those of the more 'advanced' West. Still under Communist rule, these places in the East were, in the strange temporality of Communist governance, at once suspended in time and transformed by it. This rule served to glorify the peasant as timeless and yet transform their lives through collectivized and enforced co-operative methods of farming. This transformation was in most places a degradation, for lip service only was given to the glorified peasant, and industry took brutal precedence over agriculture.

Figures tell the European story in stark fashion. It is good to dwell on them a while, for all their limitations, for they help explicate smaller stories within the big story of the great decline of the old agricultural world.[12] First, the so-called industrial nations. In France, once the greatest peasant country in Europe, the percentage of people in agriculture in 1950 (out of total employment) was 23 per cent and only 3 per cent in 2019. In 1913 that figure was 41 per cent, and in the same year in Germany still 37 per cent. By 1950 in Germany this had shrunk to 14 per cent, and a mere 1 per cent in 2019. Austria was more a peasant land, with almost a quarter in agriculture in 1950. This was only 4 per cent by 2019. The figures for the UK show the peculiar history of Britain, with only 5 per cent in 1950 and 1 per cent in 2019 (in 1913 it was 10.2 per cent).

In terms of longer-term change, for instance, Ireland in 1913 had 47.5 per cent of its workforce in agriculture, Spain 67 per cent and Italy 55 per cent. The centre and East of Europe were transformed as well as the South. In 1913 in Romania, Bulgaria, Poland and Yugoslavia around four-fifths of the working population were in agriculture. By 2006 that figure had dropped to 10.7 per cent in Bulgaria, only 7 per cent in 2019, and just less than 10 per cent in Poland in the same year. In Romania, however, in 2019 a remarkable 22 per cent of the workforce were employed in agriculture, though many were as much underemployed as employed. None of the former countries that made up the former Yugoslavia had more than 5 per cent in agriculture. Lithuania, as always, was the most agricultural of the Baltic nations, and another bastion of the old order, with just below 20 per cent of its workforce in agriculture in 2000. However, by 2019 this had shrunk to less than 7 per cent, slightly exceeded by Latvia in the same year.[13] Even fewer were those employed in agriculture in the Scandinavian countries.

In all cases the rate of decline after 1950 was considerable, gathering even more momentum as time advanced, particularly as one moves further east in Europe. By 2019, in once deep-peasant Russia, only 6 per cent of employment was in agriculture, and in Ukraine 14 per cent, down a quarter since 2000. In 2000, Georgia, however, still had 52.1 per cent of its workers in agriculture. But the 76 per cent of Turkey's employed population in agriculture in 1950 had dropped to only 22 per cent by 2019 – an altogether remarkable change in the ancestral home of European farming. Today, as one rides up the Bosphorus towards the Black Sea, on the port side of the ferry the vast new Istanbul of tower blocks and shopping malls seems never to end. One almost reaches the Black Sea before the near sixteen million of the city's population are left behind. In Europe, broadly defined, including its East and Turkey, the proportion of those working in agriculture was around 10 per cent by 2006. By 2021 agriculture accounted for only a little over 1 per cent of GDP in the EU.[14]

These changes have happened worldwide.[15] Latin America, and much of the Caribbean, was transformed from a continent of peasants after 1950. By 2019, in Brazil, only 10 per cent of the employed population was in agriculture, in Argentina scarcely anyone at all. The figure in Colombia meanwhile was 15 per cent. Poorer Peru had 27 per cent and Bolivia 30 per cent. Further north, Mexico recorded only 13 per cent, though the impoverished small Central American states were considerably more dependent on agriculture than Mexico. Poor peasant migrants of countries like Guatemala, Honduras and El Salvador have been pulled north to Mexico and the

USA by economic necessity, many of them dying on the way in the cruellest of circumstances.

In North Africa and the Middle East the same has happened, with Iraq, Syria and Iran transformed. The vast central belt of Africa, down to South Africa itself, is still made up of peasant strongholds. The Democratic Republic of Congo, for instance, recorded 65 per cent of employed people in 2019 (though populous and more 'developed' Nigeria many fewer, at 35 per cent). Historically, among these African peasantries, populations were less differentiated socially and economically than elsewhere, and a cash economy less developed.[16] 'High-income nations' worldwide recorded only 3 per cent in agriculture in 2019. Japan, for instance, has utterly changed over the last century, with farmers making up over 50 per cent of the workforce in 1947, 9 per cent in 1985 and only 3 per cent by 2019. In Japan the expansion of the number of women employed in cities served greatly to deplete the rural areas. In South Korea it is striking that, as recently as 1961, 60 per cent of the population still worked in the fields: now it is only 5 per cent.

The poorest countries in the world are almost always the most agricultural: Moldova in Europe, Somalia in Africa. The figures for agricultural productivity indicate the connection between poverty and productivity (these are arrived at by comparing the value added to national economies and the number employed in agriculture): outside Europe the differences between high- and low-income countries are dramatic, and even in Europe very striking, low productivity being greatly marked in Poland, Serbia, Russia, Ukraine and Romania, especially. It should be remembered that 'low productivity' does not mean that peasant farming is inept or deficient somehow. That which creates maximum reward from what is available to the farmer is surely 'efficient', to use a word that does not come out of peasant lexicons.

Over one billion of the world's population, however, still make their living in agricultural work, of which the great majority are in just two nations: India and China. India is the greatest peasant nation still remaining on Earth, with 43 per cent of its population in agriculture. The peasant populations of Pakistan and Bangladesh, if still big, are in sharper decline than India's. And in China the flight to and the growth of great cities is well known. The proportion of the labour force engaged in agriculture there fell from over 70 per cent in 1978, to 36.7 per cent in 2010, and 29.5 per cent in 2014. Nonetheless, somewhat over a third of the population remains rural, though villages in less developed areas came to be inhabited only by the very young and the elderly, as most able-bodied adults went out to work. Almost an entire generation of rural youth across the country grew up never having tilled the soil: by 2012, over 87 per cent of rural sixteen- to thirty-five-year-olds were employed full time off-farm.[17]

As always, statistics hide matters as well as revealing them: what the reality is in this case is that, for many, agriculture is only part of their employment, the 'five o'clock farmer' being numerous everywhere, not least Poland, Ireland and Italy. Should we call these people peasants, miners, factory workers? Perhaps the 'death' of the European peasantry has been exaggerated. Nonetheless, in Europe an ending is everywhere clear, and it is not melodramatic to call this death.

These social changes have been accompanied by huge shifts in big agricultural business. In 1996, the ten biggest seed companies in the world had a market share of less than 30 per cent. Today the three largest control more than 50 per cent of the market. By 2006 five corporations controlled 90 per cent of the world's grain trade, and three countries exported 70 per cent of the world's corn. Meanwhile, the thirty largest food retailers controlled a third of world grocery sales. When agribusiness flourishes, so does agropoly, and the small producers pay the price, relentlessly ground down as they are under the mills of the great corporations. These corporations are now vertically as well as horizontally integrated, meaning that in the search for ever-cheaper raw materials they control large parts of the 'value chain' leading up from the primary producer to the consumer, for instance, the processing, packaging and distribution of food as well as the provision of seeds and fertilizer.[18]

The intensive-production model has spread from the USA, and great swathes of the rural landscape have been transformed by it, particularly in the form of monoculture, one-crop production in a single expanse. Three-quarters of the world's poultry meat and almost the same proportion of its eggs are produced intensively in a tiny handful of countries. Large supermarkets have emerged globally, even in rural Romania, robbing farmers of local outlets. In Europe, as everywhere else, the industrialization of agriculture has transformed everything: vastly increased production is accomplished by vastly fewer workers on the basis of new technologies, mechanization and bioscience.

These changes emerged during the Third Agricultural Revolution, of 1945 to 1970. (The first revolution was the original Neolithic agricultural revolution and the next was the British agricultural revolution, concentrated in the eighteenth century.) New initiatives included high-yielding varieties of cereals, including wheat and rice, chemical fertilizers and much-increased mechanization. Modern 'scientific' farming, combined with massive land accumulation and capital intensification, displaced peasants everywhere. The period of this third revolution coincides with the time frame when many scientists argue the Anthropocene began, the era when human activity became the dominant influence on climate and the environment. The era when our living planet has been in peril.

The EU's Common Agricultural Policy and its multitude of other subsidies kept many small farmers on the land. At least for a while, anyway. Ireland was especially nimble – particularly 'cute', as they say there – when it came to making use of these subsidies. In Europe between 1999 and 2001 EEC Common Agricultural Policy subsidies accounted for 36 per cent of the total value of European agricultural output, and similar subsidies in the US accounted for 22 per cent. With national subsidies added, around 50 per cent of farm income came from state and EU sources. These interventions occurred in relatively rich countries, largely for political reasons. In authoritarian countries, Fascist and Communist both, people were long kept on the land uneconomically. The result, after the transition out of Communism in east and central Europe, and the vicious, state-imposed neoliberalism of the 1990s, is the empty village, the village only of the old, with the young and hopeful gone to the West. The Romanian peasant must become something he does not know the meaning of, namely a 'farmer', one who practises what the EU preaches, who must show 'transparency' in his dealings and standardization in what he produces.[19] This has been happening for a long time. Only now it is the turn of that part of Europe which was the most profoundly peasant of all, the Europe of serfdom and late industrial development.

In Ireland, by 2010, almost two-thirds of the population were urbanized and today rural Ireland has receded from people's daily awareness. Large tracts of the countryside are mainly concerned no longer with agricultural production, but with the consumption of lifestyle, with leisure and tourism. In the 'tiger years', the economic boom between 1993 and 2008, the number of Irish farms declined by more than a third. By 2015 only around one-third of Irish farms were economically viable, while another third were unviable, but sustainable through the means of off-farm income. The remaining third are unviable but heavily subsidized.[20] Of the viable, it is estimated that in the near future over three-quarters will be part-time in operation. The grand-nephews of my father in Dúiche Seoighe now refer to themselves sardonically as 'hobby farmers', for though deeply attached to the land they must find a living beyond the land as well as on it. They still farm, but are the last generation to have been raised in the old rural culture of the island, the last generation to have grown up thinking that the land would be their fate.

Halfway between Belderrig and my father's house in Dùiche Seoighe is Westport. In the town there is a factory which, with the labour of peasants and the children of peasants, produces the entire world's production of Botox. The managing director in Westport was brought up on a 26-acre farm close to the town. The equivalent of a quarter of the town's population are employed by Allergan Ltd, which first set up business in 1977. Two, now sometimes three, generations of the same family are employed in the factory. While so many towns in rural Ireland have fallen into a terrible decay, this place thrives. This is a world beyond the imagination of the parents and grandparents of those who work there, and one scarcely credible to me.

The products made in factories such as this, which keep people on the land in a kind of suspended animation, are various. Take, for instance, the sophisticated surgical products made only a little to the south by the vast Boston Instruments installation in Galway City. Ireland has become what is called 'Treasure Ireland', a haven of low corporate taxation in which the American connection is milked for all it is worth. Yet in Ireland the old ways have not been forgotten, and pride is taken in them. Only now, in the country as a whole, they endure as relics that must be preserved, things to be put in museums.

Not only was Seán Seoighe's span of life led concurrent with the vanishing of peasant Europe. The bachelor life he led was itself a sort of emblem of what happened far beyond Irish shores. Pierre Bourdieu, born in 1930, was the son of a village postmaster in the ancient province of Béarn in France's extreme south-west. Béarn neighbours the Basque regions and the Pyrenees, and the land is pastoral and upland, like the West of Ireland. It is, or rather was, an area with long-established traditions of peasant landownership, traditions much older than Irish ones. Bourdieu is generally regarded as one of the major intellectual figures of his time, a great sociologist. In a book called *The Bachelors' Ball*, he collected his work from the early 1960s to the 1980s on his native region.[21]

Bourdieu had a deep care for the people of the world he was born into. He writes that he wanted to protect his people from ill-intentioned or voyeuristic readings. He is full of anger at what peasant France had become in his lifetime, a treasury of relics to be consigned to the theme park. In France, as in Ireland. Almost despite himself, Bourdieu confesses his 'pent-up tenderness' in the description he gives of what is the symbolic centre of his story, his account of the 'ball'. It's a small-town dance night, in which the peasant bachelors assemble in the hope of finding wives, an unavailing hope, for who wanted a clumsy peasant from the back of nowhere in the modern days of the 1960s and 70s? The peasant ball, the country dance, becomes in his hands the great symbol of the death of the peasant world. Failure to marry removes the central axis of peasant culture, he says. Failure to marry because the young women had almost all gone, drawn by employment opportunities open to women in the cities.

These peasants were raised in a culture where male and female society was much more strictly demarcated than in ours, and where to us now relations between the sexes seem to have lacked naturalness and freedom. Church, school and rural custom were the policemen of the division. In the towns and the villages of Béarn, a more liberal culture was taking hold, making the peasant's body a burden to him and a deterrent in the marriage market. In the ballrooms of rural and small-town Ireland similar things were being enacted at the same time. These ballrooms of romance have been described by William Trevor as places where the bachelor felt the heavy weight of his own body.

In his account of the ball, Bourdieu catches the gaucheness and discomfort of the peasant body and demeanour when confronting a culture that is not his own, meeting people not like him, but still part of his local world, one from which he hopes to find a bride.[22] The author captures the mixture of pride and shame the peasant feels at the ball, or, if not always shame, then an acute awareness of his shortcomings. Contempt and homage are mingled together before the people of the town, the ball a reflection of everyday life. In his ordinary dealings the peasant is clumsy and embarrassed facing the townspeople. Peasants' bodies are like that of Seán Joyce, possessed by the labours they must perform. In these French upland areas, these bodies bear heavy loads across uneven and sloping ground, so that they are slow and ponderous in movement, not to the men themselves, but to outsiders.

Bourdieu tells of how the peasant internalizes the devalued image that others form of him through the prism of urban categories, and comes to perceive his own body as an 'en-peasanted' one, burdened with the traces of agricultural life. He sees his body through the eyes of the beholders at the ball. The consciousness that he gains of his body leads him to break solidarity with it and to adopt an introverted attitude that amplifies his shyness and gaucheness. In a phrase that is truly terrible the author writes of this as a social mutilation, bachelorhood inducing in many cases an attitude of resignation and renunciation resulting from the absence of a long-term future. Peasants use the same words of insult upon their own kind as are directed to them: *cul-terreux*, *plouc*, *péouse* and others. Earth, territory, heavy clods and heavy gait, the peasant even speaks with an *accent du terroir*.

In Béarn as elsewhere in peasant Europe, the house – 'la maysou' in the Béarnese dialect – and the family name were the same, the lineage and patrimony of the family house ('la maison') together. The name and the house live on together even when the family that personifies and perpetuates them has gone. The house carries the name, even if uninhabited. But with time the uninhabited house falls into decay and the name is gone, the bachelors' ball now long a thing of the past.

2.

What Is a Peasant?

'Peasant' is a tricky word, one that is troublesome to me as I am using it to describe my own forebears, when they would mostly not have used the term, and would perhaps not even have known what it meant. Those who were called peasants elsewhere would be called 'country people' in Ireland, or just farmers, and in the Irish language there is no word beyond *tuathánach* (a country person), which is neutral and not pejorative. The disgrace that some attach to the word 'peasant' means that the word itself is shunned. This shunning is at bottom absurd.

The word 'peasant' in English is a borrowing from French, derived from the twelfth-century Anglo-Norman *paisant* and Middle French *païsant*, and variants thereof. Peasant is from *pays*, countryside, and itself comes from the Latin *pagus*, or outlying administrative district, and in post-classical Latin *pagensis*, of or relating to the country or a country district.

Italian *paesano* and Spanish *paisano* went a similar semantic route to English and were also influenced by the French usage. A peasant is also called a *contadino* (someone from a county) in Italian, a *campesino* (from *campo*, countryside) in Spanish and this term is used throughout Latin America as well as Spain. It is a *camponês* in Portuguese. In German, *Bauer* is used, and is synonymous with 'farmer'. In France we have *paysan* and the feminine *paysanne.* A peasant is a country person, a person of the land. That is all the word in its original innocence means.

Peasant

There are strict definitions of 'peasants' as forming a distinct class and there are broad ones, which concern how the word has been used over time. Both are important. Alexander Chayanov, the great early-twentieth-century Russian agrarian economist, offered a strict, and very influential, definition of a peasant mode of production in which a peasant is seen as primarily oriented to securing the subsistence needs of the family unit. The peasant occupies the land he or she works and consumes the products this work creates. Peasants seek not to maximize income or profit, but to ensure that all family members are adequately fed and employed. As a result, peasants are less prone to market forces and, thereby, less likely to fall victim to the external pressures, both market and political, that turn a few into successful commercial farmers and many into labourers. To ensure their survival, peasants must be conservative in their farming practices, sowing those crops or rearing those animals that minimize risks rather than maximize gains.[1]

Defining peasants was in the twentieth century a dangerous business, in Mao's China or in Stalin's Russia. Chayanov believed that the logic of peasant production was not conducive to the production of a surplus through collectivized agriculture; they produced what they needed to survive. He was right, but this did not endear him to Stalin, who had him shot on concocted charges in 1937, as a supposed defender of the 'kulak' (the largely imagined rich, capitalist peasant). His wife Olga spent eighteen years in labour camps.

Here is the broader cultural definition, in the form of the *Oxford English Dictionary* description of how the term has been used, the length of which is more than warranted:

> A person who lives in the country and works on the land, esp. as a smallholder or a labourer; (chiefly *Sociology*) a member of an agricultural class dependent on subsistence farming. Now used esp. with reference to foreign countries (or to Britain and Ireland in earlier

> times), and often to denote members of the lowest and poorest rank of society (sometimes contrasted with *prince* or *noble*). In specific contexts the term may be variously defined. Although modern sociologists agree that a peasant works the land, more wealthy peasants may also be landowners, rentiers, hirers of labour, etc., and in these capacities share interests with completely different social groups. Hence, in the analysis of many rural societies, divisions within the class frequently have to be made.

A peasant can in this view be a labourer, with or without land, a farm servant, a subsistence farmer – as Chayanov observed – a rural person of low rank, a rentier, a hirer of labour, indeed a bit of a capitalist. (It would be difficult to find peasants almost anywhere in Europe who did not have access to and in some measure depend on markets, which in the West especially were capitalistically organized from early on.) On the other hand, a serf was incontrovertibly a peasant in Europe's East and centre. This broad definition fits the multiplicity of peasant society. Most of these figures in the landscape of the peasant world would historically have called themselves peasants, and been called such by those who were not peasants, including academics in their many studies of them. So, it does not seem a bad idea to call them peasants. The problem with Chayanov's definition is that if strictly applied it would leave Europe in recent centuries pretty much bereft of peasants, contrary to common sense and common usage.

As we will see, occupation, consumption, production and the family rarely lined up in the tidy way that Chayanov described. As for occupation of land, this happened in umpteen different forms. So did what we today call 'ownership'. Peasant society is deeply various. Nonetheless, the strict, analytic definition is useful, and this is so because what it highlights is the family and the family economy. The family anchors things in the peasant world. The essential point is that land – whether it is self-owned, rented, aspired to or enserfed – is understood to be a social rather than an economic entity. Reproduction as well as production comes into the picture.

*

Because land is of social value, the loss as well as the gain of land is critical: with the loss of land the family may hold on economically but its capacity to act in the world may be fatally reduced. With the loss of land social significance is lost too, and so what social power the family may have. Marriage becomes difficult and if things go badly enough may be eventually impossible; whatever part the family has in ceremonial occasions and observances is deeply compromised. With the loss of land one may become dependent on strangers, a day labourer perhaps or a farm servant. In short, the family economy denotes a way of life, and if we talk of subsistence what subsists most of all is the means of life itself, which is the family, the habitation and the land *together*: a family economy and not a business. Ideas of social value, of the group, are what count, more than the individual or the accumulation of capital and its reinvestment. What is accumulated is usually more land, not capital that may be used to buy something other than land. In this, England as is well known is the odd man out, the early emergence of capitalist social relations having led to the trinity of large landowner, commercial farmer and waged agricultural labourer.[2] However, as we shall see later, this is something of an oversimplification.

To touch on 'ownership' for a moment: this meant different things in different places and changed over time. Custom might at times be ownership's master: there was once a field in the Galician north of Spain, in the province of La Coruña, which proved deeply puzzling in this respect. In 1904 officials from the Spanish Ministry of Agriculture, Commerce and Public Works scratched their heads over this field. Was it a 'field'? It occupied 340 square feet. Who 'owned' it? This field had an 'owner', who enjoyed the right to till the soil. But another 'owner' harvested the fruit from a chestnut tree that grew there, and yet another received the rent from this field, which was an annual payment of six eggs in alternate years from the farmer and the 'owner' of the chestnut tree. To the men from the ministry such customary arrangements were an overwhelming demonstration of what they had come to understand as the 'inefficiency' of peasant farming.[3]

Ownership was not a straightforward matter, nor was what a 'lease' might in practice amount to. The ideal was the case where a man or woman actually owned the land themselves. The lives of the landless, the sharecropper and the many other manifestations of 'peasant' revolved around this ideal of landownership as planets around the sun. They measured themselves by it, aspired to it, entered into it, exited from it. They may perhaps have never had any realistic hope of owning even a scrap of land, but hope was still there.

It is helpful to think of peasanthood as denoting a condition and not a fixed thing. This condition was both left and entered into: the children of parents who have land but who do not themselves inherit often have little choice but to labour for someone else, the inheriting brother, perhaps, or a neighbour, if they do not emigrate. Tenant farmers may labour far away, for others, then return to their own land in the winter, the women and children keeping things going in the interim. This was so in my father's Connaught, which by his time had already for two centuries time been a centre of seasonal agricultural migration to England and Scotland. These men (some no more than boys) were known as *spailpíní* or spalpeens. They were farmers and labourers both. On Achill Island, in Connaught's own west, the men might be gone eight months of the year.[4] The girls as often dispersed from the home place as stayed, emigrating, becoming servants, marrying out, sometimes.

It is time to let a peasant say what a peasant is. Émile Guillaumin was extremely unusual, a sharecropper, a *metayer*, who left a memoir first published in 1904.[5] Guillaumin, under the guise of fiction, wrote his story as Étienne Bertin, a French peasant born fifty years before him in 1823. The account was written to counteract the contemporary romanticization of peasants in France. Émile/Étienne works as a sharecropper in the Loire from his youth to the end of a long life, moving from farm to farm and paying his rent with his labour, use of his horse and tools, or a part of the crop. Though he was only a *metayer*, he would not stoop to marrying a servant girl, as only the daughters of *metayers* are of the same status. Having to work as a labourer, nonetheless at times he refuses that label, being, as he says, forced by circumstance to adopt this work. Eventually he decides to marry, and so has to find a dowry to bring to the marriage settlement, for Victoire expects a down payment (a bed perhaps, or a cupboard) before they can marry. Just like any respectable peasant.

He marries and rents a property for three years. He comes into his foredestined role, and is no longer a mere labourer, proudly telling the reader that he made his own plough, ladder, barrow and three hay rakes, and that his wife sells milk around the local town. He is now a proper peasant, he says. On the one hand, the social distinctions are clear, but on the other there is little difference in outlook between him and those who rent for cash or own their own small farm, even if the latter may consider themselves superior to Guillaumin. Guillaumin is bound into the tensions and differences of a hierarchy, but alongside what divides is that which brings together, namely the concept of the 'house', the household as the unit of production and reproduction, even if the house is, as it were, in this case a moveable one. It is the house so considered that enables that degree of independence which helps a person fulfil themselves.

So far, the answers to the question of what a peasant is have been socio-economic. Other kinds of answers are possible too. The answers of painters, for instance, answers of great value when the painters have been peasants themselves.

This painting opposite is by Jean-François Millet and it is called *Man with a Hoe*. It is less well known than others in Millet's renowned series on peasant life, replicas of which were said to be in almost every peasant household in France in the late nineteenth century; for example, *The Sower* of 1850 and *The Angelus* of 1857–9. *Man with a Hoe* was painted after these and is more direct and unyielding. Millet was the eldest son of Normandy peasants and worked the land as a youth. There is nothing idyllic about the man with a hoe's toil. Before the fields can be ploughed they must first be cleared of weeds and stubble. This is brutally hard work, and the hoe can be seen to have a blade almost as wide as a shovel. It is of great weight

too. The hoe is in fact an adze, a tool that has been used since the Stone Age. The man, who is looking up in blank exhaustion, is at once supported and drawn to the earth by the hoe. There is another painting by Millet, called *Landscape with Two Peasant Women*, that is in conversation with this one. It is all sky and rough, brown earth below, the figures of the two women merely brown smears, the colour of earth themselves. It is as if they are swallowed up by earth, earth, not the ennobling Earth. Being of the base earth, the peasant has, over long stretches of historical time, been the one who is cursed.

Cursed

'Peasant', when uttered, almost invariably carries a host of denigratory synonyms. Here are just a few, in English English: a lout, a boor, a yokel, a dolt, a churl, a clodhopper. In Irish English: a bosthoon, a bogman, a culchie. My father's Mayo is generally acknowledged in Ireland as the true homeland of the culchie (a distinction proudly affirmed by the Westerners). A bosthoon (Irish: *bastún*) is 'an awkward fellow; a tactless, senseless person'. Or 'a soft, worthless, spiritless fellow', in much the same sense as poltroon. The word comes from Anglo-French *bastun*, a stick, a staff, from the Late Latin *bastum.*[6] Its literal meaning is a switch of green rushes made into a rod or whip, but it is also a metaphoric rod that dealt real blows of contempt and abuse.

In American English there are: hayseed, rube, hillbilly, hick. In the US 'rube' appeared around the turn of the nineteenth century as a slur for a gullible country boy. Its origin is similar to that of hick. Both are diminutive forms of names that were associated with country folk at the time: Rube for Reuben, Hick for Richard. Like bosthoon, these slurs overlap with others: rubes can also be 'rednecks', or 'white trash'. Though the name is not used, the USA had many peasants, southern sharecroppers among them, the kind of people written about by James Agee and photographed by Walker Evans in the 1930s in their book *Let Us Now Praise Famous Men* (1941).[7] The sympathy of Agee's (lavishly literary) prose at bottom romances the sharecropper into the figure of the primitive, the peasant as elemental man.

From a later time these are the words Hannibal Lecter uses in the film *The Silence of the Lambs* to describe Clarice Starling, a native of rural West Virginia, the primitive here as the bestial, degradation entire:

> You know what you look like to me, with your good bag and your cheap shoes? You look like a rube. A well-scrubbed, hustling rube with a little taste. Good nutrition's given you some length of bone, but you're not more than one generation from poor white trash, are you, Agent Starling? And that accent you've tried so desperately to shed: pure West Virginia. What is your father, dear? Is he a coal miner? Does he stink of the lamp?

Even seemingly neutral terms carry a great weight of denigration, *campesino* and *contadino*, for example. So do the cognates deriving from them. *Paleto* and *palurdo*, 'bumpkin' and 'boor' in Spanish, are derived from *paisano*. *Cafone*, originally a neutral Italian word meaning a poor peasant, evolved to mean an uncouth, boorish, ill-mannered person and the word with that same meaning can be found in American English slang. The German *Bauer* derives from *Bur* in Low German. In English it is pronounced like *boor*, which is where the English word 'boor' derives from.

In Middle French the connotations of stupidity were already there with 'peasant' itself. As a verb in late medieval times, 'to peasant' in English meant to subjugate, so that someone who is a peasant is subjugated as well as stupid. When the word 'peasant' is used in English it has from at least the fourteenth century carried the same charge as its synonyms, as in, 'Thou ignoble horse-rubbing peasant . . . being but a vilipendious mechanicall Hostler', from John Taylor's wonderfully named *Laugh, and Be Fat* of 1612, a book of 'comical intrigues' and 'witty epigrams'.

It is much the same worldwide. In the Ottoman period *fellahin* was the term used throughout the Middle East. *Fellahin* were distinguished from the *effendi*, the landowning class. Most urban Egyptians today are fairly recent incomers from the countryside but see *fellahin* as offensive, so call themselves *masri* (Egyptians) instead. Most world languages follow a similar pattern: lord: high, peasant: low.

Subjugation or at least inferior social worth is reflected in the antonyms of 'peasant', which describe what he is not: a *patron*, a lord, a gentleman, a landowner and so on. Underlying this opposition is a deeper one, that of the master and the slave. For the peasant suffers the curse of Ham (or Cham), the curse of being the servants of servants. This was so particularly where serfdom had reigned. The curse of Ham is the curse of Noah upon Canaan, the son of Ham. Noah's other sons, Shem and Japheth, propagate the great races named in the tenth chapter of Genesis. Ham's descendants, however, are condemned to servitude. The curse has been used over millennia, not only to justify serfdom but also as an explanation for black skin and thus as a justification for the subjection of the slave, notably in the United States, where it was used as divine justification.

In Genesis 9:25–7 of the King James Version of the Bible we read: 'And he said, Cursed be Canaan; a servant of servants shall he be unto his brethren. And he said, Blessed be the Lord God of Shem; and Canaan shall be his servant. God shall enlarge Japheth, and he shall dwell in the tents of Shem; and Canaan shall be his servant.' In medieval Europe, serfs were held to be descended from Ham, nobles from Japheth and free men from Shem. The curse holds on still. The older and then standard collective name for peasants in Polish is *chłopi*, which derives from *kholopy*, the slaves of old Slavonic society.

It is easy to forget the conjoined history of slavery and serfdom, easy because the two are not often mentioned in the same breath. Serfdom ended in Europe only with the Russian emancipation in 1861, slavery in the USA in 1863, in Brazil as late as 1888. The abolition of both was propelled in part by the drive to augment centralized state power, whether this power was autocratic, imperial or democratic. This augmentation could only be accomplished by breaking the power of the great landlords, the plantation owners on the one hand, the nobility on the other. The end of both slavery and serfdom also signalled the acceleration of economic modernization by means of the creation of more market-based economies, these markets being both free and protected, the latter in the case of the Russian empire. Industrialization accelerated as a consequence of both abolitions, if at different paces, the growth of industrial capitalism in the incipient American empire remarkable as a consequence of the breaking of the old order. And, whether for the former slave or serf, the economic gains of emancipation were in practice decidedly limited. The stigma of slave and serf remained.

As for the age-old Jewish-peasant relationship of eastern Europe, the profoundly negative image of peasants held by many in the urban and smaller *shtetl* Jewish populations of the East should not go unremarked. This from 1901 is not at all untypical:

> The peasant, because of his servitude and baseness, was like a wild donkey from birth. In the brutishness of his feeling and the baseness of his spirit, he was like a beast. Not only did he not know how to read and write, but his mind was incapable of counting and calculating. Because he was despised and the appearance of his clothes and shoes pitiful, so was he like one deprived of human rights in the eyes of many . . . despised and low were the peasants, wretched, oppressed, and tormented. The bread of men they did not eat and the lives of men they did not live; they are like the beasts of the field.[8]

This is the judgement of one historian of Jewish–Gentile relations: 'Throughout most of their history, Jews had usually shown little interest in – and quite often utter contempt toward – the surrounding lower-class and lower-stratum non-Jews. In eastern Europe, the *muzhik/poyer* (peasant) usually embodied those low-class Gentiles.'[9] This judgement is sweeping, and for those Jews who lived in close proximity to peasants, where they often performed a traditional middleman role, a more nuanced picture is apparent.[10] The historical reality is complex, and the contempt that Jews felt towards peasants was amply returned.

As regards the peasant and the general populations of European states, and here with the example of Poland in mind, the lord/peasant distinction, that of the *pan* and the *cham*, is commonly regarded as structuring Polish culture, even up to the present day. It has long been at the centre of elite/poor distinctions there and over time has given semantic form both to elite antisemitism (with Jews as *cham*-like boors), and to various types of elite class hatred directed at non-Jews. For Poles, *pan* is still an indispensable trait of Polishness. The Polish addiction to *pan* is accompanied by the popular delusion of being descended from nobles, the ranks of the *szlachta*, even though most of Polish society is of peasant origin. The landowner ideology emanating from the Polish-Lithuanian Commonwealth, known as Sarmatism, held on centuries after the end of the Commonwealth in 1795: Poles were to be regarded as the true inheritors of a class of warriors who were cultivated, free and landowning.

In Poland in Communist times, attempts were made to repress the usage of *pan*, which was seen as a vestige of a class society, but a fierce resistance was put up and the attempt failed. The very opposite of the obscure *chłopi*, who would not want the pedigree of a lord? I write here of how the noble/peasant distinction has structured Polish culture, and in this structuring has disfigured it. However, something similar can be said across Europe as a whole, and indeed across the world. The slave/master distinction has been, and still is, poisonous.

However, in the depiction of peasants over time something other than denigration alone is evident. There is also the peasant's elevation. Often the latter is more deleterious to the peasant than the former. Frequently, too, denigration and elevation are opposite sides of the same coin. In Poland the post-Second World War generations were all too willing to passively forget the peasant past in order to replace it with new images of the modern, ones that in the form of rapid urbanization and industrialization involved the destruction of the foundations of peasant culture. However, these same people were subjected by the new Communist state to a relentless diet of peasant 'folklore', *faux* rural 'traditions' being avidly fostered.[11] The peasant, invariably attired in 'folk costume', becomes in this manifestation the familiar creator of tasteful artefacts for sophisticated modern buyers and collectors. Thus in the midst of their denigration the peasant becomes the exalted one, the real noble, ennobled by their simplicity, by the peasant's closeness to what is held to be authentic in human existence. This picture of unspoiled contentment echoes down the ages. In Oliver Goldsmith's *The Vicar of Wakefield*, first published in 1766, we read that 'The ignorant peasant, without fault, is greater than the philosopher.'

Being philosophers of the earth, peasants are wise, instinctive, natural as well as elemental. The 'simple folk' have been the ideal of conservative political purposes for centuries, but as the model of authentic existence peasants have also served liberal, socialist and Communist purposes. 'Folklore' is another product of this search for authenticity, the peasantry exiled to the land of the museum, the 'folklife' and 'living history' versions in particular, so that, as Bourdieu writes, the peasants 'are assigned to their reserves where they will be free to dance and sing their *bourrées* and gavottes for the greater satisfaction of ethnologists and urban tourists, so long as their existence is economically and symbolically profitable'. In this way the last peasants are converted into the guardians of a nature transformed for the consumption of city dwellers, environmentalists these days among them.

The great Irish comic writer Flann O'Brien was surely the equal of anyone in excoriating the employment of peasant wisdom for political purposes, scourge of the blarneyed peasant of Irish ethno-romantic nationalism as he was. In a story of his from 1933 called 'The Tale of Black Peter', Peter gets up early in the morning, dons 'his Aran jumper and his woollen rags', eats a bowl of stirabout in which there are twelve nettles, 'lovely nourishing nettles of the kind that do be had on the Bog'. When Black Peter has at last had enough of things he goes to the priest and asks, 'WHO CREATED ME AND THIS MISERABLE COUNTRY?' The priest tells him God was not responsible but two gentlemen in Dublin, one an author, one a poet. Peter grabs his double-barrelled shotgun and heads to the city.[12]

In the excoriation stakes, O'Brien had an equal, however: another Irishman, Samuel Beckett. Beckett wrote this of peasant-nationalist Ireland in his novella of the 1970s *First Love*: 'What constitutes the charm of our country, apart of course from its scant population, and this without the help of the meanest contraceptive, is that all is derelict, with the sole exception of history's faeces. These are ardently sought after, stuffed and carried in procession. Wherever nauseated time has dropped a nice fat turd you will find our patriots, sniffing it up on all fours, their faces on fire. Elysium of the roofless.'[13]

'Elysium of the roofless': in Bourdieu's eyes, the French rendition of the wisdom of the peasant took form in their cultivation of silence. Silence, the repository of peasant wisdom, comes from a deep well in the peasant soul. As he puts it, the peasant may be as adept in finding mushrooms or setting bones as in his mastery of what is wrapped in this silence, beliefs so ancient that they defy time; whereas actual peasant silence is another matter. In his *History of Silence*, Alain Corbin describes the silence of peasants: silence is more a tactic linked to the necessity for secrecy than it is an expression of the peasant soul, a necessity born of the need not to disclose family secrets and also to repel all attacks on the family. Silence preserves group solidarity, within both the family and the village. Silence averts envy, which poisons the commune's soul. Silence may also conceal a desire for vengeance. Ambitions and revenge are slow to mature in rural societies, and it is essential not to show your hand too soon.

There is also the silence before outsiders, tax officials and policemen, say, the fear of saying too much, the distrust of those who ask questions, the distrust of one's own capacities too, the vast incomprehension produced by the encounters of one mismatched code and another. Corbin notes how peasants will speak when they wish to be credible in a certain way, a long prior silence pointing up the boldness of speaking. The taciturn may appear silent without actually being silent, based as taciturnity is on knowledge of other codes than those which govern speech. The peasant is frequently a man of few words, speech often seeming pointless to him, even in the act of prayer. Corbin cites the example of a peasant looking at the Eucharist silently: 'I perceive him, and he perceives me', and nothing more need be said.[14]

In oral cultures, agreements are often concluded without resort to writing or even speech, as in practices of tacit or automatic renewals of lease, or the hiring of a labourer or servant, the hand spat upon and then grasping the other hand to seal the bargain. There is also the reassuring silence of the farm, and, within their own circles, peasants are anything but silent, of course. There is a great silence surrounding peasants historically, produced by their own silence, and this is amplified by the refusal of elites to record peasant speech, which is regarded as impoverished, inept, incomprehensible (proverbs are the exception, full of 'peasant wisdom' as these are held to be). Peasants have been referred to as hidden from history by historians, part of what has been called 'Hidden Ireland' in one instance.[15]

Historically, peasants do not generally speak, they are spoken to. Peasants are in their nature people who are to one degree or another under the power of others. Among the privileges of those who are powerful is the privilege to control how they wish to be known and seen by others. And how such people see themselves is in relation to what they are not, the powerless, who have historically usually been peasants. This control over how people are seen takes many forms: legal, political and aesthetic among them. Those who have little or no power must reckon with this, for the world comes to be 'objectively' seen through the lens the powerful hold up, so that peasants must contend with a truth about themselves which they have not themselves made.[16]

Peasants are the most dominated class because they are the least able to control how they are represented to the world (they are poorer, less educated, more subject, from oral cultures and so on). Similar to the victims of racism, they must work with the image of themselves created by others. Oftentimes peasants' existence is dependent on the conflicts that are fought over them by others, conflicts often fought in the peasants' own name.

Peasants have everywhere suffered greatly from the namings that have been inflicted upon them, including the naming of 'experts' of all sorts as well as politicians: eighteenth-century 'agriculturalists', modern agronomists, modernizing gentry and development planners. In early modern Europe, peasants were regularly despised by townspeople, who, as Braudel writes, ruled their rural territories with a fist of iron, in the same autocratic fashion as the European powers would rule their colonies.[17] Peasants are and have been the objects of history, that which is to be socially designed and re-designed, in Europe the design of which was to be, in eighteenth- and nineteenth-century parlance, 'improved'. Made, as would later be said, 'modern' and 'developed', no longer backward. A great deal of this started early and started in England, building as it did there on the already solid foundations of a precocious capitalist agriculture and the earlier retreat of seigneurial obligations. Peasants were everywhere those who dwelt, as one nineteenth-century observer put it, in a state of 'almost idiotic wretchedness'.[18]

The object of the social engineering of said wretchedness was the creation of a society of economically productive property owners in land, productivity itself being defined in terms of the maximum operation of free markets, and damn the majority left behind. Damn the vast majority of the Irish in the Great Famine of Ireland: Ireland, England's first colony. Damned by the self-evidently true dicta of political economy and Providence, religion and classical economics working as one mighty engine of the True and the Good. The moral ethos of Enlightenment across Europe – the French Physiocrats, the German Cameralists, the English 'agriculturalists' – was that humanity existed so that it could be improved. In this rush to improve, peasants were impediments, whether they represented the roadblocks of 'tradition' or what Marx and Engels in the *Communist Manifesto* of 1848 called 'the idiocy of rural life'. The Irish peasant, for instance, was believed to have been made 'lazy' by the too-easy cultivation of the potato. (The ridges on which the potato was planted were called 'lazy beds'.)

Rural conditions were, in places, parlous, but peasants usually knew best what was best for them and had everywhere developed appropriate and sophisticated methods to handle want and ensure survival, methods that could have been worked with to deliver a different meaning to the term 'improvement'. And as for idiotic wretchedness: when the improver took the nose-holding time to enter the houses of the rural poor they might indeed encounter squalor, squalor by any standards, sometimes, but more often these encounters were informed by the wilful incomprehension of those who took their own standards as the markers of what civilization was.

How has this all come to be? What is behind the curse? Time itself has a lot to do with the answer. In the course of history, from at least the scientific revolution of the seventeenth century, circular conceptions of time were replaced by ideas of time as linear, irreversible, the arrow of time as it is called. Peasant time kept to the old temporal registers, while increasingly having to survive in the new. Which, being adaptable, peasants did – though not without great cost. When the rate of historical change (population, production) began to accelerate in the eighteenth century, the principle of historical progress was born, and the timeless and unchanging were incorporated into historical time. Historical writing itself was a cause and a product of these new conceptions of time. Progressive, linear time ran roughshod over older ways of conceiving and living time, which were seen as superstition, fatalism, evidence of being 'backwards' indeed, as opposed to moving forward, as time (and people) should.

But we must note too that a curious thing happened with the consolidation of historical time: peasants, being part of 'tradition', could not partake of the history that was the hallmark of modernity. They were outside history. They were at once that which retarded progress and that by which progress could be measured and criticized. Either way, they were outside time, a barrier in the road of progress or the signpost setting progress on the right track.

In the latter guise their outsiderness took the form of the new idea of the 'folk'. The origins of 'the folk' go back to Johann Gottfried Herder in the late eighteenth century. The peasant was not the only representative of the folk, but by far the most important one. Across Europe the folk came to emblematize the nation in the course of the nineteenth century. The peasant, being steeped in the wisdom of the ages, was of a culture that was held to be the bedrock of the nation, something communal, anonymous, bearing the future because not losing sight of the past. The peasant, being 'authentic', verified the authenticity of the nation.

As for peasants themselves, they continued to live in the old order of time, an order that today is largely lost to us, the time of the seasons, of the family, of the house and its fortunes, of the commune. I am drawn once more to the words of John Berger on peasants:

> Before time and history were conflated, the rate of historical change was slow enough for an individual's awareness of time passing to remain quite distinct from their awareness of historical change . . . History used to pay its respects to mortality: the enduring honoured the value of what was brief. Graves were a mark of such respect. Moments which defied time in the individual life were like glimpses through a window; these windows let into the life, looked across history, which changed slowly, towards the timeless which would never change.[19]

Windows let into a life, in which one could look across history to the timeless. This is a beautifully wrought way of saying it, especially the idea of looking *across*, for, as time went onwards, the wall between time and history grew ever higher so that it became difficult to any longer look across. But nonetheless, we all still live in different time registers, even though the arrow of time propels us forward, progressing we now no longer know where.[20] Beyond what is socially official time, clock time, there are the times of the body, of the family, of the imagined life, no less real for being imagined.

It is true that social justice was only to be had when the possibility of change could be let into time and a better future be conceived of. There should be no idealization of a class that has to define itself as the class of those who survive. Peasant history is one of want and exploitation, among other things. These other things include the wit to survive and sometimes prosper. And to determine their own fate when that was possible. When peasants got education and became organized, from the late nineteenth century onwards, they showed themselves highly adept at getting what they wanted. When they got what they wanted they did not stop being peasants. What *they* wanted, not what others deigned they should have in the name of progress. On balance, however, the consequences of the temporal and spatial revolution that makes up 'modernity' have been more devastating than liberating for peasants. Devastation has in fact been liberty's price. The curse of Ham has been a heavy one.

PART TWO
Worlds that Have Gone

3.

The Church of the Peasants: Society

Writing in 1930 of peasants, the once greatly famed Italian writer Ignazio Silone put things so: 'Poor peasants, who make the soil productive and suffer from hunger . . . are alike all over the world: they form a nation, a race, a church of their own, but two poor men identical in every respect have never yet been seen.'[1] No two peasants and no two peasantries, but nonetheless the church of the peasants abides. Silone was born into the peasant society he describes and knew hardship as a child and young man. Many of his family were killed in the catastrophic Avezzano earthquake of 1915, including his father Paolo Tranquilli, along with tens of thousands of others (Ignazio Silone was a nom de plume). A brother of his, Romolo, died in a Fascist jail in 1931.[2]

The *Oxford English Dictionary* definition of 'peasant' ends, as we have seen, with these words: 'Hence, in the analysis of many rural societies, divisions within the class frequently have to be made.' Indeed they do. Divisions galore. As a leftist political organizer Silone knew these divisions intimately; he was a founder member of the Italian Communist Party, from which he was subsequently expelled for opposition to Stalin.

Here is a list of some terms used to describe those who over recent centuries laboured on the land in England: cotter, commoner, husbandman, yeoman, tenant farmer, sharecropper, copyholder, grazier, herdsman, wage labourer, farm servant, statesman, farm cooperator and numerous, and usually waged, occupations such as huntsman, shepherd, drover, dairymaid, forester/woodman, apprentice in husbandry. These designations, locally inflected, would have applied across most of Europe.

The distinctions between peasants are as various and obscure to us as are the criteria of measurement they employed in defining the land that meant everything to them. In Poland one *łan* was reckoned by custom to be enough to make a farmer independent. In Irish a *cológ*, a collop in English, in Ulster a *sum*, was the measure of land deemed sufficient to support one family, based on what was needed for the grazing of one mature cow. What being 'independent' meant varied according to place and circumstance of course, but actually owning land was the gold standard, or, if not that, then having long-term tenancies.

Below the independent man in the Poland of the late nineteenth century was the *zagrodnik*, someone owning half a *łan*, one who might work for others as well as himself. *Komornicy* were tenant farmers, with no cultivated land in their own ownership, but usually enough to build a house and have a garden and a farmyard, so that the concept of the 'house' was still very real to them. Further gradations downwards followed until the completely landless, below whom was the beggar (who in fact had their own special standing). Below even the beggar was the pauper, the utterly destitute and low.

However, these landless people would have had few reservations about calling themselves peasants, or cognates like 'villagers'. They were members of a peasant commune, which, with all its tensions and contradictions, governed their lives. What drew them together was the sense of a common fate, the fate of being us against them, the big landowners. The lord was not one of them, nor was the priest, nor what petty officials there might be in the village. Nor were the local townspeople part of 'them'. The 'we' arose because people felt, as they were eminently right to feel, exploited. Whether landed or not, and those with land were little better off than those without, they drank in the same inns, wore the same clothes, talked in the same way, sang the same songs and laughed at the same jokes.

It is a case of balancing the forces of division and unity in understanding peasant society. Across each example of a peasantry, whether we give these peasantries a national adjective or not, the church of the peasants is clearly a pretty various one. If such a church abides, then one has to be attentive to its many different doctrines and observances. There is difference among peasants but also fluidity and change, so that roles are entered into and left throughout a lifetime (for example, temporary farm service itself). Again, thinking about 'peasant' as a condition is helpful. In 1971 Teodor Shanin edited a volume called *Peasants and Peasant Societies*.[3] The book defined the academic study of peasants for decades, and Shanin was a founder of the journal that continues to do this.[4] Shanin was a Jew from Vilnius, no ordinary academic. He knew peasants during the great violence of the Second World War, a war in which he and his family were exiled to Siberia.[5] Above all, he knew Russian peasants. His father had fought alongside them in the Russian Revolution of 1917.

Shanin shows how peasants can become paupers, how they can be marginalized, as they are relentlessly subject to the advances of the modern world as small-scale agriculture declines. Peasanthood is mutable, therefore, peasantries heterogeneous. Peasants' strategies might involve dual employment in the city and the country, seasonal emigration or full emigration. Money sent home from those who have left is a major source of subsistence in the world today, including for the last peasants of East and central Europe. (Outside Europe, as one example, almost a quarter of the GDP of Central America's El Salvador is made up of remittances from abroad.) It is not for nothing that Shanin called peasants the 'awkward class', awkward because they are not easily socially categorizable, and awkward in their politics too.

Since Shanin's time in the 1970s there has been a great increase in knowledge about peasants, almost all of it in academic books and journals, the products of which are for most people either too expensive to access or too specialist and abstruse for all but the most patient and dedicated of readers.[6] The gist of much of this literature is that peasanthood is not a changeless condition, and that peasants do not and always did not exist immobile in time. Peasants, if given the chance (which mostly is not the case), can be adaptive, flexible, innovative.[7]

Peasants are not strangers to capitalism. There is much to be gained by producing for the capitalist market: essentials of life that can only be had with money – iron tools, seeds, salt – or at least things that are deemed essential – tea, coffee, tobacco, mirrors. The list varies from place to place. Though peasants have traditionally fled from military conscription, mutilating themselves to avoid it, even, joining up has been a survival strategy for centuries, as in Ireland. In the aftermath of the Great Famine in Ireland, for instance, the land market entered a state of extreme fluidity in which some gained and many lost, none more than the landless labourers, the cottier class so-called, who faced decimation or beggardom at home, emigration or the army abroad. The British army in India was peopled by such men. And of course small peasants become big peasants, with more land, and some of them (a few, historically) capitalist farmers.

Division existed at the very heart of peasant society itself. On the one hand, there were the individual interests and strategies of peasant households. On the other, there were the interests of the commune in defending peasant households against powerful outsiders, the community acting as an insurance against misfortune. The household and the commune complemented but also contradicted one another. There were also the tensions produced by the presence of a local landowning class, the different fates and circumstances of households, depending, as these did, on the fortunes of their own inheritance practices and farming methods. There were in most communal settings almost always rich, middling and poor peasants.[8]

Italy 1945

There are two ways of showing something of the discordances and concordances that marked peasant society, the situation within national borders, and the variations across Europe as a whole. We'll first examine the particular, in the form of Italy, before venturing on to peasant Europe at large. Around 1945, Italy was still substantially a peasant country, before the great decline of *Les Trente Glorieuses*, the three decades of post-war economic growth which saw massive waves of peasant migration from the Italian South to the North. In Italy there was relatively limited peasant proprietorship, and most of it was to be found in the central parts of the country.[9] There were considerable differences between here and the South (and the landless peasants of the northern plain). Sharecropping was practised everywhere, but in the central band the estates were not vast, and annual contracts were in practice fairly long term so that de facto peasant proprietorship was prevalent. The *mezzadri* in Tuscany were for centuries considered a privileged caste, in contrast to those who had no security on the land, in Tuscany the *pigionali*, in Umbria the *casengoli*.

Unlike in the South, life was lived not in villages or agro-towns, but in separate farmsteads, in which the *capoccia* and *massaia* reigned (the male and female heads of household, the names for these peasant dignitaries varying from nation to nation, region to region, even within a few miles). A united front was maintained before the non-peasant world, and the subjection of family members within the household was as strong as the external united front. The labour of women in the fields and at home was astonishingly hard. Nonetheless, the landlords were a daily presence, and in the towns were not absentees, so that close ties often bound landowner and peasant. Landlords were decidedly a part of this peasant world. Indeed, Ginsborg writes of the 'profound subjection', the deep paternalism, of the relationship. However, it depended on both sides of this paternalist relationship honouring their obligations, and conflict was never totally absent.

Multigenerational families lived within single households, often in large houses extended several times, just as in parts of France. (France was marked by high peasant proprietorship.) Despite living in separate and sometimes isolated dwellings, families were integrated into communities, and rich networks of exchanges and mutual assistance were customary. These people were not Marx's potatoes in a sack, incapable of joint action.

The heritage of the *latifondi* in the South, on the other hand, was apparent in vast, absentee-owned estates geared to national and international capitalist markets from early on. The *Latifondo* system was the landholding system that prevailed in much of the South, inherited from Roman times, where it in part was dependent on slave labour. In South America the *hacienda* was the equivalent of the *latifondo*. Estates were not only huge but labour intensive and autocratic in management.

Family size in the South was smaller than further north, and families were of the nuclear type. In eastern Sicily's Siracusa province in the early 1940s, 80 per cent of the entire male workforce were agricultural labourers. In the villages and small towns the labourer left early in the morning and worked on until late into the night, perhaps many miles away, walking to and fro, on their return their wives helping them with the burdens they carried, people reduced almost to animals. The controls of the landowners and the priests were less marked than further north in Italy. This is the Sicily of Carlo Levi's *Christ Stopped at Eboli*, a work that was the fruit of his exile in Basilicata in the South in the early 1940s: 'no message human or divine, has reached this stubborn poverty . . . Christ did not come. Christ stopped at Eboli.'[10] Contemporary sources speak of one-room 'houses'; one large windowless room, the kitchen, sleeping area and stables all crammed together as one.

Unlike in central Italy, there was little security and continuity of labour. The extraordinary continuity of the *latifondo* system (it was abolished only in 1950) was possible because of the limited work available, the political authority that was concentrated in the landowners, and the elasticity and quick responsiveness of labour supply. If the villages and agro-towns brought people together, their work drove them apart, in constant competition as they were for jobs. The result was a lack of civic trust, and isolation from, suspicion of and resistance to the institution of the state; in western Sicily the common response to greeting someone on meeting them was 'Cuntrastamu': 'We are resisting.' The first *mafiosi* were those offering protection from the large tenant farmers, the *gabellotti*, who had taken over as stewards from the big landowners in western Sicily.

The *mafiosi* meant solidarity against outsiders, protection, above all of course protection from the Mafia itself.

Distinctions abounded however in the rural South, especially between the more fertile, tree-shaded 'covered South' and the 'naked South' of pasturage and grain. Poor as the covered South was, the naked South was poorer, only emigration keeping villages going, until access to the United States was curtailed after the First World War. The naked South, in turn, was divided between the plains and the mountains and hills, where forms of ownership were more varied than on the plains of the *latifondi*. Though occupying a tenth of the area of the Mezzogiorno, 50 per cent of the population lived in the covered South, crowded together on smaller and smaller landholdings. Here 'mixed forms' existed and a peasant could be at one and the same time an owner, a sharecropper and a poor labourer. The family economy was still the greatest recourse, and the small plot provided independence of a sort.

Despite usually not owning land these peasants were as hungry for it as those who did, their hunger nurtured in what collective solidarity made possible. In 1806, under the rule of Joseph Bonaparte, a promise was made that a quarter of the land would be given over to the peasants, and this promise was what has been called 'a diamond in the collective consciousness of the peasantry'. Peasants rose repeatedly in the nineteenth century to demand that this promise be fulfilled. Indeed, the great protest peasant movement of 1893–4, the Fasci Siciliani, harked back to this past and looked forward to the future under the influence of an anarcho-syndicalism as suspicious of the state as it was. The future brought them only more of the same, however; the Second World War served only to reproduce the old system, thanks to the active participation of the Allied powers, in collusion with the large landowners and the Mafia as they were.

The Communist deputy Fausto Gullo said of the songs of Calabria in 1950, 'all the folk-songs are laments, there is not a single popular song that has a sense of joy about it; they are all pervaded by a most profound sadness, by a harrowing melancholy which sometimes borders on despair.'[11]

This South is the land of 'La Miseria' (just as Polish peasant poverty in the Galicia of the nineteenth century was referred to as the 'Galician Misery').[12] On the one hand, the Italian South has been understood as among the most 'backward' in Europe, in Edward Banfield's influential book of 1958 on Basilicata, *The Moral Basis of a Backward Society*, a world marked by so-called 'amoral familism', the war of each family against all, in which politics was seen as useless. This was a place, in this account, incapable of action in support of the common good.[13]

On the other hand, in the mentality of non-Southerners, especially those from the Italian North, the South has often been taken as representing a model of humankind's capacity to endure, which in many ways it indeed did, but in seeing it as such it has also been exoticized as the essence of the 'pre-modern', the place beyond Eboli, the home of the essential peasant, the ultimate primitive. However, there were other ways of seeing things; for instance, that of an acute American anthropologist named Frank Cancian, who visited Basilicata around the same time as Banfield, of whom he was very critical:

> The delicate sense of the hierarchy of things, natural and human, is well expressed in the remark of a landless peasant who, in attempting to describe his daily routine, had started by saying: 'We hoe the earth' – then had interrupted himself with the apology to me (the gentleman) – 'if you will forgive the expression, like beasts.' Someone who wants to explain a difficult question to a visitor often starts by saying: 'I am only a peasant.' However, this matter-of-fact recognition of one's proper place in the general scheme of things has no taint of submissiveness of the poor to the rich. First of all, the criterion of social order, in the minds of the peasants, is not primarily an economic one, as it is for the baron or great proprietor, who for this reason does not participate in the dignity of the peasant and is not treated with the same kind of simple human regard that peasants are accustomed to show each other.[14]

In 1957, as a young student, Cancian spent a year in the village of Lacedonia, to the east of Naples. There he lived, worked and photographed the peasants of the village. The photographs form a fine record.[15] Cancian had an eye to match his words, whereas Banfield's vision was marred by the politics of the libertarian right, of which he was a vocal and influential advocate (he went on to be an adviser to Ronald Reagan). For Banfield, it was the peasants who were to blame for their own condition, not the state or the prevailing forms of economic exploitation. This view is familiar when outsiders who have power define those who have little power themselves. The peasants join their cousins in powerlessness, the hapless peasant beside the hapless worker and the hapless black.

In such places, work might indeed be cursed, for working for others was itself a curse.[16] Frank Cancian reported on 'the almost absolute taboo on talking about work. Men spend entire days during the winter season standing in the square talking in small groups, but competitive discussion of farming techniques and yields, and expression of hopes or plans for the coming season are almost entirely absent.'[17] Cancian's photographs are often, and eloquently, simply of people waiting. But then these people he sees waiting are as often as not landless labourers. This is a world to which the term 'fatalism' is so often applied. To which one may reply that there was a lot to be fatalistic about and that fatalism was itself an entirely rational response in the circumstances.

Peasant Europe

'Peasant Europe'; what is it? There seem to be several peasant Europes, not one. There are many ways of thinking about the diversity of peasants' situations across Europe as a whole, with the first, the variety of tenures, which might simply and usefully be divided into good and bad ones.[18] Good tenure involved forms of landowning by which the peasant had a permanent and often hereditable right to the use of his land. Bad tenures were those where peasants held land for limited periods, or at the will of the proprietor. Different tenures coexisted within regions or even localities. To make matters more complicated, one form of tenure frequently shaded into another. In general, however, historically, in the lands of western Europe good tenures were more common, and in the East bad ones. The line between good and bad tenures can be regarded as sharecropping, where for the use of the land the worker forfeited a share of the crop. Sharecropping itself differed in degrees of security from place to place, but was still better than the aptly named tenancy at will, the will in question being that of the landowner. Below the relatively few well-off peasants, the middling peasants had enough land to survive and reproduce, prospering at times. The smaller landholders sometimes had enough to enable survival, and, when not enough, work outside the farm was needed as a supplement. Then there were the completely landless.

The feudal system distinguished Europe north of the Mediterranean basin and the latifundia system the lands of the Mediterranean itself. Both left enduring legacies, as we have seen in the case of the *latifondi* in Italy.[19] The enormously large estate in the hands of the few was in southern situations accompanied by *minifundismo*, the tiny holdings of the many. Across most of Europe north of Italy the open-field system was the dominant form for over 2,000 years, continuing through feudalism, and thereafter being very slowly eroded by land consolidation, private ownership and capitalist farming. It continued in Russia, Iran and Turkey into the twentieth century, however. North-west Europe was in the vanguard of this change, particularly England. There, the enclosure of manor fields for livestock grazing and for larger arable plots made the economy of small strips of land in open fields less attractive to landowners by the sixteenth century.

Individual peasant holdings in the form of strips were scattered among the different fields in the open-field system, and annual crop rotation and common grazing were practised. In this system, coordinated action was essential to survival, hence the particular centrality of the village in these cultures, especially across central and eastern Europe. This system, however, varied by degrees from low to high across Europe from west to east, continuing as a dominant form in large areas of eastern Europe even up to the present time. Poland today, when seen from the air, is a breathtaking mosaic of these long narrow strips.

The open-field system had stretched from the English Midlands to the heart of Russia, and tillage was dominant across the great central European plain. Nonetheless, in the many highland areas, more isolated farms on enclosed holdings proliferated. In Ireland and Scotland, the system known as rundale also operated, where the land is divided into discontinuous plots, and cultivated and occupied by a number of tenants to whom it is leased jointly. This is the system into which my West of Ireland grandparents were born. There is an intensively cultivated 'infield' around the clusterings of clachan households, and a shared 'outfield' for pasturage on mountains and wastes. Common tenancies reached a peak on the other side of Europe. Russian serfs paid their masters rent and by their labour, but the obligations and taxes owed to the state were negotiated through the elders of the communal unit. Land in the Russian heartland of Muscovy was communally held and repartitioned between the families of the *mir* (the self-governing commune centred on the village). Common tenancies were also found in continental Europe in Hungary, Moldova, the Bukovina (now in Romania), the Serbian *zadruga* and parts of Polish Galicia.

The East–West distinction is most of all apparent with serfdom, England being among the earliest territories to have done with it (by 1400 or so, most of western Europe by 1500). As serfdom retreated in the West it was imposed in the East, in the so-called 'second serfdom'. This 'neo-feudalism', as it is also called, profoundly differentiated eastern from western European history, a differentiation that extends to this day. In the West, modernity came by means of the towns and their bourgeois dwellers, in the East via the decline of the landowning class, a difference of vast and fateful proportions.

Nonetheless, in the West what might often be heavy seigneurial obligations continued and were not finally swept away in France until the revolution there. What was serfdom? Essentially it was a system of indentured servitude and debt bondage. In return for their obligations to the landowner, peasants were entitled to protection and held certain rights in respect to the land they cultivated, land which they worked only after fulfilling their labour obligations to the lord. In Poland each lord was almost a sovereign in the hyper-decentralized political system of the Polish-Lithuanian Commonwealth. This sovereignty was, nevertheless, curbed by the state-centralist Prussian, Russian and Austrian partitionings of Poland, commencing from the late eighteenth century and enduring to 1918. Peasant emancipation was the hammer by which this curbing was accomplished.

Nonetheless serfdom itself varied greatly over time and place and in some places obligations were light. By 1800, seigneurial rights and peasant obligations were tied to land rather than status in the West and parts of the East. Obligations were commuted to rent in some places, in others not fully enforced, especially where there was access to princely or manorial courts. Across parts of central and eastern Europe, a high level of hereditary tenures co-existed with personal subjection. Hungarian serfs were allowed free movement. Among Polish-speaking peasants in 1791, 16 per cent were free peasants, and in the vast territory of the Polish-Lithuanian Commonwealth around a quarter were free.

The emancipation of the Austro-Hungarian serfs in 1848 did not make things much better than they were before, with rent servitude replacing serfdom. As in Ireland, earlier population growth in Galicia resulted in small peasant plots and agricultural techniques did not improve. There was little interest in agricultural reform from the major Galician landholders and the Austrian government. In 1899, 80 per cent of peasant plots in Poland were less than 5 acres in size. In the second half of the nineteenth century, despite only a marginal increase of arable land (about 7 per cent), the population of peasants living on plots doubled. Many peasants were heavily in debt, or had lost their land to moneylenders. The Imperial State of

Vienna tapped the eastern grain plains of Galicia in fully colonial style and drained the region of manpower through conscription. What went on in Poland was fairly typical of the East in general. Peasant emancipation turned upon state reduction and the redesign of seigneurial power.

On the other hand, after 1800 landlords' powers and restrictions on peasants were considerable within much of the western half of Europe, for instance, in southern Spain, including Castile, southern Italy and Sweden. The traditional view of North and South Europe is blurred too, although largely there were more peasant proprietors and better tenures in the North, sharecropping and *latifundismo* in the South. This is apparent within France and, to a lesser degree, Spain. Sharecropping *was* to be found in the north-west of France, particularly in parts of Brittany, where Martine Segalen has written of 'fifteen generations of Bretons' in a small and isolated commune in the far west. There the people followed the land, as it were, with people mobile from one sharecropped farm to another (but, with remarkable persistence over these many generations, moving only within the charmed circle of a strictly defined, and small, territory).[20] The category 'sharecropper' is itself far from precise. In the Department of the Loire in the mid-nineteenth century a farm might consist of around 5 hectares of owned, and usually inherited, land, some more rented for money, perhaps from kin, and some other land taken under sharecropping arrangements, worked with the help of other farmers when the necessity arose.

What is known as proto-industrialization was evident across Europe from the sixteenth century onwards, so that the rural world was by no means solely agricultural. Whether rural industry was truly a part of industrialization proper is a point argued over by historians. Handicraft activity was always apparent in peasant villages and rural industry was often simply an extension of this, creating work in slack seasons for peasants. Rapid progress in rural industry was apparent in more-developed economies from the eighteenth century onwards, including the 'putting-out' system in textiles, where in Britain it clearly was part of the industrialization process.

Certain areas in peasant society stand out as more distinct amid this great variety. The largest proprietor class was to be found in France, parts of Sweden and Bulgaria. There were vast numbers of landless labourers in Andalucía, the Po Valley, the Great Hungarian Plain and much of the Italian South. The North Sea basin, including south-east England, was, on the other hand, the most precocious in developing large-scale commercial farming, and so ahead of the rest of Europe by around 1800 in its capacity to beat the Malthusian population trap, unlike Ireland, of course. (The trap is sprung when population increase outpaces agricultural production.)

Whatever the differences are across the church of the peasants, it was almost everywhere a poor one. In France in 1892, 85 per cent of landholdings were less than 5 hectares in size (around 12 acres), 12.5 per cent were between 5 and 100 hectares, and a mere 2.4 per cent over 100 hectares. However, this 2.4 per cent held 43 per cent of agricultural land. In somewhat more evenly divided Germany in 1905 these figures were respectively 74 per cent, 25 per cent and 0.5 per cent, the last with 25 per cent of land overall. The 25 per cent in the middle held 61 per cent of the total, and its owners varied from peasants who were poor to comfortable. Austria and Denmark were somewhat similar. Poland was a sort of halfway house, with 51 per cent of those in the middle range accounting for 43 per cent of land, but with a massive 44 per cent held by less than 1 per cent of the population. Hungary and Romania were very emphatically lands of 5-hectare holdings.[21]

And then there is precociously capitalist England, which is commonly held not to have had a peasantry in modern times, and by some never to have had one. Scotland, Wales and Ireland had large groups of agriculturalists that can only be called peasants. These people were themselves far from quiescent, and besides the better-known Irish Land War of the 1870s and 1880s there was the Crofters' Land War in Scotland and the Welsh Tithe War of the same decades as the Irish troubles. These peasants were prepared to go to war. On the other hand, the common account of England is that capitalist farming had so reshaped agriculture by the mid-nineteenth century that the trinity of landowners, capitalist farmers and a large mass of landless dominated. It is certainly true that landownership in Britain was more concentrated than anywhere else in Europe: in 1861, 710 individuals owned a quarter of England and Wales and almost three-quarters of the British Isles was in the hands of fewer than 5,000 people. (Spain ranked second for its concentration of landownership, Prussia third.)

There is, all the same, a north and south divide for English agriculture, just as for most things in England, in this case the line being drawn roughly between the Wash and the River Severn. To the north there was a greater presence of small farmers and farm servants who lived as part of the farmer's household. Even in the South very small farmers existed in numbers in several areas. It can be argued, and has been argued, that this small-farmer class and farm servants were, in essence, peasants.

Of course 'peasant' has not much lingered in the social imagination of who the English think they are for a simple reason: by the late nineteenth century Britain was already an overwhelmingly urban and non-agricultural nation. But, in fact, 'peasant' was a word actually used by nineteenth-century English writers towards their countrymen, including Francis George Heath, whose anti-romantic *'Romance' of Peasant Life in the West of England* of 1872 was a thunderous attack on the wilful neglect that had led to the immiseration of the landless agricultural labourers in that region. He was an advocate of agricultural trade unionism, then on the rise, but used the term 'peasant' freely. As did others, including eminent twentieth-century rural historians.[22]

So, 'Peasant Europe'; what is it? It seems to be made up of several different things; for instance the marked, if at times blurred, distinctions between Europe's North and South, and its East and West. And it can be asked if peasant Europe is solely a matter of geographical Europe. The characteristics of European peasantries have been exported throughout the world. Old, indigenous peasantries, in place there before the Europeans arrived, were not always destroyed but adapted. There are millions upon millions of black 'European-style' peasants, in the Caribbean and Brazil, for instance, peasantries emerging out of the syncretism of African, Amerindian and European cultures, including the main organizational form that followed European slavery, namely the plantation-cum-*hacienda*-cum-*latifundio*. These people were often ex-slaves, African rural culture re-emerging after emancipation as people creatively adapted to new circumstances. In the eighteenth and nineteenth centuries poor Caribbeans and Latin Americans, of all ethnic backgrounds, fought incessantly to achieve the status of the landed peasant, the real meaning of emancipation. After the end of slavery in the United States, having a plot of land to own or rent, even with the harsh realities of southern sharecropping, was the dream of many, though the realities of new forms of subjugation and violence eventually drove so many north into the cities and industry.

The church of the peasants is ecumenical when it comes to colonialism within as well as without Europe. One does not need to spell this out to the Irish. But then there is the colonialism of eastern Europe. This colonialism is forgotten in the West, particularly in Britain, so fixated as it is on its own empire that it forgets the other empires its history was shaped by, the empires at its back door in Europe. There was the ancient colonizing push of Germans into the East in search of land, into Transylvania, for example, a thousand years ago. Then the colonialism of the Russian and Soviet empires, also the colonialism of the other land empires of Prussia–Germany and Austria–Hungary. Land empires, all hungry for more land, *Lebensraum* in the later Nazi empire. Poles and others from central Europe were colonizers as well as colonized, pushing into modern Belarus and Ukraine. Peasants were usually the victims, but sometimes the perpetrators.

And what do we make of the serfdom of the East itself? The word 'colony' derives from the Latin *colere*, to cultivate, from which comes *colonus*, a settler or farmer. In serfdom, one farmer, the landowner, battened on another farmer for profit. The great landowner, very pointedly in Poland, never laboured, work being the opposite of being a person of leisured culture. The serf always worked. In Poland, serfs were not free: they might not flee their villages, change profession, marry without permission, they might be held in manorial prisons, were legally beaten, were unable to trade in land without permission, had limited and mostly no rights of ownership. Military conscription in Polish Galicia might be as long as fourteen years, the local landowners acting as the imperial recruiting sergeants, another reason to hate the landlords.

The list of unfreedoms is long. The list of encroachments on peasant rights is long, such rights as they were. The body was enserfed: a Russian traveller to Galicia in the 1860s heard a description of a manorial whip from a peasant who drove him in a cart: 'like my horsewhip, only the handle was very, very short, and the strap was long, about the length of a man's body, plaited, with a knot at the end.'[23] The nobility and their officials beat peasants just like draught animals were beaten, convinced that only this would work. Colonialism came from within, without and across Europe geographically, but also within peasant society itself in the centre and the East.

We speak of French, Polish, Italian peasants and so on, and peasants became, in time, distinguished as citizens as well as peasants. These citizens fought and killed one another. The polities of European states left an indelible mark on each national peasantry. Still, how long it took for peasants to become French, Italian, Polish and all the other nationalities! Not until well into the twentieth century in many cases, not even until the twenty-first in others, not even now in some places.

The Historian James R. Lehning describes this process in *Peasant and French*: 'Our intention should not be to discover when and how peasants became French, but to discover the ways in which they served to define what being French meant, and the ways in which French culture defined what being a peasant meant.'[24] One was a peasant *and* French, not just one thing made into another. Things were not simply a one-way street, the peasant just driven to the wall as modernity pushed by.

Thus the differences that marked peasant Europe were tempered politically by resistance to the encroachments of the state. Indeed, one thing peasants had to survive was nationalism itself, the very thing that was supposed to make them as one in relation to others often making them at one among themselves. And then there is the experience of being colonized too, something else in common. I began this book by calling peasants a class of survivors, the most basic thing that gives them a common identity. Can we therefore talk of peasant Europe in a more unitary sense than we have so far, not as one identical thing, but as something evincing a pattern in the weave of peasant society? A pattern that is the land and how the land was worked?

The Labour of the Land

Norman Davies is the leading English-language historian of Poland. In the second volume of his monumental *God's Playground* he writes, 'Polish peasants were not just the members of a socio-economic class. Like their Russian counterparts, whom until the mid-nineteenth century they closely resembled, they were the bearers of a separate civilization, as distinct and as ancient as that of their noble masters', and adds, 'their powers of passive resistance were proverbial', likewise 'their imperviousness to the modern concepts of law and property'. Above all was their 'ineradicable conviction that the land was theirs, irrespective of the technical details of its legal ownership'. All these things made for 'an ultra-conservative culture, whose values were obstinately preserved in spite of the dispositions of well-intentioned reformers . . . Contemporary reformers, and modern social theorists, have ignored these factors at their peril.'[25]

I like the word 'civilization' because it thumbs the nose at those who imagine peasants to be uncivilized. And it is once-enserfed Poland that is being written about. But then 'distinct', 'ancient', 'resisting', 'impervious': these are attributes that apply to peasants across the continent. Above all, and for Europe too, and crowning all, is the ineradicable conviction that the land is theirs, all of the peasants, the ones who make it flourish.

The means of survival is land. Peasants do not see land like we do. We see land in terms of 'nature', something separated from the artificiality of humankind's creations, or, if these creations are included, then the natural, the supernatural and the unnatural are distinguished one from another. 'Nature' does not convey peasant reality, though we like to think it does. It is for peasants a semantically empty category, and there is little iconic or verbal representation of it in what records peasants have left (although educated peasants writing for an audience of non-peasants do embrace the idea sometimes).[26] From the point of view of the vast majority of peasants, there are, on the other hand, meadows, a river, the sky. For peasants the land is useless without their own work upon it, it will not be domesticated, 'It will not open and it will not close', as is said in Poland.[27] Marcin Brocki cites peasant words collected by the anthropologist Jacek Olędzki in the Poland of the 1960s: 'I like it where the plain is; when I was in America I saw a mountain, and this was an awful view. And when it's flat wherever you look, so that you could roll an apple, that is beautiful. Where you are perfectly flat, a lake, that's beautiful. And when there are mountains, sands, forests, you don't even want to come back.'[28] There is fear and even hatred of the wild, so unlike our veneration of wildness and the wilderness. The wild as our sublime makes no sense to the peasant.

'Domestication' for peasants represents what has been brought under control, what is useful, what is familiar. Through domestication people are recognizing and bringing about order in an uncertain world. The land isn't merely a tool or something useful; the entire well-being of the person and the community is wrapped up in it.

In all peasant societies there is the ideal of the 'good peasant'. In France the good peasant is the one who is not and does not want to be a *lou moussie*, a gentleman. His virtues are hard work, confidence, the capacity to run a farm well, all underpinned by the belief that whoever owns the land it is really the peasant's own, because he is the one who takes the land out of chaos into order. As for women, being a good peasant involves taking the good male peasant in marriage and not the gentleman, or upstart.[29]

Knowledge of the land was reflected in the naming of things, especially the naming of fields and of places and things within them. Naming was most intimate in the names coming from local languages and dialects. Land was also profoundly connected to structures of peasant belief that, if always rooted in local circumstances, show striking similarities across great regions of time and space, encompassing all of Europe. These beliefs were Christian, pre-Christian and para-Christian. Natural and spiritual. They were rooted in understandings of what land meant, something inseparable from understandings of nature and its cycles. We will encounter these beliefs later. For now, the photograph below will speak better than my words. It is of the peasant custom in the Upper Silesia of the early 1930s of marking the first sheaf of the harvest by erecting a cross on the sheaf, and so asking a blessing on the harvest. The picture is composed but the seriousness of the participants' devotions

should not be doubted.[30] All there will work in the field the man has scythed, the child included.

Men and women in the fields or on the pastures seldom describe their work in whatever reports of them we have, those few memoirs included. They are too busy doing it. Peasants who get more than a rudimentary education sometimes write, but even these do not write much about their experience, usually desiring to put their labour behind them. Those who leave accounts who remain peasants are rare. The description of work by Émile Guillaumin (whom we met in the previous chapter) is itself brief.[31] There is the arduous slowness of flailing corn by hand that he describes, the dull regularity of the regular downward beat; but then there is the satisfaction of winnowing, where the clean, golden grain mounts in a pile as he goes along. Flailing was, nonetheless, superior to the toil of hoeing with the adze, as in Millet's masterful painting. Children were inducted into work from a very early age. Women also had to command physical tasks: if the peasant is too poor to have a horse,

donkey or ox the man and woman must both be horses, taking it in turns to pull the plough. The woman usually does the brainwork, however, managing the accounts, something difficult when you do not have literacy or are innumerate, as Émile Guillaumin's family, among many others, were. On the previous page is a photograph of three women pulling a plough in France, taken sometime between 1917 and 1919. The men are perhaps away at the war.

Mastering work is key for men, but is essentially another form of self-mastery. Self-mastery is essential to survival. The culture is one of control: of emotions, of mind, of body. Physical strength is very important. In Poland it is said that the highest compliment you can pay a man is that he has *hart ducha*, which roughly translates as fortitude. It denotes strength of spirit, mastery of self, a person who will not flinch or surrender. Even if one must work for another person, the job itself is to be respected. One performs work with gratitude; there are prohibitions against cursing work. There is also a respect for property, for one is only a temporary custodian of the home, of what land there is, and of the Earth itself. Personal property is unwillingly loaned by peasants.[32] To destroy a beehive is a crime worse than murder.[33] Human labour is put into property, a rented house and land as well as what is directly owned. Peasants everywhere who are tenants come to believe the land is really theirs, chaos made into order as always, and it is they who may well have lived on the same land for generations. Many tenants, historically, had, as we have seen, a sort of de facto ownership anyway, given the prevalence of customary and long-term tenancy arrangements.

But oppressive work could be cursed. In the time of serfdom, before the early and mid-nineteenth-century emancipations, serfdom itself dramatized work as humiliation, work as hated. Serfs endured the everyday suffering of men who must feed other, and usually idle, mouths before they feed the mouths of their own. Sometimes, their work was a waste of time for all concerned, for the master in Poland had to take the serf back again after each and every extraction of compulsory labour from him or her (or else there would be no one else to labour for him), and this was always the case, no matter how badly the work was done, and it was often deliberately done badly and with contempt – as a sort of peasant revenge.

Peasant cultures are almost always cultures of scarcity. The fruits of the Earth are finite and should not be unequally shared, so that private initiative is always suspect, even if communities were not necessarily egalitarian in outlook. The idea of 'the limited good' appears again and again in peasant societies.[34] There was held to be only a limited supply of the goods of the Earth, so while one man prospered another went without. Thus the accumulation of capital was something alien, indeed, in most forms, viewed as inimical to the community. It followed that cultural displays of vanity and social distinction were hated, the peasant civil code rejecting signs of distinction and difference (even if distinctions abounded, people did not like to see them displayed, as the boat should not be rocked). In nineteenth-century Ireland there were strong punishments for those taking over the holdings of evicted persons. The Irish term for the English, a *Sasanach* (Saxon), implied this lack of generosity.

'No class has been or is more economically conscious than the peasantry,' Berger writes. '[T]he peasant's economic relation to the rest of society was always transparent . . . A peasant might think of his imposed obligations as a natural duty, or as some inevitable injustice, but in either case they were something that had to be endured.'[35] Taxes, dues, conscription were the fate of all. Scarcity means that peasants are always watchful, cognizant of change, change in the weather, in the sky, change in the earth itself, the soil, change on the earth, in the animals. These are often minute changes not visible to anyone else. Peasants must therefore protect themselves against these changes, and the insecurity they bring. They do this by customs, practices of work, by beliefs, religious and natural, by the attentive living of a conception of time which is cyclical and repetitive, like the labour they perform.

In order to understand the meaning of this labour better I turn to a remarkable study on the lives of Polish peasants, a five-volume work published between 1918 and 1920 called *The Polish Peasant in Europe and America* by William I. Thomas and Florian Znaniecki.[36]

Florian Znaniecki entered the Imperial University of Warsaw in 1902, but was expelled after involvement in protests against the governing Russian administration. Fleeing from conscription, he left Poland and subsequently faked his own death, briefly served in the French Foreign Legion, worked in flea markets, on a farm, and in a travelling circus, before he became an academic.

For the Polish peasant of the early twentieth century, the landholding, the farm, was the primordial cell of life. Land was not property as we understand property. It was symbolic as well as material, social rather than economic. Among Polish peasants, we learn from Znaniecki, if a mortgage was to be taken out, then the quality of the property was in a sense partly destroyed, for it no longer belonged completely to the nominal proprietor. The more distant the source of the mortgage was, the greater the degree of destruction of the symbolic quality of the land. There was a distrust of the distant instrument of the market, a bank, say, or state bodies, even if interest rates might be lower. (What in economic terms we might have regarded as irrational behaviour was apparent: the peasant, despite the availability of low interest rates elsewhere, wanted to pay off the whole of the mortgage as soon as possible.) Land, in this symbolic economy, was only held 'temporarily', in virtue of others, the family. There was the dense web of obligations and rights connecting household members. No amount of work would entitle a brother to wages in the Poland of the early twentieth century, for wages contravened what it meant to support and be supported.

The same was true for money. Money did not have the character of capital, but was really a substitute for other kinds of property. As it was a substitute like this, it was individualized according to its source and destination; the sum received from selling a cow was quite different from dowry money. Money for a dowry could only be used to buy land. Money was in a sense not fluid, not mobile, though increasing economic activity from outside the community always tended in this direction. Money was not made to fructify, to reproduce itself. In the Poland of the time it was kept at home, if possible, and if loaned out it was lent without interest or at very low rates, or payment was taken in goods and services instead. Peasants therefore were (and are) not capitalists.

Nonetheless, income in the form of cash must often be had, especially for taxes. As the influences of towns radiated into the countryside there grew the demand for commodities of a different and often alluring life, even if these might only be a mirror, or a length of cloth, which to the peasant woman might seem the object of dreams. Some bits of decent furniture, perhaps some wall pictures. Peasants are proverbial for their supposed stinginess, but, like the other myths, this is not true, or true only in a particular sense; money is set aside for the primary purpose of enhancing the land, and to have to spend it on anything else is considered a misfortune.

All this is replicated across Europe, Ireland included. Conrad M. Arensberg and Solon T. Kimball's classic anthropological work *Family and Community in Ireland* was published in 1940.[37] Again, in this study of the area around Ennis in County Clare, there is the family economy, with land, labour and family inextricably linked. The father directs the family, does the heavy tasks, the care of the cattle, for instance. His boys watch him, observe, mind themselves as they say in Ireland, so that the skill of the farmer is on display to the sons, but also to the rest of the family and to one's neighbours. The boy in Arensberg and Kimball's Clare community might remain a 'boy', even when the father is old, as long as the father has the farm. The boy moves to become a man; the son is subordinate to the mother, is her constant companion until the age of seven. She is the one who nurtures and praises, until marriage breaks the bond. 'Father' and 'son' are emotional symbols of great power. The sons are treated all the same; there is no necessary primogeniture. Solidarity between the sons is mandated, even though all but one must eventually relinquish any rights to the farm in the interests of the family and its identification with the land. But the new head of the family has obligations as well as rights, and must assure the well-being of those family members who have to remain.

And the daughters? The long years ahead on the farm might be contemplated with sadness if a marriage is not made and independence made possible, or if emigration is not the recourse. Even after the parents die, their children are slow to leave. No one wants to be the first to leave, male or female, at least this is the preordained etiquette: the smaller the farm, however, the keener the children are to leave, and the lucky ones may be the ones who go. The boy's relationship to his sister is based on the one with his mother; the sister's relationship to her brother follows the pattern of hers with her father, but as marriage and departure are held to be the ultimate destination of most women, the daughter does not have the same intense relationship with her father that the son will have. There is a marriage *group*, as it were, the extended family so-called, and this includes those outside the immediate family circle, who are called 'friends', the meaning of which differs from common English-language use. The marrying man inherits his wife's family as 'friends'.

The circles of obligation start with the 'friends' and then move on to cooperation with wider circles. A peasant has a right to this cooperation, it is fitting and part of the tradition. Cooperation between friends and neighbours is customary (the townland – the smallest administrative unit of land division in Ireland – is the most immediate and intimate marker of neighbourhood), as tasks too large to be done alone, like haymaking on bigger farms, are accomplished by reciprocal cooperative labour with others. There are various English and Irish names for this: for example, in Clare: cooring, cottilage, *comhair*. *Cóir* in Irish is a term for a traditional right or duty: *duine cóir* is a worthy man who fulfils his obligations; and *cóir mhaith* conveys that there is a good feed there for me, but the message is about the social situation rather than the food taken literally. The kinship naming system reflects all this.

Lives and their courses, families and their histories. It is time to turn to these stories of lives. These lives are not only lived in houses, but the houses themselves represent the lives. Down to the stones, the timbers, all the things of the Earth that peasants take from it in order to dwell upon it.

4.
Lives: The House

What does it mean to say that the houses represent the lives of peasants? The simple answer is that the house is the symbolic as well as the material centre of the peasant family economy, the family economy being at the centre of peasanthood. The house itself is at once the physical shelter from the world and the organizing principle of peasant culture, and as such is the heart of what it is to dwell in the world.

There is something striking about the word 'dwelling'. The same word is used for the act as the means of being in the world, and both act and means denote perhaps the most fundamental part of the sense of place that we possess. This is especially so with the experience of the first dwelling or at least the dwellings we experience childhood in. The existential sense of place itself, of being 'here' in the world, is inseparable from the dwelling, therefore, the place where one is sheltered from the world, protected. Or not sheltered and protected, for the absence of these things leaves its mark as well. This is so for us all, but especially so for peasants, who practise a family economy, the centre of which is the house itself, the dwelling house but also the other houses that might surround the main house, for animals, for crops and so on. What we call the 'farm', in fact, the farm unfolding, as it were, in layers from the dwelling house to the fields, then the mountains, the forests, the wastelands.

The dwelling is also a constitutive part of the relationship between past and present generations, between the living and the dead. Something handed on, or hoped to be handed on, something to be received. When the dead have a foundational role in human life, as is the case with peasants, then the house takes on a cosmological significance. But the house remains eminently material at the same time. There is also that other house, the one where the dead dwell, the graveyard. So, the place of burial is yet another dwelling place in the peasant village, one always of the greatest importance. The word human comes from the Latin word *humus*, meaning earth or ground. We are made from the earth to which we will return. The place of inhumation is, or at least was, as surely as the dwelling house, an indication of the sense of having a place in the world, of taking possession of a place and securing it as one's own.[1]

There is a story by Pirandello in which he refers to a Sicilian baron who refused to let the peasants bury their dead on his land, because he knew that if they did they would come to regard it as their own by natural right – to regard it as their house.[2] The peasants who oppose him, even though the land is in the baron's ownership, in fact regard the land as already theirs, the dead needing to be buried on 'our land', so that the living can be near them in order that they may be watched over and cared for. In times not so far in the past, where land was owned the custom was that the dead be buried there and not in a cemetery. At the same time as the living watch over the dead, the dead watch over and care for the living; in Corsican culture the dead elders of the house retain in death the authority they once possessed in life.

Opposite is a photograph of the interior of a peasant house. I start my discussion of houses with those I have known or which are similar to ones I have known, the sort of houses my parents grew up in.

Houses

The photograph above was taken in 1935 and the kitchen is shown. The woman in the image is known. She is Mrs Breathnach from Maam Cross in County Galway, in the south of the Country, Dúiche Seoighe, Úna her first name. The centre of the physical house is apparent in the image, which is always the kitchen, at the centre of which is the hearth. The woman sits at the centre. She sits on a tiny stool, the crude bench is before her, the bellows by the fire, above the cut-away barrel holding the turf for fuel ('turf' is peat). The fire looks as if it has gone out but is merely dozing, for the teapot is on the stone flags before it to keep warm, and the great black kettle is apparent. In the face of Úna Breathnach there is something of 'devilment', fun, the playing of tricks in the gaze, and there is a certain distance there too. She sports with aplomb what is usually regarded as a man's pipe.

I remember such kitchens thirty years on in the West, by then the walls smoothed off, the floor better laid, although the cooking range-cum-stove was only just coming in.[3] The old farmhouses in my mother's Wexford were often rather grander affairs than in Mayo and Galway, if too cut to the same basic pattern: entrance almost always directly into the kitchen, the rooms for sleeping at either side. The old Wexford hobs (hearths) might be enormous and comfortable, with room for four or more to sit by the fire, the kitchens themselves large, the furniture simple but stout, the walls kept white and clean. Geraniums were proudly on display in every window, the elaborate dresser with the 'delph', the crockery, on display in the kitchen ('delph' from Delft ware in Holland). What the house amounted to depended on economic circumstance, of course, but just as much on the pride of the woman of the house, the wife or the grandmother who might be the real governor.

My mother's family had a newly built house in Wexford in the 1950s which was in many essentials little different. One lived still in the old, limited order of consumption. Despite it being built in 1950 'modern conveniences' were not thought of as the first priority. The house was made with the old-style black open hearth, the fire irons hanging down, the fire the house's only source of energy, aside from the hand-driven bellows located under the floor, the handle of which I turned at first with delight and then complaint when told not to flag and keep at it. The sound of the bellows wheel turning woke me in the morning. A modern convenience. The Tilley lamp, a mid-nineteenth century Polish development, in fact, shed its lemony-coloured light as the late evenings drew in, a thousand moths and other winged creatures, drawn up from the river below us, smashing themselves hopelessly against the always closed windows. One went outside summer and winter to relieve oneself. Although the chamber pot was of great relief in the middle of the night. Seamus Heaney has some fine lines about women urinating together at the gable end of the house, their strict preserve.[4]

The only refinement of the house, apart from the comfort of being newly built, was additional room on one side which acted as a parlour or best room, one that seemed never to be used. The house was a decided improvement on our living conditions back in a blighted post-war London. The irony was that we thought the visited relations the lucky ones, whereas they envied us the gold-paved streets of London. Electricity came to rural Wexford only in the 1950s, two decades later to my father's place in the west.

My memory is a poor guide to these matters, however, and so I turn to one who spent much time in Irish houses, a professional at the job of house contemplation. The folklorist-anthropologist Henry Glassie offers an understanding of the Irish rural house which is striking.[5] His resounding genius for reading cultures through things is apparent, things like walls, windows, kitchen dressers.[6] He wrote about County Fermanagh in Northern Ireland in the 1970s.

For Glassie, time since the 1970s has meant that generosity and openness, the soul of the old house, has given way to comfort and privacy. He writes of the old houses, still a majority in Fermanagh then. Historically, the openness of Irish houses, which means always a measure of disarray, has been taken by outsiders to signify the squalor of the feckless Irish. In the Fermanagh house, wherever you were positioned in the world depended on where you were in relation to the hearth, 'down' when going away, 'up' coming towards it. You go into the house and are on familiar ground as all houses are more or less the same. You enter directly into the room where all of life, but for sleeping, is led, the kitchen; the sleeping rooms as usual on either side. Room doors may be open to adjust the fire's draught, but are usually shut, icy boxes in winter, though less so the room behind the fire, which may be reserved for the old people.

It is bad manners to knock and for the host to keep you waiting at the door. You go into the house to the fire, the fire the centre of the hearth, the hearth the centre of the kitchen, the kitchen of the house, the house of the farm ('the home place'), and so onwards goes what Glassie calls a culture of centres, one around which cyclical time revolves. Only illness brings you into the bedrooms in daylight, and being confined to 'the room' for any reason is 'like walking the road on your lone'. 'It put me in that much despair, I could go up into the room,' one woman says to Glassie. One should stay by the fire, 'in company'.[7] I have written of the Irish house transplanted to the worn and cramped London flat of my immigrant parents, my dear, sick father too often confined to 'the room', away from the fire.[8]

The following diagram, made by the Irish Folklore Commission in the 1940s, shows the interior of a smaller, two-roomed house, and what is within this house, and the arrangement of the things of the house is fairly common across Ireland. A table is before the window (the luxury of two kitchen windows and tables is apparent in this charmingly drawn plan).[9] There is a bench, a settle, placed by the wall opposite the front door. Opposite the fire is the dresser, and beside this 'cood' is marked, which is a sleeping place used only at night. Two little stools, 'creepies', are on either side of the fire. In the second room is a 'covered-car bed'. Behind the fire is not a second room but a contiguous but separately entered chamber which is for animals and storage.

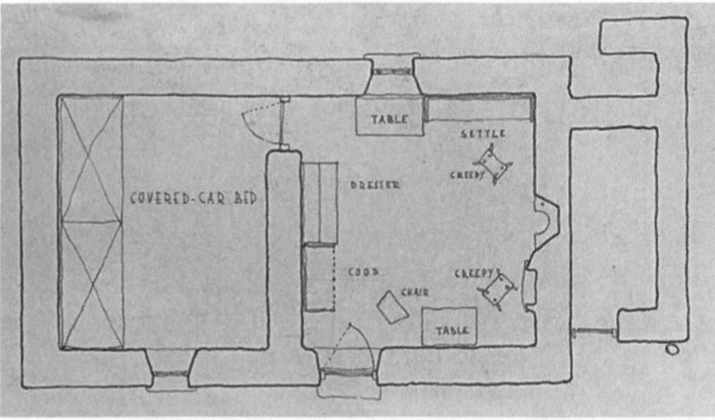

The dresser is of great significance, the site of public show, and Glassie reports that a Mrs Cutler is 'happy as money' when she takes her delph down from the dresser.[10] The dresser dignified the kitchen, and by Glassie's time many of the houses he describes had a 'best' room, where family photographs might be laid out and cherished ornaments kept, as was usually the case in one of the sleeping rooms when best room there was none.

The contrasts, but mostly the underlying similarities, with Poland are noticeable. A fairly typical peasant house in Poland around the same time as the photo of the Breathnach house in Maam Cross was taken would have been made up of two rooms, known as the white room and the black room, the *izba czarna*, the black room, and the *izba biała*, the white. The *komora* was a storage area between the two, and the *sień* a passageway to the door, also between the two rooms. The *sień* was literally the 'windcatcher', direct entry, unlike in the Irish house, prohibited by the cold and wind of winter, also the mud.

The white room is seen in the image that follows: the bed is an object of display with its giant mattress and pillows. The bed is the great symbol of comfort and worth, most often there being more than one pillow, and pillows being carefully arranged in descending order of size in what appear to be remarkable acts of balancing in many cases. The white sheets and covers are carefully kept white, as are the white walls. The hand-embroidered hangings aloft, the decent bits of furniture, all attest to the differences being marked. The purpose of such rooms was not sleeping, but necessity might drive people to that purpose.

In the white room the great events of lives took place and were marked, the events signifying the reproduction of the house-as-family. Here, in the best room, in Poland, the young aspirant couple would come to seek marriage permission and blessings from parents, the obedient children embracing the knees of the elders in supplication and respect.[11] This was the dying and laying-out room also, with the 'mourning woman' in attendance, praying, singing, bearing the expertise of how to die and how properly to be thought of after death. In both the white room and the black, as in Irish rural houses of every type, holy objects decorated the walls, pictures, prayers, figurines of Mary, Christ and the saints, holy water for use on entering and leaving, St Brigid's cross near the door.

What we call nature we would regard as being outside the house. For peasants, though, inside and outside flowed one into the other much more freely than for us. Production as well as reproduction take place in the dwelling house, especially in the winter when production outside is curtailed by the weather and the crop cycle. Hens and dogs wander in and out, and are constantly shooed away. Everything must find a shelter, animals and humans both. The house is open to the outside to allow for this flow, winter conditions permitting, that is. Houses themselves grow out of the ground, built by what is to hand: wood, stone, sods of earth, mud. They are adapted to the climate in the most knowledgeable of ways, to the constant westerlies in Ireland, to the Polish winters, to the summer sun of the South. The Donegal house represented below shows the adaptation needed to negotiate the Atlantic wind, this type being commonly found along the north-west seaboard, rounded roof ridge and roped thatch evident.

There is complete dependence on the source of water outside, whether there is a yard well or just the spring itself. Fuel as well as food and water must be gathered, as with the turf in Ireland, wood in Poland. (Rural Ireland was only electrified completely in the 1960s and 70s.) In many photographs of peasant houses in Poland, herbs

and garden produce are to be seen ripening in the sun on the roofs of houses. Things needed were made out of what came to hand, even scarcely found straw in Ireland, which was used to make all manner of farm objects, including horse collars. Glassie tells the story of the outsider – himself perhaps – who asked where he might relieve himself and was told anywhere between this door and the mountain over there on the horizon.

When it comes to the photographic record of these places, we see faces and houses. Faces usually at a distance, for when peasants are photographed it is often outside, frequently by the doors of their houses, less often at work. They are posed by the photographer, a tableau of faces, bodies, doors, houses. We do not get so many peasant interiors, for technical but also social reasons, like that of the house kitchen in Maam Cross. Here below is one such arrangement of person and house, taken in the East of Poland

sometime in the interwar years. The man is in his work clothes and stands before his house. The image is striking, the quality better than most. The white top and trousers of the man are summer wear, made at home of rough flax. The man's face is a little hidden by the cap he wears, the cap itself a symbol of the Polish peasant. His shoulders are narrow but he looks a powerful man, the hands as usual strikingly sized. The sun and the camera combine to reveal a culture which is one of wood. The large axe in the man's hand is a similar reminder. The big, regular and well-set timbers of the house emphasize the man's acquaintance with the form of nature that most shapes his life. The home-made moccasins on his feet are typical of the Polish East.

It looks like summer in the photo, but the man may have recently been cutting wood for winter fuel. And to keep the stove going in summer. It is fire, out of all the natural things, that is most at the centre of life in these two cultures. Hence the universal symbolic significance of the source of heat, light, nature transformed into culture, the raw into the cooked. It is difficult now to comprehend the world before electricity, the immense darkness of winter nights, and only the fire and oil lamp for light. The fire in the hearth demands constant attention and must not go out, except in Ireland for one day a year, the first of May. Turf fires fall apart easily and clog with ash, and so need vigilance. The fire is the metronome of the kitchen, says Glassie, and there is a continuing need to clean and tidy up. In the wonderful local English of Fermanagh, the kitchen is said to be 'tossicated' when in need of tidying up, wanting a good 'retting out'.

Fire can be turned against people as well as benefiting them. There is a fine study of Upper Bavarian peasants before the First World War, *The Village in Court*, in which the great magnitude of the crime of arson is displayed.[12] Arson strikes at the heart of peasant culture, revealed, for instance, in the revenge of the landless man against the bigger peasant who employs him, for there is no greater revenge than the destruction of the house and farm buildings. And there is no greater motive for arson than being excluded from the circle of the fire, which is in effect the household in which the servant works. Many farm labourers and servants lived with peasant landowners and were treated on near-family terms. The psychological wound of being excluded from the hearth, the source of shelter and care, was deep. The motives for arson reveal the fault lines going through village culture but also its essential unity, for in the very act of using fire maliciously the arsonist affirms the centrality of the peasant hearth and house.

The stove in Poland is the equivalent of the fire in Ireland. The wooden houses of Poland themselves are generically named after fire, as 'smoke houses'. The stove, built in the corner of the black room, might occupy one-third of the room's space. The old and the young, and sick animals, would sleep around the stove in the bitterness of winter. 'He lives like one behind God's stove' is said of a person who has security, ease and freedom from responsibility. Just like the open turf fire, the stove needed a watchful eye, and women were the traditional tenders of fire, the first bearers of food and warmth.

The following photo is of a Polish peasant stove, an unrepresentative one in that it is white (in the black room, the usually dishevelled room in which the whole family ate, slept and laboured in winter). But the image is also representative, for the stove is an ordinary one but has been cleaned up and painted for Easter or for a wedding, which was the custom. The richness and beauty of the decoration are testimony to the standing of the god in the corner. The ceiling is painted too. Glass art in Polish peasant painting is renowned, typically showing images of saints, the glass of windows being the medium that would preserve the saint's image best whereas everything else to hand would be useless against the smoke and dirt. Glass can be cleaned, the image kept undisturbed.

There is a curious metaphorical richness to the smoke that gives the black room its name, as if smoke occludes our vision of

peasant life, just as it obscured the senses in the black room itself. When a house had no chimney, people lived their lives in the black rooms of Poland, their bodies held in a particular way, bowed so as to avoid the rising smoke. Experts on peasants, and folklore, certainly the older sort upon whom so much of our basic historical knowledge depends, did not, with few exceptions, write of smoke, nor of dirt, defecation, delousing or sex. The list of omissions is long. If these experts had asked peasants about these things, they would not have been told anything anyway, some things being kept to oneself, and a certain decorum maintained. What was not (and is not) told to investigators would fill many more volumes than what was, but we depend on this 'what was' bit, and in truth should be grateful for that.

Fire itself has a certain holiness. In Poland one is said to pray *through* the fire; one prays in front of the fire, and that which is evil or bad is on the other side, so that fire builds a wall of protection. Special prayers are said when a fire is started, and the sign of the cross is used: 'Let every spark burn to your glory.' Blessings are related to the tongues and sparks of fire. No dirty water should be thrown on the fire, for this will pollute it and fire will have its revenge. You should not spit in the fire, your tongue will fall out or pimples will grow on your face. You should not piss on the fire, your penis will fall off. You must be respectful of fire in your language, and should not curse in front of it. When moving house, a remnant of the old fire is carried to the new. On marriage, burned fragments of their families' fires are given to start the couple's new fire. Fire is healing, cleansing; you burn your sickness off into the fire. Fire heals particular skin diseases: flax, made into a loop or rose, when burned, will heal. Recovery from typhus may be secured by walking through fire.

There are different sorts of fire. Fire, light and heat protect. The burned or heated axe placed under the child's cradle protects against evil. You take the burning brand around every corner of the house to secure its protection. The whistling pot on the fire is the howl of souls in hell, the crackling in the burning fire is a soul begging for mercy. Fire divines: a woman blows a candle and the direction in which the smoke goes is where her future husband will come from.

This is an Irish traditional prayer called 'Banking the Fire':

> With the powers that were granted to Patrick I bank this fire.
> May the angels keep it in, no enemy scatter it.
> May God be the roof of our house
> For all within
> And all without,
> Christ's sword on the door
> Till tomorrow's light.[13]

Lives

Houses, bodies, faces; we know them in words and images, in modern times, above all, in the photographic image. The names of the persons whose images were taken are not usually known (photographs are 'taken', as we say in English). We do know the name of Mrs Breathnach and that of her husband Mícheál, a renowned storyteller locally. The photographer's name is also known, Caoimhín Ó Danachair of the Irish Folklore Commission. James Hamilton Delargy, the driving force behind the Commission, frequently visited Dúiche Seoighe to collect 'folklore'. He stayed with the family in their house and was regarded as a friend. Ó Danachair and other Folklore Commission photographers almost invariably 'pose' their subjects, pose in a broad sense, that of presenting a particular subject as set out in the various folklore guides of the time (farming techniques, house types, dress, beliefs and so on).

In short, the photograph is a document. The eye of the camera is a different eye from those of the family snap and the art photos of peasants. The Folklore Commission photo deliberately documents places and people, and the photographs that follow for Poland are similar. Though they are mostly the product of newspaper archives, they purport to make a record of what it was really like, the unlying photograph making its own truth manifest. The photo colludes with the words 'record' and 'document' to create a social and historical version of what is true, one built, however, at a remove, around the idea of the nation (Poland was newly independent and Ireland too). The eye of the camera, being political and social, tends to categorize and classify, so that the images that follow convey a sort of social history of the peasant. Which is one vital way of seeing peasants, but only one.

Lives in houses, lives revolving around the house. Images now of people before houses, the houses helping to explicate the lives. A class system of peasants is one version of the truth the documentary photograph produces. The two following images come from the Podlesie region of Poland, which was, if anything, even poorer than famously poor Galicia, which is to its south. The man's clothes are ragged and his folded arms are trying to keep his ragged coat closed to keep warm, or perhaps to hide his poverty. The photograph was taken sometime between 1918 and 1939. The man stands before a house of some sort, the dreadful state of which is apparent. Big towns were thin on the ground in the region, which lacked a developed trade system, and agrarian depression had followed world depression in these years.

The next photo was taken in Podlesie in 1933, and shows a woman alone in front of a house, arms folded, seemingly once again as an act of self-protection. She is alone, she and the house, and, as in the first picture, the house is in a poor state, the door seeming to fall in on itself, the roof crudely made and the timbers looking rotten. This picture, and the previous one, may both be of dwelling houses, incredible as this seems. Mud is everywhere. The house behind looks scarcely better than the one in front.

The photograph following that of the lone woman is a frightful picture of peasant poverty. I first saw it in the National Museum of Ireland – Country Life, located in my father's County Mayo, outside Castlebar. It was placed there by the museum authorities to serve as a warning not to romanticize peasants. The young woman – a mother, a sister? – lies as if she were ill, and beside her a young boy in rags warms himself by the fire, the new sods of turf stacked upon

it. The fireplace is primitive, the hearthstones crude. Both boy and woman are in bare feet. The photo was taken on Gorumna Island, a remote spot in remote Connemara. The year was 1910, and there were near-famine conditions around this time in southern Connemara, the potato and the sea harvests both spoiled, the former by heavy unseasonal rains. The beauty of the young woman is evident, particularly in her jet-black hair.

The contrast with Mrs Breathnach's fire and kitchen is apparent: she with the tidy fire, and the warm, heavy jumper, the voluminous and warm petticoats and the decent shoes. Maam Cross was hardly a place of riches but she is more representative of what we can call the middling condition, the one most peasants would be in. In Poland, though, all peasants were poor, some more than others, and things were somewhat better as you went east to west. The next image looks to be one of 'middling' peasants, only now they are in town, dressed probably for market day, though the market square behind is almost empty. Dress is of the greatest importance to peasants, good clothes being reserved for business in town, Mass or special events. Outside the house, subject to the eyes of strangers, one should look one's best.

They are in the town of Gródek Jagielloński in Galicia, and the year is 1934. The good boots of both, the woman's petticoats, the warm-looking shawl and his coat suggest a certain standing and contrast with the clothes of the town dwellers behind, which were pretty much standard across Europe at this time. Again, the apartness of peasants is suggested. Once more we are in the then east of Poland, 25 miles west of Lviv. Horodok is the Ukrainian name of the town now, the Poles and the Jews long gone.

As for the interior of a better-off peasant's house, the following is representative. The photo was taken in the district of Łowicz, halfway between Warsaw and Łódź, and the year is probably 1921. 'Middling' and 'better off' are subjective categories, and varied by region. Łowicz would have been more prosperous than Galicia, to the south, so that what is 'better off' here would be well off elsewhere. For Łowicz the interior would not be unusual for the region. Clearly this vision of order is posed, but the impression of order registers what is real. The uniform, dark everyday working dress of the women indicates domestic order and the pride it would have engendered. The young girl in the front is reading, her eyes modestly cast down on the words. She wears a necklace, and here prosperity has its measure of modest display. Beside the girl in the background, on the wall, there is a little cut-out figure of what seems to be a peasant, an idealized, rather jovial-looking little man. The walls and floor are smooth and clean, and the walls are decorated faintly at the top. The windows have clean, matching curtains. The emotional centre of the image is the older woman who is spinning; the girl who is not reading appears to be doing the same. The house here is unambiguously presented as the domain of the women.

What follows in the next photograph can be taken as a pretty typical peasant village in the Polish South.

The man in this photo is shod and decently clothed and the houses are in good repair, the thatched roofs in particular. Such roofs are distinctive of local tradition (there were rich regional variations). There is an electricity pole, so the village is 'modern', but no lines stretch to the houses, and it looks more like a telegraph line, which is in itself impressive, even though none of these people would have received telegrams. Like most of Poland, the houses were made of wood, in contrast to the stone houses further west in Europe, for example, in Ireland and Italy (and the brick of Silesia).[14]

The photo indicates a particular kind of village, typical of Poland, that of the 'street' type. The picket fences are striking, and the entry to the dwelling house and what other farm buildings there may be behind suggests a balance of separateness and commonality, for the houses are hardly what we would call private. More often there was no fence outside, each house having a bench in front for commerce with the passing life of the street. The usual pattern is for there to be a long strip of cultivated land behind each house, and many outlying strips around the village, each separately managed, but needing much cooperation between villagers to be manageable.

The palisaded street above is in contrast to the more scattered farms of Ireland, though there was and still is much clustering of houses there too, something going back to the clachan tradition. The next photograph is of An Chloch Bhreac (Cloghbrack), a settlement almost directly opposite my father's place, across the half mile or so of lower Lough Mask. Cousins and siblings watched upon family members from one side of the lake to the other. A candle left burning all night marked a death in a house, the light of the candle signalling this across the water. The absence of trees in the photograph is noticeable, though some have grown back since, the people gone, the trees returning, so that nature has replaced man. The bracken and rushes have multiplied. What is most notable, at least to my eye, is the neatness, the tidiness of it all, the effect being enhanced by the symmetry of the walls and

houses. Also the wide road, and the neat rows of potatoes growing everywhere, life still revolving around them. The difference to today is striking: there is only grass where once the staple of life was grown.

'Middling' when referring to peasants is a term that is relative between as well as within nations. The people of An Chloch Bhreac would have been of the middling kind in Poland, but in Ireland regarded as poor in comparison with many in the east of the country. However, in this image, the people of An Chloch Bhreac are clearly seen to live in an ordered and long-civilized natural setting. The name of the place, present in tiny letters in the bottom left-hand corner, is given as 'America', and this tells another part of the story. The settlement was also known as 'America Village', because so many from there had emigrated to the US, leaving at the fork in the road at An Chloch Bhreac. The departure of the many was the precondition of the limited prosperity the relatively few who stayed had.

The poorest of poor houses in Ireland was the sod house, the dwelling sometimes no more than if an animal had burrowed into the ground to cover itself.

This, and the simple stone house without a chimney or windows, were said to be the type of abode of over a third of the population in 1840, before the famine changed things. Such houses were to be found across Europe, then and much later, the floors often only beaten earth, animals and people sharing space, but segregated as much as possible. Nevertheless, sod houses could sometimes be elaborate, and their construction sophisticated. The heavy rains of the West of Ireland and the long and freezing Polish winters were made the best of in such habitations. In his writing, Ignazio Silone describes the poor houses of the Abruzzo a few decades after the previous image was made: the one-storey dwelling with a single opening which is a door, a chimney and a window all together.[15]

There is the story the physical house helps tell us, and then there is the story of the rhythm of the seasons and the rhythm of the life course.[16] This is also the rhythm of the house, the house now as the symbolic as well as the material anchor of life. The three great ceremonials of the peasant's calendar are christening, marriage and burial. There are these proverbs of Russian peasants which, like many proverbs, explain it best: 'May God permit me to marry once, / Be baptized once, and to die once.' And, 'A person undergoes three wonders: when he / Is born, when he marries and when he dies.'[17]

Most of what I will describe in Poland persisted, sometimes remarkably, up to the middle of the twentieth century. However, what I describe about Poland in regard to the course of peasants' lives could be said of those who lived across Europe too. The underlying similarities – with notable variations – are there everywhere, in the Iberian peninsula, say, in which the late continuance of very old cultures is as apparent as in Poland. Fascism in Spain and Portugal had played its part in this continuation, just as, to some degree, did Communism in the East.[18] There are many stories to tell.[19]

First of all, to Poland and children: the term *przezdzietnica* means the 'childless one', for whom contempt was mixed with pity. The illegitimate child was a calamity, but there were ways around calamity – hushing it up, or just living with it. If a woman's pregnancy did not show much, abortion might be sanctioned. Going far back, there is research on peasants before 1800 that conveys the actual flexibility of their behaviour, as opposed to their codes, vital as these were (and that 'calamity' was relative).[20] There is no reason to think this flexibility decreased.

Outward signs were seen as portents of what lay beneath, which was the case with everything, reality being multiple. It revealed what was beneath *and* what was to come, not exactly predestination, but something like what we would call fate, *fortuna* in Italy. It was thought that the pregnant woman should be shielded from death and the dead, and from those living humans considered ugly or abnormal. There were multiple beliefs and practices around the circumstances of birth, especially the position of the baby. A baby born in an unusual position might have 'evil eyes'. The disabled at birth could be seen as an expression of God's anger and malformation as a harbinger of future bad fortune, the crooked body and the crooked spirit going together. The pregnant woman was said to be 'in hope' – for any good birth, but especially that of a boy.

She was to be gratified and cosseted, but she was also unclean. Protection came from her and yet might also be needed against her. At the birth, the doors, windows and chimney are closed to prevent evil, and the bed is curtained off. The fear of the baby as a changeling is widely apparent in peasant cultures. The *babka* would attend, the 'wise woman' who knows not only about birth but much else too, a woman whose importance in the village cannot be overestimated (the *babka* was often preferred to midwives when these later became available). If labour was difficult the woman might be laid on the ground so that the magical strength of the 'holy earth' would flow into her. In some places, the *babka* ordered the husband to bed beside his wife with the words, 'Suffer ye both'.

There are in effect two christenings in rural Poland, one in church and one at home, the baby's first bath. The home ritual of the first bath is elaborate. It sometimes takes place in the bread trough so that the child will grow like dough rises when cooked. Everyone entering the house puts money in the trough. If the baby cries during its first bath it will have a temper, but it will also thrive and grow. The bathwater is carefully disposed of because it is identified with the child's future, and because the unbaptized baby is still unclean. There is formal acceptance of the child into the family at the time of its first bath or immediately after baptism.

Unbaptized babies were once buried like suicides in the fields or woods, without the usual ceremonies, just like in Ireland and elsewhere. In Poland, their souls were believed to haunt the world in the shape of birds, mice or shooting stars, begging piteously for baptism. If you heard the cry, you were meant to baptize the poor child's soul with water, saying: 'If a boy, you are John, / If a girl, you are Ann.' The choosing of the name at baptism is of the greatest importance, the name of the saint whose day the child is born on usually being chosen. The name is sometimes kept secret until the moment of baptism.

The child grows up in the world of the elders, early on sharing their reality and responsibilities, and only an infant is fondled and caressed. There is abundant love for children but certain formalities to do with parenting are to be observed. The child addresses his or her parents by the respectful rather than the informal pronoun. Nonetheless, formality also dictated that the dignity of the child should be recognized. The child was never to be publicly scolded or humiliated.

The beating of children as of wives was permitted, the former more prevalent. The latter was however a two-way street, for wives beat husbands, and it depended on who got the upper hand. It was a question of power, psychological and economic. The spoils went to the fittest. In the Loire region there was the custom of the *balai*, the *culotte*, the trousers: a pair of men's trousers was raised on high and the newly-weds competed to reach the trousers first. The one who wins gets the authority.[21] The one who loses gets the broom. It may not be a fair fight, as men and women are usually of different heights. Despite that, there were ways around this, and male dominance was (and is) very often more formal than real.

Nonetheless, public hierarchies were to be respected: when the woman went to church she walked a little behind her husband; the wife was referred to as the wife of her husband, for example, as Markov's wife, or Slomka's wife. It was said that a kind intention of the husband should be accompanied by a hard word.

A woman's position is ambiguous when she goes as a bride to her husband, for she is an outsider who comes within, yet is then the guardian of the prosperity of the family. If ends are to meet, she makes them meet, as circumstances will allow. Another telling Russian proverb alludes to this: 'Without a husband is without a head: without a wife is without a brain.' In France the man was known in official records as the *proprietor/cultivator*. The husband's domain is the land, and his rule extends formally to the home, but the authority of the wife embraces the household, which involves both house and land.[22]

There is a high value put upon a wife's counsel in Poland. She is the one who, as the mother, makes sacrifices, and there is compensation for her formal subordination to the husband in her authority as mother. To use a wife's given name is disrespectful after the age of thirty-five, when she is well established as a mother. She is the *stara*, the old (and therefore respected) one, and is always called 'Mother' in front of the children. Among the peasants of the Loire, it is similar, the woman is known as the *ménagère*, the house boss, her domain including the farmyard, the garden and the well. Of course, women might work in the fields also, just as men built the houses and worked in them in the evenings, especially in winter. As everywhere, when the wife had a child, her position got stronger.

In a fine study of four Italian peasant villages that covers the same time period as the Polish ethnographies I have drawn on, the fragility of male dominance is also evident. Male authority is almost always apparent, but authority and dominance are not the same things.[23] Public respect must be shown to the husband: using the polite form of 'you' to his face, but 'the mule' behind his back. The suspected *cornuto*, the cuckold, is the butt of endless jokes: the honour of the proud groom is at the mercy of the bride's bedsheet. Only a wife's pregnancy can sustain her husband's masculinity. Everything is subordinate to the procreation of the house.

The child grows up: as soon as it 'moves by itself', as it is said, the mother in Poland stops paying direct attention. Only babies are cosseted and greatly fussed over: when the baby 'comes into his mind' it is the elder children who look after him or her, sometimes a three- or four-year-old acting as a parent. Relationships with siblings formed in this way may last powerfully throughout life. The child's sense of security is vested less in one person than the solidarity and stability of the family unit, the 'we' that counts. He or she is responsible for the family, and the family are responsible for him or her.

At the age of seven, discipline of a son passes to the father. The boy is then regarded as old enough to care for the animals, and this is a big moment. Girls tend cattle too, but increasingly, from the age of seven, daughters move into the mother's orbit. In peasant memoirs, the most touching accounts of the fears of these early days are revealed. Émile Guillaumin wrote *The Life of a Simple Man* at the end of his life but childhood memory irradiates his writing. The fear of the wolf and the snake stays with him, a fear branded on his mind by the experience of being sent out alone at the age of seven to mind the sheep, having sometimes to stay with them at night. He describes the agony of waiting in the dark, which he must do. He tells us that he used to weep, overcome by fear and misery. He had a pet lamb as a friend. Nonetheless, there was a small parcel of land he loved dearly, Le Breure, he calls it, especially in the early morning, on what he calls a 'summer dawn', his dog beside him.

He has a special song for the ladybird and clearly delights in nature, even though he is sent out so early without breakfast, and only gets it at home by 9 a.m. In the summer when the sheep are too hot to feed properly he endures the heat alongside them. At the age of nine he takes over the care of the pigs, which means he has to be out in all weathers. With the pigs, as with the sheep, there is a world of daily knowledge, a constant attentiveness he must master. From the age of ten the child is actively brought into the ways of the world by his parents; at the fair, say, looking on, the boy sees how a bargain may be struck (the drinking of the *litkup* in Poland was as good as a written contract).[24]

There is an equivalent of sorts to Guillaumin among Polish peasantry, a man called Jan Słomka. Born under serfdom in 1842, he lived most of his long life in the nineteenth century, as did Émile Guillaumin. Słomka spent the whole of his life in Dzików, a village in what for most of his lifetime was Galicia, and so under Austrian rule until 1918. Słomka progressed from poor beginnings to amass a piece of land and so he prospered, becoming a man who thought himself a bit above his fellows. He eventually became 'mayor' of Dzików, and was even visited by the president of Poland, who pinned a medal on his chest, as you can see in the following photograph.

His memoir is plain, without literary artifice, and dense with invaluable detail about the village that was his world. The memoir is not to be swallowed whole, for Jan was a man very aware of

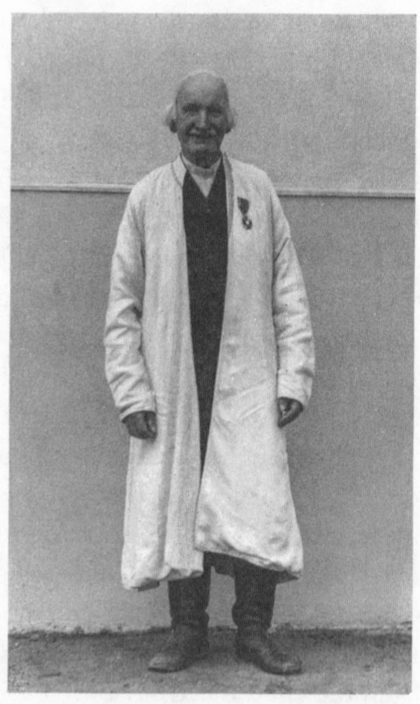

having got on in life, even though this getting on was pretty small beer by most standards. The memoir is nonetheless all the better for being unadorned, and Słomka's periodic prejudices are worn on his sleeve. Carousers, skivers, Jews and the 'superstitious' are among others not to his liking. We will have occasion to revisit Jan Słomka later, and for now it is childhood and the journey into manhood through work that is my concern. He wrote as follows:

> From my sixth year I began to pasture the stock – pigs, cattle and horses. The custom was that every house should provide one cowherd – a boy or a girl. No village boy or girl escaped without herding – it was a sort of apprenticeship. At thirteen, I made an end of herding, and began to work in the fields and about the house. From the time when I stopped herding my business was to drive the team for the plough, to harrow, to summer-fallow, to help plant, and hoe and dig the potatoes, to help with the haying and harvesting, with the hauling out of

> manure, etc. In addition, night by night I had to take the horses out to pasture and sleep by them, no matter what the weather.[25]

Słomka also testifies to the importance of the house and all those who lived in it, the life courses of whom ran alongside the life course of the physical house. It is striking how frequently even poor peasants had 'servants', and how often these actually lived in the house of those they worked for. I see this in the 1901 census of my own people in Ireland, in Wexford, where my grandfather Patrick was an only child; his mother died giving birth to him, and so a measure of prosperity was to be had in a family of few. A servant might be someone poorer, but could also be a young boy or girl of equal status to the family they worked for, taken in when help was required. Being a 'farm servant' was often part of the early life cycle of the children of those who took in the hired man or woman in the first place. And in the world of the village the servant might be someone the child had known from birth. This is how Słomka describes the treatment of hired help:

> Where hired help was hard-working and had found good employ, they would stay in the same place for years. The relation between master and man was a family one. They worked together, they ate from the same dish, and custom did not permit that master and mistress should have better food than their servants. The hired-man got as a rule fifteen guilders a year, and his working clothes of homespun linen in addition. These included three shirts, three pairs of trousers, a waistcoat, a pair of new boots, and new soles for his old ones. There was a cap as well. A sheepskin coat he could buy for himself, or a cloak if he wanted it. The hired-girl got from five to ten guilders yearly, and three dresses of home-woven linen.[26]

The child is taught how to live by their parents (not the school, not the Church). In Poland, and everywhere among peasants, etiquette is a most serious matter. Etiquette is morality (and too weak a word, therefore). This is in complete and utter opposition to the deeply insulting stereotype of the peasant as boor, as oaf. Courtesy, indeed a kind of courtliness, is what is called for. Self-mastery is central to life, to the continuance and survival of the house and of the commune. This regime is strict, not to the liking of an age of individual freedom. Desire and emotional need take second place to decorum, in eating, walking, speaking, even dying. Actions are to be performed with dignity. Indeed, with grace, so that dignity and grace are fundamental to correct human conduct.

And here we might step back a moment and consider that something of great weight may be going on here, with this matter of the morality of ordinary life, and with the word 'grace' in particular. For a word that is traditionally applied to the lord seems equally and perhaps more applicable to the peasant, one who is decorous, courtly even. Where does being civilized really reside? Where is 'civilization' to be found? The anthropologist Julian Pitt-Rivers was deeply interested in the concept of what he called grace in what he termed traditional societies.[27] The subject of Pitt-Rivers' anthropology was the peasants of twentieth-century Andalucían Spain, not its aristocrats. As he puts it, 'grace is inspired by the notion of something over and above what is due, economically, legally, or morally; it is neither foreseeable, predictable by reasoning, nor subject to guarantee.' It is the gift freely given, a sort of cousin to 'honour'. As such it infuses peasants' social relations. Rather than being based on the expectation of reciprocity, it is instead rooted in sacrifice, which is at the root of grace. What is involved is 'an expression of friendship, respect, appreciation, love, which comes from the heart, not from a sense of obligation; as such, it is a vehicle of grace, and it can be returned, as it must be, only in the form of grace.'[28] What nullifies grace is the parasite, the witch, the sycophant, the usurer, the graceless ones of this world, big and small.

The anthropologist Sula Benet produced a nuanced and sensitive account of peasant Poland in 1951.[29] She tells us how there are certain expressions that must be used at certain times and in certain places, for instance, the short dialogue after the customary greeting, also the formulaic use of rhymed proverbs on these occasions.

Grace is thereby shown to others, and thanks rendered (the term for thanks in several languages is, of course, derived from 'grace'). Throughout Poland there is a great respect for the right words in the right places; words, as we have seen, being a kind of object, a thing out there in the world that must be treated with the greatest respect.

Even people close to each other do not show heartiness in greeting or leaving. Correct conversation is slow and gradual, and peasants are reluctant to open up before strangers.[30] Personal questions are tactless and result in silence. Happy and cheerful people are regarded as shallow and stupid: 'He laughs like an idiot, a dunce.' Nor should you be too sad, however, and the best thing is to be mildly restrained. Children are taught to show restraint in all things, their tempers and their tongues, and physical relaxation is restricted to the domain of what privacy there is. Good manners require that in company one should be direct and poised, though not necessarily tense (Benet is acutely observant). The knees must never be too far apart and a seated woman must keep her knees together. To yawn, stretch, scratch oneself or cross one's legs is the mark of a boor.

It is bad manners to show hunger or eagerness for food, and one must eat slowly, occasionally putting down the spoon to show one is the master of appetite. Each person has their own spoon, rigidly reserved, with its special place in the rack hanging on the wall. Children do not always sit at the table and sometimes eat standing up. Orders of seniority are strictly observed. Food is neither forced on children nor denied them. When they have had enough, they say, after putting their spoons down, that they have had enough. The grown-up wipes his mouth with the back of his hand to indicate eating is finished. No child or adult would leave the table without thanking the women of the house first. Etiquette achieves the levels of a theatrical performance on the infrequent occasions when there are guests. Even a poor household would strain their resources to entertain guests, and peasants would rather stint themselves than let the servant do without. This is the showing of respect, you give it to others and expect that it be given to you. One is insulted if the forms of managing daily conduct are not respected. The visiting ethnologist who declares how hungry he or she is and then tucks in will create outrage at their total lack of breeding.

We need to be aware that peasant societies are societies of the gift, not the commodity, like our societies. What is given should be given freely: that which is given without expectation of return feeds the giver again and again. One sees this reflected across cultures, for example, in the Irish 'folk tale' of Peigi, a woman who is given a gift for her alone by the *slua sí*, the fairy host, the 'wee gentry', as they are also known.[31] She is generous with the gift to her neighbours, who admire her as a provider, for the fairy pot in the story signifies munificence. That which is given freely in the end feeds all, that which is kept or hoarded feeds only once and leaves us hungry thereafter. Peigi's story has a moral: her husband thoughtlessly puts his hand in the pot and the gift is corrupted, now useless. The right order of things must be followed. The gift aims to bind society together. This is the aim of its many and elaborate protocols. The 'folk tale' teaches the lesson of the gift, just as all such stories help to regulate the social order of peasants (though they may be fun too, and are one of the peasant arts).

The act of eating is not an incidental one but, as John Berger saw, a fundamental act of peasant culture.[32] The main meal is in the middle of the day, not at the end, as with us, the latter marking the transition to leisure. Placed in the middle of the day, '[The peasant meal] is placed in the day's stomach.' It is in the middle of work, in the middle of the production that enables reproduction. To the peasant all food represents work accomplished, because food represents physical work; the peasant body already knows the food it is going to eat. As Berger writes, 'His food is familiar like his own body. Its action on his body is *continuous* with the previous action of the body on the food', on the production of the food.[33]

Peasants eat and live domestic life in the room in which the food is prepared and cooked. There is little division between the eater and the food. The difference with our culture is great, where food is an abstracted entity, insulated from its production, for all its cultural valorization. To the peasant, food represents work done and therefore, for a short time, repose. For us it is a stimulus, an expression of wealth. 'What wealth has obtained from nature is an affidavit that overproduction and infinite increase are natural,' as Berger puts it. 'The variety, the quantity, the waste of food, prove the *naturalness* of wealth . . . *happy the world which feeds you*.'

Birth, marriage, death, the course of lives, and the bodies that lived these lives. How little we know about these bodies, these bodies that do the eating! Our ignorance is fed by our assumption that peasant bodies were the same as our bodies. They were not. The difference can be summarized thus: we have bodies, which we carry about in our minds, whereas they *were* their bodies. The head had not yet won victory over the medieval notion of the bowels as the centre of the body. Food, in the eating, went straight to this centre. In France in the late nineteenth century, the head still did not have much to do with reason.[34] In Gascony, there was no patois word for brain, and 'ideas' weighed not on the mind, but on the stomach.

In peasant Italy, tripe, taken from the stomach of the cow, had tremendous symbolic and ceremonial significance, the bowels, the belly, being the very stuff of life, although the generative belly is linked to death too. Tripe is from the centre of the body, where the upper and lower parts meet, and it plays a central part in wedding ceremonies: father and son share the same plate of tripe so that fecundity will be passed on. Rabelais emphasized the stomach as itself a symbolic centre of peasant vitality, transgression and excess.[35]

In Gascony, peasants had a deep awareness of the unbridled body, the body that is outside control. The etiquette of the peasant should be understood in this context, an etiquette that is at once a deep morality and a need to have control over a threatening world. Suffering is not, as in modern societies, unacceptable or avoidable. There is little faith in medicine.

Peasant etiquette is therefore integral to the entire moral and physical universe of peasant life. It is contrary to the overlapping and sometimes contradictory mores that dictate how town dwellers should live; they lack a single ordering power. But peasant children who are learning the categorical imperatives of existence perceive themselves as part of a stable, God-given order, an order which applies to others as well as themselves. This order recognizes other people's rights as well as one's own, including the rights of children. Children are taken to church in order to see their own place in the society around them. They are 'shown', 'led', unlike children now, who already know, who are made adults long before their time. The order of seating at church is one example of the many blueprints they are given to live by, the order of seating reproducing the social structure of the village in material form.

As a peasant child became an adolescent, restraints against the mingling of the sexes relaxed, eagerly, as was the case in Jan Słomka's memoir of his life. Adulthood was marriage and marriage was adulthood in this culture. Celibacy in Poland was considered contrary to nature, and the spinster and the bachelor were looked askance upon. The wife is regarded as not the lover, but the mother, and there are accounts in the more recent ethnographic literature of men and women not seeing each other's bodies, even in the most intimate circumstances. (But how ethnographers would know is another question, and the early ethnographers were not interested in such dubious matters, or at least, if interested, prevented by their own form of decorum from asking.)

Marriage. The Polish wedding is a play in seven acts, a great event publicly enacted.[36] The first act is *wywiady*, the enquiry and proposal.[37] As in ancient theatre, the play has a chorus. During *wywiady*, the future bride and groom have their separate retinues, who, throughout the seven stages of the drama, may actually perform as a chorus, sing as a chorus, dance as a chorus or witness as a chorus. Both parties bring a dowry to the marriage, and if the woman's is the greater the man may well have a subordinate status. If a woman receives land as part of her dowry or inheritance it is hers for life, the man only manages it, and her children inherit it. There is *babizma*, the mother's land, and *ojcowizna*, the father's land. This is hardly patriarchy, nor is it matriarchy. There are certainly separate spheres for men and women but there are many crossings from one sphere to another.

Marriage was a serious business, a transaction, in fact, marked by law, public notaries and certainly custom, the 'good word', as it was called in Poland. The father has discretion in determining the dowry of a daughter, and, if she gets it in full, she signs a document that says she has no further claims (in Poland she could, in certain periods, go to law if she was not awarded a particular fixed amount). The dowry chest the wife brings to the new house is called 'the hope chest'. It is of intricate design, and images of the married couple may be drawn on it, also depictions of the animals that are brought in as part of the dowry, animals the bride may sometimes have raised from her childhood, a pet calf or lamb, perhaps. The landless labourer who marries up is 'he who gets himself into the house'. His position may not be as enviable as it first appears.

Betrothal, after full agreement has been reached, is the second act. The prospective bridegroom comes to the house of his bride's parents, preceded by a fiddler, and embraces the knees of each of his future parents-in-law in turn. The young couple place their hands on a loaf of bread, bread being the symbol of life. The *starosta* ties their hands together with a long ceremonial towel, then cuts the bread and gives each of them half.

The 'maiden evening' is the third act, the unbraiding of the girl's hair a symbol of the leaving of maiden status. The wedding wreath is a symbol of female beauty and in everyday speech a symbol of virginity. 'She died in a wreath' means she died a virgin. There is the symbolism of leaves, especially the evergreen leaf.

The baking of the wedding cake is the fourth act, and it is as elaborate and involved as all the other acts. For instance, the bride's mother goes to the women of the village who are happy in marriage and asks them to come to knead the dough for the cake. The cake is enormous, and pieces are given to everybody. The ritual and symbolism of the cake are considerable: the moon and the sun represent the bride and the groom, and may figure on the cake.

The greatest act of all, the fifth, is the marriage ceremony itself. The first guest to arrive will affect the couple's future: if it is a man, the husband will rule the household; if a woman, the wife will be dominant. A book would be needed to describe the marriage ceremony itself.

And so to bed, a scene within the sixth act, which is the putting to bed, the laying down of the bridal couple, their withdrawal alone and the endless jokes and pranks played upon them. In earlier days there was the formal announcement of the bride's loss of virginity.

Then the seventh and last act is played out, the capping ceremony. This follows the wedding night and marks the initiation of the novice into the sisterhood of married women. It also marks the full acceptance of her husband's role and rights. She submits to this with loud weeping and lamentation, not altogether convincingly. There was once a custom of cutting the bride's hair at the capping ceremony, but by the mid-twentieth century the hair was merely rearranged and the head covered, as the covered head of the woman signified the married state. The famous and elaborate headdresses of married Breton women were worn with great pride. Headdresses similar to the Breton *c'hoef* (or coif) were also seen in Poland, but among the unmarried there.[38]

The wedding was much the same across Europe. In the Loire, a century before the Polish instance I draw on, the wedding ceremony had the same public significance: the drama of the wedding was played out to the commune as a whole. There was the same erecting of mock barricades to affirm, and dissolve, territorial boundaries, and the wedding party paraded publicly to and from the church ceremony. The cultural topography of the village was and is affirmed by these practices. The church and the official office, the *mairie* in France, will be visited, and often the local graveyard too. Food and drink are central, the village itself laying out food for the wedding procession, something at times done with satiric intent. Food and drink are communication.

Birth, marriage, then death. In Poland, as elsewhere, there is devout respect for the old, but this sits beside the ignominy with which old age is also associated. This ignominy in Poland is perhaps more marked than elsewhere. Partible inheritance, which is equal division among the male children and not solely inheritance for the eldest (primogeniture), is part of the explanation for this. In this system, common in all of Poland, but especially marked in Galicia, the land is constantly subdivided, so that all the children must get some share. Even if there was only one inheritor there would be some equitable settlement for the others. Property and authority can with age therefore be stripped away. When the last child is married, the parents are left without land or home, unless an arrangement is entered into; so the father and mother make arrangements in advance as far as possible.

But it wasn't always possible so to do. In Polish, there is the same word for 'old man' and 'beggar', its use depending on context. Polish peasants, especially in the South, lived in conditions of near-perennial scarcity, one bag of grain away from starvation, as the saying goes. If a settlement could not be reached, or there was simply not enough to go round, too many mouths to feed, beggardom might be the condition of lives towards their end. The Polish beggar was, however, a different thing to the beggar in the West, greatly superior, in fact. Before the days of developed communication beggars were valued as carriers of news and gossip, as they floated between villages. Beggars were always considered a working part of the population. The beggar's function was to receive charity, in return for which prayers were given, pilgrimages undertaken, songs and stories rendered, especially stories about the lives of the saints. The work of a beggar, 'living on charity', was legally recognized through long usage, better-off peasants giving shelter to an old man or woman in return for light tasks, playing with the children, say, or guarding the house. Such people became the 'little grandfather' or 'little grandmother' to the household.

Litigation might attend old age as well as beggary. The famous notoriety of peasants for litigiousness is warranted. In Poland litigation might follow the farmer's settlement upon his children (although it was noted that even if family members might be fighting in the courts, they would band together against an outsider who attacked any one of them). The public notary was involved, there was public enjoyment of the whole procedure, though in the end it was what the village mandated that mattered as much as what the law decreed.

There is no hiding the awfulness of the poverty, however. Sometimes the parent-turned-beggar would prosper sufficiently to go back home with gifts for the children and grandchildren, and sometimes this would be a form of revenge upon those they felt had cast them out, and, at other times, it was to ingratiate themselves so that they would be taken back in.[39] Often s/he was a welcome visitor, but one who would then, of necessity, have to leave again. The suffering involved in the experience of a rootless old age is impenetrable to our understanding. This was still in most essentials the world of Polish peasants up to the middle of the twentieth century, into my own lifetime.

Death was at once feared and met with resignation. Most old women made, and cherished, their own burial outfit: the better-off the peasant, the more elaborate the funeral regalia (it was the same with weddings, of course). To die with dignity was important, and the funeral itself was of great significance. The contract poor tenant farmers in Poland made with their landlords sometimes stipulated that they would be given an honourable funeral, a policy not unusual throughout Europe.

Sudden, violent or untimely death was a different matter and 'unnatural' death deeply dreaded. Parents were warned against grieving too deeply for their children, and the early death of children was not unusual. There is the story in Poland of a dead daughter who was condemned in the next world to carry her mother's tears about in buckets. Death, as it so often is in these peasant cultures, is feminine: in Poland, a tall woman. There were also many tales about imprisoning Death so that no one else should die. In one story, when nobody died the Earth began to complain that it could not carry so many people, so God ordered that Death be released. (Death had by this time been locked up in a snuffbox for seven years.)

When Death finally comes she knocks three times on the window, calls the person three times by name, and then gives him or her the final blow, usually on the cheek, or she may just stand next to him or her (though as long as she stands at their feet he or she cannot yet die). Steps are taken to help death along, sometimes: the dying person may ask to be laid on the ground to gain the benefit of contact with 'holy earth', and so avoid the knots of pain felt by the dying which tie the soul to the suffering body. If an infant is dying hard the baby is taken in its crib and placed with its head halfway out of the door so that the infant can more easily make its way to the end.

However, death is more than just an ending. Lives are lived, and over, but as with all of life – childhood, adult life and then death – things move, not in the linear way that is ours, but in the way of a circle. There is the circle of lives, of the land, of nature and the seasons, and time is populated not just by the living, but also the dead.

5.

The World: The Lark that Sees into Heaven

'The lark, which soars so high, is the favourite bird of the angels; during a storm they hold it in their hands, and when, with every lightning-flash, the heaven opens, it is allowed to look in.' So it was said in early twentieth-century Poland. Larks are messengers in many cultures. Among the Lakota, a Great Plains Native American tribe, larks are the messengers of the sun, the bringers of warmth, light and life. Seeing a lark is good news everywhere, because the lark, arriving in spring, brings the promise of abundance for the impending harvest. Shakespeare's song from *Cymbeline* places the bird at the boundary between two realms: 'The lark at heaven's gate sings.'

The lark has connected Earth and sky, Earth and heaven, for much longer than the time of Shakespeare, and it has ascended in peasants' imaginations just as it did before their eyes. I write about Earth and sky in this chapter, which is to say, peasants' beliefs about how the world is perceived; in the next about Earth and heaven, which is to say, peasants' beliefs about God and the divine. Cosmogony now, then religion. 'Cosmogony' is the begetting of the world, of the order of things. But, in practice, the two constantly merge, Earth and the cosmos that contains it on the one hand, and heaven, the realm of the divine, on the other. The divine of Christianity, that is, which, even after millennia of influence, by the twentieth century still did not have complete dominion over the Earth and skies above in peasants' minds.[1]

In the Poland of the early twentieth century there were essentially two aspects to beliefs that were not religious: naturalism, in which the lark was just a lark, and then belief in a world of spirits, in which the lark was a spirit. These spirits may be useful, may be harmful, may be both at once. They are different from natural objects on the one hand and religion on the other. This is the realm of what is sometimes called 'magic', a perhaps misleading word. If the natural, the spirits and God, in practice, merged one into the other, then they do represent a distinct threefold system of what we can call peasant belief.[2]

A Polish Cosmogony

What was this system, one that was not usually all that systematic? The opening quote in this book give a sense of it: 'Every field knows its owner, the Earth is indignant at every crime committed on its face . . . Nothing bad should be said near water. The wind listens and talks . . . While animals do not know as much as man they know things he does not.'

These are some more of the elements of the natural part of the cosmogony of Polish peasants, that part in which the Earth and the stars above it may be 'indignant': after the death of the peasant farmer his heir must inform the domestic animals of the event so that they will know that he is now the master. This is also done so that they will accept him and not follow their dead owner by dying themselves. Sometimes the orchard and farm buildings are also notified. A strict protocol is needful so that order will be maintained and chaos not be invited in. A furrowed ridge ploughed around the edge of a field by a team of oxen insures against hail, and if by twin brother oxen against pests too. Nesting storks will lead to a full barn. Birds can be kept from eating seeds by burning a few shavings from a coffin over the field; vermin can be destroyed by pouring the water in which the dead body was washed on the four corners of the house.

As to the fauna, so it is with the flora. The plants and trees show gratitude for proper treatment. When an animal, for instance, a cow, is sick, the peasant finds a plant, bends it down and fastens its top to the ground with the words: 'I will release you when you make my cow well.' The same evening, the cow will recover: then the man or woman must go to release the plant the next day or the cow will fall sick and die. Similarly, animals are interested in plants and can influence them. Non-living things also have knowledge, indeed animals and objects know each other, and have prevision of the future. All this, Florian Znaniecki says, 'must be taken literally, not metaphorically'. So is it that peasants learn about the world by always being alert, listening and watching, always heedful of being warned, chided, praised.

If there is an ultimate solidarity of humankind with the natural world, then this has to be earned, indeed fought for. The sun should not look upon dead animals, because it will be disturbed by the sight; it will set in blood, and may send hail and rain. There is a solidarity between fire and water, and between both of these and all living things. But there is also the inevitable division between the two, an indication of the depths beneath. The principle of solidarity between beings of the same class is the strongest, plants with plants, animals with animals. The house snake is in solidarity with the cattle and the poultry. When there is danger, animals call to one another, especially those close to each other. Man is *not* the king of creation, and if privileged is part of a solidarity based on sympathetic help and respect. Again, all this is not a metaphor. It is real.

In the world of the Polish peasant any breaking with the solidarity of nature is to be punished, for such breaking of the rules is a harbinger of chaos. Killing a stork is a crime that can never be pardoned. A man who kills a dog or cat is to be avoided unless he shoots these animals, elsewise a lack of solidarity with nature is shown. This naturalism persisted for a long time, well after the second decade of the twentieth century when it was written about. It persists in remnants even now. I use 'naturalism' here simply to denote what is not supernatural, whether what is 'above' nature is of the spirits or of religion. The rites of a tradition can persist much longer than what they express. In Poland, it is the rites that are forgotten, or they are absorbed in Christianity, and it is the old beliefs that persist. For among these peasants, Christianity has been unable to destroy them: there is, according to Znaniecki, a particular seriousness in the peasants' actions upon nature, a gratitude to it. A 'peculiar respect' is also shown, a 'curious pride', when nature favours a man, when a bounty going far beyond a simple award for effort is given. This pride is similar to that which a person feels when they are favoured by their human community. The respect due to nature is reflected in the tiniest details of life: shown, for example, in the fear of letting even the smallest particle of food go to waste.

Astonishingly, time is involved, too, as it is part of nature. Individualized periods of time become natural objects: one-third of the days of the year are individually distinguished, and certain days are favourable or not. The same day returns the following year and can avenge or reward. Anniversaries are therefore of huge significance. The 'objects' of peasants are also assuredly not ours, which are outside ourselves, objectified, precisely as we describe them as 'objects', things simply 'out there' and not of us. For peasants, however, objects made by humans have the character of animation, if less so than natural ones (this animation is not the same as what is called animism, which involves an underlying supernatural quality). If not exactly conscious and alive, the human-made object – a knife or a broom, say – may maintain its own existence, such objects in tales sometimes having a form of speech and intention. Animation decreases in objects whose manufacture is easily seen, almost completely so in what one makes oneself.

Death begins to show us the transitions between the natural and the world of spirits. There was fear and repugnance towards death. Death needs accompanying quotation marks here, however, for it is not a generalized death, a spirit being called 'Death', but *decay* that is feared. There is solidarity within nature because of the common struggle against the process of decay, of which death is the most absolute form: sickness, destruction, misery, winter, night and pestilence – these are the main phenomena correlated with death. And these are what chaos is. Aversion to death is still evident, as in a reluctance to talk about it, and in feeling distress near a cemetery.

Anyone who by occupation is connected with death may be feared and despised. These functions are therefore performed by men who have little to lose, outcasts, and, in Polish nineteenth-century society, significantly, by Jews: 'Up to the present, in Russian Poland the dog-catchers are often men who at the bidding of the authorities act as the executioners of political offenders, and most of the butchers and skin-dealers are still Jews.'[3]

Despite an aversion to death, concern with it as the natural principle of decay (not as an overarching spirit) exemplifies how solidarity within nature exists in order that the regeneration of all nature can take place. Generation and regeneration are intimately connected, part of that circle of life which is the peasant's ('The great wheel of life', *Roth mór an tsaoil*, in Irish). Securing the continuity of generations, of the house, becomes at one with nature's regeneration. The continuity of the family is paramount, despite the death of its individual members. Death from this angle on the world is no big deal.

This is from the memoir of Jan Słomka again and concerns the death of the elderly:

> Whenever an older person was taken sick, people said that his time had come and that nothing could help him . . . Folk would pass away without fear, and with extraordinary calm. When the farmer felt that he was near the end, he would call his wife, children, servants, relatives and neighbours. Telling them that he was not long for this world, he would say goodbye to them, ask forgiveness if he had done anyone a wrong, and beg his folks to help his wife lay him safe in the cemetery. In a word, he would depart for the next world with the same calmness as if it were only a short journey and he was to return. Nowadays lots of people make far more fuss when leaving for Prussia or America![4]

The spirits then begin to make an appearance, and we are aware that the distinction between the spiritual and the natural, while profoundly real, is also accompanied by many gradations and different mixtures of the two (as is also the case of these two with the divine). As regards death, on the one hand, people have no spirit distinct from their bodies, but they do have a 'vapour', which leaves them temporarily in dreams (rather like how in sleep we lose voluntary movement). It is this ill-defined 'vapour' that passes out of the body in death, in doing so forming a medium of connection to the spirit world. Nonetheless, so long as the body exists, including its existence in the grave, it may not yet be fully 'dead' and so still natural.

Vampire belief in particular illustrates how nature and spirits merge; hence the great range of beliefs about 'vampires' involving different kinds of vampires made up of varying mixtures of spirit and human. For instance, those with strong vitality when they are alive come out at night to feed. They will have big teeth, a red face and strength: the natural features of the person when living present in the vampire after death. Though not generalized as a spirit, Death in peasant Poland is anthropomorphically represented in particular spirit forms, for instance as a nebulous woman in white, or a skeleton. The *bean sí*, or banshee, is the parallel figure in Ireland. My mother, born in 1910 and a child of those early times, had more than half a belief in the banshee.

Some spirits have markedly natural characteristics: for instance, the *boginki*, who have human bodies but can become invisible. These interact with the human world and may in part follow the pattern of human society. 'The good people', 'the noble people', those 'of the gentry', the 'fairies' of Ireland and Scotland are of a similar breed, though subtly different too. (W. B. Yeats thought that the Irish versions were more fun than the Scots.) Faeries in Ireland, as in Poland, were part of everyday life, they call at the door, they loan their cows, save people from death, bestow magical gifts and mend pots. Again, there is a problem with words here. These fairies are not the familiar fairy sprites at the bottom of the garden of anglophone and Protestant imaginations, but rather forces that are much darker.

The Polish fairies seem scarcely more fun than the darker, Irish ones, of which there are plenty, Yeats notwithstanding. The *boginki*, like their Irish peers, exchange their children for human ones, especially when these are not baptized. The changed child can be recognized from its bad temper, growing ugliness and enormous appetite. The spirit may also take the place of a woman, and is also bad-tempered, capricious and evil. In order to force the spirit to give the child back, the *boginka*'s child must be mistreated and beaten, so that the spirit brings the real child back and takes her own away. Even then the *boginka* may avenge herself by biting off a finger of the real child, or making it as bad-tempered as her own.

The *topczyki* are unbaptized children born of illegal relations. They are natural beings, have a human body and their actions are physical, not magical, spoiling the hay, drawing by their strength animals and men into the water. Magical rites are of no particular power against them. The cast of such beings is enormous, their shades almost endless in variety: cloud beings, *płanetniki* or *latawce*, dwelling in the clouds, sometimes spirits directing the clouds, sometimes spirits of children who died without baptism. The *kania* is a beautiful woman who steals children, the *wił* a being that comes in the night and terrifies children and hinders people from sleeping. The nightmare, *zmora*, strangles sleeping men and rides at night upon horses. The *skrzat* is the house being, *leśny*, the wood being.

If these beings are more or less materially conceived, they are acted upon mainly by magical means, not by appeals to natural solidarity. Christianity mobilizes against them, trying to assign their actions to the Devil, but privately and secretly peasants keep their old duties of solidarity towards them, and try to win their help, even if acceptance of this help is sinful in the eyes of the Church. As to beliefs about the human soul itself, there are in Poland at least six varieties of beings corresponding to the concept of the soul. The relative degree to which these spirits are detached from the body and leading independent existences is the reason for the diversity. Local spirits are the most material, the least spiritual. They are attached to particular places, such as old trees, marshes or ruins. There is one locality remarked upon where Russian soldiers killed in battle against the Polish in the eighteenth century lie buried.

Their souls cannot find rest anywhere, for they were christened according to the rites of the Orthodox Church. They cannot be helped and must await the Last Judgement.

Jan Słomka remarks of the beliefs of his neighbours, 'In the matter of their ideas about the supernatural, our peasants from earliest times have stuck to various superstitions, believing in spirits, ghosts, magic workers, fairies and the like. Everyone was expected to hold to the old convictions, and not doubt them; else he would be thought an evil and perverted fellow.' And further, 'In Dzik[ów] there were several places where ghosts were believed to live. Everyone "saw" something at this spot . . . [a] dog would grind his teeth at something and growl fiercely . . . All this would happen at night. During the day at the noon hour the "white dames" would frighten people . . . Most of all in those days did people believe in the witches who stole the milk from the cows, so that someone good with these animals might be considered a witch and hated by her neighbours.'[5]

The 'general animation of natural objects' forms an overarching solidarity, Znaniecki observed of Polish peasant beliefs. 'There is a solidarity between the earth, the sun, and all living beings', so that 'the earth can communicate its fecundity to animals, the sterile cow, say, and the fecundity of women can be communicated to a sterile field.'[6] This looks on the face of it uplifting, something comforting to modern minds. This solidarity should not, however, be misunderstood. The destructive forces of nature abide everywhere: for instance, upon the ridges between fields, which are places defiled by human hate because it is there, on the borders of landholdings, that conflicts occur. The signs of solidarity are hidden, darkened, difficult to read, things to be earned by respecting the Earth, the spirits, God and the Devil. Chaos is, as it were, the hidden presence of order, the presence of what is out of kilter, what does not fit in.[7]

The peasant search for order in the cosmos looks for similitude and correspondence between all things, correspondences that are to be seen in the stars or the planets, among other human beings, and in the inanimate as well as the animate world. This search for order is a search for safety in a for ever uncertain world, the world of the survivor. As we have seen, the outward sign is a portent of what is beneath, with the crooked body the herald of the crooked spirit. Once, this was the world view of most people of the world itself, then as modernity developed it became the peasants' own.

Chaos is threat, fear, horror, incoherence, the possibility of disorder. At an everyday level, chaos may take the form of what is outside the village, outside the house at other times, the fear of strange ideas, the fear of time when it is conceived as irreversible, when things become changed into a form they did not hold before and this form endures. The Devil, and evil itself, have to be given their due. For peasants, nature is the bedrock of need, and peasants are constantly exposed to nature as struggle, living on land that, as we have seen, is no good without their being able to 'open' it to fecundity. The peasants' view of 'nature' is that it is evil as well as good, not the 'nature' we have adopted. We live in societies in which we aspire to join our internal lives, our personal subjectivities, with nature, so that we can be 'at one' with it. Especially in the anglophone world, nature is a manifestation of a designed universe. This is the universe of Isaac Newton and Providence. The universe of the Protestant Reformation that neutralized nature, cleansing and desacralizing it. What do you do with a Great Design? You admire it, you contemplate it; in recent times, you 'wonder' at it and are 'enchanted' by it. This is a universe that in the present takes the sentimental view of nature as alternatively a garden or a wilderness.

We have transformed our vision of nature to our own great peril, whether as something to be instrumentally acted on or enchanted by. In an age of climate crisis, and the almost untrammelled capitalism and political self-interest driving it, something is to be learned from peasants' connection to the cosmos. All the same, we cannot go back and be peasants. I did not write this book to make peasants tutors to the present. Nonetheless, as John Berger saw, the breaking of the vast continuity of peasant existence has an 'unprecedented and unexpected urgency', one now almost thirty years after he wrote these words even more marked than then. This urgency seems to me to lie in seeing that we are not in nature, but of it; that there were and are many more versions of 'nature' in the world than ours; and perhaps most of all that the vision of the cosmos that peasants had comprehended order and chaos, beauty and terror. That vision included the recognition that the dead, and so, with them, the past itself, have what I termed earlier a foundational role in human existence. The dead and the past are part of 'nature'.

We no longer inhabit a world of spirits and our gods are not like peasant ones, still bound to the Earth, but the search for ways of realizing what Znaniecki called the 'overarching solidarity' of ourselves and the Earth would do well to keep peasants in mind. Seamus Heaney understood the landscape in which as a child in small-farm Derry he grew up as 'sacramental, a system of signs that called automatically upon systems of thinking and feeling'.[8] Kevin Williams has remarked how the Catholicism of Heaney's upbringing was part of an environment that was paradoxically not 'specifically Christian'.[9]

Heaney wrote that 'Much of the flora of the place had a religious force, especially if we think of the root of the word religious in *religare*, to bind fast. The single thorn tree bound us to a notion of the potent world of the fairies – and when the Blessed Virgin appeared in a thorn bush in Ardboe, a few miles up the country, the fairy tree took on a new set of subliminal attributes. The green rushes bound us to the beneficent spirit of St Brigid: cut on Brigid's Eve, they were worked into Brigid's crosses that would deck the rooms and out houses for the rest of the year.' The poet also tells us that his upbringing conferred on him a sense of never feeling 'alone in the universe for a second' even as he 'heard the clay hit the barefaced coffin'.[10]

Most of us are not poets, we were not brought up as he, and as long ago as he, a man born in 1939. Six years his junior in time, I also knew that old world, if at a distance, being a country boy only in the summer interludes of being a city one. But my parents brought the old world with them when they left, fervent in retaining it as they negotiated the alien urban life into which they came. Heaney, like me, lost the Catholic faith early and without great struggle, but the peculiar nature of rural Irish Catholicism, in which God, the spirits and the natural world were not completely sundered, has left its mark on me just as it did on him. That mark lies in the sense of the possibility of binding, of *religare*, just as the thorn tree and the green rushes bound Heaney.

What I am describing in the cosmogonies of peasants is the outlook of those who cannot bend the world to their will. It is part of the culture of those who suffer, and yet are not helpless. Peasants are indeed connected to the Earth, the world, but above all to the place where they are born. Regarding the matter of peasant identity, the answer to the question 'Who are you?' is that I am from here, I am a peasant or a farmer, but also, in the European context, that I am a child of God, for the world is made rather than being a world to make, and God, or some overarching force, has made the world, the cosmos. 'My fatherland is the land of my fathers' as the saying goes. A peasant may answer the question of who they are by saying who their father and mother were, who their ancestors were.

These lives were literally more raw and less mediated than ours. When it comes to the lives of those who cannot bend the world to their will, so much of reality is grounded in their bodies, bodies exposed to the vicissitudes of the natural world in ways we no longer experience, or indeed have any inkling of. This degree of exposure was of course felt by far more people than solely peasants in the past, but their exposure was more direct. Paved roads, electricity, the conveniences of town life – countless taken-for-granted things were absent.

Peasant society was also simply more violent than ours, daily, commonplace violence, that is, not our collective sort, anonymous and institutionalized. But then societies in the past were themselves more violent. Violence was seen as natural, ordinary, even banal. Among peasants, anger was considered to be a strength, not an involuntary emotion. There was a much greater focus on negative emotions than on positive feelings, emotions like jealousy, because these are the things that have to be guarded against if the community is to survive. There is violence within marriage, as we have seen in the account of peasant Poland, even though women constantly and successfully negotiated power in these societies.

Among French peasants, the parts of the body that were targets of sexual desire were different from ours: the stomach, for instance, and also, more surprisingly, the nose were highly sexualized. The ankles, and especially the thighs and the calves, of women were greatly admired. There was little squeamishness about sex: there were terms aplenty for vagina and penis, and no shortage of knowledge. A good deal of playful euphemism around sex was also apparent. Absolute nudity was unusual and not considered necessary for sex, and there is abundant evidence that sex was enjoyed, and transgressive behaviour was tolerated. If the feminine man was not welcomed, he was accommodated. As farmers, peasants were surrounded by sex.[11]

In the course of the nineteenth century, the body was medicalized and objectivized, a process memorably charted by Michel Foucault.[12] Sex was a large part of this. Where before there were sexual practices, now people came to understand their own identities in sexual terms, and this understanding has only intensified in present-day society. The logic of this situation in peasant society is that, since sex did not yet confer identity, it followed that the category of 'homosexual' had no meaning for these people.

John Berger recognized, having lived beside and worked with peasants for many years, that, while their belief systems always tended towards suspicion of change, this did not mean that they were not open to it. Indeed, because each time they act they have to improvise, change always surrounds them. As Berger writes, peasant ingenuity makes them open to change, but their imaginations demand continuity. The actions of the peasant are oriented towards the future. They are forever anticipating and never finished. There is no assured security or arrival point in the future, only the hope of survival, so that it is better for the dead to return to the past where they are not at risk, for they *are* at risk in the unknown future. They return to the past because it is safe.

As time is cyclical, like the seasons, life is an interlude. Looking back from this interlude into the past, the dream is of not being disabled; looking forward it is of handing on the means of survival. The ideal, for peasants, lies in the past, their hopes in the future, and after their death there will be a return to the past, not a transposition into the future. But the past and the future are always connected, for things go around in a circle. Experience of change is the constant experience of the unknown, and this makes peasants aware that the condition of humankind is one of ignorance. Too much is and will remain unknown to make progress credible. Therefore the peasant is a conservative, not a progressive; slow to move, but once roused, unstoppable, as in the peasant revolt, the *jacquerie*. Peasants are not ignorant, for they often admire knowledge, and, as Berger says, there is no antagonism against those who possess knowledge or those who lack it.[13]

Stories

How do we know all these many things about peasant beliefs, the things we might learn from? We know in part through the stories peasants tell. These stories in turn invite questions about those who have collected and interpreted these stories. There are stories to tell about these people as well, our knowledge of the original stories coming to us through them, their lives, their ways of seeing the world. So, before the peasant stories, the stories of the others, or at least of a few of them among the many.

As we saw in the previous chapter, Úna Breathnach sits in her kitchen in the Maam Cross of 1935. Not far to the north of Maam Cross is the townland of Seanadh Farracháin, Shanafaraghaun, birthplace of my paternal grandmother, Bridget Burke, a woman who died long before I was born and of whom there is no photograph. Nor did I ever meet her husband, my grandfather, of whom there is no photograph either. They are both obscure parts of myself, made less obscure by the people who have helped bring their stories into the light. Pat Liam Seoighe's townland, Kilbride, is a mile or so further east from Seanadh Farracháin as one travels along one lakeshore to another. The townland was and is the fundamental unit of social identity in rural Ireland.

Below is a photograph of Mícheál Breathnach sitting beside an eminent visiting American folklorist, Stith Thompson (1885–1976). They are both smart dressers, especially the American, who seems dressed for the streets of Chicago or LA, in his fine silk socks and hat, the cut of which is almost matched by that of Mícheál's, who is in his Sunday best. Even so, the difference is there in the faces, but especially the hands. Mícheál's hands are huge. The image is from 1935. Stith Thompson was indeed eminent, as he was the author of the *Motif-Index of Folk-Literature*, which indexes folktales by type, and is still the worldwide authority in the field. There is a printed record of the meeting.[14]

The Joyce Country was honey to the bee of the folklorist. The bee is drawn to the honey of what is old, that which is evidence of the origin, and so is supposedly authentic. The authentic was most authentic where Irish was spoken, so that elsewhere, where it had died out, got less attention – my mother's Wexford, for instance. The authentic was to be found in the evidence of the *ur*-nation that was peasant culture. These sorts of convictions were remarkably long-lasting, continuing into the time when Thompson and Breathnach sat on the same hill together. Small, new nations eagerly embraced folklore. (The Irish, the Estonians, the Hungarians, for instance.) Thompson was a creator of typologies, an analyst.

The Folklore Commission people were forever interested in 'survivals', antiquities, old wisdom, but were also consumed with a desire for accuracy by recording what seems, at times, to be everything – tools used, houses, occupations, designs of gate hinges – so that present life was memorably recorded, the parts people were willing to talk about, that is. However, behind this recording of the present was the feeling of the folklorists that the old was better, and must be recorded before being lost. On the whole they did not like what the advance of modern life brought with it, not unreasonably, in many cases. But they were not anthropologists, not intent on finding out what all this life they recorded meant, how it all fitted together. They were men of the nineteenth century, in many ways (and almost all men), still in part living in the age of the nineteenth-century 'collector'. Folklorists have changed, have wised up theoretically, and women now count as both the student and the studied. My knowledge of stories of Joyce Country owes much to one of these women, Ailbhe Nic Giolla Chomhaill, whose mother is a Joyce, from a townland very close to Seanadh Farracháin.[15] The generations move on.

The following is a photograph in the old sense, a paper one, a material thing that would have been kept near the heart, or perhaps stored away in a drawer somewhere, but, if so, this one has, from its appearance, seen plenty of use. It is a physical object, one of a kind, one that not only carries the years with it but in it. The photograph shows the Rauszer family, of whom Michał, like Ailbhe, has been my guide as I have tried to tell my own story about peasants. His story emerges, alongside mine and Ailbhe's, for we three are – if at different removes – the children of peasants, children who have lived to study and write about them.

The family come from Poland's Upper Silesia, and have been miners, factory workers and technicians, but affinities with peasant existence are strongly felt. Anyway, in this area, where mining, industry and farming have for approaching two hundred years all been mixed together, it is difficult to know where 'peasant' stops and starts. Full-time peasants lived in the same villages as industrial workers, who themselves were often 'five o'clock farmers', regarding themselves as at one with peasants, 'villagers' all of them. Such 'workers' had, and have cows, geese, pigs and grew their own food.

Michał is half my number of years, one of those who will take the story on beyond my time. He was raised in large part by his maternal grandmother, who is on the extreme left of the family portrait. She was in youth a seamstress from a poor peasant family, and was bilingual in German and Silesian, but knew some Polish too. His great-grandparents are at the centre in the front row of the picture, the woman dressed in Silesian peasant fashion. One side of the family were poor peasants from the Russia-partitioned kingdom of Poland, and of German origin. They emigrated to escape Russian domination in the nineteenth century to Upper Silesia, then part of Prussia.

These are their great-grandson's words: 'All of us are Silesians, that means that we speak in a different language and we think about ourselves as quite different than Poles. Usually our accent was used as an example of being a stupid peasant or worker. But we learned how to adapt. I learned how to speak properly in Polish in high school, and until I got to university learned how to hide my accent.'[16] His grandmother, as a peasant, was sent to Germany to undertake forced labour in the Second World War. His grandfather was conscripted into the German army, but escaped to fight alongside the Allies.

Michał is an academic anthropologist, the bearer of a long and honourable Polish heritage of investigation into the lives of peasants. This lineage runs through the Bursztа family, going back to the renowned Józef Burszta, an ethnographer and sociologist. Burszta (1914–1987) was born in a village in deepest rural Galicia. He fought alongside peasant partisans in the Second World War, and defended their interests against the excesses of Communist rule. He was a major scholar of his day. Józef's son Wojciech also achieved eminence as an anthropologist. Wojciech was Michał's teacher. Both of the Bursztas in turn were instrumental in editing and republishing the vast and fundamental folklore collection of Oskar Kolberg. So, Michał and I are, in turn, the students of Kolberg. It is needful then to tell something of the story of Oskar Kolberg, who lived between 1814 and 1890.

Kolberg's stupendous life work was published in thirty-three large volumes between 1857 and 1890, and after his death in 1890 a further three volumes were added.[17] These were subsequently republished in eighty-six volumes, making up well over 300,000 pages of published material, covering all of the vast territory of partitioned Poland.[18] The original folklorists were children of their time, like all of us, dressing the peasant up in clothes of their own choosing. Immodest subjects were to be avoided. Religion, like patriotism, was a good thing. What was 'modern' corrupted the soul of the peasant. Peasant protest was to be avoided. But nonetheless what stupendous work the great ones did. Before men like Kolberg, one must bend the knee: what life-long fervour, what seriousness of mind, what sympathy and respect for peasants.

Kolberg was a studious man, a man of absolute devotion to his task, a man said to be 'humble', also 'silent', which is not a bad way to be if you are listening to others attentively. He was a child of the Polish Enlightenment and of Romanticism. His father was German, and had come from Mecklenburg to Poland in 1796 to pursue a scientific career, becoming one of the first professors at the new University of Warsaw after its foundation in 1816. The city was then under Prussian hegemony (to be succeeded until 1918 by the Russian variant). Educated in what was supposed to be the Prussianizing Warsaw Lyceum, Oskar, like so many this institution educated, turned out to be an ardent Polish patriot. The Kolbergs grew up with the Chopin family: folk music, in practice, peasant music, was the inspiration of both families. Oskar studied and played music as did Frédéric Chopin, but it was his collection of peasant music, and his pioneering system of music notation, that set him apart.

From this interest in music grew his eighty-six volumes, the fruit of fifty years of almost ceaseless movement across the then considerable territory of divided Poland in order to record his observations *in situ*, an early version of 'field research'. The culture that nurtured him, in some cases the people who taught him, produced the staples of Polish nationalism, dictionaries of the Polish language, dialect studies, histories of the Polish nation, all monuments alongside his monumental work. These architects of national culture were to be found in all the European nationalisms. In Poland such men died in considerable numbers in the numerous revolts of the liberal intelligentsia against foreign domination. In these revolts they attempted to get the peasants they exalted on their side: naturally enough, as peasants represented the vast majority of the population. The peasants usually gave the gentlemen, among whom were enlightened landowners, short shrift, as we will see.

Kolberg, a Protestant German, Polish patriot, a dedicated lover of tradition, worked for a time in the management of the Warsaw-Vienna Railway, the first railway line in Poland and only the second one in the Russian empire. The railway was the great harbinger of contemporary change. However, tickets were expensive, and until the 1870s and 80s the coverage limited (by contemporary standards, skeletal). Many peasants would have encountered the railway for the first time only as they emigrated from the country of their birth.[19]

And now the stories of peasants and what they tell us about peasant beliefs. Like folklore, and indeed, for me, *folk* anything, 'belief' is a tricky word. Belief is something we tend to think of as residing in the head, whereas in peasant culture it is distributed in the body and the landscape, something that inhabits places – remember that 'In Dzik[ów] there were several places where ghosts were believed to live. Everyone "saw" something at this spot . . . [a] dog would grind his teeth at something and growl fiercely.' One lived in a landscape that was not mute, that contained the stories and objects through which beliefs are made manifest. Belief resides in the physical world. And, as we will see, this residence or 'in-dwelling' applies to organized religion as well.

What does it mean for belief to be 'in-dwelt'? The great folklorist (cum-anthropolgist) Henry Glassie strikes the right note here, observing how people without great physical resources accomplish complexity in their mental operations which we, viewing them as 'primitive', are not easily able to grasp and usually dismiss. We think through words and ideas, those of biology, say, or sociology, and, these days especially, psychology. Peasants think through *things*, by comparing nature and culture. As Claude Lévi-Strauss argued, natural things are a resource for thinking for such people. Knowledge, including myths and stories about these things, forms 'a mode of thought, functioning as scholarship as science and art do in our world'.[20]

Stories: Henry Glassie and others along Ireland's northern border have listened with great attention to the content, form and context of stories. In Glassie's and other articulations the story is at once a form of entertainment, a means to social arrangements which are negotiated in the present, and a sort of continuously remade history of the places in which the stories are told. The immutable and the transitory merge into one thing, and the events of time and change are read in terms of what is passed down from a long past. Glassie describes how at collective gatherings stories gradually emerge, the less spontaneous storytellers sometimes joining in, especially when alcohol is involved. Past, present and future have to be attended to in the story, because even today in these areas of Ireland the culture is still, in many ways, an oral one. The teller speaks of the past to the present so that the story will be transmitted into the future. There are many types of stories, among them the tale for children, the riddle story, the humorous story (with or without a message), the religious story and those of historical origins.[21]

Seanchas is the Irish word for what is feebly called folklore. In modern Irish, *seanchas* is used with a variety of meanings: "history, lore, ancient law, a record or register, a minute description, a pedigree, an ancient tale; [an] act of storytelling, gossiping; inquiring (about one's condition, health etc.)". I quote here from the work of Guy Beiner, the eminent Israeli historian of Irish 'beliefs' and local history-making, testifying as he does to the moral coherence of this local and deep-rooted popular intellectual activity. A *seanchaí* is the teller of these accounts, a term frequently translated as 'historian', but perhaps more accurately as a custodian of that which is carried forward from the past. A 'storyteller', in fact.[22]

Stories are serious business, and there is a conscious effort to base them on truth. Storytellers were, and still are, particularly important in oral cultures, where they are the custodians of what is memorable, memorable in the sense of what is to be remembered and what can be easily remembered, registered on the senses so that it stays. Repetitions, striking gestures and voices, remembered bodies, code-holders all. The storytellers are deeply versed in their art. Stories must have an attribution, a person, for instance ('There was a man lived down on the Great Island one time, name of Bowe'), or a particular event, and it is necessary for the truth that the right attribution of the source is made. 'History' is a particular issue among these Irish storytellers. The truest of the true accounts are the historical ones, because the continuance of the community depends upon them. These truths have no authors, are held communally, but have to be gathered not only from reliable sources but told by reliable persons, who are the storytellers acting as historians. The true story will stick in your head. Other stories that are among the innately true ones are those of saints, of God's word.

All this 'belief' is counter to our versions of rationality. However, what must be emphasized is that peasant cosmogonies are entirely 'rational', which is to say, they are coherent, grounded in experience. They are a clear-eyed means of getting things done using methods that have worked. Our reason is based on the idea that nature is accessible to rational calculation and so to control, and is, as Max Weber put it, purposive-rational, in other words, means are purposefully designed so as to secure efficient, utilitarian ends. Calculative reason, in Weber's view, resulted in the 'disenchantment of the world', the term denoting the outlook of modernized, bureaucratic, secularized western society.[23] For peasants, entry into the world of 'belief', that is, the world of nature and spirits, provides a degree of management over lives that are often lived on the margins of control. Beliefs and stories enabled key moments in life to be negotiated, childbirth and death, for instance, both of special significance in peasant societies. A scholar of beliefs and stories in Ireland, Angela Bourke, describes these beliefs as akin to databases. People draw on the databases to be able to know about and act upon matters of everyday life, including hygiene, disability, madness, what a 'stranger' is and how to deal with strangers.[24]

Stories therefore enable people to handle those parts of life when reality and established meaning seem to break down, when, for instance, horror overcomes people, at times of murder, famine or war. Bourke writes about what she calls 'oral fairy legend' and how it gives people access to a paradigm outside reality with which to manage awful memories. In these stories, in this case, of the fairy host in Ireland, the overwhelmingly incomprehensible sits alongside the mundane and necessary in a single narrative. Yet the two are kept separate. 'Fairy legends allowed traumatized people to express nightmare horrors alongside fantasies of plenty,' she says, and the incomprehensible is rendered less painful by its alignment alongside the necessary and the ordinary.[25] What was true for fairy legends was true for similar story forms across Europe.

Stories about babies taken away and replaced with changelings carry memories of real children whose appearance changed as they starved, in the Great Famine, perhaps, when 'wrinkled with care they appeared like aged persons'.[26] The figure of the changeling child enabled women, and men, to cope with unfathomable loss. Unlike folk tales, where things happen in threes, and the protagonists are the children of either kings or poor widows, the kinds of stories Bourke describes are realistic, indeed claim to be true, and so are full of exact detail about real people and places. Again, the local landscape is not mute, the stories and beliefs being manifested in this tree, that house, so that belief was distributed and so verified in the territory in which people daily lived.

For centuries, folk culture was said to be communal, collective and thus anonymously authored: however, the storyteller is not anonymous. What is said, sung or played is the product of certain key voices, though it is true that such figures hold prominence only insofar as they retain the trust the group has in them. Thomas and Znaniecki's *The Polish Peasant* introduces us to the three main figures of 'popular' wisdom in Poland around 1920: the wise person, usually older than others and often of a higher social and economic position; the 'narrator', who is more a source of information than advice, perhaps the one who has travelled, a sailor maybe or a pilgrim, perhaps the venerable and wandering beggar. Another, having arrived in more recent days (just before the Great War), is the one who is literate, the 'reader'. As reading developed, the narrator was replaced by the reader. Then there is the 'explainer', the 'philosopher', also newly developed, the self-taught man, who may even be a newspaper letter-writer. This figure is not yet fully established in 1918.[27] Some of these figures will be active in peasant politics.

The people of Dzików or Maam Cross did not dwell in the endless repose of unchanging time. Events occurred and changed things, just as they did everywhere else. Life went on. Dzików is on the Vistula River. People travelled up and down it all the time, often as far as the Baltic, to the north. Being a raftsman *and* a peasant was not unusual, the raftsmen carried back new habits and new things. They walked back the hundreds of miles from the far north when their work was over, stopping at taverns along the way, picking up news and views. The same was so for army recruits (Dzików had to produce one and a half conscripts annually for the Habsburgs). The 'people without history' do have, in fact, a history. But these men returned, as did the women who went away, perhaps to earn a dowry (in the same way that women went to America from Joyce Country to earn a dowry and then returned). The village was still the centre of the world. Peasants combined the immutable and the transitory in ways that transformed both into something new. That is their genius. Stories help us understand this.

There is an essay by John Berger called 'The Storyteller' which bears on this (Berger was himself a master storyteller). In the essay, the village is seen to reproduce itself in stories, at least informally, as opposed to the formality of ceremony and ritual, which serve to do the same job in another way. The village is a 'living portrait of itself'. This is because all are involved and all are known, everyone portrays and is portrayed. This never stops. The village's story is the great collective talk that keeps everything going and everything together; it comprises gossip and news. The talk is collective, but the teller is the one who best articulates it for the collective.[28]

Berger's account of what he calls 'mystery' in 'The Storyteller' is particularly telling, for, although the village is the centre of the world, the mystery of the human species is nonetheless apparent. The village and what happens in it for those who live there are typical of human experience. What it means to be human is what interests the peasant, the typology of human character, the common destiny shared by all. Peasants are not cut off from the world, as is so often thought, and are interested in it, but in their own fashion and following their own needs. 'The foreground portrait of the village is very specific, the background consists of the most open, general and never entirely answerable questions. Therein is the acknowledged mystery,' Berger writes, and the old peasant man that stands before him 'knows that I know this as sharply as he does'.[29]

And then finally there are the words themselves, the elements that make up the stories, words the nature of which we take for granted. Just like the bodies of peasants, their words are not the same as ours. To understand the difference is to begin to appreciate the power of the story, and of peasant beliefs more generally, but begin to appreciate only. William Pooley, the man who has written so perceptively of peasant bodies, writes also about peasant words. He confesses in the end to the 'irreducible otherness' in trying to explain what things meant in the society he considers (that of Gascony in all the richness of its dialectal forms). This is so because the associations of words are so strange and difficult to comprehend. 'Making foxes' is vomiting, 'making almanacs' is to faint, and being ill is being 'unbound'. There are fifty-six phrases for being drunk in the local dialect. There is a particular word for the vomit of drunk people. How to better understand this 'irreducible otherness', and so make it a little less other?[30]

As Znaniecki and many others have shown us, words, for peasants, are things. Just as the objects that surrounded peasants may be animate, so too for peasants with language itself, in which there is an immanent life. Znaniecki shows how in Poland words are animated and conscious, so that our familiar conceptual distinctions and the reassurance they bring dissolve before our eyes. Words have their own quality of being and the dignity or obloquy that accompanies this. Changing the pronunciation of words and playing with them is disliked by peasants; the pun is seldom used by them, and great words should not be applied to small things. Hence the significance of spells, curses, the order and manner of storytelling, that they be given their correct word forms. Language is performative, it *does* things. Thus stories, which are made up of words, living things out there in the world, have a power that we can hardly imagine, so different is it from our conceptual universe. (But perhaps not completely different, for we have literature, which is a sort of paler version of this old verbal order, and of course for those who are religious there is the word as incantation and performance.)

The word is not a symbol, as it is to us. The word exists in its own right. We are in a world where folk tales can be carried around in a bag, forgotten in a forest, and then found again; in the account of one particular storyteller, a story is mysteriously contained in his little finger. So Anna Engelking tells us in her study of the 'folk magic of the word' in the eastern borderlands of Poland, Belarus and Ukraine. And Engelking is not describing the 1950s, nor the 1910s, but the very late twentieth century. Words, remarkably, can themselves show a willingness to talk. 'Magical realism' is centuries old. Stories can be experienced through other senses, touch as well as sight. One touches the teller to verify the account.

Words can also be dangerous: the death of a villager would be announced in such a way that the inhabitants of the neighbouring houses would notify those who lived in the next house in the same verbal form. The news would thus travel, and it had to make its way to every house in the village before sunset, failure to do so having grievous consequences. Words therefore carry power. There is the terrible power of the curse. Peasants live in a world where the noun is king and not the adjective or verb. The name and the thing are conjoined. The character of the Irish language itself reveals the power of the nominative, and so in that culture, as in all peasant cultures, there is an enormous metaphoric richness to talk itself (the pre-eminent noun constantly reverberates with meanings), which is the result of the peasant law of constantly comparing things. There is also the consequence of the remarkable individuation of things noted by anthropologists. Fields, trees, rocks, houses are known individually, and so named. Place and word are fused.[31]

*

Half a century before the photograph of Seán Joyce in Chapter 1 was taken there is another image of him, the following:

My father holds me on his lap. I shelter from the light because of an eye problem, a light shield shading my eyes. Seán Joyce, Big Seán, stands beside us, a lanky boy of eight or nine. It was 1948 or 1949. Seán is barefoot, as children were in summer. I approach my long-dead father through the means of the photographic image, but then I move towards the even more obscure parts of myself that are his father and mother, Pat Liam and Brigid, and I do so through the stories I have described and the world they came out of. And then the 'Liam' in Pat Liam's name comes into view, Pat's father. Pat Liam was born in the old Kilbride house in 1869, and his father, Liam, Liam na haille, born in 1825, had the farm before him ('Liam of the cliff', as Seán Joyce translated it for me, the cliff being a rocky cleft on the mountain marking off the boundary of both the farm and the townland). Liam's own father was also a Liam, born, as far as I know, in the last decade of the eighteenth century. I have no reason to believe the place was not a Joyce place from at least that time. At least 200 years in the one place.

I venerate the ancestors, their endurance, their survival. The Wexford ones I do not forget either, the Kilkenny Halligans over the River Barrow on my grandmother's side, the Kents who were in the old Loughstown before my grandfather the drinker Patrick Bowe turned up in the 1870s. These elders approach, tellers of stories like Mícheál Breathnach bid them forward, but their images, like their selves, are still obscured, as things gone sadly are. Perhaps one of them, or a brother or sister, was a *senchaí*. Knowledge of the world of the in between lessens the obscurity.

In between

What anthropologists call the liminal is where categories overlap, where boundaries are drawn, boundaries in daily life that are to do with sex and sexuality, with purity and impurity, with childbirth and the life of the newborn child. With the difference between life and death. The world of the emotions is involved, and sometimes the erotic dimensions of life receive a special kind of articulation. The Polish water spirits, *boginki*, and the 'wee people' in Ireland are close kin, inhabitants of material and spiritual realms both, where it is the boundaries and the in betweenness itself that count.

Ireland has long been considered a place where in betweenness is marked. A story helps show this, a story about *fóidín meartha*, in English 'the stray sod', a place where a person is liable to be put astray (a sod is a piece of earth torn or cut from the ground). It is a 'true' story and not a made-up tale, but the line between the two is well-nigh impossible to trace in the world of the in between. Mícheál Breathnach told a local collector this tale of his experience in the industrial town of Jarrow in north-east England. (There was a tradition of seasonal migration to shipbuilding Jarrow from the Joyce Country, Jarrow of the once-famous 'Jarrow March' against unemployment in the stricken 1930s.)

> I saw *fóidín meartha* on a man in the middle of the city. I was working in Jarrow and at around 10 o'clock at night I left my lodging house and I saw a man standing with his back to a lamp post. I knew him, I was working in the same place as him. There were scores of people

> going by. He didn't know any of them. I recognized him and I asked him what had come on him. He said he didn't know. 'I've walked the whole town,' said he, 'and I'm unable to make out my lodging house.' I knew he was a man that wouldn't drink much. 'Come along,' I said, 'I'll bring you home.' We weren't 200 yards along when he told me to return home. 'The fog has gone down now,' he said, 'I know where I am.' Those were the very words he said to me.

The idea of the *fóidín meartha* is that the 'good people' have put a spell on a sod of earth. Whoever steps upon this spot goes into a sort of trance, occupying a place that is in between human and spirit. They are kept in this state until the fairies release them, though there are certain actions that can bring about release too. Accounts of these phenomena are to be found throughout Ireland. I draw at random from the Irish Folklore Commission accounts of the 1930s:

> One evening a girl from our place was going to a wake and she fell asleep while she was walking. She walked over water and she was not a bit wet. She kept walking until morning. As soon as the sun shone in the morning she woke and went to the nearest house. There she was told that she was six miles from her own home. She was shivering when she woke and she was put to bed and she never left it until she died.

Or again, 'Quinn kept walking on, but the wood was still in front of him. This time he sighted the dance house, but he was aroused by music and laughing that was behind him.'[32] The wood appeared to keep in front of him, although he walked into it; he saw the dance house before him but its sounds came from somewhere behind him. Where fields, trees, rocks are known and named individually, disturbance to the ground was of great meaning.

The *fóidín meartha* might be associated with places where certain people were buried; for example unbaptized children, the graveyards of whom, *cillíní*, are to be found everywhere in present-day Ireland. Or the place might be where a coffin was placed, while those who were carrying it rested (coffins had to be carried over long distances for burial where roads were poor, this journey itself being one of great ritual significance). If you stood on *fóidín mearbhaill* you would be 'lifted' as it is called, led astray. There is also the 'hungry sod' or the *fod ghorta* as it is called. If a person happens to stand on this sod, he is seized with hunger and weakness.

Mícheál Breathnach's account is unusual as the *slua sí*, the fairy host, the *daoine maithe*, do not usually travel abroad. That they do so here reveals the need for them in the stranger's land. Implicit in Mícheál's account is his immediate understanding of what his compatriot is experiencing in a strange new world where countless people go by unrecognized, just as he is not recognized. It is a big thing to come from a place where you are always known to one where you are never known. The immigrant is drawn to the immigrant by the intuitive sense of what is happening and what needs to be done to rescue the man. Ailbhe Nic Giolla Chomhaill tells us that the storyteller's verbatim repetition of the man's words, as well as his assertion that this was a man 'that wouldn't drink much', verifies the truth of the incident.[33]

Mícheál's own life helps link the world of his beliefs to the realities of existence in Joyce Country. He was in England in the 1890s, when he first went to Jarrow in search of work, he and his wife Úna then not long married and with two young children. He spent a few years working in Jarrow before returning home, where he got a job as a supervisor on a roadworks project. In 1914, however, Mícheál's second son, also named Mícheál (then seventeen), left home to go to Scotland. The father was terrified that his son would be enlisted in the British army, for he had a strong hatred of what, reaching back to 1798 in one of his own long 'historical' stories, he called the 'red coats' (*bhí gráin aige ar an gcóta dearg*, the hated the redcoat'). He followed his son to Scotland, where both men found work, moving down together to Jarrow, where the older Mícheál made the then quite astronomic sum of £5 a week, hard labouring as a furnaceman. His son died in Jarrow in the great influenza epidemic of the post-war years and is buried there, far from the home place. The father was heartbroken, returning home to Maam and never again returning to England. There his stories continued to be collected by the insatiable folklorists of the 1930s.[34] Though they tended to be neglected by the collector, there were many women in Joyce Country who had large oral-narrative repertoires, at least four in the Maam area in 1935 alone, including a Mrs Spelman of Claggan, who was born at the time the Great Famine raged.

The *fóidín meartha* was only one small part of the world of Irish in betweenness. Fairy belief and official religion have coexisted in Ireland for perhaps 1,600 years, since Patrick landed in AD 432. In the not-so-distant past, priests were regarded as being wise in the ways of the fairies, indeed the priest himself might be considered to have magical powers: earth from a priest's grave was used in curses. The fairies inhabit a reality parallel to human reality and live alongside humans in the same physical world, but in special places. There are estimated to be 60,000 hill forts, or 'raths', in Ireland, where the fairies are said to live.[35] Most of these date from the second half of the first millennium after Christ and were dwelling enclosures, the standing stones of which remain. These places are given an added charge by people having actually lived in them in the far-distant past, so that a tradition of continuous habitation links belief, landscape and history. There is a degree of obscurity in the actual naming of these places; they have no single, settled, generic name. They are untouched places, places covered with vegetation, places that may be dangerous. In these sites two worlds may clash. The whinbush or thornbush, as with Heaney's thorn tree which binds, might mark these dwelling places of the fairies, although the bush has its own magic power and should not be cut down, even if in the middle of an arable field.

Peasant intellectual activity, constantly comparing nature and culture as it does, proceeds by exploring the interrelations of the human and non-human dimensions of the world through metamorphosis. For instance, farmers in 1970s Fermanagh, in Ireland's North, imagined the *broc*, the badger, to be a sort of farmer, metamorphosed as such. By the light of the big harvest moon, the '*broc*'s moon', the badger 'pulls grass out of the hedge and makes "the *broc*'s fodder" by spreading it on the stubble of the cornfields, where it is "won" to provision him through the winter', just as a farmer would do.[36] The badger may mean good or bad luck: if you heard a badger call, and then heard the hoot of the owl you were not long for this world.[37] That these beliefs were extant in the 1970s shows how gradual their retreat has been.

Angela Bourke's remarkable *The Burning of Bridget Cleary* dramatizes an earlier stage in the erosion of the old peasant beliefs. It is a study of how in 1895 in rural Tipperary the badly burned body of twenty-six-year-old Bridget Cleary was found buried in a shallow grave. Her death may have been unintended but there is no doubt her husband Michael and the others involved, acting on the belief that she was possessed by fairies, used the prescribed method of fire to exorcize the evil and strangeness they believed to be in her. Everyday fears and jealousies, hopes and longings, were tied up in the case, which revolved around a wide range of issues, from childlessness to the tensions produced by the new levels of social mobility becoming apparent at the time. Matters came to a head because the Clearys had built a house on top of a fairy rath.

At the centre of the Cleary narrative is the story of Jack Dunne, a poor and isolated old man, but still a master of spells, and so a principal actor in these events. In his very age, his social isolation and marginalization, he is a symbol of the slow ebbing of the old world and the coming of the new, for the case, in essence the clash of two worlds colliding, dramatizes the reality of the late coming of modernity to rural Ireland. Both Jack Dunne's command of magic and Michael Cleary's employment of his knowledge involve securing control over life, a need heightened by the rapidity with which the familiar landmarks of existence were being lost. The dramatic retreat of the Irish language was at the centre of this. There was no landmark more familiar, and none the loss of which was so grievous.

In 1800 almost half the Irish population spoke Irish as their first or only language, but by 1900 this had declined to fewer than a sixth. Literacy in English soared over the course of that century, growing from less than half of the population to most of the people in the country. New and powerful forms of official religiosity developed out of the chaos that followed the Great Famine, the so-called Catholic 'devotional revolution'. The powers of the Church were centralized and new devotional organizations such as the lay confraternity and the sodality flourished alongside new religious services like Benediction and the Stations of the Cross. New aids to private devotion like the scapular, the holy medal and the rosary emerged. The cult of the Virgin Mary thrived. Church building increased dramatically. The Church authorities looked upon the old beliefs as a threat to their power.

But, as Bourke recognizes, Tipperary, in the fertile South, was advanced in its 'modernization' when compared with the Irish-speaking western parts of the island, my father's world. And even in the prosperous parts of the country there was not so much the replacement of the old beliefs by established religion as a continuation of them in new forms. Only now religion had the upper hand at last. But upper hand or not, the kingdom of the in between continued in the form of the nod and the wink, the no man's land of half- and quarter-belief.

A rather nervous jokiness is involved sometimes in talking about the old beliefs. The face-saving denial is made, but often the insurance policy of still believing in the old ways is quietly taken out. Belief in these may be tacit, unspoken, and there is the underlying desire to believe, as with my own mother and father and the parents of my wife, who, like my own parents, were shaped in the latter days of the old beliefs, when to believe was to do so with less certainty than their own parents, but still to believe. In a poem called 'Keeping Going', published in his 1996 collection *The Spirit Level*, Heaney writes of how one day a tree was cut down that should have been left alone. It is the thorn tree once again, a tree marking a place where another race of beings may have had their abode:

> When the thorn tree was cut down
> You broke your arm. I shared the dread
> When a strange bird perched for days on the byre roof.

The good people had still to be 'minded'. You had to look out for them or you would come to harm, 'look out' both in being aware of them and in looking after them. There is the story of the farmer who showed no respect and cut the whinbush down and then woke up in the morning to find the hair of his head, all of it, shed around him on the pillow. Travellers, then called 'tinkers' or sometimes 'gypsies', struck a special fear into others as they too summoned up the in between. In some houses the place was blessed after they left, though the same people were a source of respect and fascination, too, for they knew the future. As a child in the Wexford summers of the 1950s I knew the hesitant incoming of the Travellers at the gate below the house to be the signal of a general womanly consternation, a flurry of trepidation which was at once something anxious and delighted.

The past holds on strongly in Wexford as well as in the West: in the immediate past of 2018 there is ample evidence of how the old beliefs are still given more than half-credence. In the wonderful filmed folklore collections of Michael Fortune, now online, people talk directly to camera with sincerity and humour, and in the distinctive speech of Wexford. There are striking accounts of raths and fairies, some from Castletown, near where my mother's family, the Bowes, came from. The *bean sí* screamed in the night for these Wexford men and women when they were young, just as for my mother a generation before them. In Wexford the *bean sí* is called the Bow (pronounced in the same way as my mother's surname, Bowe (like an archer's bow). One man tells Fortune a story of an old man and the Bow: 'He really believed it. I was young at the time and had to believe in it so. Whether it was true or not I don't know.' Another man complains how there 'are people who fucking tell you there are no such thing', but 'I really believe. I know.' He relates how he was told by a man he knew the precise time a dying neighbour's life would end, based on this man's knowledge of how the Bow cried: 'Not a word of a lie, that woman died at that time.'[38]

In conclusion I turn westwards again. In the spring of 1940, twenty-four families, 127 people in all, departed on buses from my father's native village of Clonbur to make a new life for themselves in the eastern Irish county of Meath. There the land is much better than in the 'congested' district of Joyce Country. The Congested Districts Board was the name of the original British state body of 1891 that governed what we would now call 'rural development', and this was the forerunner of the Land Commission of the new republic that sent these Clonbur people on their way in 1940. The Meath exodus (there were several other, bigger ones) was designed by the republic to form a new Gaeltacht, a little linguistic oasis of Catholic nationalism among the insufficiently Gaelic people of the East. Martin O'Halloran (Mártan Mhailic Sheáin Leachlainn) describes the world of what he calls 'The Lost Gaeltacht', the world of his upbringing.[39]

Most of those who travelled east came from the townland directly across Maskeen from the Kilbride of my father, Cloghbrack, as it is anglicized (its image in 1904 is in the previous chapter, on page 87 above). Some of these emigrants came from Kilbride itself. My grandfather's brother was among them. The Meath people themselves cleaved to the old ways, just as the first generation of peasant exiles would do, my parents included, where in London they carried the old time with them and kept it beside them until their earthly time ended.

Martin tells me that the Meath people believed that the people of Seanadh Farracháin were great adepts at 'throwing the handful' and making a curse. In this townland there lived a woman called Maire Dubh. It was generally believed that the Devil had appeared to Maire, and that she had the power to snatch children and leave changelings. My grandmother, from the same townland, would have known Maire. Cloghbrack and Kilbride are remote, Seanadh Farracháin even more so, set as it is at the far, western end of a steeply glaciated lake-filled valley. The lake there is called Lough Nafooey, Loch na Fuaiche in Irish, 'Lake of the winnowing winds', or, in another rendering, one in this instance apt, the 'grave-shaped lake'. Not far west of Seanadh Farracháin lies Glentreague, in a similar setting of great natural beauty. Bid Laffey was Glentreague's version of Maire Dubh.

It should be said that all the people of Joyce Country were devout Catholics and had been so for many centuries. Bid Laffey, Bid a gheata (Bid the gatekeeper), was the sister of Martin O'Halloran's grandfather. He writes of how the grandchildren of this woman were forbidden to see their grandmother throw a spell and so make a cure. One of them, out of curiosity, peeked through the door as she practised and heard in Irish the words (written here in English), 'Live fire, dead fire, evil fire into the ground, the person saved, and the fire dead.'[40] All this was coming to an end. Bid a gheata's own son, a good Catholic, was outraged by his mother's works and said they would be 'disgraced' if the priest got to hear of it. Nonetheless, all around had great faith in her, and, as she said, 'Never mind the priest, what is the harm, am I not helping people?' This woman called on the dying and very ill to comfort them. She laid out the dead for burial. But then she also lent out special rosary beads to people, beads that had come from her daughter, who was a nun. It is hard to see who was winning here, the Church or the old order.

In Joyce Country, the bonfire on St John's Eve was kept up into the second half of the twentieth century, on the 23rd of June, as near the summer solstice as Catholic propriety would allow. Pebbles were thrown on the fire, which had to be circled the proper number of times. On the feast of St Martin of Tours in November blood must be shed, and a fowl is killed by an old woman. A man in Joyce Country of my own age remembers his parents' talk in the 1960s and 70s of *An Stail Bhreac*, the 'Speckled Stallion', a rough and bawdy game played at wakes for the dead when a masked man would enter the wake house and prod people into such agitation that violence might ensue as old animosities were settled or new ones provoked.

All this was much to the disapproval of the One True Catholic Church. The peculiar conditions of far-western-Connaught Catholicism meant it had a good deal in common with religion across Europe, especially in the East. In Ireland the participants in the duel between folk belief and religion had fought and made up and fought again for almost a millennium and a half by the time of Maire Dubh and Bid a gheata. The cohabitation lasted longer than a thousand years in Poland; in Italy, the best part of two millennia. It is to this strange marriage that I now turn.

6.

God: I Have Created the Vermin and the Birds for People to Prosper

In the Poland of the second decade of the twentieth century, old beliefs were interpreted from a Christian standpoint: a peasant might say to a child who wants to kill a frog: 'Don't do it, this creature also praises our Lord Jesus.' Christian legends were connected to many of the natural beings who make up the solidarity of nature and man: for example, stories about the healing properties of plants might be related to the legend that the head of St John was cut off and fell among the plants in question, imparting them with its power. The whole process of the natural, agricultural year, the building of the house, the preparation and eating of food, everything is accompanied by religious ceremonies, thanksgivings, blessings, expiations.

Nonetheless, Christianity is undergirded by the older axioms. For instance, lightning can be seen as the instrument of God's punishment but the long-held beliefs survive in the idea that lightning is that which purifies, so that a man struck by lightning goes straight to heaven. The same is the case for the snake, which is a symbol for the Devil but still a benefactor in nature. Things of God can be enrolled in the cause of the Devil. Prayers said backwards, for instance, may be magically efficacious and counter to the authority of the Church. Rosary beads and amulets may be appropriated for other than the official uses.

Every day of the year is consecrated to a Christian saint, so that the name is substituted for the date, but the day itself, even time itself, may have an animate character as it operates in and on the world. This symbiosis with Christianity was ever-present. Oskar Kolberg tells us how, in earlier times, 'The day (Sunday) is holy, as are its parts: morning, noon and evening. So, if for example one says something unseemly at noontime, one should add, "with my apologies this sacred noontime".'[1] As the great anthropologist of southern Italian peasant religion Ernesto de Martino put it, it is mere delusion to imagine that, for instance, that the magical incantation for breast milk is on the one hand pure magic and on the other that the recitation of the rosary is pure religion.[2]

We remember the upbringing of Seamus Heaney, experience of the natural world being for him what he called 'sacramental, a system of signs that called automatically upon systems of thinking and feeling'. What was sacramental was the landscape and God, both together, symbiotic. There are thus many kinds of overlap and concordance between the three spheres of the natural or physical world, the spirit world and the world of religion. In the thorn tree of Heaney's Derry live the fairies and there too in the same tree appears the Blessed Virgin, the tree in the process taking on what he called 'a new set of subliminal attributes'. Here concordance reigned, and with it an intensification of spiritual power. But the tree is no less a tree because the fairies may have their abode there, just as in Poland the snake, even if symbolic in some contexts, remains resolutely part of nature, and of humankind's solidarity with nature.

Peasants might also encounter contradictions and sometimes incoherence between the different realms of belief. This is when things went awry and the codes that guided the different realms got mixed up. Chaos threatened; the Devil might take over. However, like us, indeed, peasants were often able to live quite happily with contradictions. Their embrace of one or the other code was a matter of context, of what best fitted which situation people were in, of that which worked. You behaved towards a fellow villager, a townsman, a priest, in different ways. Sometimes the wise woman was consulted, sometimes a priest, sometimes you kicked the wall in frustration.

Nonetheless, because codes could collide it was necessary to create boundaries. This was where religion came into its own, because, being an institution, it had organization, and thus the power that went with it. This enabled it to create and police boundaries. The Devil was to be made the monopolist of evil, God the monopolist of good. The divine was to be strictly guarded as the preserve of organized religion only. Moral authority could be established all the better with the social authority it had achieved and the political power it had secured. Religion usually had the law on its side, and so it also had the support of those who uphold the law, the landowners and the state.

The power of religious institutions represented at times a radical assault on the spirits and the natural realm, and at other times an accommodation with them, for if the divine was to be guarded compromise was often needed, something that usually went against the grain of established religion and which was not easily forthcoming. Accommodation marked peasant religion in general. Accommodation from the peasants' side was as much as possible on their own terms, integrating their established beliefs into Christianity where they felt the fit was best. Studies of what is usually called folk religion everywhere remark on its lack of dogma, its indifference to theology, its human-centred God. The attempts of the Protestant Reformation and Catholic Counter-Reformation to make belief into doctrine were more effective upon higher and more-educated social groups than on peasants. Peasant religion was something else.

In thinking of this 'something else', it is instructive to turn to what may be termed peasant wisdom, a sort of philosophy in fact, though an unusual one, being made up of proverbs, stories, the wisdom of wise men and women and not infrequently of jokes. The cast of much of this peasant wisdom can be summed up by a Polish peasant saying, 'The wind always blows in a poor man's face!' Jan Słomka helps us again here, on the subject of proverbs. Proverbs 'typical of peasant thinking', as he puts it, include, '"Even a stone will grow if it stays put!"; meaning that whether farmer or servant, a man will make something of himself if he stays in one place and doesn't become a rolling stone.'

Don't tempt fate, stick with your own kind. The past anchors one, and certainly hope lies in the future but it is not with any great certainty of improvement.[3]

One is disabused, one knows the score of bearing the curse of Ham. The cards are stacked against you. The idea of fate enters in, with good reason, and fatalism has often been remarked as characteristic of peasant society. It is certainly the case that, to peasants, many things seemed guided towards an ending somehow foretold for them. Prevision, a prediction but often just a feeling about what is to come, was strong in peasant thinking. If the christened child has a certain feature then it will likely grow up in accordance with the associations of that feature; the lame mind following upon the lame body, the crooked babe being followed in life by all things that are crooked. This is fate, *fortuna*, but one is not helpless, for following another course of action, doing a certain deed, saying particular words, creates a chance fate can be reshaped into a better form. It is possible to know as best as one can what will come and to guard against the worst outcomes.

This peasant imagination, which amounts to a demand for continuity, has in turn elicited the scholarly imagination of many, not only folklorists and social scientists, but also writers of fiction. Mircea Eliade was a profoundly influential historian of myths and religions. Born in 1907, he grew up in a still deeply peasant Romania, and as a child he was fascinated by Romanian folklore and peasant Christian belief. This is what Eliade wrote about peasant religion:

> It is true that most of these rural European populations have been Christianized for over a thousand years. But they succeeded in incorporating into their Christianity a considerable part of their pre-Christian religious heritage, which was of immemorial antiquity. It would be wrong to suppose that for this reason European peasants are not Christians. But we must recognize that their religion is not confined to the historical forms of Christianity, that it still retains a cosmic structure that has been almost entirely lost in the experience of urban Christians.[4]

In practice, peasant wisdom can be seen to have been rooted in deep-seated peasant beliefs that themselves drew on old religious traditions of a pre-Christian sort. This is what Eliade means when he states that peasants were indeed Christians, but that their religion still retained a cosmic structure lost to our contemporary experience. In short, within peasant religion other forms of the sacred were present than the sacred of the Christian God, who, for Christians, monopolizes the divine, the realm of God or the gods. The sacred is that which is other to material existence, the word coming from the Latin *sacer*, that which is 'set off, restricted'. Set off from the common and the material world, the sacred expresses the total value of life, a value represented in what is an eternal reality.

Understandings of peasant time help explain how recourse to the sacred meant that one was not helpless before the workings of fate. Religious belief of all sorts is closely integrated with conceptions of time. The reckoning of time among peasants might be according to the needs of the task, and so measured by the time of doing a task, ploughing an acre, say. Time is also reckoned by the light of the day, when the first light hits certain parts of the land, or, with more precision, when the light comes in at a certain angle through the opened door, or the sun first hits an object on the wall, a holy image perhaps.

And then more comprehensive periods of time are linked to the phases of the moon, the reappearance of certain types of bird, the blossoming of particular bushes and trees, periods of warmth and cold, wet and dry times, or longer-term cycles involved in working the land, which were marked by corresponding festive rituals.[5] (In the long periods of isolation and separation from normal routine during the Covid pandemic, there were many reports of people knowing again these former ways of experiencing time; via birds, flowers, animals, the weather making a comeback, something itself often reported as 'spiritual'.) In practice, therefore, peasants lived in several kinds of time, just like we do, but their times were greatly different to ours. By the twentieth century, many peasants were also often well familiar with the new time order of the clock. The world of railway timetables, newspapers ('periodicals', so-called), political elections, armies, was well known to them. But this knowledge was lived alongside much older ways of experiencing time, sometimes with, sometimes without contradiction.

In short, time was, for peasants, experienced concretely and had multiple dimensions, rather than the abstract and unitary clock time that dominates us. Their various ways of experiencing and registering time, along with time's personal, communal and generational dimensions, were integrated and legitimated by sacred time. This provided the means by which disorder and threats to the community and the person could be kept at bay. Sacred time was secured by creation myths, in which everything done by the gods had irreversible validity. What Eliade called 'the eternal return' is a central part of this, the idea that it is possible to experience creation time again, to gain sustenance from this experience, and thereby create order in a present that has become disordered. In this sense, time is reversible, unlike western time.

Reversibility is enacted on the occasions (observances, rituals, festivals) in which 'the same is met again that was made evident in the festival of the previous year or in the festival of a hundred years ago.' Deviations from the rules of the sacred may, therefore, in this universe be reversed or at least adjusted through such festivals, or by rites of atonement, the payment of penalties, or sacrifices of one sort or another.

Suffering is at the centre of religion, our own suffering and, in the European tradition, that of Christ and the saints. Time also has a great deal to do with suffering, because suffering is the result of the constant uncertainty that time brings. Peasants' dependence on the cycles of nature means uncertainty is doubly marked. Their survival is at stake. Eliade writes that suffering in what he calls traditional societies is tolerated morally 'because *it is not absurd*'.[6] Such societies had, and have, only limited concepts of calculated risk, because they see an intentionality behind misfortune. There is an order to things which underlies the vicissitudes of fortune and the suffering they bring. Suffering is given meaning by being understood as the consequence of the breaking of a taboo or the magical action of an enemy or entry into a forbidden area, provoking the wrath of the Supreme Being. The complementarity of 'traditional' religion and here the organized religion of Christianity will not have escaped the reader, and thus how the former might serve as the template for the latter, for all their great differences.

As we have seen, for peasants the world and God are full of signs that are there for a reason. You act on the signs. It is to this world of signs, wonders and terrors I now turn, moving from these general remarks towards seeing peasant Christianity in action in the concrete forms of particular places and times. I will focus mostly on Catholicism, the predominant peasant faith in Europe. Of course, many European peasants were not of this faith: for example, the population in Poland that preceded 1945 was at times only 70 per cent Roman Catholic, with strong Orthodox and somewhat less significant Protestant minorities. And the main denominations themselves split into different Churches: in Ireland, the Catholic majority lived side by side with Protestants for centuries. Italy, with Rome at its centre, was almost totally Catholic. There were great swathes of Protestantism across northern Europe, especially around the North Sea basin. Muslim peasants inhabited south-east Europe, and, of course, Orthodoxy dominated in Greece, as in the Europe east and south of modern Poland. There were also a small number of Jewish peasants, forgotten as they have been, who had much in common with other peasants, irrespective of denominational allegiance. It would be unwise to try to cover the ground of this great mosaic, so I will concentrate on the predominating Catholicism, though also with some attention to Protestantism.

There are three features of Catholicism that are characteristic of Catholicism pretty much everywhere: cults, pilgrimages and the power of the image. I begin with the cult, in relation to Italy, the South of Italy being particularly rich in these. Then I look at pilgrims and pilgrimages in relation to Ireland, including the pilgrimage site of Croagh Patrick on the furthest rim of Europe, which is the place of pilgrimage of my own West of Ireland kin. However, this section is mainly taken up with an example of pilgrimages in Slovakia (the locations of which in fact are just across the border from Poland). Here I am also guided in my choice by the richness of the source of my knowledge, the extraordinary photography of Markéta Luskačová. I confess to being guided by the same logic of choice in the case of the cults of southern Italy as well, namely the luminous anthropology of Ernesto de Martino, itself replete with photos.

As for the image and its power, Catholic Poland presents itself immediately in the form of the image of the Blessed Virgin, Mary, who is officially the Mother of Poland. Finally there is the word, as opposed to the image, the distinction between the two usually marking out the divide between Protestantism and Catholicism, and in particular the direct authority of the word of the Bible, as opposed to the vast and powerful mediations of the 'One True Church of Rome'. The idea of the 'word' takes me to Lutheran Poland and Anglican England. But there is a different 'word' too, as we shall see, in the Catholic folk bible of central and eastern Europe: and this helps us to see that, once all the great distinctions of faith and sect are acknowledged, there are certain similarities across the board that identify 'peasant religion'. So, four small windows briefly opened on domains of extraordinary human richness: the cult, the pilgrimage, the image, the word.

The Cult

Cults can be official and orthodox, unofficial and heterodox. Official religion can be at ease with cults or uncomfortable about them. The following photograph is of a cult in action. The image forms an essential part of a renowned anthropological study on the religion of the people of the Salentino peninsula in southern Italy called *The Land of Remorse*. It is not an art photograph, a family snap, nor exactly documentary photography. Perhaps it could be called anthrophotography: it is an academic image. The man standing on the corbel of the altar is called Donato of Matino and the woman

sitting on the tabernacle is Caterina of Nardó. Donato has just before entered the Chapel of St Paul in 'spectacular fashion', crawling slowly on his back towards the altar, his arms in the shape of a cross and then raised in the air with his fists clenched. Periodically he bursts forth with 'the long stereotypical cry of the *tarantati* in crisis'. The woman, however, is the person who is having the crisis. She sits 'immersed in her anxious depression . . . immobile'.[7]

Tarantismo is a rural possession cult involving a nervous disorder believed to be brought about through the bite of the tarantula. Through music and trance-dancing it is believed the afflicted person can be cured. It is women who are mostly afflicted (therefore Donato is a kind of master of ceremonies rather than a *tarantato* himself). On the feast of St Peter and Paul every June, men and women who have acted out the possession rituals in their homes have for centuries gathered at the Chapel of San Paolo in the village of Galatina. During the so-called 'home therapies' people would publicly perform uncontrolled dances, scream and move in convulsive ways simulating possession by (and eventually the trampling upon) a spider. During their wild, often obscene gestures these 'tarantuled' persons would hold an imaginary dialogue with St Paul, the patron saint against spiders and snake bites.

The people involved were peasants. The picture was taken in 1959. All these ritual actions, it should be noted, take place in a consecrated place of worship, and are accompanied by the support of the clergy, if not always with their complete approval. The author of the study the image comes from is Ernesto de Martino, born, in Naples, only a year after Eliade, and like him a great historian-cum-philosopher of religion. He was a man of the left – though there was a mild flirtation with Fascism in his youth.

The photo is of poor quality, as de Martino's research team tried to be as unobtrusive as possible, dodging out from behind a curtain from time to time to take the photographs. The author was aware of what he calls the 'violence' done to what is observed by the presence of the observer.[8] But in another sense this does not matter, for the photographer's showing is just another act of showing besides that of the actors in the cult. As Mircea Eliade puts it, 'showing', making the spiritual manifest, is central to all religions. Religion involves making the sacred manifest, revealing the innate sacrality of things.

The dancers in the ritual, mostly women, are consciously displaying themselves, in anguished yet erotic fashion. The public role of women in this culture was very limited, and public courtship by women was then forbidden or at least frowned upon. The rituals around pregnancy, childbirth and child-rearing were near innumerable, as in most peasant cultures. De Martino maintains that the cult and its rituals deals with existential crises of various sorts, and so express the feeling of not belonging to the world, being overwhelmed and out of control, a state that de Martino referred to as the loss of, or crisis of, presence.

The afflicted are commonly surrounded by a band of musicians playing drums and violins in an attempt to cure them. The next photograph is a more artful image than the previous one, but no less a case of 'showing':

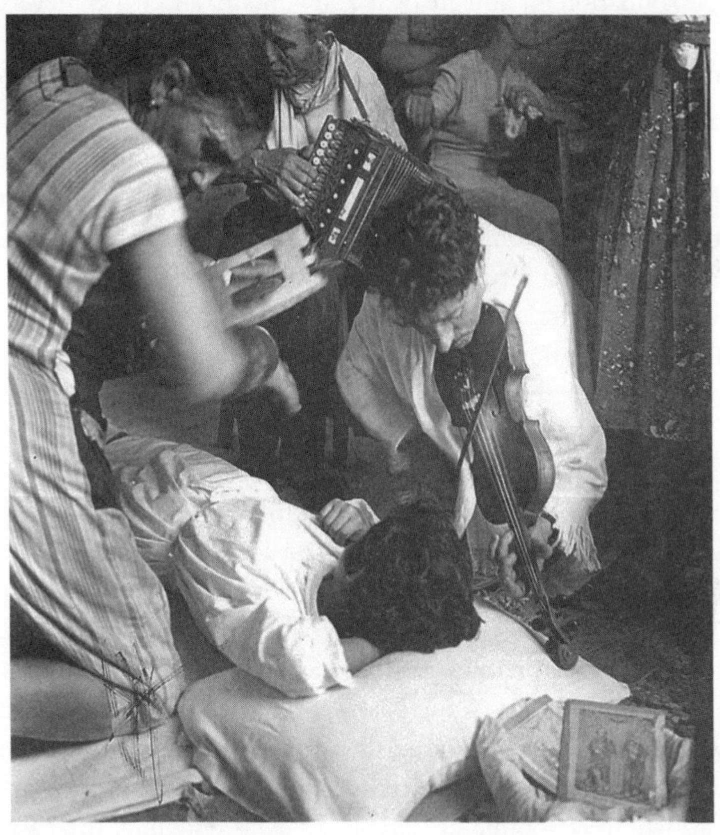

These photographs ask questions of us. The most immediate question is 'What is going on?' What is going on is deeply enigmatic. Photographs take us some of the way in understanding the mystery, great photographs somewhat further. In helping us understand a little better, they proceed by, as Susan Sontag puts it, 'conferring on each moment the character of a mystery', uttering in effect, 'There it is, a surface, now think – or rather feel it, intuit it – what is beyond it. What the reality must be like if it looks this way.'[9] I use her words beside those used by de Martino on the *tarantismo* itself, the mystery of which he attempted to probe, in part, by the means of photography, 'This symbol [of the *taranta*] offers a perspective for imagining, hearing and watching what we lack imagination for and are deaf and blind to, and which nevertheless asks to be imagined, heard and seen.'[10]

The photographs of de Martino nonetheless play their perspectival part in helping us imagine what asks to be heard by us who lack imagination. The images carry the truth of a moment, a moment that came only once but is recorded potentially for ever, and thus demands interpretation. The photographer offers us a mystery to decipher, or rather intuit, asking 'What is going on?', 'What must it have been like if it looks this way?'

The interpretation of photographs de Martino offers – de Martino being a pioneer in the use of photography and film for interpretation – would go something like this: the sense of a personal self in peasant societies is always subject to collective constraint, so that this self is something different to ours to begin with. The personal is less 'individualized'. This collective constraint involves the relations of men and women, which is one among all the other elements making up the balance of the personal and the collective. De Martino thought that the *crisi della presenza* could be experienced both individually and by the community as a whole. Both the person and the communal were engaged in Galatina and at the places where home therapies were administered. In the extreme conditions of the impoverished South, where economic precariousness was endemic, the balance of the self and the communal was constantly threatened by breakdown, hence the precipitation of crises, and so the existence, the necessity, of the cult itself. The simultaneous propinquity and indifference of the Catholic clergy of the day also played its part, people turning to a form of magic that was also Christian: a magical Christianity.

De Martino viewed the 'magico-religious' world view of peasants in the South of Italy as resting on the hardship of their lives: 'The immense power of the negative throughout the individual life, with its procession of shocks, defeats, frustrations, and poverty. This is the foundation of magic and religion.' A crisis in peasant life is interpreted in terms of the disruption of an ideal stable order by some kind of either natural or supernatural agency. Magic is used, de Martino maintains, to deny the location of this crisis in historical and social circumstances, in order that what is negative be suspended or eliminated, and the ideal order re-established.[11] It does not matter if this magic is Christian or not. Secular time is abolished and mythical time reinstituted. The matter of the difference between magic and religion is one of degree, not kind, though the degree is great. As de Martino puts it, 'What is different is the degree and complexity of the magical techniques, the quality of degree of the mediated value; the quality of moral feeling.'[12]

In effect, on the plane of magic, all pregnancies are happily brought to term, all newborns will live, all illnesses heal, all uncertain prospects become clear, all storms will break over uninhabited places; that is to say, exactly the opposite of what happens in life.[13] A visit to a sacred place at a time outside ordinary profane time, such as a Christian pilgrimage on a feast day, releases the pilgrim from everyday social life. Profane or secular time is held at bay and the power of mythical time is released, with rituals releasing the participant back into social life renewed by contact with sacred time. There is a peculiar intensity to the 'magico-religious' world view of peasants when conditions are most extreme, the most parlous, the most uncertain. We remember that the songs of the South in the 1950s were pervaded by what Carlo Levi called 'a most profound sadness'.

In *Christ Stopped at Eboli*, Levi wrote these words: 'No message, human or divine, has reached this stubborn poverty . . . Christ did not come. Christ stopped at Eboli.' Levi was a major inspiration for de Martino, and did more than anyone else in Italy to open the eyes of the Italian North to the extreme poverty of the South. He was a northerner, but an outsider there too, a leftist Jew, and someone deeply sympathetic to the South. He wrote in the 1930s at the time of his exile by the Fascists to Basilicata, his place of confinement the village of Aliano, which he called Gagliano. Published in 1945, *Christ*

Stopped at Eboli has shaped the perceptions of peasants held by generations.

These are Levi's words:

> Eternally patient, hedged in by custom and sorrow, cut off from history and the state, eternally patient, in a land without comfort or solace, the peasant lives out his motionless civilisation on barren ground in remote poverty, and in the presence of death. We are not Christians, the people of Basilicata say, for Christ stopped short of here. Christian means human beings, but they are not human beings. Christ and humanity have passed them by, but they are fervent Christians nonetheless.

These are the same people that de Martino writes of, his not far to the west of Levi's. There is perhaps something of the essential peasant, the ultimate primitive, in even Levi's perceptions, a people without history once again, living in a 'motionless civilization'. But who can deny the mystery of the cry of the *tarantati* in crisis, and the deprivations of the life that mandated that cry?

The deities of the city and the state find no worshippers here, Levi writes, for the state is a form of fate, like the wind that devours the harvest here 'where the wolf and the black boar reign supreme, where there is no wall between the world of men and the world of animals and spirits, between the leaves of the trees above and the roots below. They cannot have even an awareness of themselves as individuals, here where all things are held together by acting upon one another and each one is a power unto itself, working imperceptibly, where there is no barrier that can not be broken down by magic. They live submerged in a world that rolls on independent of their will, where man is in no way separate from his sun, his beast, his malaria.'[14]

Yet here, where 'there is only the grim passivity of a sorrowful Nature', there is nonetheless what Levi calls, 'a lively human feeling for the common fate of mankind and its common acceptance.

This is strictly a feeling rather than an act of will; they do not express it in words but they carry it with them at every moment and in every motion of their lives, through all the unbroken days that pass over these wastes.'[15] A lively human feeling that also, it should be said, took the form of the considerable resentment of the peasants of Aliano at Levi's depictions of them.

The South of Italy was, and still is, a land of Catholic cults, albeit today the Church has better control of 'folk religion' than previously (although the Cult of the Dead in Naples was put down only in 1969). Italy today, North and South, especially the far South, has the largest clustering of shrines to the Virgin Mary in Europe. There are reputedly somewhere around one thousand. When I say 'shrine', I do not mean a small affair, a roadside statue, say, but established sites with long histories, often in the custodial care of the clergy and where a miracle has occurred. The site of the Santuario Madonna delle Lacrime in Siracusa is now dominated by a massive, concrete church said to be in the image of a tear hitting the ground. The church houses a statue of the Virgin Mary that allegedly wept for four days in 1953, and bestowed hundreds of miraculous cures. The tears were for a poor local couple, a fisherman and his wife. If the tears at these shrines have not been shed for fishermen, then they are usually for other poor people. And most often it is a peasant who is the first witness of the holy apparition of Mary, as at Lourdes in France, Fátima in Portugal, Knock in Ireland. This is the church of the poor.

Pilgrims

The following is another photograph of Catholic devotion, by Markéta Luskačová, from her published exhibition catalogue *Pilgrims*.[16] It mostly covers the daily life of a central Slovakian village called Šumiac, as well as peasants on pilgrimage from different parts of Slovakia. In the book, the village is seen through its religion, the religion seen through the village. The photograph shows the arrival of the annual procession from the town of Košice in Slovakia to the Marian shrine of Levoča, and was taken in 1968. Many of those in the photograph will have joined the procession along the 60-odd miles of its way. In Communist times it was a brave thing to do. The pilgrims are prostrate in adoration. It seems as if a river of human bodies has entered the church and then the river has stopped before a power that is greater than it. The river halts before an image, that of the fifteenth-century statue of the Virgin Mary of Levoča. The carved arms of Mary's statue are open to greet them when they come. It is the image of the Virgin that they have come to see, an image they love. Images are central to peasant faith.

Near this site, Mariánska hora, the Marian hill, a group of shepherds many centuries ago were said to have witnessed an apparition of the Virgin Mary. Again, it is the common people who are visited by these apparitions, historically and now, for these manifestations go on occurring today. It is often peasants who are the privileged ones who see.

In the centre of Levoča is the fourteenth-century Basilica of

St James. It contains the great altar of Master Paul of Levoča, completed in 1517. This is the world's tallest carved wooden Christian altar and is of stunning beauty. A Greek Catholic chapel lies at the top of Mariánska hora, and in the town there is a Lutheran church as well. The Greek Catholics are one of the Eastern Catholic Churches (the Uniate Churches) and follow the Byzantine-Greek liturgy but are in full communion with Rome. There are many Greek Catholics in this area, too, and some of the pilgrims in the photograph may be of that persuasion. Šumiac is itself not far from Levoča, and was a strongly Greek Catholic village. Slovakia, like Poland almost immediately to the north of Levoča (over the Carpathians), is overwhelmingly Catholic, both Greek and Roman. In July 1995, some 650,000 pilgrims crowded into Levoča for Pope John Paul II's visit.

The next photograph by Luskačová is of peasants in the village of Obišovce in eastern Slovakia. The village is just north of Košice, itself not far south of the Slovak Tatras Mountains, and across this range lies what was once Galicia. The Slovak and Polish Tatras are part of the great sweep, the great loop, of the Carpathians as they

head east into the peasant heartlands of Europe. From here they pass into what once was eastern Galicia and is now western Ukraine, and then south into Romania before they curl back upon themselves into Transylvania, once under Hungarian rule.

The figures in the Obišovce image sit and stand in a church that seems intimate. The church around the figures looks somehow of their own making, the intimacy born of their being at home there (its pews look newly carved, or at least lovingly polished). The church is a Roman Catholic one. In the photograph the women sit; the man stands, and seems to read. He is old and looks poor, at least as we understand it, his collar awry, his face thin and lined. But he has a suit on; respect must be shown in the village church. He does not speak from what he holds, but rather sings, for the man had a good voice and liked to sing in church.[17] Markéta Luskačová gives us the man's name in her book: Mr Ferenz. Markéta often gives the names of those she photographs, for her subjects are indeed subjects, not objects, and one feels she is able to work from within what she shows rather than from outside it, the view from outside almost always being the way peasants are seen.

Šumiac lies west of Obišovce and is much further into the highlands. Between the two is Levoča. In the Šumiac photos, those who live in the village in the ordinary course of life seem in effect to be pilgrims, a pilgrimage being the ancient metaphor for life's journey. In ordinary life, the people yet seem to be on the way to some preordained place. Šumiac sits on high ground and has an ancient pastoral economy. And a perilous economy too, not unlike the sheep-farming country of the deeply indented valleys of Dùiche Seoighe. The following is another photo by Luskačová, one of peasant pilgrims, taken only a minute or so after the women had received Holy Communion. Markéta draws my attention to the still partly open months of the communicants and the exalted looks on their faces. She calls this photo simply 'Women after Communion'. The travel bags of pilgrims are laid on the ground beside the women.

The image is what we like to call 'timeless', and this is because it travels across time and still speaks eloquently to us now. In Markéta

Luskačová's *Pilgrims* catalogue, there is a quotation from Paul Valéry: '[P]hotography encourages us to stop trying to describe what can clearly describe itself.' Yes, this is true, but it is a parallel truth that these images travel and speak, courtesy of their timefulness as well, which is caught in the tired faces and attitudes of the women, and in the time-laden 'basketball boot' of the woman on the right. The 'western' shoe appears in the east, a harbinger of the drift of American culture across all of Europe in those post-war decades even if it is a cheap Eastern European imitation (the shoe is, I am told, a Converse sneaker, but we in working-class post-war London called them basketball boots). In the same way, in the background of Koudelka's image of Seán Seoighe, Paddy Kenny and Martin Mangan kneeling in the timeless pose of the Crucifixion there is in view a young woman in a short skirt, reminding us that this is the 1970s. Timelessness is made up of the juxtaposition of precise moments of time.

On the cover of *Pilgrims* there is a photograph of a man curled-up, asleep, his right hand cradling his head, his left laid on his leg. He must have come far, for he seems to sleep the sleep of the exhausted.

But he is also exhausted because he has spent the night praying at the shrine, and, as well as exhaustion, there is peace in his sleep; the peace that comes after prayer. The pilgrim has a suit on, just as the three men atop Croagh Patrick did. (The photos were taken at much the same time.) This man's suit looks to be a rather shabby one, and much crumpled. The sleeping figure appears to be a poor man. He carries what he needs for his journey in an improvised rucksack held by a string around his back. His head is shorn, his boots big. He has probably walked here, some part of the way, just as Seán, Paddy and Martin walked a long way overland on their pilgrimage.

What we see in the photograph is an impromptu place of rest. Behind the figure, looking like tree stumps at first sight, are the backs of two women also resting, their heads covered in the scarves we associate with peasants. And there appear to be other women further on into the photograph. The whole group, the man and the women behind, seem to be contained in and by their surroundings, embedded in the woodland in which they rest. The ground rests them, and they seem borne aloft by it, most of all the sleeping man, who, cradling himself, seems to be cradled by the land.

The conjunction of person and faith, nature and land, in the photograph is no accident. Other images invoke the deep relationship between nature, work and religion in peasant culture, such as the one opposite of people processing through the fields outside another sub-Carpathian village, Čirč, nature and supernature in harmony. For religion as presented here is about the village and not God alone, just as all peasant religion is. The curve of the hayricks and that of the children and adults in procession are the same curve, religion and nature one. The line of people follows the contours of the land up and down, from far to near, past into present.

There is another photograph in *Pilgrims*, that of a kneeling man with a cross. Behind him a group of women kneel on a small rise in the land. All face the camera. They are once again enveloped, contained in and by the countryside. Markéta Luskačová writes of a village woman eating bread, 'the ritual of her hand movement struck me as being devout.' The woman is cutting bread and spreading it with cheese; 'later with the same movement I saw her saying the rosary.' Religious devotion is in the body, in its deportment, the motion of its limbs, part of a daily life in which work and devotion are not separate.

Luskačová writes of how meeting the peasants of Šumiac changed her life, and how she wished to learn from those who practised 'the religious customs of their ancestors'. She is there in Šumiac to find, she says, 'the remaining fragments of Christian-peasant culture'.[18] By the time the photographs were shown she had lived eight years in England. When asked if she missed Czechoslovakia, she says that she does, not Prague, but instead, Šumiac, 'that village at the bottom of Králova Hola'.

In an essay called 'Christ of the Peasants', John Berger wrote about the work of Markéta Luskačová. After considering how the experience of peasants, including their faith, has been so very little understood over many centuries he writes of Luskačová as being summoned by the dead. The people she photographs are not 'there', but 'elsewhere': nonetheless, still with their neighbours, for the living and the dead are equally neighbours. (The figure of the sleeping man shows this, for it seems equally possible that he reposes after death as before it, so static, thin and borne aloft does he seem.) In this manifestation, one is aware that religion is a way in which peasants remember themselves, memorialize themselves. Its rituals and observances might thus be regarded as a form of history: peasant history. An archive of the things they love and hold on to which enables them to hold on to the dead, whom they love.

Berger knew at the time of his writing that the end of peasant Europe was at hand. Markéta Luskačová herself writes that her wish is to preserve, and she refuses what she calls social amnesia. She writes that, 'In the Czech language, the verb "to photograph" means to immortalize. When I came to Britain in 1975, I was shocked to learn that in English, the equivalent is to shoot. Even after 37 years here, I find that notion fairly foreign.' The majority of the images in Luskačová's book were made in the late 1960s and early 1970s, many in the long 'Prague Spring', which in political reality lasted from 1962 to 1968. Afterwards the repression was brutal, the fear great.

In *Pilgrims*, Luskačová reports that one of the villagers, Tetka Kata, 'will be cross for having shown the photographs, for Tetka Kata is in tune with the modern and does not want to know my reasons for photographing the old ways, perhaps the village children or their children will understand'. Perhaps they will understand her wish to convey 'immortality' and why their forebears deserve to receive it. Luskačová's practice seems to me the opposite of the photographic image as an appropriation. These photographs are a gift rather than something taken. Like Berger with the French peasants he wrote of, she lived and worked with those she photographed. She kept in contact with the people, following their lives after the photographs were taken. She was liked in the village for the photographs that she took privately of the women there. They always showed off the women well.

The people in the images in *Pilgrims* make up a kind of historical document, and indeed Markéta was at the time a student of sociology: they are often named, the occasions of the images are also named, and places and dates always given. The people usually face the camera and look out with confidence and without artifice. Their involvement in what is going on is apparent. Through these images, one gets to know something substantial about Šumiac. And about peasant religion. Nonetheless, a conversation with Markéta Luskačová in her London apartment revealed more.

As she described to me, the villagers had few illusions about their life. Farming these uplands was hard work, tractors being no use even if one could be found. The land was so poor that the Communists did not bother to collectivize it for a long time. This meant that the old ways continued there, though clearly there were some, like Tetka, who preferred the modern ones. People greeted the eventual coming of the state farms after 1974 with resignation. After all, they knew that their family relations in the lowland cooperatives had an easier life than they did. In Šumiac, they lived under constant pressure, taxes being ruthlessly levelled on them by the Communist government, and in order to pay them people had to go to work in the factories, or, at least, one member of the family had to go.

By this time, the old wooden houses were already on their way out, for the state provided family houses of a new, more 'rational' type. It also provided easily available plans for a 'modern' house, what Markéta called the 'squares', an architectural template people could adapt when building new houses themselves. These houses were ugly and made of breeze blocks: difficult and strange to live in compared with the old. The children of peasants, like all children whose parents openly practised religion, were not encouraged to advance in their studies, and their education was deliberately a basic one.

There was a Roma settlement on the edge of the village. From there each day, 'Rosa the Radio' emerged to inform the village of what was going on. In return for news, she collected food. By that time many of the gypsies worked in the factories. Nonetheless, in the 1960s and 70s women still spun thread and wove cloth, especially in the quiet winter months, when all the households were involved. Cloth was woven in patterns unique to each village. But now, Markéta says, no one can weave any more.

Markéta tells me that, before she came to the village in the 1960s, she did not know that this old peasant world was still almost intact. She talks of the 'absolute apparition' of these people's religion when she first saw it in action, thinking previously that it had vanished. She immediately wanted to let people know something of what was going on, and this was easier after the start of the long Prague Spring. People in local religious processions tentatively took to the roads then, walking with their simple wooden crosses. Before then, the crosses would be hidden when they came to a road, people walking into the woods to avoid notice. Crosses that had been hidden on the lower slopes would reappear on the higher slopes, at the small shrines that punctuated the uplands.

In 1968, the former Greek Catholic parishes were allowed to restore official communion with Rome. Before Dubček's reforms only the Catholic, Protestant and Orthodox faiths were recognized. Greek Catholic priests were forced to convert to Russian Orthodoxy: if they did not sign the conversion document within twenty-four hours, they were sent to serve their sentences in the uranium mines. Critically, the Uniate Churches had allowed their clergy to marry. Of course, married priests sometimes did renounce their faith, but what could a man do who had a wife and several children dependent on him? Single priests, meanwhile, often did resist, refusing to renounce their faith. In *Pilgrims*, there are images of the local priest, a handsome man, attractive to the men because he was a man's man, and to the women for his looks, but also for the strength of the faith accompanying these looks. Markéta spoke with real feeling for the deep spirituality of the man – a spirituality present in his voice as well, for he sang beautifully and relayed his voice around the village by a series of loudspeakers, much to the annoyance of the Communist authorities. The priest's name was Stefan Havrilla. He died in his early sixties, a month before democracy returned to Czechoslovakia in 1989, his health destroyed by the work in the mines.

The villagers made pilgrimage not only to Catholic Levoča. They also made the difficult journey over the Tatras into Galicia, via what is now the fashionable mountain resort of Zakopane. From there they travelled by crowded bus, sometimes by night as their journey was frowned upon by the authorities (the Czechoslovak Communists were harder on religion than the Polish). Their destination was the Sanctuary of Kalwaria Zebrzydowska. Started in 1605 and completed in 1641 by the nobleman Mikołaj Zebrzydowski and his son, the site was laid out as a scale replica of the holy sites of Jerusalem. The first chapels were erected in this sequence: Pilate's Palace, the Sepulchre of Jesus Christ, the Mount of Olives, the Capture of Jesus Christ and the House of Anna. There is also a chapel called the Weight of the Cross. Below is a photograph Markéta took on a pilgrimage to Kalwaria Zebrzydowska around 1970. To repeat Valéry, '[P]hotography encourages us to stop trying to describe what can clearly describe itself.'

Half a century earlier, Florian Znaniecki gave a generalized view of the relationship between the village and organized religion, one

that complements this one of Luskačová's images, and bears it out. Writing of peasants who were very similar, those on the other side of the Carpathians, he showed us that the buildings of the parish signified the social bond of village and religion: above all, the place of worship itself. The graveyard was the moral property of the parish as a whole and not the religious authorities, and was simply managed by the priest. Limits to untrammelled priestly power were apparent. As God's representative the priest led the acts of common worship. The priest was listened to as the voice of Jesus and this influence was extended into the whole social activity of the priest – although some powers were not clearly established; for example, whether the priest outside the church was still in the same sense a representative of Jesus as within it. The priest had a social obligation to perform his acts conscientiously for the parish.

The gestures and intonations of the priest were performed according to an unwritten code as well as a written one, the congregation reacting by gestures, sighs, sometimes even exclamations. This amounted to an unofficial code and the priest who did not know it could not have as much influence as one who did. It helps, as in Šumiac, if the priest was a manly man to the men, an attractive one to the women, a defender of the common interest of the parish. It hindered the Church if, as so often happened, the priest was distant, without sympathy, wedded to other interests than the well-being of the parish and village. (There is an old Irish proverb: 'Where four priests are gathered together, there is greed.') The actual daily running of the parish also owed much to older men and women and they were to be listened to. The peasant lost immensely when he emigrated from one parish to another, never mind emigration proper. He always wanted to go back in his old age.

In Šumiac now, as in twenty-first-century Ireland, tourism has in large measure appropriated the old peasant culture. But, again as in Ireland, it is not that the old ways have been forgotten, or that pride is not taken in them. Only now these old ways are relics that must be preserved. Religion is still strong in both these remote regions, but with the coming of time this has waned too, even if the annual summer pilgrimage to Levoča is still an enormous event. Levoča itself is now a UNESCO World Heritage Site, like Kalwaria Zebrzydowska. Meanwhile, in Šumiac there is a state subsidy to cut grass on the higher slopes, grass once harvested as hay. A government helicopter patrols the skies to make sure that the cutting is done. But now there is nothing to do with the hay when it is cut. The wooden buildings of old still remain, yet few live in them now, and the buildings have become relics, 'heritage', so-called. And the houses visitors stay in must be 'authentic'.

Markéta took the following photograph also, which is of the ancient pilgrimage site of Croagh Patrick in my father's county of Mayo. By what to me is a case of extraordinary chance the picture was taken at almost exactly the same time as Josef Koudelka's image of my kin kneeling at the top of the sacred mountain. In 1972 both photographers had travelled together for the same purpose, staying in the nearby town of Westport.

Again the pilgrims are what one can only call well dressed, even though they have laboured a long way up the Reek. One man huddles, for the day is probably cold and the photo is taken at the top of the mountain, by the side of the small chapel that is the only monument there. They have reached the end of one journey, though the way down is not easy either. Most notable is the handsome man who kneels across the line of the other figures, for he will have walked up the mountain in his bare feet all or some of the way. The men's hats are off, and it looks likely they are in prayer. They look no different from Joyce, Kenny and Mangan in the Koudelka trinity: the black hair, the gaunt features, the abstracted gaze, the cut of their faces, western Irish faces.

During pilgrimage, which is about being on the move to a desired goal, pilgrims commonly have a sense of time being suspended and changed. Their experience of space is changed as well. New geographies of faith are created, new landscapes of devotion take shape. Movement reshapes time, the special, remembered time of pilgrimage. Oskar Kolberg has described the highly organized character of peasant pilgrimage, now almost two hundred years ago: the pilgrimage company was typically usually one of twenty to thirty people from one parish or village. There was one lay leader who led prayers and songs. People's own village church images of Mary were proudly carried. Polish peasant villages were, and still are, marked out by holy images at their boundaries, most of all those of the locally venerated saint. Pleasure was mixed with pain, for these pilgrimages were convivial as well as ascetic, and drunkenness was not infrequently reported.

By Jan Słomka's time the Sanctuary of Our Lady of Dzików was already centuries old as a centre of pilgrimage. In the earlier part of the twentieth century, the day of Our Lady of the Sowing had been kept in the neighbouring town of Tarnobrzeg. But great sulphur deposits were discovered in the area after 1945, and it was despoiled. Our Lady of Dzików became known as the Queen of the Sulphur Fields. The image of Our Lady of Dzików is simple, unaffected, unlike the dazzling, golden, jewel-encrusted images of more august places.

Peasant pilgrims on the way from Dzików 'followed the highway at a slow pace, kept time with their singing so that the sound was fair to hear, and gave an impression of fineness and goodwill. From the villages people would go out to look at them and to listen to the hymns, and to serve the thirsty with milk or water to drink. The way to Lezaysk from our village took two days. Everyone had his own provisions, no one was allowed to enter a tavern, and during fast days the rules were strictly kept.'[19] Słomka reports he took his own group from Dzików and the neighbouring villages a few times. The rules were no doubt well kept on these occasions.[20]

The religious journey called pilgrimage taps the root, and perhaps is itself the root, of a central motif of European culture, that of the transformative journey. Moses journeying into the wilderness, Odysseus to the ends of the Earth, alike going into the unknown and coming to an edge. Ireland is at the edge of Europe and the most emblematic religious sites of Ireland are at its western edge, Croagh Patrick in Mayo and Lough Derg in Donegal.[21] The former is quite literally at an edge, sloping into the North Atlantic. Ireland's Marian shrine is also in the Mayo village of Knock, not far from Croagh Patrick. My own Joyce Country and Connemara make another edge. The edge of the West of Ireland is the poor and mountainous areas in which apparitions of Mary so often manifested, territories of peasants and places known intimately by them.

How different to the religious sites in Poland are the Irish ones! Even in the village of Dzików, the church is of a grandeur and at the same time a delicacy that seem to me unparalleled in Ireland. How different the great weight of historicity in religious buildings and holy objects there is in most of Europe compared to Ireland. Its religion, like its history, is different from most of the rest of Europe, particularly its immediate neighbour, England. Faith in Ireland was relegated to nature and the landscape to a greater degree than anywhere else on the European mainland. Unlike any other European Roman Catholics, the Irish were virtually cut off from their mother church for almost a century and a half while laws penalizing the Catholic religion operated. This left the old traditions of worship substantially intact when the Penal Laws were lifted in 1829, not long before the Great Famine.

The faith publicly proscribed, the churches unbuilt, the Counter-Reformation that transformed Catholic Europe was almost completely absent. Rural Ireland had itself been blocked from direct access to the economic and technical developments that were transforming western Europe in the two centuries before the Great Famine. And then the famine struck, in the end mortally affecting the old Gaelic culture, but unevenly, western Ireland holding out longest.

In his superb ethnography of religion in the far west of County Donegal, Lawrence Taylor tells us that religious images in public places are not as common in Ireland as in mainland Europe.[22] The plenteous supply of early Irish saints are nonetheless themselves very little pictured. The natural landscape was most significant. The old saints are addressed only in formulaic discourse, you don't think about them: they are part of the landscape, which is what people actually say about them. For they are literally in the landscape, in its places, in the stories about these places, in the ruins associated with the saints and the stories. Walking the land was itself a kind of pilgrimage. One did not have to go far to be a pilgrim.

In Ireland, the consolidation of official Catholicism became a power struggle between competing stories about what the land was to mean. Taylor gives a detailed account of this struggle, one of special significance to those who live most deeply in the meanings the land has. The Church reclaims the landscape; the rath, the hill fort, is anathematized, as is the ancient holy well. My own father's townland of Kilbride is an example, the name denoting the church of St Brigid. The stones of an ancient place of worship lie there beside an ancient burial place, both disused now for a century. Over time a new charismatic landscape has emerged, that of the village church, with its nearby graveyard. The Church's attempt at the desacralization of the landscape involved the attempted appropriation of the meanings of the old sites. This is to be seen in Croagh Patrick today, where the largely post-religious pilgrims drawn to the 'spirituality' of the place these days are feeding the hopes of the Irish Church in its post-abuse disarray.

Nonetheless, the landscape resisted, and resists, and, just as elsewhere in Europe, 'popular' and official piety are two different things. Croagh Patrick is still very much a Connaught pilgrimage. The bright quartz and conical shape of the mountain are visible for miles around, just as in prehistoric times. The shape is of a mountain in a dream: the essence of 'mountain'. The size of the pilgrimage, on the main day of the year, is only around 30,000.[23] There are also smaller pilgrimage days for local people. But three and a half million people visit Częstochowa, Poland's greatest Marian pilgrimage site, each year. Croagh Patrick is simple, unadorned, elemental even. The hilltop chapel is a complete contrast to Polish magnificence. There has been a primitive oratory at the top of the conical hill for longer than a millennium. Also on the hillside is Boheh, St Patrick's Chair, one of the most significant ancient rock-art sites in Ireland.

Between the small chapel at the bottom and the oratory at the top are the stone *turais*, 'stations', which mark the long walk up. The climb is steep and rocky. Taylor records how in the decades before the 1960s, groups of local men walked barefoot, 40 miles there and back, to the purgatory of Lough Derg. Up to 1974, a night pilgrimage took place on Croagh Patrick, with people walking up with torches. Both Patrician sites have long held a particularly strong attraction for Travellers, especially newly-wed couples. The place is alive with meanings, old and new. Despite attempts at a new spiritualization, it is still a place of stark self-privation, self-purgation. One undertakes the walk to do penance and seek forgiveness, not simply for oneself but for others too. At one time, in Donegal's Glencolmcille, different weights of stone were carried to the site of pilgrimage of Saint Columba, stones of weights proportionate to the burdens of the sins for which forgiveness was sought.

The Image

The following is an object which my mother loved, her Mass and prayer missal, *The Treasury of the Sacred Heart*, a new edition published by 'Vanpoulle Bros., 200 Vauxhall Bridge Road, London S.W.'. Such things had to have an official 'imprimatur'. This one was given to her by Cardinal Cullen, the high priest of Ireland in his day, a man of very conservative leanings, a Gallican zealot. The Sacred Heart devotions inside the missal have been approved by one Dr Delany, 'Lord Bishop of Cork', no less, who was a man every bit as conservative as Cullen.

Catholicism is a religion of the image rather than the word. These images are in themselves also physical objects, like statues or paintings. Or images are carried within objects, statues within caskets, say, or as here with the missal, which inside is full of images, some of which are in fact shaped as smaller objects within the greater one of the book, which is itself emblazoned with the image of the flaming heart of Jesus. As a physical object the book makes God real for the believer. Because over historical time the image and the object have been more real to peasants than words, the written word that is there is a way in which Catholicism has been more in tune with traditional peasant beliefs than Protestantism.

The missal is a devotional tool, a tabernacle and a shrine, all in one. My mother carried the Sacred Heart of Jesus around with her, in the form of a tiny metal heart enclosed within a shrine recessed into the front cover. Inside the back cover, it is similar, only there a recessed crucifix is set in a linen background. Touch and sight are engaged. The book is a library, too, an archive, for in it treasured prayer cards and newspaper cuttings are stored. My mother's scapular was kept inside the book. The scapular is a devotional object worn at the front and the back, joined by two bands of cloth over the shoulders. She always wore one, as did I as a child. The missal's frequent use is evident from the black insulating tape that kept the spine of the book firm in its old age.

The Treasury of the Sacred Heart is a 'retreat of afflicted souls', it says in the book, and to guard against her own sorrows my mother must remember to pray for the souls that have gone before her, which in her case would include the soul of her husband, my father, who died too early. Christ is implored to comfort her and her fellow sufferers, to 'save, answer for me, comfort me'. The images and object together give her the promise of peace by means of their innate physicality, their immediate reality. And so an old woman was comforted.

Old women remembering those who have gone before. Remembering with their missals, remembering at graves. Women who sit alone in churches, women perched in churchyards alone, women who tend graves, like my mother – these old women – it sometimes seems – are the soul of faith across Europe. The beautiful image following was made in Polish Upper Silesia in the 1930s. The suffering Christ is evident. Mary, his mother, the one who intercedes for us, stands below Him at the head of the grave.

The centrality of the Catholic faith to the idea of Poland itself has often been remarked upon. Poland has been called 'God's playground'.[24] There is something about the image, or rather the image-object, that spoke with particular eloquence to Polish peasants. This relationship towards images emerged, in part, from the cultural and geographical closeness of Catholicism and the Orthodox tradition of Christianity in eastern Europe. In Orthodox tradition the image itself, the icon, is holy. Peter Brown, the great historian of religion, wrote of the icon that it was 'a hole in the dyke separating the visible world from the divine, and through this hole there oozed precious driblets from the great sea of God's mercy: icons were active.'[25] Images therefore seem to take on a life of their own, something clearly already in the grain of peasant belief.

The object of attention in peasant religion is humanity, more than God, and God is more heavenly than earthly, at times benign, at times wrathful. A person goes to Jesus, Mary and the saints when they are in distress and need. It is Mary that matters, not God, and this is perhaps above all so in Poland: Mary, the Mother of God, who is also 'Mary, the Mother of Poland' – above all, she is a mother.[26] Humanity is expressed by these images of the Virgin, Christ, the great army of saints, God in human form. In Poland, the saints and the Mother of God acquire such levels of sanctity that one might almost talk of a form of polytheism. Those who are sanctified are treated in human, and even instrumental, ways. They are asked for favours and promised things for these favours in return.[27] Using the saints or Mary as a means to an end is in harmony with peasant culture. Objects and images lead their own lives: they bleed, they cry, they talk, they disappear and reappear in new places. One picture of the Virgin Mary has one task, a different one another, and one can be more powerful than another.

A different ontology to ours is in play. For us there is an equivalence of the thing and its likeness, but reality does not lie in the likeness, as it does for peasants. Religion is always real for peasants, just as reality is for them necessarily ever-present, constantly pressing in on all sides, tumultuous in its immediacy. Marina Warner attempts to convey this apprehension of reality by comparing it to the overwhelming sense of the presence of the dead loved one in the opened wardrobe, or to the familiar room entered again, but these examples pale in relation to those who believe they have actually *seen* Christ's face imprinted on the veil of Veronica. The name Veronica itself derives from the Latin *vera icon*, true image.

The 'true image' is a contradiction in terms for contemporary mentalities, for only the original can be true, that which is authentic, and a copy is just that, a copy. But in Catholicism the copy is real too. It picks up its reality by a kind of osmosis, based on contact with the original holy thing, a lineage of holiness being established. It is as if the aura of the original never fades but is constantly renewed. The vision of the saint and the presence of Mary, these are the 'originals'; the vision and the presence are then painted or carved and retain that which is holy; the painted or carved image may come into contact with other objects, a piece of cloth, say, a veil, and these objects in turn receive, and retain, the original charge, indeed they may increase it, for the charge does not wear out. In Kolberg's words, 'A person returning from a patron saint festival (particularly if it was celebrated in a miraculous place) is considered "a blessed person" and other people brush against them.'[28]

In popular belief the lowly are themselves felt to have a privileged role in this process of transmission of the holy. For instance, the virtue of the unknown craftsman who refuses payment for making the holy image imparts a further degree of holiness to it. The great Marian shrines were located at places where peasant children in their humility knew how to see the holy. In Poland, the holy image itself was often said to be found in lowly and unbecoming places, 'in humiliation', as it was put, in a 'sorry state'.[29]

The human physicality, and so humanity, of this kind of devotion, is marked outside Poland too, of course. The eyes of the Virgin of Siracusa in 1953 are said to have wept. The arm of Mary's statue is in several places believed to physically break out in sweat as she tries to restrain her angry son, who is trying to protect his mother. All the aspects of Mary herself are transmitted to the statue, as well as her 'sanctity'. The tears from her statue become healing, beneficent. The statue is alive: she cries, viewers partake in her tears. These tears speak directly to the person. One talks to Mary, listens to her, senses her feelings, and she speaks back.

Religion is a matter of worshipping the divine in the service of everyday purposes, whether of the individual or the group. Religiosity is not doctrine, but ritual.[30] Every member of the peasant family in Poland was expected to participate in the ritual. Individual devotion was most fully realized through the group. You followed the way that your family acted. There was a sharing of collective responsibility for the moral behaviour of members of the group.

The next image, of the blessing of the fields with holy water in the Upper Silesia of 1931, shows how the divine and the everyday worked together.

The Word

This all seems far away from the Reformation faiths, although it is not completely distant, given the unity of peasant systems of belief across Europe. In Poland, once colonized in the West by Protestant Prussia, Lutheranism was a strong minority presence, particularly in Upper Silesia. I spoke with Grażyna Kubica, an anthropologist who is from a Lutheran village in the region, and is passionately attached to both Silesia and its Protestant religious tradition. She tells me the story of her great-grandmother, and of the old Lutheran wish that each person of the family should read the Bible from one end to the other in the course of every year. This is the literal Word, which must be followed, over and above the dictates of institutions. The book of her family bible was itself large, heavy, wooden-covered, the written Word, but also and very much an object.

The history of this Silesian Protestant faith is important to her people: Lutheranism existed as an underground Church under

Habsburg rule, followed by official toleration, from the late eighteenth century onwards. Not unlike Ireland, a tradition of illegal and clandestine worship emerged during times when these practices were banned. This tradition is remembered today, and, although pilgrimage does not figure in the faith, visits to the old sites of once-proscribed worship – in the woods and other hidden places – are a kind of pilgrimage, a journey to meet their old selves, and affirm themselves in the present. Here Lutheranism was very much the preserve of the lower classes, especially peasants, but there were some Protestant landowners who supported their co-religionists in setting up churches and schools. However, the Silesian nobility were Germanized early on, and this marked a difference from the peasants, who, as across Europe, were most loyal to what was nearest, in this case, the identity of being Silesian.

The literal Word meant that education was important. One had to be able to read the Book. In Silesia, schools were systematically attached to churches and literacy levels were high from early on, very different from most of Catholic Poland. Even in the nineteenth century, inclusion of girls in local schools was not uncommon. The Word was consumed collectively and individually, in silence and out loud. Hymns were sung, written down and learned. The key distinction from Catholicism seems to have been that the Silesian clergy were drawn from the ranks of the peasants and the villagers. They were often called 'Daddy' and 'Mummy' by their parishioners, Grażyna tells me. They owned and depended on local farms for a living, if not usually working them themselves, so that they were deeply integrated in to agrarian culture. If services could not be held by a pastor, then there was the 'home service', the head of the household holding the service, and if the man was absent his wife took his place.

All the same, this faith was not divorced from peasant beliefs in spirits and the natural world, but the old beliefs operated at a greater distance than in Catholicism. This meant that customary belief lost a good deal of its power. However, in Lutheran funeral rites, practices familiar across Catholic Europe were followed. There was also little distinction between Catholic and Protestant peasants as regards the customs marking the agricultural year. The first slice of bread at the Christmas Eve dinner was put away safely and then taken out again at the first ploughing. Grażyna tells me that it was only the more evangelical of the Lutherans who stigmatized 'folk belief'.

There was, and is, however, a keen appreciation of Protestantism being more 'advanced' than Catholicism, more 'modern'. Neighbourly everyday relations in the village were and are firmly maintained, although 'mixed marriages', if not unknown, are not numerous these days. The Catholic Church in Poland has been assiduous in its political manoeuvring, so that present-day Polish legislation deems that the children of such marriages be brought up Catholic. A degree of resentment at this is rightly felt. Even so, it is politically correct not to openly express feelings of Lutheran superiority.

This is one form of Protestantism. Anglicanism, the state-established Church in England, is another. And what differences there are between the two! I dwell on a very fine study of nineteenth-century rural Lincolnshire, an exception to the tendency in Britain for rural belief and religion to be less subject to the ethnographic imagination than in most of Europe. Contrary to expectations ('This stuff happened over there, not in England'), the people of rural Lincolnshire turned out to be little different from the rest of Europe. The Lincolnshire people involved in the study were rural labourers, people who would have been called peasants in Europe. Just as Polish peasants were careful to inform the animals when the head of a household had died, so it was in Lincolnshire; and when it came to the larger annual ritual cycle of the seasons and its attendant customs, beliefs and observances, it mirrored the European pattern.

In that part of the UK, the Devil, the 'Owd Lad', or the 'Old 'Un', was alive and well. He aroused a mixture of fear and awe but there was also a familiarity towards him. He was a person more than a principle and you might meet and talk with him on the roads or in the fields (rather like the God of the eastern folk bible). He was someone who could dispense wisdom as well as evil. He might also have appeared as a gentleman in a black coat, which does not reflect well on the black-coated Anglican clergy. Spirits, ghosts, witches, wise men, oracles, omens, dreams, all were there, just as across Europe. Death was treated in the same ways too: the day of death, the night, the final hours, what to do afterwards, all are pretty similar. There was, however, an unusual Lincolnshire belief that two of the same family should not be buried in the same grave, husband and wife, for example.

There was therefore limited belief in Christian ideas of the resurrection, and not a great deal of knowledge of or interest in the Christian afterlife. There seems to have been little concern with the reality of sin, too, or at least what counted as sin in the eyes of the Church. Short of the main life events taking place in the parish church, there was little attraction for rural people in Lincolnshire in the rites and sacraments of the Church. Nature was alive, the Christian sacraments dead. A Christian person was simply thought of as a decent, honest, unselfish woman or man. These people were still, in a broad sense, Protestant. Their dislike of ritual and display, for them manifest in the Anglican sacraments, was more Protestant than the Protestants. At times, their appropriations of Anglicanism involved a political anti-Catholicism, Rome being the headquarters of ritual and display, the home of the image and of the autocrat Pope (who was himself the Antichrist). The Bible was prized for its distance from organized religion, even though prior to the Education Act of 1870 levels of literacy were far below those apparent in Silesia. There was, however, collective reading of the Bible. If they did attend formal worship, people might go to the Anglican service in the morning, and a Methodist prayer meeting in the afternoon or evening.[31]

As for the clergy, the difference with the Lutheran clergy in Silesia was considerable. The English clergy were not drawn from the common people and were part of the social world of the improving, capitalist-minded farmers, who from the second quarter of the nineteenth century onwards separated their social existence from those of the labourers and the village community. The parson was not seen by the lower-class inhabitants as the true representative of the parish. There were strong ties to the parish as a bedrock of identity, but this had more to do with welfare legislation and generations of attachment to the parish church and its burial ground, and also to the centuries-long role of the parish in local government.[32] Most Anglican clergy were both unable and unwilling to adapt to popular beliefs and mores.

Notwithstanding their dislike of Catholic ritual and display and their strong attachment to the written Word of the Bible, the Protestant Word of these English agricultural labourers had essentially more in common with another 'word' than is sometimes acknowledged, the word of the Catholic folk bible of eastern Europe. Over the centuries, idiosyncratic mixtures of belief have enabled people to survive in the face of the most appalling of calamities. This is, however, true for Protestant peasants as well as for Catholic ones. The Protestant Bible could itself be decidedly idiosyncratic. The Word was, in theory, strict truth, but following it to the letter is another matter, for it is notoriously incomplete and decidedly ambiguous. In vernacular versions of Protestantism the most baroque of reinventions of biblical characters and events are apparent.[33] The story of Noah's Ark, for instance, has been a particularly fertile source of elaboration; the aim of course being to make faith serve people's real as opposed to official needs.

In the case of eastern Europe, its folk bible gave people a God in tune with the cyclical rhythms of time and space that defined peasant culture. Themes from the Old and New Testament intermingle in these para-biblical beliefs, and events from the Gospels are superimposed on stories about the olden days, before heaven and Earth were separated, and God walked among the people as an old man, an aged beggar. The non-canonical biblical works known as the Apocrypha were included, those writings that are not accepted as scripture, at least not by Protestants (they were accepted in the Orthodox faith, however, and have some standing in Catholicism). Jewish religious traditions are also evident within it, as is only logical in areas where Jews and Christians had lived side by side for centuries.

This is not something of the distant past. These beliefs have been observed by scholars like Magdalena Zowczak in Polish rural communities from central Poland, and from the peasant diasporas in Lithuania, Belarus and Ukraine, in the years between 1989 and 1996.[34] In this cosmos, the Devil plays a sort of game with God. The Devil is indeed almost akin to God's alter ego. While contradicting God, and acting to discredit him, he creates the inferior part of the world, a failed creation in which suffering reigns. In this realm, God, like many a peasant, turns out to be a rather luckless and bumbling individual. There is also a Ukrainian story in which Jesus and St Peter, 'not knowing what to do, out of boredom decided to create the Earth'. The Bored God acts, alongside his sidekick St Peter. The causes of human imperfections are shoved off humankind, including original sin, and put down to episodes from the history of creation, a history that shows how this very human God did not get it quite right, through plain negligence or just bungling the job. Human frailty is endorsed. The incompetence of the Creator is a reflection of the conception of the fall or the progressive degeneracy of the human race, dominant in the folk bible and peasant culture almost everywhere. It is God's negligence and not original sin that explains this fall. In another story, the serpent tempts Eve during the absence of Adam, who has walked away from her, thoughtlessly, to 'take his nap on the lawn'.

A forgetful God, in a different testimony, comes back to the scene of creation and finds that the Devil has enacted pain and suffering in the world. He asks the Devil ' "[was] that you in your wickedness [that] did it?" The Devil replies: "Oh God, this man created by you will forget you if he suffers no pain. As numerous as my stabs here, he will have as many causes for pain and suffering: growths (paraugu), parasites (dyminičiu), matted hair, pimples (nižu), scabs, ulcers (arba pokuniu pikutiu), a variety of diseases, poverty and trouble. I have created the vermin and the birds for people to prosper." '[35]

'Passive suffering makes the world go round.' These are the words of Seamus Heaney in a poem called 'Weighing In'. Mircea Eliade, as we recall, wrote that suffering is tolerated morally when it has meaning, when 'it is not absurd'. In 'Weighing In', Heaney wrote in the context of the violence in Northern Ireland, and in his poem the question of the boundaries of suffering is raised. Passive suffering does in truth make the world go round, and religion is one of those things that are most often at the root of this passive bearing of suffering. If all who suffer were not passive most of the time, the world would stop. Striking back, as Heaney writes, would be a violation. Yet not to strike back carries its own hurt, but the validity of passive suffering is real: 'When soldiers mocked / Blindfolded Jesus and he didn't strike back . . . Something was made manifest – the power / Of power not exercised, of hope inferred.'

This hope of the powerless has limits, however, and is not eternal. Peace no longer holds when suffering is absurd: which is to say unreasonable, illogical. Absurdity may lead to abjection and negation but also to action and purpose. This is how Heaney puts it:

> Peace on Earth, men of good will, all that
> Holds only as long as the balance holds,
> The scales ride steady and the angels' strain
> Prolongs itself at an unearthly pitch.[36]

The angels' strain is unearthly, and we live *now*, on Earth and not above with the angels, so that peace topples and we must act, must, as the title of the poem says, 'weigh in', act, act violently sometimes, following through with the associations of 'weighing in', as in both preparing for and engaging in a physical fight. There is suffering, and there is resistance to suffering once boundaries are crossed. The question of justice is raised. But suffering first.

7.
Suffering and Its Redress: The Devil in Our Purses

Passive suffering was how things were for peasants most of the time, and how things had to be. There was ordinary, everyday suffering, the frequent lot of the survivor class that peasants were. Then there was extraordinary suffering, that of famine, war and natural disaster. Pierre-Jakez Hélias, a Breton peasant, produced a remarkable memoir of life in a Breton village. The book was first published in 1975, and became a bestseller in France, the author going on to have some considerable celebrity back in the day, a celebrity due, ironically, to the recognition that the last days of the French peasantry were at hand. The book's author was thought of as writing the peasantry's obituary. Hélias writes of how poverty, misfortune and the despair they brought was the Devil. To feel this despair was to have the Devil in your purse and in your pocket.[1] He also wrote of poverty as a large and threatening animal lurking by one's side, ever ready to pounce. The animal was a dog, a bitch: 'bitch' carrying the malevolence of its contemporary meaning. The 'World Bitch' is the term he uses. The title of the book is *The Horse of Pride*, and the horse was the shoulders which his grandfather Alain carried him on, the only horse many of his kind ever had.

Hélias writes of how his grandfather was poverty-stricken in his youth, a poor day labourer who hired himself out to others, and then saved and borrowed enough money to get a small place. His son, Pierre-Jakez's father, struggled, but succeeded in keeping the place going. The son came into this inheritance, and knew this poverty at first hand, even though it had somewhat lessened by then compared to earlier on in the century (the area was dominated by absentee owners and large tenant farmers). The grandson writes of how the slightest blow of fate was enough to bring down those who were already victims of the Devil, but did not yet have him, as the saying went, 'living in their purses'. When there was nothing at all in your purse, then the Devil lived in it. Any disease, to human or animal, a bad harvest, an overly harsh employer or merely a single one of 'the seven daily misfortunes', as he called them, would force you out on to the road begging with 'a prayer between your teeth, and your eyes shut to block out the humiliation'.

This was the despair ordinary suffering could drive people to, and it was deeply buried in the psyche by the constant wear upon the soul that bad fortune brought, like the despair de Martino found in Basilicata. There might be no way out: sometimes the men chose to hang themselves, and there was always a rope in the shed, which was there for the asking. The women preferred to drown themselves, and there was ever a well in the farmyard or a wash trough at the bottom of the field. Poverty was so ever-present that one might meet it at any turn in the road, 'in the form of a raw-boned, shaggy bitch, its chops curled back, showing yellow teeth: the World Bitch'. It was mute and sly, this bitch, and you could never safely defend yourself from her.

His grandfather, Alain Le Goff, told him several times of how, when he happened to be alone in the middle of the fields, he didn't dare stop working, because the World Bitch always crept in the very moment there was a pause. His grandfather said, 'Whenever you hear a cry for help and there's no one anywhere around, it's your own unhappiness that' howling inside you. Or else it's the World Bitch, which has just jumped on somebody you know.' Pierre-Jakez Hélias reports the words of his grandfather thus: '"Whenever that happened to me, I grabbed hold of my spade and started turning up the ground as if I were about to kill." He was a placid and gentle man, that grandfather of mine. And such types are often the most dangerous. That damned slut, the World Bitch, must have known it.'[2]

Alain Le Goff managed to ensure that none of his own children went hungry, even if it meant that when he got home he claimed that he had already eaten, and when the 10-pound loaf of bread was down to the heel he would say he had no appetite. The children never asked any questions. At one time he was a road-repair man, leaving home at 3 a.m. to be ready for work at sunrise. Alain's son worked just as hard as his father, but when it came to Hélias' aunts and uncles, emigration was their lot (just as it was with my own parents and my aunts and uncles). His father's brothers and sisters were called by family members according to the locations of the towns and cities they emigrated to in France. They did not, however, have to leave their own country, whatever consolation that was to them. His father and mother were married in 1913, and had what was known at the time as a 'poor man's wedding', one for which the couple and the guests between themselves paid the costs of the feast, usually a two-day feast that would sometimes end in a pitched battle between parishes and villages, just as with the faction fighting in Ireland.

Hélias, an educated and successful man, writes that he feels like an heir to the Irish Celts (he admired Yeats). He is at pains to tell us that, despite all the tribulations of the women each day, they always wore the elaborate head coif that has come to be seen as the symbol of the Breton peasant. In Brittany, seven peals of the church bell signalled the death of a woman, nine that of a man. People stopped work when the bell tolled and said an 'Our Father' and a 'Hail Mary' for the soul of the dead person.

In Brittany, habitations were clustered around the church. Hélias tells us that workers in the fields assumed exactly the pose of the peasants in Millet's magnificent painting *The Angelus* when the Angelus bell tolled (at noon and 6 p.m). People recognized themselves in the dignity the painting conferred on them. Many a local house had a copy of the painting on its walls, though, as he says of the painter, 'as a matter of fact, not one of us used even to know his name'. Religion was what helped the suffering to be borne. Passive suffering had to be the way, at least a lot of the time, even as their unhappiness howled within them.

There is an intimate connection between peasant labour and the body that has performed the work. If we consider the Gascony of only a few decades before the Brittany of Alain Le Goff, at that time it was said by peasants about their own kind that, 'the earth calls to them'. The body pulls you down to the ground: it is a burden, as in Millet's great painting. There is a sort of dream of uprightness. Being usually bent by toil, the upright body is greatly to be welcomed, as a cessation of toil, a relief. But being lazy is associated with verticality, and there is a moral judgement on this. There is an ironic Gascon simile: 'as straight as a sickle'. The horizontal is what is prized. Where so much relies on physical work, and there is little difference between physical and mental agility, to be short is not good and the clumsy are sometimes regarded as idiots. Unsurprisingly, a peasant's arms are associated with work, and hard work in Gascony requires 'arm oil'. The tool, the agricultural tool in particular, supplied many metaphors for the body, ploughs and shovels especially.

People worried about what work was doing to their bodies, and they were aware that they might sometimes work like donkeys. And they did not want to see themselves as such. However, to be hard as iron was good. Resilience and endurance were prized above all. The peasants of Gascony experienced a double exploitation, as sharecroppers and as workers in the capitalist forestry work, which they became engaged in during the late nineteenth century. For them, the tall and straight pine tree was the ultimate symbol of well-being, though they were aware that the pine could be sapped and stunted, and that the body was a finite and precious resource.

A remarkable Irish memoir depicting life a few decades before this time in Brittany and Gascony dwells on another finite peasant resource: money. The book is set in the remote Fánaid peninsula of Ireland's County Donegal and written by a man called Hugh Dorian, who, like Hélias, had got a bit of education (he became a schoolmaster). The memoir was handwritten and completed in 1890 and only published in 2000, nearly a century after his death in 1914. In it he describes the tyranny of rent day, perhaps one of 'the seven daily misfortunes' of Hélias in Brittany. Dorian writes of

'That great unlost sight of overhanging cloud never to be banished from the mind, never to be forgotten, always oppressing the brain, from the month of May to November and from November to May: the rent – the rent'.[3] Many landlords served precautionary notices to their tenants to quit their rented property in advance of the much-feared first of May, thereby increasing their tenants' dread. This was a routine manoeuvre so that the landlords could have immediate recourse to the law in case an agreement about the rent might not be reached. It also served as a deterrent to any behaviour unwelcome to the landlord. These notices were called 'white messengers', a spectral symbol of the great overhanging cloud.

Rent had to be paid in cash, so that people would deny themselves the benefit of what they produced, that which was cultivated with their own hands and yet had to be given up. The best of everything was surrendered to the rent devil; if there were two fields of potatoes, the better-quality ones would be left untouched to be sold and the family would get by on the smaller, watery ones. If there was butter it had to be marketed, poultry and eggs sold too. Women wove cloth to dress their families, but cash might be had this way as well. Dorian lived a long time, from 1834 to 1914, and saw much. He died in poverty and almost complete obscurity in Derry's Bogside, his grave unmarked. The economy Dorian describes is pretty much the same as that of Joyce Country. The 1892 Report of the Congested Districts Board for Joyce Country shows this in some detail, the same women's weaving, egg hoarding, the same restricted, but by then at least not unhealthy diet.[4] The district was 'congested', even after the famine: 'congested' a pointed, if hardly sensitive, word to describe a human community.

The fear of famine was also a fact of ordinary suffering. Each year there was a sort of phantom image of real famine. This was before the annual harvest when food ran short. Then the immeasurably precious seeds for new planting might perhaps have to be sacrificed. Jan Słomka wrote this of his village in Galicia, at much the same time as Dorian described the ills of the Fánaid peninsula:

> There would be every year with rare exceptions 'pre-harvest famine' . . . During the 'pre-harvest famine', folk lived from grass or various greens – we felt the lack of nourishment, almost every year, from spring till the crop came in. Grain and other things would jump in price, just double, and could be had only from the Jews. As a result everyone gleaned his fields with care, since it was held a sin that any be left on the stubble to waste. In our day we can have no conception of the hunger-times of old, and of the famines folk went through.[5]

There are accounts of peasant mothers in Poland who, to distract their children until they fell asleep, would keep the pot boiling on the stove when there was nothing in it, the children deceived into thinking there was. Sometimes stones would be put in the boiling pot to enhance the subterfuge. Stone soup. The sorrow of women was keenly felt, especially for a lost child, even when so many children were lost. The loss of a stillborn child, or a child that died at birth, is conveyed by that great recounter of the suffering of Irish peasant women, Máirtín Ó Cadhain, in his stories of Connemara, his own birthplace.[6] The father's sorrow at the loss of a child was great too, but the woman was the one who had carried, given birth, reared, or hoped to rear, the baby. Ó Cadhain was a remarkable man: peasant born and raised, he became a teacher, then an active (and later interned) Irish Republican Marxist-cum-agrarian populist.

Around 1900, among Ukrainian peasants, for a mother to mourn the death of her baptized children under the age of seven was considered pointless. These sinless children were destined to go straight to heaven and become angels. It was said that if a mother cried for such a child, her tears would drown or burn the child. In Ukraine, professional keeners were hired to communicate publicly between the worlds of the living and the dead. They addressed the dead as if they were alive, asking them for forgiveness, praising them with tender words, expressing love with the use of the diminutives of the dead child's name. In the Ukrainian province of Podolia (once part of Poland), a grieving woman is recorded as having addressed her dead daughter thus:

> My daughter, my dissatisfied [daughter]! Did you fear that [by living] you would deprive me of years?! Were you afraid that I would lose days?! Did you worry about interfering in my work?! Where are you going, my child? I rejoiced in you and looked after you. What will happen to you now? Why aren't you laughing . . . ? Why aren't you stretching out your small arms?[7]

At the same time when grief is expressed, a public reckoning is made. The mother points out to her neighbours that she had loved and cared for her child, though guilt is accounted for publicly also. Children could be felt to be a burden as well as a gift. Hard work had to be done in the house and in the fields at the same time that children had to be cared for. In a lament from the Russian province of Kaluga, a mother blames herself for her children's deaths, agreeing publicly that she had not fed them properly.

The father's death is the occasion of great lamentation, too, for he is the one who sows and reaps. Near the beginning of the twentieth century, a daughter from Skvirsk district in the Ukrainian province of Kiev bemoans the death of her father, as the whole family depends on his labour and guidance: 'Our father, dearest, why did you abandon us little ones? Who will look after us, who will plough for us, who will grind [the grain] for us, who will mow for us, who will give us away in marriage, and who will guide us along the path?' In still other laments, those left behind are said to be destined to walk around naked, cold and hungry. The burden put on the widow was immense. Economic disaster loomed.

Then there is the suffering of men. These are two verses of a song sung by a man called Joe Heaney (Seosamh Ó hÉanaí), who was born near the village of Carna in coastal Connemara twelve years after my father. I heard him sing it and many other songs in the London of sixty years ago. Most of his singing was in Irish, but it did not matter to me as I listened, entranced, entering the world of my father, who had only recently died, through his singing. I grieved through Heaney's singing. The song captures the same existential dread as Pierre-Jakez Hélias captures. The song is called 'The Rocks of Bawn' (as for all music, the printed page cannot hope to catch the intensity of what went on in that room on that long-ago night):

> My shoes they are well worn now, my stockings they are thin
> My heart is always trembling, afraid I might give in
> My heart is always trembling, from clear daylight till the dawn
> For I'm afraid I'll ne'er be able to plough the Rocks of Bawn.
>
> I wish the Queen of England would send for me in time
> And put me in some regiment all in my youth and prime
> I would fight for Ireland's glory, from the clear daylight till the dawn
> And I ne'er would return again to plough the Rocks of Bawn.[8]

To plough the rocks of Bawn means the Devil is in your purse. Your own unhappiness howls within you.

What follows is another dimension of the suffering of men, different in setting, though war connects the two. This is a photograph of peasants at work in a field reaping corn. The men are in a line, working in unison, with a powerfully built and striking man in the forefront, the first of the three men with scythes. He seems to lead. Work is cooperative but also individual. And work is also a source of pride and creativity on the one hand, and of suffering on the other. Look, however, on the right of the photograph. A uniformed figure strides up purposefully. It is 1942 or 1943 and Poland is occupied by forces that the figure represents, a German, Polish or Ukrainian police auxiliary, or a soldier perhaps.

Poland was the killing ground of the twentieth century, where more died per head of population than in any other nation except Belarus, parts of which were then in Poland anyway. Going on for 20 per cent of the population were killed. And among those killed, half of them were Jews. This toll leaves out of the account the

Russian prisoners butchered in their millions, and the forced labourers of Polish and other nationalities dying in the vast system of labour/extermination camps which extended over almost all of Poland. Peasant boys, Russians, most of them, like so many of the Poles who died, like the German peasant boys also, like the glorious dead of the French in the Great War. Like the Jewish village boys. Peasant armies: there is conscription, but also enlistment, which is usually a matter of necessity. You enlisted or were conscripted and then slaughter might await, as in the Galicia of the First and the Second of the Great Wars.[9]

One may make a little better sense of how suffering was borne by peasants by means of the ideas of fate and of honour. Fortune can, as we have seen, be placated with the right action or the right incantation, so that what may come can be guarded against. In his novel *Fontamara*, Ignazio Silone writes of his own Abruzzo village of Pescina. He describes the order of things there:

> God, the Lord of Heaven . . . Then come . . . Prince Torlonia, lord of the earth.

Then comes Prince Torlonia's guards.
Then comes Prince Torlonia's guards' dogs.
Then, nothing at all.
Then nothing at all.
Then nothing at all.
Then come the *cafoni* [low-class peasants]. And that's all.[10]

Silone describes the fatalism of his mother, something that he says was shared by the 8,000 families of the region who cultivated the 35,000 acres of Prince Torlonia. Fate ran deep, and the business of being a peasant in the first place is part of this: the idea that one could simply become a shoemaker and no longer be a peasant simply did not occur. What manages, assuages, suffering, what enables the humiliations of life to be borne, is chiefly honour, especially in Mediterranean peasant cultures. However, shame is the corollary of honour, and humiliation the other side of pride's coin. Honour is inseparable from one's 'reputation', which is 'possessed' as if it were a property.

So attests the historian Rudolph M. Bell, who has written about honour in the Italian South across the century that preceded the 1970s. Honour allows even the poorest *contadino* to conquer time itself, as Bell puts it.[11] Honour is the special recourse of the poorer families, sometimes all they have left. There is the rage of the poor cottager who might be wrongly accused of begging, for whom rage is still a salve, even if it is impotent against insults. Children will avenge their parents, however poor both parties are. Death can be accepted, and suffering may be *un dolore accetto*, a suffering accepted. But an accepted suffering is not necessarily an acceptable one. 'Fatalism' is, in fact, perfectly rational. It makes no sense to kick against misfortune's wrongs if kicking does no good and puts you further in the mire.

Nor did fatalism rule out politics. Antonio Gramsci, a founder of the Italian Communist Party, knew the force of the past for peasants, and, too, how the past could be the source of a better life in the future. Sacrifice is the root element: honour involves obligations to the sacrifices of the forefathers.[12] At times, the Italian Communist Party was able to work well with this sense of *il destino*. In one of the villages Bell studied in the 1970s, there was a peasant who dedicated the rosary to Marx, Lenin, Gramsci and all the saints.[13] As Bell puts it: what matters are not plans, but prayers – defiant celebration, not resigned stupor. Not concerted offences, but familial defences.

There is ordinary suffering and then there is extraordinary suffering. Some regard the human-caused peasant famine that was a consequence of China's Great Leap Forward of 1958 until 1962 as the greatest in human history, though the total dead of the human-made famines in Soviet Russia and in Soviet Ukraine in the 1920s and 1930s exceeded the number of the Chinese dead.[14] The Irish famine of the century before, proportionate to the total population, was far worse than that in the Chinese case.[15] The suffering in these famines is inconceivable. And then there was endemic famine: famines occurred in Polish Galicia in 1847, 1848, 1849, 1850, 1855, 1865, 1876 and 1889. A large famine affected many eastern European territories as late as 1913. The years between 1911 and 1914 are said to have seen the emigration of 25 per cent of the Galician population, though much of this was within Poland, including Russian Poland, or westwards to neighbouring Bohemia, Moravia and German Silesia. Vast numbers, as in the West of Ireland, went to the USA.

In 1853, a few years after the Irish famine, the London Law Life Assurance Society sent a young Scottish surveyor called Thomas Colville Scott to survey the vast Martin Estate in Connemara with a view to its sale. The estate, the largest in Ireland, covered most of Connemara, and had been put up for sale in 1849. Colville Scott's journal was edited by the late Tim Robinson, the unparalleled chronicler of Connemara and the Aran Islands (whose name may be recalled from Chapter 1).[16] In his introduction to the journal, Robinson tells us that the people had been already cleared from the land by the disaster, so that the estate was 'a blank canvas on which

Capital could paint a fair and profitable landscape' – however, the place, little but bog, lake and mountain, was so poor, it could not be got off the books for another twenty years. Colville Scott was not an unsympathetic observer, though riddled with the prejudices of his time: Catholicism was benighted, Protestants enlightened, peasants feckless, Ireland backward.

In his journal, Colville Scott recounts the experience of seeing a young chimney sweep boy, an 'Irish curiosity', as he rather strangely calls him, who had run away from his job in Galway City, from which he was by then 60 miles distant. The boy ran along the side of the road as Colville Scott drove by, perhaps begging. Snow was falling, and the boy was without a stitch of clothing, except for a belt of sacking about a foot in width which was tied around his middle. Colville Scott stopped and enquired about his history. He does not seem to have stopped on his way often, though if he had travelled six or seven years earlier he would have met the dying all along the roads he travelled. (However, he did, as we have seen, write of how, during the famine, dogs ate the corpses by the sides of Connemara's roads. It is recorded that pigs ate the dead elsewhere, although in fact those who survived the famine went to extraordinary lengths to give their kin a decent burial.)

Colville Scott reported that the little boy managed to laugh through his awful condition. Robinson adds his own words to Colville Scott's: 'Surely this apparition is William Blake's chimney-sweep, mysteriously transported from London: ". . . little black thing among the snow, / Crying 'weep, weep' in notes of woe!" – except that, in Connemara, he is laughing. Colville Scott sensibly arranges to have him scrubbed and provided with a coat; and, in his journal, brings home to us that appalling laughter.'[17] Robinson does not report the lines that follow in Blake's poem, the little black thing speaking of his fellow sweep Tom Dacre and how when Tom slept he dreamt:

> That thousands of sweepers, Dick, Joe, Ned, & Jack,
> Were all of them locked up in coffins of black;

. . .

And the Angel told Tom, if he'd be a good boy,
He'd have God for his father & never want joy.

It is scenes like the following that the young Irish sweep would himself have seen: in the autumn of 1847, at the height of the famine, the Quaker philanthropist James H. Tuke visited the counties of Galway and Mayo. He reported back to the Central Relief Committee of the Society of Friends in Dublin. He wrote of the north-east part of Mayo that conditions there represented the '*ultima Thule* of human misery', the place itself, geographically, the 'furthest Thule' or the 'furthest of the far places'.[18] This area is not far from Céide Fields, where this book begins. During the Great Famine, *An Gorta Mór*, or *An Drochshaol* (Time of the Bad Life), my father's Mayo was the hardest hit of any county in Ireland. In some places a third of the population was lost, roughly half by death, half by emigration.

'Ultima Thule' was located in the barony of Erris. James H. Tuke continues, 'This barony is situated upon the extreme north-west coast of Mayo, bounded on two sides by the Atlantic ocean. The population last year was computed at about 28,000; of that number, it is said, at least 2,000 have emigrated, principally to England, being too poor to proceed to America; *and that 6,000 have perished by starvation, dysentery, and fever*. There is left a miserable remnant of little more than 20,000; of whom 10,000, at least, are, strictly speaking, on the very verge of starvation. Ten thousand people within forty-eight hours' journey of the metropolis of the world, living, or rather starving, upon turnip-tops, sand-eels, and sea-weed.'

Redress

In his depiction of the famine in Donegal, Hugh Dorian reports how the dead went quietly, and quietest of all went those without land, the subtenants, the landless labourers, the cottier class, so-called. People in effect were just got rid of – 'without much talk and without much trouble, and no cry of any injustice for the reason that they did not possess anything, and no more thought about them. It was just removing the dead, as if for the benefit of the living.'[19] Sometimes, most of the time, there was no redress. And, in the face of such privation as famine, if those who remained had enough between them to make life anew, then the matter of redress had to be put to one side. Put to one side for so long that the wrongs perpetrated by those who had themselves experienced famine were forgotten, the wrongs of land-grabbing farmers in Donegal, for instance, those who took the land of the dead. No woman or man wants to die unheard, unremembered, without the hope that the future will somehow redress the wrongs done to them. There in Donegal it was the unheard who went the quietest of all. It is up to us to speak for them.

Suffering was inflicted on peasants by peasants, therefore, and not just by the bailiff or land agent, who might himself come from the same stock as the smaller farmer. There was the land grabber of course and, beyond these immediate circumstances of famine, the local 'big man' who could throw his weight around. On Saturday 19 February 1853, Colville Scott wrote in his Connemara journal that he 'drove a long time through the territory of Lord Leitrim, now in Joyce country . . . We alighted at the King of the Joyce's door who though living on a farm of the Earl of Leitrim is also a tenant on the Martin estate to the extent of 1594 acres at £100 a year. We found his Majesty at home. There we were regaled with boiled eggs and whiskey.'[20]

Big Jack Joyce was invariably visited by those writing travel literature on the West of Ireland, a genre that became increasingly popular from the early nineteenth century onwards, in part in the wake of Sir Walter Scott's imagined peasants and equally imagined wildness. I have no wish to slander Jack, but he was typical of the 'big men' who rose to prominence in many peasant societies. Such men might be leaders of, or batteners upon, the communities in which they nonetheless remained rooted. Sometimes they were both at once, men able to make a few quid when the chance came, but also men who might defend local interests against outsiders, among whom they were the go-betweens for their own kind.[21]

The self-inflicted suffering of peasant on peasant was at once expressed and managed by the peasant feud. Revenge was part of the code of honour by which fate was managed and redress was to be had. Often, in the face of self-inflicted suffering, silence was the only response, although, in part, this was the silence of closed ranks against outsiders. The matter would be settled, or not settled, and so fester within the community itself. This festering and eventual settling is what happened in my father's place in the 1880s. In early 1882, just over the hill of Kilbride to the north, on the edge of Joyce Country, a slaughter took place. In the so-named 'Maamtrasna Murders', an international cause célèbre of its day, a band of men attacked and brutally killed five members of the family of John Joyce in the townland of Maamtrasna.

Several of the attackers were Joyces. Another Joyce, Myles Joyce, was wrongly hanged for the murders, and other Joyces falsely imprisoned. There was but limited justice to be had from the obtaining legal system. These following are the prison photos of one of the men falsely imprisoned for twenty years, Patrick (Paudeen) Joyce, a brother of the executed Myles. Imprisoned beside Paudeen were his brother Martin and his own son Thomas, the Cappanacreha Joyces. In the first photo, Paudeen looks down, his arms folded as per prison photography convention, and above his name the word 'Life' is written. The neighbouring photo shows him on his release in 1902, now an old man in his sixties; his life, like that of the others falsely accused, in ruins, those of the Cappanacreha Joyces most of all. The year of his release was only three years before that of my father's birth.

By all accounts, on his release Paudeen lived a troubled and vexatious life, estranged from his family and dying alone and in poverty. In his long life he knew only the Irish language, the years of the English-language regime of prison touching him not. Nor did literacy touch him, in either Irish or English. The accused were tried in English, a language several more of them than Paudeen alone did not understand, including the executed Myles Joyce. The translations made for them were poor in the extreme. The trial was in Dublin; the jury was heavily Protestant in its make-up. By all accounts it was the man who got off free, 'Big Tom Casey', who had led the murdering band, the action being motivated by a feud over land.[22] The murdered John Joyce had himself a reputation for sheep-stealing, which in the impoverished highland of Maamtrasna (where the grazing was poor) was a blow to the heart of survival itself, and so a source of profound anger.

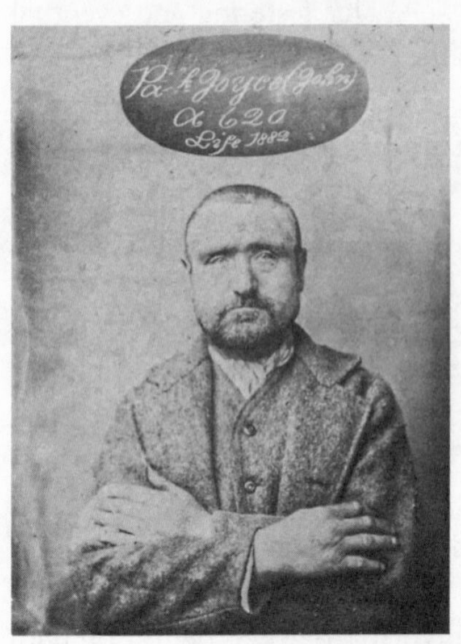

ARRESTED FOR THE MURDER.

Patrick Joyce, Shanvallycahill,	executed, guilty
Patrick Casey,	executed, guilty
Myles Joyce,	executed, innocent
Michael Casey,	penal servitude, guilty
Martin Joyce (brother to Myles),	penal servitude, innocent
Patrick Joyce, Cappanacreha (another brother),	penal servitude, innocent
Tom Joyce (son of Patrick),	penal servitude, innocent
John Casey (little), Cappanacreha,	penal servitude, innocent
Anthony Philbin,	approver
Thomas Casey,	approver

There may have been a political element to the murders too, for, as we shall see, violent anti-landlord protest was rife in Joyce Country in precisely these years. If this was so, then betrayal was perhaps the key: John Joyce's wife was talked about as a police informer, acting against those who had assassinated a landlord's agent and his son, only a short distance away from Maamtrasna. John Joyce himself was also believed to be politically involved. Whatever the case, the privations the system of landownership had reduced people to meant that the extreme of violent anger was, in effect, a condition of life throughout those years. 'Feud' only inadequately describes what was going on.[23]

That other Joyce fellow, James, wrote from Trieste with great anger about the treatment of the accused (*his* Joyces had gone down to Cork in earlier times than those of Maamtrasna, and prospered). James Joyce the bourgeois showed no sign of ever understanding our lot, whom he regarded as from another world to 'ours', namely the modern one.

The case in a nutshell – the list of destinies compiled by the nationalist MP Tim Harrington in 1884 – is printed in a pamphlet on the case which Harrington authored and is reproduced below. The densely woven web of family relationships among those involved is immediately apparent. Thomas Casey was an 'approver', one implicated in the crime, but then allowed to testify against others.

There are two kinds of redress apparent: that of peasants' own resources and collective silence, and that of the law, which here got it so badly wrong. Thomas Casey was a tyrant, but if Big Jack Joyce, the tenant of Lord Leitrim, had thrown his weight around, he was but an innocent babe in arms compared to his landlord; Lord Leitrim, the most reviled landlord of his day, ended up assassinated for his sins. Lord Leitrim, the Third Earl, owned parts of the Rosshill Estate in the barony of Ross some miles inland from where 'His Majesty' Jack Joyce reigned. In fact, the estate included the townland next to my father's Kilbride, only a wall separating us from the regime of Lord Leitrim. Leitrim had vast estates and was a notorious evicting landlord.[24] In April 1878, after surviving previous attempts on his life, Leitrim was shot and killed along with his clerk and driver on their way to the Donegal village of Milford, a place which he owned in its entirety. The crowd at his Dublin funeral wanted to throw the corpse into the street. The scales had been smashed, the balance tipped.

In his memory of famine-era Donegal, Hugh Dorian poses a question: 'If we have the real feeling to thoroughly understand all these sufferings, we might well ask humanly speaking, how was it that man could govern flesh and blood so as to submit to such slavery, that in the whole world, the Celtic Irish and they alone could do so: instead of, as a man guided by nature alone would mean to do. And the answer can only be accounted for and traced to the teachings of and consolations given them by their clergy.'

Indeed, how could they have done this without, as he puts it, 'reaching into deeds of revenge'?[25] Religion enabled the passive suffering that made the world go around, but this did not mean that people did not enact revenge once boundaries were crossed. The boundaries themselves involved what can be called the peasant sense of justice.

What is justice for peasants? In academic discourse, some idea of balance, equilibrium, is commonly invoked to describe this. Intrinsic to keeping balance is reciprocity, the idea that there is a give and take, which has limits. Obedience and even respect may be given to those in authority if the code is followed. But there is a code, and the powerful must recognize it. The ostensibly powerless are given a source of power when they hold others to the code: you, the master, must know there are limits and so be curbed by them. 'Moral economy' is one term used to describe this reciprocity, denoting that something else beyond the amoral political economy of the market is going on.[26]

Codes like this are a 'weapon of the weak'.[27] These codes are backed by the resources the seemingly powerless have: there are 'official' and 'unofficial' channels through which they may express themselves: the law and the breaking of the law, the latter seen throughout Europe in acts of arson, the maiming of animals, the withholding of rents, and, in my father's vicinity, in a place called the Neale, the original invention of the 'boycott', the word and the act bequeathed to posterity from this tiny quarter of the world. Charles Cunningham Boycott was the land agent of Lord Erne. Boycott was systematically ostracized by both the local tenants and shopkeepers, as part of the activities of the National Land League.

There were also the little acts of revolt such as saying one thing and doing another, pilfering, dragging one's feet, a bit of quiet sabotage on the side, slander or playing dumb. If these failed, then there was the escalation from violence upon animals and property to the threat of violence upon humans, and then the actual use of violence. Eventually, more collectively organized institutionalized routes were opened up, by no means all of which were peaceful. Political anarchism, with its objections to the state, was very influential in southern Europe too, not surprisingly, given peasant distrust of the state. Cooperatives, unions and political parties were established across Europe. And, as for the law, recourse to it was taken at all times, if possible, even if in practice the dice were loaded against peasants when it came to legal systems.

Sometimes reactions were so explosive, so frenzied and all-consuming, as to seem to deny all codes, all ideas of redress. The degree of frenzy and ferocity was in proportion to the sufferings undergone. There is a kind of elemental anger in the incipient violence of men such as Alain Le Goff, as he grabs hold of his spade and turns over the ground as if he were about to kill when the fear and despair come on him. This rage, and the existential dread behind it, was the basis of an escalating scale of violence in peasant societies: first the desire to kill, then the individual act of doing so, then the inchoate actions of bands of men and women, and then the transition into organized rebellion itself.

We can see this taking terrible form in an example drawn from nineteenth-century France. What is terrible is the sudden eruption on a mass scale of the kind of anger Alain Le Goff carried around with him throughout the many days of his life. Alain Corbin's *Village of Cannibals* concerns the torture and murder of Alain de Monéys, a young French nobleman in the commune of Hautefaye on 16 August 1870.[28] The commune was in the Dordogne, the poorest corner of what many regarded as the poorest region of France. De Monéys was tortured and then burned alive by a group of hundreds of villagers. De Monéys' death was a terrible one. At the time, the murder was regarded as an act of the utmost barbarity, proof of the brute nature of the peasant. However, as Corbin brilliantly analyses these events, he reveals that they have their own inner logic and coherence, a logic subsequently buried in the historical record, buried alongside the scores who were executed and imprisoned for the murder. The guillotine was erected at the place of the murder itself, one barbarity exchanged for another. What was at work below the surface is what the author calls 'a forgotten and inarticulate assertion of identity'.[29]

The atrocity belonged not so much to the history of the commune as to the history of the peasant market or fair. The fair was the one place a peasant could be a peasant, the one place he could act without constraint, fear or deference. De Monéys' crime was to have shouted '*Vive la République!*' in a place and at a time when the republic was loathed. He was known to be a man of considerable wealth and privilege and his utterance was regarded as a gross violation of peasant space, and so an assault on the very idea of what it was to be a peasant, which, inarticulate as it was, involved the shared understanding of being one who had 'suffered deeply'. The sudden violence was testimony to the sense of the communion of those who had suffered in this way. Decades of hatred against the nobles and their lackey curés came to the fore.

Vengeance for suffering expressed itself ritually: De Monéys' body was communally beaten, and quite systematically subjected to pain, for this man was made to suffer just like those he had made to suffer, those who now had power over him, a man who was still the greatest threat to the peasants, but now at their mercy. This was not blind fury. What happened reached back to much older traditions of conduct than those then becoming dominant throughout France. The post-Enlightenment, post-Revolution rise of the sensitive soul, *l'âme sensible*, in which cruelty and violence were increasingly coming into question, could not comprehend violence as expiation, as exemplary, in its very intensity setting right a sacrilege upon man as well as God. When no other justice was to be found, you made your own justice. Expiatory violence, torture; the monster is expelled from the community, which is thereby purified. Cruel the events indeed were, but as the sensitive souls of France and Europe recoiled in horror at the cannibalistic villagers of the Dordogne, they were simultaneously mobilizing hundreds of thousands of men for the organized violence of war, men who were mostly peasants. In this matter, the brute is difficult to identify.

The anger gets colder, the violence more organized, when ratcheted up to the level of planned attacks like that upon Lord Leitrim. Leitrim's death in the Ireland of 1878 was but one of many examples. Joyce Country itself was at the time called 'the most bloodstained of the districts of Ireland'.[30] At the time, the major landowners in Joyce Country were the Guinness family and the Clements family; Lord Leitrim was a Clements. In early 1882, Joseph Huddy, the land agent of Arthur Guinness, was assassinated almost directly opposite my father's Kilbride house, barely a mile across the lake below. The land agent's grandson, then seventeen years old, was killed alongside him. Both were shot. Another landlord was slain on his way back to his Ebor Hall residence on the northern shore of Lough Corrib. The crown prosecutor in the Huddy trial case, George Bolton, later reported that in the course of the investigation every male in the valleys of Joyce Country was arrested and interrogated, and many held for long periods.[31] This does not seem to have been much of a deterrent: Thomas Gibbons, a bailiff, was attacked on St Patrick's Day, 1882, eleven weeks after Huddy was attacked. Another bailiff, named Flynn, was also assaulted near the place of the Huddy shootings, a few weeks after the hangings of those found guilty of the murder of the land agent and his grandson. George Bolton was a busy man in these years: he was also the crown solicitor in the Joyce murders in Maamtrasna. In all these cases, communal silence met investigation by the forces of the state.

There is no evidence that secret agrarian protest societies were involved, but such violence was typical of this long Irish tradition of the band of brothers sworn to avenge wrong (in the Maamtrasna case there was some talk of Ribbonmen involvement). The Defenders, the Ribbonmen, the Whiteboys, the followers of the mythical Captain Rock, the list of these agrarian, and usually violent, secret societies in Ireland is long. Such societies were active at different times in most peasant societies worldwide. Brigandage, usually issuing out of the unsettled aftermath of war, crosses over with the agrarian secret society, as does social banditry, as it is called. Long ago, the historian Eric Hobsbawm opened up the study of what he called primitive rebels, among whom were peasant groups.[32] These primitives were felt by him to be 'blind and groping forwards' towards modern forms of political mobilization, the destination of the groping looking suspiciously like the Communist Party, of which Hobsbawm was a member. Once again, the primitive peasant is to be corrected and set firmly down on the right political path, namely the one that will terminate in modernity.

One story helps illuminate further the fury that drove people to kill. A brief and local account goes like this: when, in 1852, Sir Benjamin Lee Guinness (the 1st Baronet, 1798–1868) bought up the large, and debt-encumbered, Ashford Estate around the village of Cong (total acreage 33,298), he summarily proceeded to evict hundreds of tenants, turning thousands of acres over to woodland, fishing and wildfowl shooting. On Sir Benjamin's death in 1868, the estate passed to his son, Lord Ardilaun, who turned the place into a vast and monstrous neo-baronial gothic pile now known as Ashford Castle. The estate regime of Ardilaun was harsh, the son following the paternal example. (The 'castle' is now a hugely expensive hotel where the distant and loaded American kin of the once insulted and injured now recreate for themselves the Ireland of their dreams.) It was Ardilaun's agent, Joseph Huddy, who was killed opposite Kilbride.

Lord Ardilaun eventually ended up owning most of County Galway between Maam Bridge and Lough Mask, which is to say, a big chunk of Joyce Country.[33] As for ravaged South Connemara, the

Law Life Assurance Society finally got the Martin Estate off its hands to the London brewer Richard Berridge in 1872, in the process making Berridge the largest landowner in Ireland, possessing 200,000 acres or so. His Ballynahinch estate gave rise to its own Victorian castle pile.

After the famine, the local tenants were crushed between the grotesquely opulent consumption of such as the Guinness family on the one hand and by 'rational' farming on the other. The foundation of the latter was the Griffith's Survey, the national land survey of the 1850s. This survey enabled the amalgamation of scattered plots into consolidated holdings, a process known locally as 'striping'. The old culture was rooted in the old scattering, and was a system of interdependence, itself being aptly known as 'throughother'. Striping involved the breaking up of villages and the pulling down of houses. The new units and the big opulent estates were both rigorously managed, conspicuous consumption being no bar to rationality.

Where once a man might allow his cow to stray onto another's land, now, if the bailiff saw this, he might be marked down as 'troublesome'. The taking of heather for kindling was policed, as was poaching. The cutting of a single sod of turf from the landlord's land was enforced in some places. The landlord himself became the central figure of authority (where once many landlords were absentee), the big landlord especially. The new system was thus one of increased surveillance and legal enforcement, and the tyranny of the petty agents of landlords – the middlemen – who ran the new regime stretched the limits of what was bearable each year. Bribery and favouritism thrived.

What I am struck by in Joyce Country, nonetheless, is the extraordinary resilience and intrepidity of the people of the area, the seeds of justice sprouting little over a decade after the end of the famine. This is brought out with great force by an extraordinary pamphlet published in London in 1860. The author is one 'Lex [pseud.]'. The title is *Doings in Partry: A Chapter of Irish History. In a Letter to the Rt. Hon. the Earl of Derby, K. G.* The author is a mouthpiece for Lord

Plunket, Lord Bishop of Tuam (otherwise known as the Bishop of Wine and Grouse), as well as for other local landowners. Partry is the area in which the Joyce family Maamtrasna Murders later took place and the Land War later raged. It is worth quoting from this voluminous publication.

In Partry, 'the population of the parish of Ballyovey, which is almost conterminous with Partry, in 1851 was 3073 . . . The inhabitants are not very civilized or enlightened . . . The tenure is from year to year, the average holding about five acres . . . as in many parts of Ireland.' The Bishop of Wine and Grouse endeavours to put an end to 'the peculiarly inconvenient system of tenure known as the rundale'. The situation is further inflamed by forced Protestant evangelism. 'Some Protestants were imported', and 'about seventy are converts, or "Jumpers", as they are popularly called.' The opposition to Plunket was therefore twofold: the local firebrand Catholic priest and the extremely inventive and obdurate local tenants.

On one occasion, 'Lex' tells us, 'a right honourable gentleman – at present a Cabinet Minister – and his lady were unfortunate enough to pass in front of the local school, and were greeted with a *cead mille faltha* of stones and curses'. The term translates as 'a hundred thousand welcomes'. 'This school' was, of course, the Catholic one. Many of Plunket's tenants refused to give up possession of the land they worked. Large police reinforcements were sent down to keep the peace and a general notice to quit was issued. Then:

> A reign of lawlessness set in. Lord Plunket's property was injured in every conceivable way: his land was burned, his plantations were destroyed, his grazing lands were trespassed upon, his bogs were used by any one that pleased, the sedge upon the mountains was cut contrary to his orders, his game was destroyed by poachers, a weir which he had erected on the river was torn down, and every device that malice and ignorance could suggest was had recourse to, to torment and annoy. The Rev. Mr. Townsend and the [Protestant] Scripture-readers were frequently assaulted, and the carrying of arms became common.

Recourse to the law had little effect: 'The proceedings in court were conducted in the midst of confusion.' One Edmund Joyce burned his own land, and 'vexatiously' summoned his lordship as a witness for his defence. '[O]ut of court a system of terrorism prevailed . . . Police escorts were but a feeble protection. On one occasion a party of police were struck, one at least was dangerously wounded; so that at last, in sheer self-defence, they were compelled to fire on the mob . . . Such, then, was the attitude assumed by the gentle peasantry of Partry and their susceptible neighbours of Ballinrobe.'

Popular tumult, the reign of lawlessness, a system of terrorism: what was going on in Partry amounted almost to an insurrection, even if a short one. However, it was not a revolt, a desire to have done with the whole system. From the lone man's rage to this rage, multiplied in the case of De Monéys' dreadful death, and then from that inchoate, spontaneous rage to the cold, organized anger of assassination in Ireland, there is a progression, a sort of ratcheting up of the stakes. The next turn of the screw is the shift from small- to large-scale organized violence, which we can properly call peasant rebellion. What happened in Partry and in the Land War was a rebellion, but one which, all the same, pales beside many of the peasant rebellions of Europe.

The German Peasants' War from 1524 to 1525 was Europe's largest popular uprising before the French Revolution, which itself was in part a peasant uprising. In Germany, hundreds of thousands died in what was a real war, a real revolt. In what has been called 'the last great European peasant uprising', the 1907 Romanian rebellion, approaching 11,000 peasants were killed by the Romanian army and police, with hardly any casualties on the authorities' or landowners' side.[34] Within the Russian empire and in the Russian civil war that followed the revolution of 1917, however, the Semirechye Revolt of 1916 is held to have resulted in 40,000 dead. The Tambov Rebellion of 1920–21 led to the deaths of nearly a quarter of a million, a consequence of the fighting itself, the executions that followed and concentration camp deaths. The movement was later portrayed by the Soviets as anarchical banditry, the work of disaffected rich farmers (*kulaks*).

The 1907 Romanian rebellion has been described as a modern *jacquerie*, a word that since the fourteenth century has become a synonym for peasant uprisings in general. It carries strong connotations of senseless savagery. As with the Soviet labelling of the Tambov Rebellion as brigandage, mass, violent peasant protest has almost invariably been conceived in the image of mindless *jacquerie*. This is so in the case of the 'Galician Slaughter of 1846', which was cast as a slaughter, not a rebellion, a rebellion in which, like the Partry people, those involved well knew what they were doing. The events of 1846 are not understandable without awareness of the suffering serfdom brought, and the loathing this brought forth. Redress took the bloodiest of forms.

This is a Ukrainian peasant song of the 1840s, from a time when Ukrainians, then known as Ruthenians, were part of Austrian Galicia:

> I, a young man, will not do corvée labour.
> I'll flee to Wallachia and live there.
> I will not do corvée labour.
> I will not, I will not.
> In the dark of night I will do the lord harm.
> I am not afraid of the mayor or the steward.
> I will not do corvée labour. I will sit at home.[35]

This was sung shortly before the abolition of serfdom by the Austrian empire in 1848. This is what an old Ruthenian peasant said to a peasant from outside his village when the visitor asked what the celebration he had stumbled upon was about (it was the anniversary of the end of serfdom): 'Aren't you a peasant just like us? Didn't the landlords beat you with cudgels and whips as they did us Ruthenians? Didn't you go out every day at dawn for corvée labour as we Ruthenians did? Didn't you spend every Sunday and holy day in the mandator's prison as we Ruthenians did? Didn't your livestock perish beneath the landlord's burden as our Ruthenian livestock did? Didn't your wives spin thread, bleach linen, grind millet, give capons, eggs, fodder, hens, and chickens [to the lord] as our Ruthenian wives did?

Or maybe they didn't take your children by force to the manor, as if into Egyptian slavery under King Pharaoh, as they did our Ruthenian children? Don't you know what day this is?'[36] Many villages in Poland erected crosses in commemoration of the day marking the end of serfdom. The Soviet authorities tore these crosses down after the end of the Second World War.

Because literacy was so rare, peasants largely relied on either educated peasants or sympathetic non-peasants to formulate their grievances. Such peasant advocates were known as *Winkelschreiber* in German, 'corner scribes' in English. These scribes have been described as the outlaw intelligentsia of Galicia. It was such a man who led the Galician rebellion, the most serious peasant uprising in nineteenth-century Poland and one that left a great subsequent mark on Polish society.

His name was Jakub Szela from the village of Smarżowa in western Galicia. What follows is an image of him made at the time of the revolt.[37]

Szela, Anführer der Bauern in Galizien.

This image gained considerable currency throughout Europe for a time. He wears the characteristic clothes of the Polish peasant: there is the long white coat of flax, the linen shirt, the high leather boots, according to legend made of a pair of oxen killed by the wearer in a fit of rage. The representation of his hands is an accurate reflection. He had fought at the Battle of Ulm in 1805, when he was taken prisoner. On his release or escape he returned home, and there cut off his little and neighbouring fingers with an axe, as well as damaging his other hand. This self-mutilation freed him from any further military service (without these fingers a rifle could not be held properly).

This is the apostle of carnage, the supposed plaything of the Austrians, the reactionary nemesis of Polish liberalism, and at the same time the patron of utopian projects of the radical left. He is reviled still in Poland, particularly by the nationalist right, when he is remembered at all. Today younger Polish academics are beginning to rescue Szela and the events of 1846 from the insults of posterity.[38] What were the events of 1846? Around 500 gentry manors were sacked and destroyed, and a thousand nobles and their officials killed. Austrian officials were spared because this uprising had been set off by another one, that of the liberal, minor gentry, who staged a rising against the Austrians in Kraków only a little time before the 'slaughter'.

For peasants, the liberal, independent Poland which was the goal of the Kraków Uprising had little or no meaning. The would-be independent 'Poles' of the uprising were to them precisely the same kind of people who had always exploited them, the landowners, the hated masters, those who enserfed them, to whom they were no more than working animals. The peasants saw the empire as their friend rather than their enemy. Ironically, the Kraków insurrectionists had advocated the abolition of serfdom, hoping to bring the peasants onto their side. Instead of joining them, the peasants killed them, believing that the Kraków events were just a pretext to eventually bring back serfdom. They had their own interest in emancipation: their hopes invested in the empire. Among the thousand killed were members of the Bogusz family, who owned the village of Siedliska-Bogusz. This was Jakub Szela's native village. In the years before the killings he had been humiliated, imprisoned and beaten by the officials of Lord Bogusz. When the time came he was personally involved in the Bogusz deaths.

The illustration above, a widely circulating one of the time, helps tell the story: the costumes of the peasants set them apart, stylized as they are, for they depict the reality of their lowest-caste social position. They hold aloft on poles or pikes the heads of their victims. One approaches the seated military officer to receive payment for a head. Bags of money lie on the ground, one on the table ready for the exchange. The soldier to the side of the seated figure lays the severed heads in a row on the ground, evidence of the bargains just completed. In the background is what appears to be a recently destroyed manor house, and the soldiers emerge from a simple wooden structure, one similar to peasant dwellings. The story is that the peasants, aided and abetted by the Austrian army, now get their base reward for their barbarous acts.

The town of Tarnów was the epicentre of events. It lies about 50 miles east of Kraków. At the time it had a large Jewish population (Jews were not attacked in the uprising). About 90 per cent of the manor houses in the Tarnów region are estimated to have been destroyed. The world was to be turned upside down, justice at last achieved. The priest of Biskupice parish noted that the result of this uprising was a contempt among the peasants for all sovereignty except the Imperial Crown. They attacked all manifestations of noble power. The landlord and his entourage were targeted, the women and children spared, although some wished to go further: 'We have killed the dogs, we must kill the bitches and puppies, we will not let them live longer than on Good Friday.'[39]

As in Gascony, the peasant's body was something different to the lord's. One parish priest, Father Zgrzebny, tried to escape in the guise of a peasant, but was betrayed by the softness of his skin and the look of his hands. His captors promised to tan his skin black before they were finished. He heard the peasants who were guarding him say to each other, 'Peasants know how to tan Polish skin, a gentleman's skin, without paying for a tanner.' The whiteness of 'Polish' skin, and its softness, were contrasted with peasants' skins, weather-beaten from working in the sun.

The manor house itself was the tormenting symbol of excess amid these people's continual want. There were several episodes where, led by Szela, bands of peasants systematically destroyed everything that was to be found in the sacked mansions. In attacking the manors, Szela was essentially leading a symbolic attack on the nobility's monopoly of power, articulating the sense that serfdom was not God-given and could be got rid of by human effort. In many attacks, the scrupulousness with which the peasants destroyed the things they imagined represented the most prized of possessions of the landowners was striking: furniture, mirrors, pianos – in one case the strings of a piano were torn to pieces by a flail before an enthusiastic throng. The weapons of the weak were here those of the farmyard: masters were scythed, flailed, pitchforked, sickled to death.

At the cemetery in the village of Siedliska, Szela had all the tombstones and crosses smashed, shouting: 'There must be equality in this.' The words of John Ball come back across the centuries, Ball the priest and leader of the Peasants' Revolt of 1381 in England: 'When Adam delved, and Eve span, who was then the gentleman? . . . And therefore I exhort you to consider that now the time is come, appointed to us by God, in which ye may (if ye will) cast off the yoke of bondage, and recover liberty.'[40] In Galicia, however, the priests remarked how peasants mocked their sermons and services. Rumours circulated that priests had poisoned the Host. Church furnishings were destroyed, acts of desacralization recorded. Again, authority was under attack, that of the noble and the cleric together. Christ was a weapon mobilized by both sides, on the one hand, the suffering of Christ seen as the suffering of the peasants, and, on the other, the priests' depiction of their own sufferings at the hands of peasants as also those of Christ. In some places peasants parodied the celebration of Mass, destroying all church belongings in the process. During an attack on the monastery in Zakliczyn, they cut off the head of St Anthony, shouting 'Do miracles for us now!'

Nonetheless, before the killing in Burzyn the peasants went to the church to obtain absolution for the murders they were about to commit, and in Dobrków they demanded a Mass from the priest for luck in their coming attack. In reports and memoirs written by priests after the robbery of churches there was frequent emphasis on how peasants did not feel regret and remorse for their actions. They claimed that they had taken justice into their hands, that they had enacted it. They had acted in this way on behalf of their forebears, on the backs of whom the masters had climbed to riches. In a few cases priests joined the peasants, one publicly announcing that the land belonged exclusively to God and to the peasants, and that murder was not a sin if one repented.

Peasants are recorded as consciously exercising justice and punishment rituals of their own. In one account, 'Mr Kotarski was allowed to confess and carry out his last instructions. Judge Gawrzycki was, at his own request, led out to the cemetery so that he could say goodbye to his wife, then to the children, and only after that was he killed. In Stara Jastrząbka, peasants attacked a priest who took refuge in the church and began to pray. They waited until the end and said, "Are you finished? Then come to our judgment now".' The parish priest from Pstrągowa, calling on his flock during his Sunday sermon to return stolen items, heard from a man called Stanisław Szczepan, a gardener: 'You sucked our blood for many years, we worked for free, but that's our reward, whoever took what.' The heirs of one landowner, Maria Bobrowicka, were ordered by the peasants to publicly milk her own cows.

The 'pacification' by the Austrian army in the spring of 1846 was severe, but despite the presence of the army whole villages refused to continue life as serfs. Being forced to do it in some places, they set fire to their own buildings and fields. Over 55,000 troops were concentrated in Galicia. Mass flogging was employed. There is an account of a man called Old Grzegorz who was forcibly placed on the flogging bench. Fifty 'heavy' lashes were counted onto his naked back. The land steward asked repeatedly, ' "Will you do serfdom, or will you rebel?" Old Grzegorz refused to answer, nor did he utter a groan.' The beating thus continued, authority now restored.[41]

At the Old Cemetery in Tarnów one can today find a monument to the victims of 1846. A collective tomb contains the remains of the owners of villages, of local civil officials and of manor servants and priests, those who 'were cruelly murdered by peasants'. After 1846, the tomb became a regular meeting place of Polish patriots. On Tarnów's tourist website the mass grave where the slain are buried is described as shameful. The peasants are the bringers of shame, and this is as far as Tarnów goes in remembering them.[42] No monument to Jakub Szela was erected in Tarnów, or anywhere else.

Towards the Great Slaughters

Only 60 miles north-east of Tarnów is Jan Słomka's village of Dzików. Słomka has faithfully recorded the long, seemingly uneventful years when nothing went on but life itself. Rebellion and collective violence were the exception, not the rule. The life of the village was slow. Literacy came to Dzików in the late nineteenth century but even then the pace was slow. Famine ended. More manufactured goods came into the village, women bought new dresses in the shops of nearby Tarnobrzeg. There the new Catholic and the old Jewish shopkeepers vied with one another for custom. Tarnobrzeg grew up into a classic Jewish *shtetl* in Słomka's lifetime.

Nonetheless, there was the inevitable quickening of time with the coming of the railways to the local town in 1887, and with the acceleration of political change from the late nineteenth century onwards. A new public sphere opened up with the coming of mass politics, but the meaning of the old peasant public presence in the market square was not lost.

Politics was built upon the age-old substratum of the divisions that had always underlain village life, but also the age-old and subtle management of these divisions. Distinctions existed between the better-off minority and the poorer majority, upon which was overlaid the distinction between the political activists and the traditional majority, which was itself also a matter of generational difference. In Dzików, Słomka reports that the older peasants 'lived their whole life, forming a wholly separate group, and caring nothing for the nation. I myself did not know that I was a Pole till I began to read books and paper. Today there are still those who got angry and cursed when the name of Poland was mentioned. They would say that only the gentry could want Poland back, so that the masses would work for them as under serfdom.'

There were, as always, divisions of gender too, women's public role being as limited in the new public sphere then emerging as in the old life. They chafed against this exclusion and did not put up with it without complaint. However, women had a clandestine route into public life because responsibility for the education of children was handed to them. They took this responsibility very seriously. The ancient rivalry of church and tavern continued, both functioning as critically important centres of cultural and political life. All the same, things were mixed up, for, much to the Church's displeasure, taverns, traditionally run by Jews, often organized Christian religious events themselves. There were of course ethnic divisions, especially in the Polish South and East, which were replicated in religious ones. Serf emancipation led to the decline of the traditional economic middleman position of Jews, and, as in Tarnobrzeg, the rise of a Catholic business class. Jews emerged more decidedly as money-lenders, better-off Jews becoming large landowners in some cases. The old Jewish tavern keeper had been an important figure in the village, usually trusted as the necessary conduit to the world outside.[43]

However, between the trade-offs of pubs and churches, of village elites and the majority, of men and women, these divisions were managed. When it came to threats from outside, division took second place to a united village front. The winter evening gatherings for communal work were also venues where ideas were exchanged and divisions settled. Political institutions were built on these old foundations and driven by a sense of moral outrage at people's treatment under serfdom. What was seen in Dzików was reflected across the nation, though peasant politics were most developed in Galicia, a consequence of the liberalism of the Austrian authorities, unlike the autocratic Russians and Prussians.

Nationalism was the most important vehicle of this new politics. By the early years of the twentieth century, at least two streams of peasant nationalism coexisted in Galician villages. Keely Stauter-Halsted, a historian of what she calls 'the nation in the village', describes these two currents thus: the first, the major stream, was reflected in the imagery and patterns of village celebrations, legends, songs and aphorisms. Its oblique references to Poland or to Polish heroes portrayed the nation as saviour, as miracle worker, as rooted in the land and the rhythms of the agricultural calendar. The second stream was associated with the social-reform agenda, reflected in people just like Słomka, those whom he called the 'intelligent people' in his village, those who had been 'true to the nation'.[44] The new politics depended on the old culture. Peasant parties emerged to very considerable national effect in the interwar years, though political divisions greatly hampered outcomes beneficial for peasants.[45]

Agrarian populism on both the right and the left emphasized the viability of peasant agriculture and its ability to survive and prosper without the increasing economic inequalities and class antagonisms of industrial society. This populism was indeed the most viable peasant route into modernity, a route mapped by themselves and tailored to their needs. As in France, one could be both of a nation and a peasant at the same time, a peasant and modern. It was believed that the modernization of traditional small farming would not come from a capitalist or a collectivist road, but via a peasant path of rising technical levels of production achieved through cooperative organization. To varying degrees and in different fashions, the cooperative wave ran through all Europe (in Ireland, very strongly).

In Poland, the peasant right was in alliance with the Catholic Church. Around the same time, in Ireland, similar things were happening. By 1918 the Irish Home Rulers had thrown in their lot with the Catholic Church hierarchy, resulting in the kind of nationalist peasant romanticism that has disfigured Ireland as well as Poland, where, unlike Ireland, it has lasted into the present. The conservative Law and Justice Party and the Church are today in an unholy alliance in Poland. If antisemitic sermons are no longer delivered (although those continued into recent times), then anti-LGBT ones have amply filled the gap. Today, the most deprived parts of Poland (the South and East) provide the electoral capital of the nationalist right. In Ireland, the Catholic Church still forms much of the para-state of social care and education wilfully vacated by the state proper.

As the nineteenth century gave way to the twentieth, the barbarities inflicted on peasants far exceeded what had gone before. These barbarities were foundational for the emergence of modern states. Peasants died in national armies on a hitherto unimagined scale in the First World War, and then on an even more horrific scale as a large number of the civilian as well as the military dead in the Second. Famine was the prelude to the Second World War. In *Bloodlands*, Timothy Snyder considers the politically purposed famine in Ukraine under the Soviet Union, the result of which involved the destruction of the body and soul of the Ukrainian peasantry. For the Orthodox and Catholics alike, the apocalypse had come: collectivization, in literal terms, was seen as a pact with the Devil, and the new machine tractor stations were regarded as the reincarnation of Gehenna.[46] Those who did not starve to death often ended up in the Soviet gulags. The majority of those who endured the gulags were indeed peasants.

Snyder quotes a song from the peasant son of a deported Ukrainian *kulak*, with which he cheers himself up in German captivity: 'If only I had wings / I would lift myself to the sky / To the clouds / Where there is no pain of punishment'.[47] In these camps the Germans deliberately starved millions of Soviet prisoners to death, most of them peasants. Ukrainian peasants who had survived the first famine were killed by this second one as Soviet prisoners.

Snyder describes the German wartime economic plans as 'the economics of apocalypse'. Their aim was to kill peasants as well as Jews. *Generalplan Ost*, as it was conceived and partially executed from the early 1940s, aimed to deport, kill, assimilate or enslave an estimated 30 to 45 million people, mostly Slavs, very many of them peasants. The future, as Hitler imagined it, would deal with Slavs as the North Americans dealt with their indigenous population. The Volga was to be Germany's Mississippi. Ultra-fertile, Ukraine itself was of the greatest significance for both Hitler and Stalin. Snyder estimates that some 14 million people were deliberately murdered in the bloodlands of Ukraine, Poland, the Baltic States and Belarus, parts of all of which were in peasant-majority Poland before the war began.

Flood, famine and war cut a murderous path through southern Poland. About 70 miles south-east of the city of Lublin lies Zamość. In 1942, as part of *Generalplan Ost*, the region around Zamość in the south-east of Poland was chosen for German colonization. This Renaissance city is one of great beauty, if these days a little careworn (it is now a World Heritage Site). In 1939, it was a great centre of Jewish settlement. Zamość was renamed 'Himmlerstadt', and then, equally absurdly, 'Plough City'. At least 60,000 ethnic Germans were to be resettled around it. Well over 100,000 peasants from the surrounding area were expelled, 300 villages depopulated in what was known as 'Action Zamość'. Some villages were simply razed to the ground and their inhabitants murdered.

A concentration camp was created in Zamość and enlarged for the imprisonment of rounded-up peasant families. Approximately 5,000 peasant children were sent there for Germanization. From this concentration camp, children no older than fourteen years of age – whose names had already been Germanized – were sent to various destinations. It is estimated that 116,000 people in total were forcibly removed from Zamojszczyzna, the surrounding area, among them 30,000 children. In the camps, it was the children who suffered the most. Separated from their parents, children were transported in cattle wagons, many were sent to the Kinder KZ (a concentration camp for children) run side by side with the Łódź Ghetto. Some families ended up in Majdanek (up to 15,000 prisoners of Action Zamość), and some in Auschwitz.

The Vistula River runs through the heart of Poland, broadening out from its beginnings through the heart of what was once Galicia and then flowing north to the Baltic. The river is of great symbolic significance in Poland. Tarnów, the centre of the Galician uprising of 1846, is upriver from Tarnobrzeg, about 60 miles distant. The Vistula is a river of sorrows. Auschwitz lies on its banks, about 120 miles south-west of Jan Słomka's birthplace, on the westernmost edge of Galicia. The ashes of those killed in Auschwitz were thrown into the Vistula, and would have drifted downriver and passed Słomka's door. Everything flows. This is the title of Vasily Grossman's great novel, which deals with Ukraine's famine in the 1930s. It is estimated that almost four million peasants died in the *Holodomor* (in English, 'death by hunger'). As far as these things can be estimated, six million children could not be born because these people died. It is necessary to remember those who died, and these invisible ones who never existed.

PART THREE
Remembering

8.
They Remember

In 2003 the celebrated British film-maker Angus Macqueen made a series of three documentary films called *The Last Peasants*. It concerns the peasants of Romania, those who stayed and those who left, and the tensions, hopes and fears that played across the two groups. The old stayed, the young left. Some of the young came back, but things would never be the same again. Have we seen the last peasants, however? Macqueen's films were made almost a quarter of a century ago, but remnants of old peasant Europe still remain. This book's subtitle refers to a vanished world, and while this is true – the integrity of peasant culture is destroyed – people whom we might still call peasants remain in Europe, particularly in its East. Whether they would call themselves peasants is another matter. They are now 'small farmers', more economically minded than previously, or perhaps little more than smallholders, getting most of their income outside agriculture. There are relatively few of them, and this is an ageing population.

The EU lost 37 per cent of its farms between 2005 and 2020, almost all of which were tiny holdings, less than 5 hectares, this size limit making up a big majority of those remaining. Large-scale production carries all before it, just as is the case worldwide. According to UN Environmental Programme figures, although small farms make up 72 per cent of all farms worldwide, they occupy just 8 per cent of all agricultural land. In contrast, large farms – which account for only 1 per cent of the world's farms – occupy 65 per cent of agricultural land.[1]

This book has been written out of a sense of urgency about this passing. In this last part I want to turn outwards, as it were, to how peasants are remembered in the societies of the present. Remembering, the elevation of memory itself, has become a hallmark of contemporary societies. It seems at times that there is only so much room for remembering, so importunate are the demands of the many powerful claimants on our memory. When they are remembered at all, peasants get the scraps of what is left. So, the next chapter is how we remember now. Nonetheless, there is first the matter of how peasants themselves remember who they were. Their way of commemorating themselves and marking their own passing is the subject of this chapter. We should not expect that the operations of remembering they brought to bear are the same as ours, nor that 'remembrance' means the same thing.

To understand this I turn first to the far east of Europe. 'The last peasants of Europe': this term has a degree of rhetoric to it, for the marking of the 'last' has been apparent in several different times and places, though the claim to 'last' in the Belarus of Europe's far east is strong. The region known as Polesie is a place where the presence of the old cultural universe of peasants seems not only to linger, but still to control memory and being. Polesie is an area which spans both modern West and East Belarus, and extends into Poland in the west, Russia in the east, Ukraine in the south. Much of it was once part of Poland, and at other times the Russian and Soviet empires.

Kolkhozniks

The author whose work I draw on in considering these 'last' peasants is Anna Engelking, another of those who have given their lives to the study of peasants; another who follows in the footsteps of the ethnographic fathers, in this case, Józef Obrębski, who studied the same region in detail decades before her.[2] The people she writes about were *kolkhozniks*, peasants of the state collective farm (the *kolkhoz*), which was the basis of their life experience from the time of the great terrors of land collectivization onwards. In recent decades, Engelking returned again and again to Belarus, compiling around 700 separate accounts, almost all those of old people.[3] Her account depends on a way of knowing that involves acute listening and keen observation, also it must be said a sort of co-creation, for the observer in time-honoured ethnographic fashion is also a participant in the process of knowing. In participation and not simply observation one takes into consideration gestures, intonation, people looking for the right words, their repetitions, '[our] meeting itself'. This is the creative encounter that elucidates what lies below the surface. It involves perceiving peasant narratives about the origins of the natural world, as well as on the origins of social institutions and customs. This is in accordance with the principle that if you know the beginning of something then you have acquired metaphysical (or magical) knowledge about its true essence and its place in the order of things. We will return to peasant cosmogonies again, all roughly similar, but each one unique, like peasants themselves.

With knowledge of the origins of things comes a sort of power, which enables a measure of control over the vicissitudes of life. Engelking writes, 'This beginning is by its nature connected with the name and features of the given "thing" – a creature or an institution – and that is why the popular science of origins is also a question of words, of peasant etymology. Despite similar interpretative patterns more broadly, origins and causes only reveal their true nature according to the unique form and idiomatic features of each language, each dialect, and each locality.'[4]

The people in Engelking's account were born between the 1920s and 1940s, and therefore many of the grandparents of the old people that she worked with would have known serfdom under Russian rule. Those now-aged grandchildren of one-time serfs would have listened to their grandparents' talk of the old times, especially as the older generation played a big role in raising children. They would have had parents who had known the First World War, as they themselves knew the Second, knew the Holocaust, therefore, which took place in their villages, towns and cities, and in their fields, the mass death, not only of Jews, but of peasants themselves.

People such as those in the photograph that follows might have been the parents of the older people Engelking met in the 1990s, many of whom themselves will by now have taken their memories with them: this is an image made in the village of Chersk in 1910, near Damachow, a small town south of Brest in Belarus, once West Polesie in Poland and by 1910 in Russian Poland. Chersk is on the east bank of the Bug (pronounced Booh), and the river divides Poland and Belarus.[5] For these now-aged ones and their parents and grandparents there was war, but there was also the Soviet atheism drive, which, like agricultural collectivization, was violently enforced by Soviet state authority. The suffering was great.

How do peasants remember, then, by which I mean, how do they share memory together? Who people think collectively they are emerges out of this sharing. Social memory is the web that at once weaves and is woven by individual memory. This weave is tighter and stronger the less individualized the society.[6] Nonetheless, in some respects, peasants remember just like us. There is, of course, generational memory, which we share with them, and also there is state or political memory, which is most commonly still national memory but sometimes imperial memory, in the case of these peasants' memory of the Russian empire, the Soviet empire and the difficult period after 1989, when Belarus' national memory, torn between east and west, has perhaps been more nebulous and elusive than other national traditions.

For these peasants, however, remembering is centred upon a much older sense of collective identity. Neither nation nor motherland, state nor language, defines these people. Instead, they identify as those who work the land and have faith in God, 'simple, hard-working people', as they call themselves. Among the Orthodox and the Catholics, the creed ran, and still runs, 'I am from here, I am a peasant, I am a Catholic', or 'I am Orthodox', and so on for other denominations. All of them are of a 'Christian nation'. Again the refrain is heard: 'My fatherland is the land of my father.' The first researcher to investigate the Belarusian peasants' sense of identity was probably Oskar Kolberg, who in the mid-nineteenth century remarked, 'Asked about who he was, a Belarusian peasant would usually reply: "I, Mister, am a local" as if the term "local" was for him the alpha and omega.'

In the Belarus that Engelking considers, she perceives how for peasants the sense of their place in the cosmos is structured by certain oppositions: those between good and evil, life and death, God and the Devil, work and holiday, chaos and order, culture and anti-culture. Meanings and actions are structured by these, which are, as it were, memory's architecture. This architecture endures. People are housed in this building, but use it in different ways – which simply means that things are historical, subject to change. And, like all buildings, there is decay, renewal and, eventually, destruction. What is astonishing is the longevity of this particular construction. Rather like the peasant house itself.

This persistence of the old as it adapted to change enabled life to be lived in the teeth of the destruction that the twentieth century brought these people. Time was preserved and carried forward in order to meet present needs and enable survival. Berger wrote this about the peasant sense of time: 'A culture of survival envisages the future as a sequence of repeated acts for survival. Each act pushes a thread through the eye of a needle and the thread is tradition', and also, 'it is by following a path, created and maintained by generations of walking feet, that some of the dangers of the surrounding forests or mountains or marshes may be avoided.'[7]

The well-trodden path of many walking feet, which we call social memory, takes the form of stories, and, like stories in general, is formed around a set of characters and plots, which form the architecture of remembering. In Polesie, the central characters of these stories were peasant and master, peasant and Jew, and Christian and non-Christian; and the plots arose out of the experience in real life of the long coexistence and interactions of these characters. The social self-image of these peasants as an enduring community over time was thus the negative of the different groups that had surrounded them over the centuries. This is how Engelking describes the process of remembering in Belarus: 'The vivid memory of traumatic change, shaped through long years of physical and psychological terror (executed through the political apparatus of the state) and transmitted to younger generations, evolved into a kind of founding myth, which became the kernel of social identity for these villagers – the people who say of themselves, "We lived through our lives and saw nothing good – just work and suffering." '[8]

The founding myth portrayed the peasant as both a victim and a member of a universal human community. The eschatological categories of the end of the world and its new beginning served to comprehend the cruel and incomprehensible forces of destruction which collectivization unleashed. Cruelty and incomprehension were felt at the removal from the local world of all landholding peasant farmers, a new, modern serfdom imposed in their place. Yet the community of *kolkhozniks*, originally bound by fear, gradually adapted to their new conditions, in accordance with the central value of peasant culture, 'solidarity with life as it occurs', as it is well put in Engelking's book. The myth of the origin of things was both negative and positive. Taking the negative first, humankind was expelled from the Garden of Eden into the fields of endless toil, on the land where, 'Thorns also and thistles shall it bring forth to thee; and thou shalt eat the herb of the field.' The curse of Ham presented the peasant's identity as a repository of negative attributes compared to those of the master (the mythical descendant of Abel/Japheth): 'In the sweat of thy face shalt thou eat bread'; 'Unto the woman he said, I will greatly multiply thy sorrow and thy conception; in sorrow thou shalt bring forth children; and thy desire shall be to thy husband, and he shall rule over thee'.[9]

'A new, modern serfdom' was more than a figure of speech for these people, because the defining story which enabled collective memory reached back to the days of actual serfdom. This is how it worked: people today, we are told (this was during the 1990s), still perceive the context of their own existence as 'a specific continuation of the ancient manor estate, in that the *predsyedatyel* (the *kolkhoz* president) plays the role of a former landowner while they, the kolkhozniks, take the positions of former serfs or farmhands'.[10] These old and lasting cognitive structures mean that in order to be able to characterize himself, the peasant first has to specify the master's characteristics. But it turns out that 'the master' need not be a master at all, not in the old sense at least, but someone merely with authority over them, or someone from 'outside', perhaps just the figure of the city dweller, or even simply an educated person. There will always be those who are higher in the social hierarchy, and those who are below. The peasant–master dichotomy is at the root of the contemporary *kolkhozniks'* collective identity, and the old patriarchal master, the rapacious 'interwar wealthy estate baron', the *predsyedatel*, the educated city man, each and all are simply different manifestations of the basic peasant–master way of seeing things.

The peasant is rude, uneducated, not 'noble', which means, 'not cultivated'. The master does not 'work', for being a master or in business does not constitute working, which is exclusively the physical toil of a person working the land. This toil is in part a curse, just as the peasant feels the lash of others' contempt as, in part, deserved, his or her given lot as a 'simple' man or woman. 'When the man lives in the countryside, he is always the last one. We are the simple, ordinary *kolkhozniks* – not even considered human beings.' *Charna rabota* – literally, 'black work' – refers to hard, repetitive physical labour and is perceptible in peasant narratives that are full of lamentation about labour without end, understood as punishment and repentance for original sin. This extreme toil is punishing or torturous work, identified with a life of suffering and associated with a sense of injustice and humiliation. 'Collective farmers self-identify as *charnaraboche ludye* (people doing punishing work), and say about themselves: *My kak byli rabami, tak budyem rabami etymi*, "Once a slave, always a slave."'

However, the positive pole of 'hard-working, simple people' in the end triumphs. 'The Lord God loves everyone. Nobles, reds, blacks, whites.' And Jews alongside Gentiles. Everyone, 'beings such as we are'. But by no means always or necessarily the master, for there is another element in the master–peasant dichotomy. The peasant is human, and when the master's behaviour is found wanting, he is not. The master may be associated with the dog, the Devil. To be human is to be hard-working and pious, and goes back to the mythical progenitor Adam, whose act of expulsion from Eden turned men into farmers. While his penance is toil by the sweat of his brow, he is the one, the cultivator, who makes the Earth flourish. There is also the biblical model of the ploughman's work as holy, so that the land the farmer works is holy too. The master may own the land, but its true possessors are those who make it flourish. The fullest incarnation of this value 'transcends the peasant–master opposition', finding its personification in the peasant who is his own master, the good *haspadar*. The work of the good peasant is not only labour, but everything that he and she produce by the work of their own hands: the house, the crops, the animals, the children.

Collectivization had, in the not-so-distant past, swept away the old class of self-supporting peasants, the peasant who was his own master, creating instead a supposedly equal group, living in the main as agricultural labourers on what was in effect one huge estate, the *kolkhoz*, which to the people affected seemed simply a reproduction of serfdom, and the sometimes near-serfdom of manorial domination that followed it. The *kolkhoz* was in fact built on either the peasants' own land or on the sequestered estates of the big landowners (who were slaughtered by the Germans in the Second World War). For the Soviet authorities, those they had swept away were the mythical *kulaks*, the rich peasants of the Soviet imagination. For the *kolkhozniks* it was a different matter, because the villain (for the Soviets) was for them the hero, the martyr. This was so because the *kulak* was seen as a manifestation of the ideal of the 'good peasant', the independent man. It is a cliché to speak of ironies as supreme, but here the word seems apposite, for the very apparatus of oppression itself, the *kolkhoz*, served to preserve the old mental universe rather than destroy it. A kind of petrifaction occurred, for in the end the *kulak* trumped the system, a vision of the *kulak* as the good peasant, the independent man, both enduring the suffering and making it endurable. The extreme geographical and social isolation of the area played its part as well as the petrifying Soviet *kolkhoz* system.

Prosperity, in this collective sense, of the good peasant was understood both as the consequence of God's blessings and as the full realization of happiness. A man was no longer an object in the hands of a master. By extraordinary feats of endurance, the category of *one's own person* remained the central value around which the *kolkhozniks'* everyday activities were focused. As self-conscious descendants of *haspadars*, in the Soviet days these people felt fulfilled when working at the only place where no master oversaw them, that was on the mini-plots adjacent to their houses, which constituted the remnants of their former property. After the end of the Soviet system, they could buy plots of land from the now cooperatively run *kolkhoz*, and did so with willingness, the old people included. 'There used to be many masters. Nowadays, everyone's his own master. Because, you go, work, and you're gonna be the master.'

Just as the masters, depending on their behaviour, might or might not be included in 'beings such as we are', so too with what the figure of the Jew represented. Like the 'master', the 'Jew' did not work: these old people say, 'The Jews did no work, nothing. They had little shops and did the trading, and our people toiled at the land.'[11] Like 'master', 'Jew' might at times just mean those who were idle, or cultivated, categories being, as always, elastic in meaning. As with the 'master', there were positive and negative aspects to the 'Jew'. The everyday aggression of Christian peasants towards Jews is well known. Peasants – so often cowed by terror as they were between 1939 and 1945 – surrendered Jews to persecution during the Second World War, but it was not they who were mostly responsible, but the townspeople among whom Jews mostly lived, and the local military and police forces the Nazis recruited, poisonously nationalist as these were, the Ukrainian ones in particular. The partisans also murdered defenceless Jews, in particular Polish partisans of the Home Army. (The Polish state tries desperately to play all this down today.)

On the other hand, the old *kolkhozniks* 'gladly recall their former Jewish neighbours', these being 'our Jews', a familiar echo in peasant history in the East. 'Our Jews' were from our village, and part of it, there since time out of mind. Jews were for the *kolkhozniks* people who were thought of as 'the same kind of people we are. They're no different. Just the same.' Just as 'our Jews' were embraced, so the categories of 'our own' and 'our traitors' were readily acknowledged – 'our' responsibility being recognized.[12] The war and the Shoah also formed innumerable personal stories, for the victims were often those personally known, just as the executioners were sometimes known. The dominating account of the fate of the Jews was a lament of sympathy and sorrow, one concerning a cosmic catastrophe shared with them, if not in equal measure, then with great peasant suffering. In the 'pacification' of the villages, fleeing Jews sometimes died alongside peasants. Jews sometimes 'married in' to Catholic families. The moving, bleeding and moaning of the Earth is spoken of in people's stories, the groaning of the air.

While the antisemitic trope of Jews as Christ's killers, the children of Abel and Judas, persisted among peasants, Jews were also seen as victims, and Christ's death on the cross was for their sake as well as that of the peasants, for that of all who were 'humans'. To have a faith is to be human and to be saved by Christ's death on the cross. The forced atheism of these people was a failure. The Soviet authorities were regarded as demonic aliens threatening the very existence of the peasants. Theirs was a war waged by the Devil against God, a battle for people's innermost souls. All this was remembered, recalled as the core of what it once was and still is to be a peasant, 'a hard-working, simple and pious person'.

Last Night's Fun

There is an architecture to remembering, but then there is the ordinary business of recalling the old times, simply talking. 'It is 1970, and two "Yanks" have moved to Donegal's Blue Stack mountains.' So starts an article by Breandán Mac Suibhne in the *Irish Times* for 17 April 2022.[13] The two Yanks in question were Robert Bernen and his wife. Born in Brooklyn, New York, in 1928, Bernen was the son of a Russian immigrant who had made money in the garment industry. He had become a historian, who had at one time taught Classics at Harvard. His was hardly the move one would have thought such a man would make, for Donegal, like my father's area further south, was in a pretty poor state in the 1970s. But then the untutored wild where the origin of the world is to be found appeals to such people as the Bernens, and all the more readily when the old world is on the point of dissolution. The couple bought an old house and redecorated it, 'stopping short of getting running water and electricity', as Mac Suibhne tells us. Whatever their delusions, and though they were derided by some in the neighbourhood as in want of their minds, Robert Bernen is a sharp observer, and a fine writer, 'if mixing fact and fiction a bit', as

Breandán Mac Suibhne puts it.[14] The untutored wild tutored him and he learned fast.

The two incomers learned the rudiments of sheep farming and began to farm. For a sheep farmer, as Robert explained to broadcaster Proinsias Ó Conluain in an RTE radio documentary of 1978, 'Every year is a small miracle.' Bernen gives an account of how things were rapidly changing. This is in the early 1980s: 'Animal and man power was giving way to machine force. The horse was yielding to the tractor, the spade to the digger. The pony and trap was disappearing in favour of the car. In time the process of change was speeded up by a slight but definite money prosperity that was affecting the entire Western world, and with it Ireland.' When prosperity spread out from the western world it arrived in Donegal, but by then it 'had spent all but its final force, keeping only the last faint ripples, [so that] it arrived slowly' and steadily but it was also reliable.

John Berger has a fine story about an old French farmer's resistance to the tractor.[15] My uncle on The Island in Wexford had the same reluctance. The farm had two great workhorses, Maggie and Mollie, named for two of the owner's sisters. My cousin rebelled, saying to my uncle that he would refuse to take on the farm unless a tractor was bought. His father relented, and the son took on the farm. I do not know the fate of Maggie and Mollie. In my mother's Wexford of the 1950s I had as a child, two decades before the tractor became commonplace, seen this old world at first hand. A neighbour's car, the first and only one on The Island, eventually replaced the pony and trap we had gone to Mass in. It was owned by the best-off of The Island's farmers, an immediate neighbour (with whom there were kinship ties as well). The donkey became redundant, its raucous braying no longer to be heard. The hand-rearing of the piglet, the *banbh*, went into decline. As much as anything what changed things was the roads, on which the bicycle, farm machinery and the motor car could now move swiftly and smoothly. This improvement in Ireland was in large part due to Ireland's new membership of the EU in 1973. As Bernen writes, 'Main roads had been widened and paved with a smoother surface, the tarmac cracks, but even the cracked tar was better from the motorist's point of view than the old unpaved roads.'[16]

The coming of better roads was significant across Europe. In *Stone upon Stone*, Wiesław Myśliwski gives an eloquent account of the effects of a new road on peasant life in post-war Poland. It is like a river to those who behold it in wonder, but it cuts the village in two. Old men will not now meet to share a smoke in the evening for fear of crossing a road on which cars are now to be seen. The old road is recalled lovingly, when walking home in the night, returning from a dance, say. The road was never in a hurry then, had not a word of complaint, stopped when you stopped. You might be drunk coming home, 'But the road never left you.'[17] So it was the way that people remembered through things like roads, real things that reminded them of former things that had been lost for ever, in what was little more than a moment.

How do peasants remember? The simplest of ways is by sharing knowledge of what has gone. I opened this book with Bernen's words as he walked at three o'clock in the morning with a neighbour by the name of Jimmy along one of the old roads. Jimmy says, 'I remember the time there be ones up and down this road all night, until dawn, until morning they be comin' and goin'. Comin' and goin', you see, ramblin', to the cards and music and dancin' and all. Piles of them. Always.' On another occasion, Bernen is on a visit with a neighbour. They call in somewhere else before the visit and at the first stop the talk is so engaging that they forget the original destination, then remember, and call on those who had expected them hours earlier. It is three or four o'clock in the morning, but the couple they call on 'greeted me much as they would had I come in rambling at a normal hour of the night. I could tell at once that they did not mind or regret the lateness of the hour . . . I realized that they were enjoying the opportunity for an all-night conversation of the kind they had had frequently when they were younger and Michael and Peggy still in the hills . . . They were talking about old times . . . The warmth of the tone of their voices as they spoke indicated that they were remembering things they liked to remember, even though they had often been hard times – times that had meant much to them and so stayed vividly in memory.'

The people at that late and early hour were talking about the work they had done. Jimmy Paddy talked first about cutting turf, how an old man watching him work had once commented that 'the first piece of turf was still in the air when the next was already flying off the spade.' The others listened attentively and made quiet comments of appreciation and recollection. There was silence and some small talk and then Peggy related how she had started working. Her mother had died when she was only thirteen – 'If it was today they would have saved her,' she said – as she was the oldest of five she took over the job of looking after the family . . . 'And so I am baking bread and working since,' she concluded with a broad smile that yet had an element of long weariness in it . . . Finally it was Peader's turn, and his mind went back to his first hiring fair, when he was no more than eleven or twelve. 'Then Michael spoke about his days in Scotland, when there was no way to make a living there in Donegal and he had had to leave his farm for a number of years to work elsewhere, and had gone to the Highlands where dam building was going on.'[18]

'They continued laughing, a soft chuckle of pleasure. What was happening was like old times, his old times, the long nights he had always enjoyed when he and all his neighbours had been younger and liked sitting up all night, made a regular thing of it, playing cards, dancing, singing, exchanging stories already told many times before, listening attentively as though each retelling of it were really the first telling, then discussing the story and marvelling over it as if never heard before and so passing the long nights, often until dawn.' At the end of the long night Bernen walks home with Peader, with the dawn coming up and thinking about how after eleven years there in the hills he still wonders about it all, a little in awe, 'a little puzzled still'. 'Peadar born into it, yet feeling something of that awe that I felt, pondering always its mysteries that were so important to him and of which he gave me only glimpses . . . as if there were something he wanted to explain to me in his own language, as if the learning of that language were a necessary and not very difficult step to the knowledge he had to impart.'

Peadar recalls the long walks into the hills looking for lost animals, slowly recollecting things seen and remembered, sudden debilitating hunger and burning thirst, 'the wild, unusual beings not known out of the hills, not seen anywhere but there'. They are reluctant, the two men, to finish their talking, for this night seems to have had something special about it, seeming 'to have redeemed some moment of an earlier time of life'. As Bernen lays down to sleep at last, he thinks of Peadar 'pondering the secrets of the earth, and I wondered about them, wondered about the secrets of the earth myself and for the first time perhaps broke through that old barrier of unbelief that I had when Peadar spoke.'[19] In an essay called 'Two Lives', Bernen compares his life to Peadar's and considers the things that Peadar does that he has never done and will never do: the crossing of himself after eating; his plaiting of the St Brigid's cross from green rushes at the beginning of February; predicting the weather by looking at how animals behave – dogs, sheep, badgers, foxes, cats. Coming on a fox at night, or a badger, and breaking its legs to immobilize it, then crushing its skull. In Peadar's mind, there subsist 'the legends of the three men whose being alive now makes the continued existence of the earth and the lives of the rest of us possible (he himself knows one of them, he told me once, but stopped himself there and gave me no further information) . . . or his belief that the Flood was preceded by the Fire (what fire? I wondered, when he first brought the subject up).'[20]

And then there were 'the other stories that seemed to me Biblical but strangely transformed, much as the bog had transformed the appearance of the wood so long buried in it: the wren that was sent out from the Ark first, never to return, and the robin then, to return with a twig of fir; or the two men who decided to build a tower to heaven, and would have reached heaven too but that a swarm of stinging midges, the first midges ever seen, came on them and put an end to their work; and along with the legends the things he himself had seen high in the hills'. The echoes of the folk bible of East and central Europe reverberate here, in Europe's far West.

Why do I find these images of Donegal nights so powerful, so moving, I wonder to myself? Listening to the kitchen talk in Wexford as a child, as I lay in bed in the next room, and then later on, as an adult, staying for hour upon hour in another kitchen, a Galway one, as people came in visiting throughout the course of the evening and the early morning. The talk was constant in the West, in English and Irish: one visitor loquacious, one reserved, one who would stay all night if he could – all were warmly included in the circle. In the East my mother and her brother Nick, the oldest sibling and given the wayward father the patriarch of the family, talked hour after hour of the old times and the old people on The Island, so that by the age of nine or ten I felt I knew everyone who lived there, past and present. Their talk was storied talk, of this one and that time, this birth and that death. Not the storyteller's stories, just the ordinary ones, the talk of the many. And all in the unique accent of Wexford, where 'sea' rhymed with 'say' and 'tea' with 'tay'. I had caught the last rays of the already long-declining light of that old life.

In that large double bed in Wexford from which I listened, alongside me lay my brother and two cousins. Last night's fun had included hours of play-acting, for which rebuke from the kitchen was instant but fruitless. I listened alone in the end as the others had long fallen asleep beside me, so that I already felt a privileged witness to another world. After I had gone to my sleep, the long struggle to stay awake ended, my uncle would stretch out beside us four to sleep as well. So that this was another world not only in what I heard but in how I heard it, four to a bed, all hugger-mugger. Awareness of the press of immediate sensation is largely lost in a time when most people sleep in individual beds in individual rooms (though in my post-war working-class Irish London many had to sleep thus, so severe was the housing shortage, especially if, as with the Irish immigrants, families were large).

Further back and much further afield, bodies in the old peasant houses, life lived together in the one room, people sleeping in groups, but also working and playing in groups, bodies straining to coordinate, to know when to touch and not to touch (as in Gascony, where the etiquette of touch was so important). The tactile sense was thus constantly active, the sense that connects the whole of the body to the world, and not just parts of it, like the other senses. Suffering, you may remember, is acceptable in peasant societies, unavoidable, unlike our understanding of it. Our existence, usually unknowingly, is woven into the senses. We know touch and smell to be intimately related to memory. This peasant world is far from our world, where we are enclosed in a sensory bubble, afraid of that which, outside us, may reveal our true nature. We deodorize to civilize, as the anthropologist of the senses David Le Breton has put it.[21]

I am also moved by the image of those Donegal nights, because what I see is a life lived after dark, so that the senses and their place in remembering come into view again, literally so with sight; the life, the vivacity, of people is expressed in a world reversed, when the night that should be given up to sleep is given up to fun. People see in the dark, see the dark, are familiar with it, know how to be on the lookout for the fox they will kill. This life after dark serves as a kind of symbol for how we remember peasants today, those whose lives were lived in the dark of history's unheedingness. Those whose sense of time defies what is held to be the rational order of life. But most of all I am moved by the sense of an ending, an ending in the dark, but one nonetheless illuminated by the light of people 'ramblin', to the cards and music and dancin''.

The Belfast poet Ciaran Carson, in an essay called 'Johnny Going to Ceili', reminds us that a *céilí*, *cèilidh* in Scottish Gaelic, in its primary sense need not include music. The word derives from *céile*, a companion. *Bean céile* is a husband or wife. Carson writes, 'Before wireless and television, the *céilí* was a *samizdat* of sorts, a news-and-scandal channel, or communications network'.[22] He goes on:

> One boy might call and make his *céilí* with his mate down the loaning; then the pair of them might carry on to somebody else's house. Others would be at the same thing. All around the townland shadows flit between the scattered lighted houses, until, late on in the evening, they converge on one house pre-arranged among themselves, or authorised by custom. Then indeed there might be music, dancing, eating, drinking, talking, or the making of 'spakes' – pithy statements, verbal stratagems, elaborate hedge-school nonsense – or the throwing out of 'guesses' or riddles.[23]

But the most fun at the *céilí* is the music. People remember through talk. They also remember through music (when memory is so often at its most piercing, because music itself pierces the body, entering it, and taking up habitation there. The tune will not leave your head).

The first chapter of Carson's volume bears the same title as his book, and refers to a 'slip jig' called 'Last Night's Fun'. A slip jig is one of the four most common Irish step dances, the others being the reel, the jig itself and the hornpipe. The slip jig is danced 'graceful and controlled, with heels very high'. With this kind of music it is best to start with the music-makers, which is where music starts anyway. The first time Ciaran Carson heard 'Last Night's Fun' was from a long-playing mono record made in 1973 of the playing of an accordion player called Joe Cooley. Cooley knew he was dying when he made the recording, as did his faithful audience.[24] He died in the December of 1973, from lung cancer, smoking the scourge of those days, especially of those playing days.

Cooley was a profound influence on generations of Irish traditional musicians, one among many of an older school that played before commercial or, for most, indeed, any recording of their music was possible, and today still exert the powers of past transmission upon the present. The Cooley recording Carson loved was made in a pub, and all the sounds of pub playing are present on it. Listening to it, Carson writes that:

> [T]he place is jumping: whoops and gulders, clicking bottles, tapping feet. The whole room was pulsing like a diaphragm, and you can almost see the punters hunched in gleeful shapes at the bar, nodding joyfully into their pints; for though this is mono, you can hear or see in stereo, as if you were some fly-on-the-wall, disembodied dreamer, some ghost from the future, floating in on the sound waves that connect the present here-and-now to the present then, some twenty years ago.

On the record Joe Cooley is heard to say, 'It's only the music that brings people to their senses, I think.'[25] In late 2022 I talked about this music with the fiddler Martin Hayes, one of the leading traditional players of the present.[26] What counts in this music he tells me is how you 'carry' the tune, how you pick it up and carry it the best you can to those you play for. Unlike formal music, there are no straight lines. It comes out 'curved', he says, like the peasant conception of time itself. This music was dearly bought, worked hard for, and so approaches the unsayable reverently, putting the self at the end of things, not the beginning. The unsayable, in the sense of the ineffable, is that which surpasses the capacity of language to express it, something that is, as we say, 'beyond' words. In his preface to Timothy O'Grady's masterpiece on the experience of the rural Irish in Britain, *I Could Read the Sky*, of 1997, John Berger compares O'Grady's words to music, for they touch upon, 'The unsayable, the invisible, the longing in music . . . Here is a book of tunes without musical notes.'[27] O'Grady, in turn, writes about music in his book, his words becoming tunes when doing so. The book's narrator, like my own father, but more than half a century on in time, follows the dangerous and peripatetic building trade in England. He thinks back to how his father back at home in Ireland played the flute. The sense of how the music was felt, what the music could do to those who listened hard to it, is conveyed beautifully:

> It was best when he was sitting in a chair on his own against the yellow wall, not you'd think to see only him. But then everything

> was swept away once he was in to the tune, He'd drive the whole world away with his music. As he built the tune you would feel it into you, twisting and curling like a wild vine running on a wall . . . I'd heard the tune since before I could walk but I never knew where the next note would come from . . . it was as right and true as the flight of a hawk. At the height of it you were away too. You were only music. When he was finished the world would come back again but it was different. Whatever it is has us walking in the world but not noticing it was away. Everything was on you like a storm.[28]

The world comes back differently, and one's eyes and heart open to it where once they had been shut. As Joe Cooley put it, 'It's only the music that brings people to their senses, I think.' This is a description of the great Connemara *sean nós* singer Joe Heaney: 'When he got immersed in a song he became possessed by that song. And it was like he was a medium. It wasn't an individual that was singing. It came out of everything that had gone before him. And anybody who ever watched him singing got that sense.'[29]

He sings out of everything that has gone before, and this everything is the well into which the stone of the song is dropped. The song is heard in the form of the echoes it makes when striking the water, the sound reverberating in the well. This might be another way of describing that which is customary, for traditional music is customary, a matter of precedent: what has gone before is precedent, is the well, but the dropping stone always disturbs the water in different patterns, the walls of the well nonetheless giving shape to these patterns. Custom is flexible, precedent alters according to need: but it is strong, change having to operate through a collective sense of what is appropriate, and what is appropriate has always to come out of 'everything that has gone before'. Music carries time and in the carrying enacts time. When framed in terms of how custom operates, music as a mode of remembering is much the same as the architecture of remembering we find in Polesie.

But then the break with the old becomes real. Over time, the walls of the well fall in. Or, the world changes so much that the well is redundant. The break with the old becomes real and lasting. The water comes through the mains, and you do not need to go out into the world to draw it in. Music that is traditional becomes 'folk', then becomes 'world music', which becomes paradoxically dislodged from the world. For peasant music is not music as we have it – whether folk, world, popular or classical – which is something *listened* to, and sometimes danced to, in the time we call 'leisure' and as something we call entertainment. Peasant music is essentially different, in that it is interwoven more deeply with life, and is a means by which life is enacted. It is embedded in life, and is a means of transacting faith, labour, the coming of life and of death.

In the Basilicata of very recent times, there is an account of three generations of singers gathered together at the same time. New generations take up the styles of what has come before, but the meanings are lost: the old people singing songs about the hardness of life, a hardness the young no longer understand; for instance, the songs of the women of Basilicata in the cool of the morning as they prepare themselves for labour in the mountains. There are other songs, wedding songs, that are now meaningless because no one has weddings like that any more. This embeddedness of music within life is all that I mean by traditional. The depth of the music is due to its being at life's centre, near the core, deep down. All this has nothing to do with the idea of authenticity, for who gets to say what is authentic?

In Poland, the music-maker is a special figure, like the other special figures that help create peasant culture, the wise man and woman, for instance. *Muzykant* is the term used.[30] There, the music-maker is embedded in the cosmogony of the peasant, all the better to embed the music in life as it plays out. The role of the Traveller in Ireland, the Sinti, the Romany, the gypsy in music across Europe, shares something of the same character as the *muzykant*, who is located between nature and culture in just the same way as their music spans, and transacts, human life and the passage of nature's year. What is also encompassed is nature and also what is outside the natural world, the *muzykant* having a reputation for contact with the supernatural, and so being a seer, one perhaps in touch with the Devil, by turns someone feared and praised, a medium. (To have the Devil in a player means he or she always comes up with the best tunes at a wedding, it is said.) Traces of the old *muzykant* world persisted in Poland right down to the immediate past.[31] But then everything changed, and what persists is no more, or rather persistence takes the form of music as we experience it now.

It is almost as if the discovery of the music by the folklorist collector is at once the moment of music's regeneration and its death. Things are never the same again. Peasant music is transformed into something it was not. However, before this happened it was avidly collected by those wishing to preserve it. Partly based on these collections, the variously timed and variously intense 'traditional revivals' have followed across the entirety of Europe.[32] There is a striking uniformity across the continent here, one that echoes another: music scholars, among them Béla Bartók, have written of the commonalities of what they call folk music across Europe, of genre, style, instrumentation, as well as the status of the musician. But if the first commonality was rooted in the individual nation, the original commonality was from the time before national borders came to mean what they mean today. From the time of the pre-modern, one may put it, in the days of what I earlier called Europe's civilization of the peasants.

Some collectors have accessed the past better than others. Among the revivalists perhaps no one was more influential than Alan Lomax, the great recorder, scholar and advocate of folk music across the world, himself the son of a distinguished US collector and scholar. In the 1950s Lomax helped record and edit the *World Library of Folk and Primitive Music*. The series was historic, the first anthology of world music in high-fidelity sound. It spanned five continents and twenty-five countries. The Lomax Digital Archive is freely available online, if it has not disappeared by the time the reader sees these words.[33] The archive is his own independent collection and includes everything he recorded, involving over 20,000 items, running from 1946 into the 1990s.

In the mid-1950s, Alan Lomax travelled extensively around Italy recording folk music. *The Folk Music of Italy* was an eight-part series produced for the BBC's Third Programme. The recordings, broadcast in 1955, are different from most. They are presented as a radio show. The commentary by Lomax is learned and deeply sympathetic, even if prone at times to the folk romanticism of the left. But what is said in commentary is integrated with the music to convey a sense of immediacy; the microphone is left running at times and there is a feel for the immediate context of the performance generally. A great deal of the material is communal in performance; for instance, the polyphonic singing which is so much a part of peasant Europe, especially in southern and eastern Europe. The immediacy is real: as if these things were just going on anyway, and Lomax was clued-up enough to get there on time. In listening to these recordings one has a strong sense of something that is very old; also that this something has died since the 1950s. These are voices of the old land.

Last night's fun: fun and sorrow are never far away in the music and song of 1950s Italy, as everywhere in peasant music. This is, after all, the music of the survivors. However, in Irish music, the slow air may break magically into the jig, life renewed. At the midsummer festivals in Calabria, there are processions featuring giant puppets of grandmothers and grandfathers doing the tarantella dance. The drummers play different rhythms for every hour of the day, and a different drumming rhythm each day. They play and the playing is relentless, hypnotic, so that to me the players and dancers sound exhausted. The music is electrifying. During the midsummer penitential rituals in Campagna, Lomax tells us of the 'Beautiful and fervent devotional songs of the pilgrims'. The songs are particular to each village. After pilgrimage there is an evening picnic, and the solo voice of a woman sings a lovely melody, accompanied by the accordion.

The darkness of winter begins in November, the month of the

dead. On an island in Venice, an old lame woman sings, 'Remember the poor darling dead, the pitiful dead.' In November, people sing for, and to, the dead. How can I describe the passion with which they sing, the longing and sadness as the unsayable is said? In the South, as December comes, the arrival of the bagpipes means Christmas. At Christmas, the villagers of Montepertusso come down to the shore at Positano and light a great bonfire. They listen out for the boats at sea, bare-footed and red-capped as they are; the fire 'explodes' and the primitive orchestra begins to play – the Jew's harp, pieces of wood rubbed together, wooden hammers clashing, then the tambourine. During the singing, Lomax tells of the voice being 'thrown down', each singer different: 'One man shakes the sound out, pinching his throat to make the sound', and there are 'glottal shakes and voice throwing'. The pulse is intense, everything. Feet hammer the ground, compounding the music, and the dancing is equally intense. Afterwards, the men sing 'How beautiful it is in the evening when the young women come to the fountain'.

Winter is ending and, in the North of the country, Carnival is over. The male effigy of Carnival is discarded: 'He was as fat as a pig', and his race is done. Gangs of farm labourers sing of the death of 'La Vecchia', the fagged-out old woman who also represents Carnival gone. In one ceremony, the figure of a drunken priest arrives to bless La Vecchia, and an elaborate cod blessing is given in song. Labour is a constant, just as nature is. In June, wheat is harvested in Sicily, accompanied by prayers. There is a harvest song, which starts as a chant, about the Virgin Mary seeking her son through the streets of a strange city. The song is sung as the wheat is cut and is a sort of lament for the death of the crop. In Sicily, men are recorded singing as the wheat has been cut, twenty men in a circle. Work songs are also songs of lamentation. One winnowers' chorus lasts an hour. Winnowers, sweepers and gleaners all have different songs. Chestnut gatherers in the hills of Avellino also sing in unison, and the song is beautiful, each singer knowing their part exactly. In the heat of summer the roadworkers in Sicily sing of how the boss eats fresh meat and leaves them only the smell. The song of the stone-breakers of Puglia is accompanied by the striking of hammers. Peasants often have to take these kinds of jobs to survive. The counting song of the burden-bearing salt miners of Trapani, in Sicily, includes the line 'We walk like the dead by night.' The cries of bitterness towards the poverty and exploitation of their lot echo across Europe. There is a Polish peasant proverb that, in a kind of reply, echoes from the East, 'Hope is the mother of the stupid.'

In Basilicata there are the bitter songs of departure, as shepherds have to leave their families to take their sheep to richer pastures. 'For wine I shall drink my sweat' is the line of one such song. When the man comes back after his long vigil, he is said to be 'sheep simple', after being so long away, but the welcome back is real and warm after the winter away on the hills.

In north-east Sardinia, the Spanish influence strikes the hearer at once in their music. The choral bass polyphony characteristic of the Basques and other isolated peoples in western Europe is also noted by Lomax. In the impoverished, mountainous interior, named the 'Land of the Barbarians' by the Romans, *Barbagia*, there are only funeral laments to be found, Lomax tells us.[34] Peasants are barbarians. Many of the men in this area of banditry are, it seems, either dead or in prison.

I learned from the ethnomusicologist Catherine Bithell about the Corsica she knows so well, its rural culture being close to that of Sardinia, just as the two islands are geographically close. In her writing, she describes how a woman once told her of how her father and brother, out on the mountain with the flock, would discuss the progress of their work in improvised song. In the evenings, they would argue in similar vein around the supper table, her mother often intervening in song. Thus are the barbarians. *Paghjella* is the polyphonic, a cappella singing tradition of Corsica and can be either spiritual or secular. It is sung by men and women, by men usually in groups of three. Sardinia has a very similar tradition which, in its sister island of Corsica, was almost extinct by the 1970s, surviving only in the interior. Men hold one another closely as they sing in the style of the *paghjella*. There are scraps of film from older times showing groups of shepherds huddled together on the pastures, their bodies and voices blending in the most stunningly beautiful and strange musical combinations. What is going on is not unlike the *windáil* in singing in Irish, the hand of the singer being held for emotional support in his or her singing of the song. People sing the language of the unsayable, body and soul one. Bodies strain together, and what has gone returns to us briefly but intensely in the recorded sound and images that are the echoes of a vanished world.

Santa María del Monte/del Condado

The presence of the past is my theme. It would be unwise, therefore, to ignore a book with the title *The Presence of the Past*. This book by Ruth Behar, first published in 1986, concerns the village of Santa María del Monte, which came to be renamed Santa María del Condado.[35] This renaming is part of the story. The story shows how the past continued, but was in the end eclipsed by the importunate present.[36] The village lies 12 miles north-east of the city of León. The region, as in most of the north-west of Spain, is one of small peasant proprietorship, where an estate or manor system never took root. This form of proprietorship was accompanied by systems of communal tenure, formed at a time when there were large uninhabited spaces lying open for settlement. Holdings were very small, and widely scattered. There was a relative lack of economic stratification, unlike in Andalucía to the south, but like the South of Italy, southern Poland and Ireland before land reform.

Consequently, the tradition of the independent man, here the *labrador*, was strong: 'People often spoke to me of the importance of having the status of *labrador* and of passing on this status to all of one's children, especially in the past when virtually everyone's prospects were rooted in the soil.' The *haspadar* of Belarus is cousin to the *labrador*. A distant cousin, given the different histories, but kin nonetheless, kinship residing in the ideal of the good peasant.

Around this ideal, remembering was organized, in Spain as in Belarus, only in Spain the material world of peasants is more visible. Material things are the scaffoldings of memory's architecture, so that remembering is done *through* things (as in Ireland, where belief is something scattered in the landscape itself).

The possibilities for remembering are shaped, not to say, determined, by solid, real things: the shapes and sizes of fields, the patterns of the irrigation canals, the actual houses in their particular forms, the kind of farming practices necessitated by systems of communal tenure. People's sense of the past was in the deep history they inhabited daily, composed of several key things that Ruth Behar describes. For instance, the physical form of a house itself perpetuated the sense of having a long continuous identity over time, the continuity there in terms of the basic design of courtyards and the interior of houses. The form of building echoed a time when family life dominated, and itself reverberated with the time of communal calendric and labour observances. These observances involved both the management of the individual's holdings and the vital business of managing the commons upon which all depended. The presence of the past was also manifest in traditional harvesting methods (for example, in the name of the 'Roman plow' as villagers termed the old, crude plough), and in the landscape itself, in particular the many paths and landmarks needed to negotiate the scattered holdings. Multiple place names were created and had to be learned in order to keep track of things. The same was the case with the elaborate system of canals needed to irrigate these holdings.

The material world summoned the past into the present, but institutions and documents mattered as well (as they were themselves, like writing on paper with ink, material things). The uses of literacy, and of illiteracy come to that, were complex. There was the institution of the village council. The *concejo* was in many aspects highly effective, even during the time period when Behar was there. It enforced attendance at funerals, wakes, supported votive Masses and the custom of harbouring the wandering poor. The village held a beggar's stick, *palo de los pobres*, 'the stick of the poor'. When beggars came to a village they would ask in whose house the stick had last been kept. Then they would retrieve the stick and take it to the next house, which was obliged to feed and house them, and so on, in a circle of turn-taking. The operations of the *concejo* were facilitated by the keeping of written records and the frequent recourse to these, records stored over long periods of time and jealously guarded. These things recorded and verified custom, which was mobilized by the actions of the *concejo*, the whole comprising what villagers described as the 'good and Christian administration of the *pueblo*'.

Ruth Behar visited the village for the first time as a young woman in 1978, and writes of how rapid major change was, a matter of no more than a few years later. 'Much has changed in Santa María since my first visit to the village six years ago. I would go so far as to say that if I had begun my research in 1984, rather than in 1978, I could not have written the kind of book I did. Not that the changes now in evidence were unfor[e]seeable years ago, or that "the presence of the past" has suddenly receded into the mists of time, but Santa María today is a different kind of village, and its people, to some extent, a different people.' She talks to an older man, who reflects on what seemed the longevity of former times: he says, ' "How must the world have been in the past; it seems it was standing still, the way they went on using the Roman plow." I asked him why things had remained static for so long. And he replied: "It must have been a punishment, I don't know, but it was only forty years ago that the world started to evolve . . . They say we are on the road to development." Another man, remembering the eighty-three *vecinos* [neighbours] in the village during the 1940s when he was starting to raise his family, remarks: "If those people hadn't left today we would be dying of hunger". Compared to past times, most have prospered since the 1970s, a fact that people readily recognize. It is a prosperity that has come upon village people very quickly. Not surprisingly, then, many of them conceive of the past as locked in a still time.'

What changed things, suddenly and irrevocably, was the consolidation of the scattered parcels of land in 1983. Consolidation represented the very opposite of what the *concejo* had always stood for. It freed the landholder of labour obligations and moral ties to the community, making each field a world unto itself. The old physical universe in which the past had been embedded no longer made sense, the old-style houses, the pathways, the canals. 'But no one has any doubt that a dehumanized landscape is more suited to the requirements of the modern world. With consolidation the fields were not only made larger; the irrigation canals were widened, the old roads enlarged and new ones plowed into existence with bulldozers where there had once been cultivated land.'[37]

Behar writes of how, on her return in 1984, 'As we drew closer I could see, with the sort of intensity that only first impressions can call up, that the village was out in the open, visible from every direction, exposed, almost naked. There had been more trees, more hedges, more gardens; now there were large fields of barley and oats reaching right up to the houses, practically touching them.' The name of the village was changed, to Santa María del Condado. As one respondent put it, lamenting the change, 'This isn't Santa María del Monte [*del monte*, of the woods] anymore, now it's *del condado* [of the county or earldom].'

For all the advantages of consolidation, inequalities and irrationalities became apparent. As one man put it, 'they say that those who lose win, but there are some who win 50,000 and some who win 500,000.' The real-estate value of the land increased in some areas, near the roads, or near the new urbanization that grew up beside the village, which in the summertime filled up with vacationers. This area bore the name Montesol (which the author translates as 'Sunnywoods'). Prior to the 1980s, people had left the village in droves for the cities, leaving many of the old houses in ruin. These people then began to come back and build new houses as summer retreats, bringing their urban tastes and money back home. These houses were known in Spanish usage as 'chalets': 'The emphasis in the chalet is on comfort and leisure, and it is the living room, the bedroom, the bathroom, the garden that matter', unlike the old houses, which 'had sheltered humans, animals, and harvests under a single roof'.

Raising cattle brought a new-won prosperity to the people, but it drew them into what the author calls 'the vicious circle of capitalism':

> For one thing, as people often told me, most of the money they make from selling milk has to be recycled back into the market because of the large amounts of fodder they must buy in order to feed the cows that give them the milk they sell. Just as contradictory is the fact that, in order to be less dependent on purchased fodder, they continue to work their rye lands with the very cows that they have raised, not as work cows, but as milk cows. And of course the harder they work their cows, the less milk they give. The money that the villagers are paid for the milk they sell comes to them like a monthly wage, almost as if they were *jornaleros*, mere day labourers.

All this impacted on the old ways of mutual assistance and the redistribution of goods and services, which before had expressed a deeply rooted feeling against commercial trading. William Christian, writing of a similar form of village life in Cantabrian Spain in 1970, remarked upon 'a kind of shame in the pure market transaction'.[38] This ethic has for long had the support of the Catholic Church, with its disdain for relations of a purely commercial sort.

For all the difficulties, knowing how to work was the essence of the old regime, the essence too of what it meant to be 'of the woods'. Ruth Behar reflected: 'When I went back to Santa María this past summer the remark I heard most frequently, almost daily, was that nowadays no one wants to work anymore, no one knows how to work anymore. People want to live like earls, not like woodcutters.' The wastefulness of the new regime is often commented upon by villagers; how in the past every ear of wheat, every stick of wood mattered, and how today thoroughness is sacrificed for speed. Those who are accustomed to working in the old style still approach the land with patience, slowly and coaxingly, giving it attention every day without fail. The large fields of the new order demand an extensive manner of working. Some people carve human-sized plots out of the new large ones, and these are worked to the fullest and nothing is wasted. There are areas that are close to the settlement, where every family used to have some land, and which everyone now recognizes should not have been consolidated. A kind of equity reigned before, which has now been erased. Again, the combine harvester played a crucial role, erasing in one great mechanical gesture the centuries-old commonality of the old forms of harvesting.

'It's all vice' – *todo es vicio* – one woman says: rather than being happy with what they have, the young want more and more. 'If there is one word that epitomizes for the old the way of life of the young it has to be *vicio*,' writes Behar. The young want too much, spend too much and still don't have enough. The common refrain is that the young don't know how to enjoy themselves without spending money. They no longer get a dance going in the village square on Sundays, as was the custom in the past: 'For people long accustomed to the moral economy of the village, with its customary forms of reciprocity, cooperation, and exchange, the materialism of their own offspring easily takes on the appearance of greed, ambition for ambition's sake, vice in short. Yet, while the older generation decries the money culture that their children have adopted, they are the first to admit that many features of that culture, if not its core values, have found a place in village life.'[39]

What has happened in Santa María del Monte is only one outcome of the dissolution of peasant Europe, if a common one. In some cases, this outcome has been relatively benign for those who survived the perishing of so many. The present situation of the urbanization of Montesol sums up certain of the positive aspects of change, at least for some. But a price was paid: this is how a village blog describes the emergence of Montesol (the tensions and contradictions at work are evident in the brief entry): 'A privileged place surrounded by scrubland between holm oaks and pines, for many the town we always wanted. Although its beginning was complicated (for many, very complicated, they were authentic farmers) with the illusions and effort of all, today we have to feel proud, we have the urbanization that we deserve. ENJOY IT.'[40]

Remembrance of Basilicata

There are many candidates for the dubious honour of being called 'the last peasants', and the rural people of Basilicata in the extreme South of Italy are among the candidates, at least for the western part of Europe. Basilicata is an area of not much less than 4,000 square miles, but today it has little more than half a million inhabitants. I quote from a recent account of the area: 'The continuing outflow of young people is still one of the greatest problems of the region, since it results in the progressive abandonment of the countryside and the overall ageing of the population.' The region remains poor, and 'Basilicata is still considered representative of some of the worst features of the Italian South, including political and economic clientelism.' However, 'Over time, these migratory patterns have created various diasporic communities that in some cases have maintained continuous relationships with their communities of origin, and especially in recent years have taken advantage of the internet and social media to rekindle their links.'[41] Peasants remember, but here in different ways and with different experiences than in Polesie, the Blue Stacks and Santa María del Contado. No doubt by now those other places will have caught up with tech-savvy Basilicata.

One of the co-authors of the words I quote is Nicola Scaldaferri. I spoke with him in January 2022. San Costantino Albanese is located on a hilltop overlooking the Sarmento Valley, across which is its sister village of San Paolo Albanese. Both were founded around the mid-sixteenth century by ethnic Albanian refugees from Greece. These people were and still are known as *Arbëreshë*, and there is still a strong connection with Albanian culture. Surnames and speech in the village reflect this connection. In the Sarmento Valley, the Sinni River is a dry riverbed during summer, but often becomes a torrent during the winter rains. Nicola tells me that he can date the real fall of the village to 1973 when a disastrous landslide and flood broke the spirit of the old place.

There were earlier ends and deaths too: the massive emigrations before the First and after the Second World War in particular. (Since the 1950s there has been a loss of at least half the population; the 1950s, of course, the time of de Martino's famous studies of the magic of Italy's South.) These days some of the old come back to live, and there are some retired people from elsewhere. There is a tourist element, but this area is much less of a tourist destination than neighbouring Puglia, or Calabria. Those who go away to be educated also sometimes return, and create a life through the means of patching together different streams of income (there is a small service and offices sector). There is more traffic from those who annually return on holiday, especially, as is usually the case, if the holiday coincides with a local festivity. The agriculture that carries on is at a much higher commercial output now. Agricultural labourers in the region tend to be immigrants, some of whom are from the continent of Africa. Some of these immigrants will themselves be peasants by origin. The situation I describe is not far different from that of the former Mediterranean peasant everywhere.

What these returning Italian emigrants rekindle, through the internet and social media, is their younger days, though by their time these younger days would in all likelihood have been spent in a village long on the way towards death. Ironically, all categories of villager will know their own world through the eyes of those like Levi and de Martino, who made the region known to the world in the first place. Not only this, but they, or perhaps more likely their children, will now know their past through the eyes and the means of representation of those who in turn have recast Levi's writing and de Martino's ethnographies in new forms of 'memory' or 'heritage tourism'. The representation becomes the reality. The postmodern peasant emerges. Levi, poor man, has been 'heritagized'. So has de Martino.

Lorenzo Ferrarini and Nicola Scaldaferri document a striking instance of what has happened. They tell the story of how the village of Colobraro, a little north-east of San Costantino, once had such a sinister reputation as the home of witches and bad luck that the people of the region refrained from mentioning it by name, referring to it simply as *quel paese* (that village): 'Among the best-known pages of the entire body of de Martino's Lucanian ethnography is the description of a troubled trip to Colobraro to record a well-known *zampogna* player, only for him to be found dead upon the researchers' arrival.' The place becomes cursed. It is now publicized as the village that dares not tell its name. The photographs of a local 'enchantress', made by Franco Pinna, who worked with de Martino, helped with the authenticity of its reputation. This 'enchantress' has today become 'an icon of Basilicata'.

More than half a century on in Colobraro the practices de Martino so meticulously documented have been absorbed as an 'identity marker' of a new vision of the peasant South, a vision 'enacted in a theatrical form during open-air shows that take tourists around the narrow alleyways of the village. Twice a week during the month of August, a group of local people, coordinated by a theatre director, take part in a performance that makes use of de Martino's terminology and is opened by an exhibition of Pinna's images. This initiative, started in 2011, has now become one of the main cultural tourism attractions in the region, drawing three thousand visitors on a single evening in 2018, a figure which represents more than twice the number of permanent residents in the village.'[42] A similar festival was started in 2012 in Albano di Lucania, another key destination of de Martino's expeditions. This is explicitly entitled 'The Nights of Magic – A Journey in the Footsteps of de Martino'. The people who take part are local people. The people who come to watch are often those who are still villagers or those who emigrated earlier. These people mingle with the outsiders in a new form of remembering peasants, which, just like the end of peasant music, is characterized by the separation of what is now represented from the reality that originally gave it purpose and meaning.

Something decidedly different is put there in place of the old. The universe of meaning that comprehended the reality of the past has been severed, leaving the old meanings as they were, now floating free and so available for appropriation in all manner of new ways. Severed from poverty, social marginalization and spiritual depth, peasant culture has been reinvented, particularly for tourism. Nevertheless, what has been going on is complex and has several layers. There are still the old festivals, but also these days the invented ones. There is now so much activity that the festivals have formed their own 'network' for self-promotion.

Maggio, so-called, is one such festival, an ancient one, held in the village of Accettura, where, at the Feast of the Pentecost, a huge oak tree (symbolizing the month of May) is raised in the main square by means of an elaborate system of manually operated winches. This takes great strength, and is planned for over much of the year. A massive oak tree is dragged from the nearby woods, borne on the shoulders of teams of both men and oxen. The symbolically male oak is 'married' to the female holly as part of the ritual. The care of these animals is a great concern of the villagers, who now number no more than 2,000 people. Ferrarini and Scaldaferri report that the Maggio has now lost all its connections to everyday agricultural practice, and all aspects of the rebellious character that characterized it in much earlier times.

The event is reproduced on websites, in films, on TV, in the shape of documentaries, and in captions for photographs, almost all of this being aimed at the tourist trade and so addressed to outside audiences. The whole thing is now deeply influenced by the heritage process and what was once alive and eminently tangible now becomes something that is called 'intangible'. 'Intangible heritage', as it is known. Those who authenticate this heritage, by giving it the necessary stamp of approval their authority brings with it, are not just de Martino and Levi, but the flood of academic investigators, film-makers, photographers and journalists who in their wake 'discovered' Lucania-cum-Basilicata for the wider world. Nicola Scaldaferri, as he is well aware, also lends credence to what is going on, for these things must be given credentials so that they will be properly 'authentic', and so really 'real'. These things began to happen rapidly in the 1970s and 1980s, when these places were in effect dying, a familiar process in history, things being recorded and so enabled to be remembered only when they are in their last days.

There is, however, another festival, the Festival of the Bells, the 'Campanaccio' of San Mauro Forte, which seems to embody more genuine meaning. The two anthropologists I refer to are anthropologists of sound, helping to pioneer understanding of the full sensory dimension of these and similar experiences. Their work reveals something else, that events such as the ones I describe take on a life of their own, and have accrued new meanings for the villages involved and those who periodically come back after emigrating. These returnees are an important part of peasant culture all over Europe, the Irish emigrants from Britain with their children on the annual summer visit, the Portuguese peasants flocking back from the France of their first great post-war migration to attend their village feast day, or to mark Christmas. More is going on than the heritage business alone, therefore. Despite the presence of the festival in the digital domain it 'seems to have retained its deepest core meaning . . . with a strong identity value for the community of San Mauro Forte. People take part for themselves, for the community and for the village, and masks, groups and places end up resonating in synchrony.'[43] As well as the Campanaccio, Basilicata has many festivals celebrating the wheat harvest. In giving an account of these, Lorenzo Ferrarini is aware that, while the agricultural world these festivals represented is all but gone, something new emerges that partakes still of the old. All the same, this creation is a perilously maintained thing: 'This juncture of affect, devotion, reuse of anthropological knowledge and touristic promotion makes these festivals emblematic of the condition of much of Basilicata's cultural heritage.'

The people involved, as the authors write, 'precariously walk a line between the celebration of rurality and becoming a defunctionalized spectacle. By engaging stereotypes and expectations of tradition through visual displays and soundmaking, the protagonists of wheat festivals enact their own visions of tradition and rurality to an external audience and to themselves.'[44] The 'precarious walk' these people take, the balance they have momentarily achieved, represents what is happening now, and it may be that the outcome will amount to 'defunctionalized spectacle' in the end, spectacle without an inner meaning or social value. Outcomes are played out within these events, and in the Campanacci those involved actively argue among themselves about what is old and authentic on the one hand and what is merely a pale 'revival' on the other. There are also arguments between the Church and those involved, the former, as always, on the lookout for the presence of the 'pagan' in these new–old rituals

What has happened and is happening to those in the Italian South who now work the land represents one of history's ironies. The old ways of exploitation are replaced by the new, which in some cases look remarkably like the old. Italy's food products now saturate European markets. Sicily, for example, is Europe's third-largest producer of vegetables. Out of an Italian agricultural workforce of around one million, nearly half are now foreign workers, most of whom are in irregular, seasonal work. A majority of these workers are men, but there is a large group of women, too. Conditions are frequently atrocious, with poor pay and living conditions and no trade-union protection. This is especially so in Italy's South, including in Basilicata. All levels of food production are intimately linked in the 'agricultural value chain': the large suppliers and buyers (including the big supermarket chains across the breadth of Europe) impose low-cost operations on the smaller producers, who then employ middlemen, who then exploit the farm-workers.[45] These chains run what are called 'double-race' online auctions to incentivize processing companies to offer the lowest possible prices, which reverberates all the way down the supply chain.

The old forms of peasant exploitation have been replaced by new ones, those of large-scale capitalist food production.

The gang-master system known as *caporalato* has in recent times become more and more elaborate, reaching out to govern all aspects of the migrants' lives. Their travel to and from the workplace is controlled, as is housing, meals, even social contact, as well as working time and wages. It is as if the vertically integrated systems of big agri-business have been copied by those who exploit people at the lower level. Small fleas on bigger fleas feed. The Mafia are never far away: Italian organized crime generated a turnover of €21.8 billion from agriculture in 2017, a 30 per cent increase on the previous year, according to one industry source.[46]

Newly arrived workers are cheaper than those who have been working in Italy for a long time, who have often developed decent relationships with local farmers and are mostly unionized. The Tunisians fall into the first category, the Romanians and immigrants from sub-Saharan Africa into the former. Regulation is especially difficult in the South, where the many small and medium-sized farms there are difficult to monitor. The children and grandchildren of once impoverished Italian peasants now, in some cases, exploit other European and African peasants or those people's children. Women face a combination of excessive overtime, harsh working and living conditions, the withholding of wages, and physical and sexual violence.

Many workers follow the harvest cycle across Italy's southern regions: Calabrian citrus production in winter, Campania's strawberries in the spring, Basilicata's tomatoes in the summer. In truth, the working and living conditions of migrant farmworkers are not much better across Europe generally, as European agriculture seeks to emulate the 'Californian model' of intensive cultivation.

In 2021, the *Guardian* ran a news story titled 'The Invisible Migrant Workers Propping Up Ireland's €4bn Meat Industry'. The story unfolded thus: 'Approximately 15,000 people work in Ireland's large-scale abattoirs and processing plants, and an estimated 70 per cent are migrants.' The chronic mistreatment of these workers was reported by the Irish trade unions. A good deal of this production ended up in the UK, which of course also employs migrant labour, in much greater numbers than Ireland. There have been many reports of their mistreatment also. Many of these workers come from eastern Europe, especially from Romania, where peasant agriculture is still significant.[47]

The understanding we have of these contemporary 'peasants' recedes into the background when confronted with the spectacle of heritage tourism, the fantasies of which are enacted in the very same places where the newly exploited now labour. In Basilicata we can see how there is now a sort of convergence of the 'they' and the 'we' that do the remembering. Heritage makes us see the past as if we are only looking at ourselves. So how do we remember in this time of the unrelenting present?

9.

We Remember

Why ought we remember peasants? We have a debt to those forgotten by history. Peasants exemplify what it is to be forgotten more than most. This feeling of there being a debt is further informed by the sense that in 'advanced' western societies the dead in general are too happily put away, banished from our easily forgetful minds. In putting away the dead we put away the past. Of the dead there is nothing more certain than that we will one day be a member. Death unites us as humans, and, just as much as when we are alive we hope to be respected, so it is when we are dead. So, in putting away the dead we also put ourselves away. Peasants were good at remembering the dead, respecting them, which is one of the best possible reasons for remembering them.

To be respected one has first to be remembered. One's chances of being remembered increase in proportion to the wealth one has in life. The poor are mostly forgotten, and this is ignominious, at least in the sense that they do not get to choose whether they are remembered or not. It just does not come up. They did not have the power to be remembered. We should not think that because it did not come up people in the past did not think that it ought to have done, that they felt that their hopes and fears should be recognized by those coming after, that it is galling to die unconsidered, ignominious to be silenced by history and so forgotten.

To be forgotten, for the majority over historical time, is to leave no trace, and for most people in the past there is no trace, or very little. And if we have a trace, it is often fleeting and obscure. Nowadays in the time of the all-consuming present paradoxically traces multiply endlessly, but whether these traces will endure is unclear.

The fleetingness with which the traces of the past reveal themselves is nowhere more poignantly evident than in the photograph. This is why I have used so many in this book, as a trace detector. Walter Benjamin writes beautifully of this fleetingness of the past in the form of the photograph. He tells of a very early photograph in the history of that medium, one taken in England, and the image is that of a Newhaven fishwife: '[E]yes cast down in indolent, seductive modesty, there is something that goes beyond the photographer's art, something that cannot be silenced, something that fills you with an unruly desire to know what her name was, the woman who was alive then, who even now is still real and will never consent to be wholly absorbed in art. And I ask: how did the beauty of that hair, those eyes, beguile our forebears: how did that mouth kiss, to which desire curls up senseless as smoke without fire. . .[1]

Elsewhere, in his 'Theses on the Philosophy of History', Benjamin asks, 'Are we not touched by the same breath of air which was among that which came before? Is there not an echo of those who have been silenced in the voices to which we lend our ears today? Have not the women, who we court, sisters who they do not recognize any more?'[2] The unruly desire to know that Benjamin writes of is paralleled by the Newhaven woman's unruly determination to never be unknown. The reciprocity of the living and the dead is realized here. They are given a deeply moral cast by Benjamin, one drawing on the force of the messianic cast of his thought, the belief that the suffering of the past is not for nothing, and that we can help save this past, the messiah that does the redeeming being no other than each of us.

He writes further of the photograph, 'The most precise technology can give its products a magical value, such as a painted picture can never again have for us. No matter how artful the photographer the beholder feels an irresistible urge to search such a picture for a tiny spark of contingency, of the Here and Now, with which reality has so to speak seared the subject, to find the inconspicuous spot where in the immediacy of that long forgotten moment the future subsists so eloquently that we, looking back, may rediscover it.'[3]

This future subsists in us, therefore, and those who come later, the ones who are looking back, who may apprehend the spark of contingency. The past connects us this way, through the nature of time, just as it does through the nature of life, our not being here part of the matter as much as our being here. Our being of the dead and the living both, the former through the latter. The past and the present connect in the photo and if we catch the past at the moment of its evanescence, its vanishing, so it is that the past catches us at the moment of our vanishing, our contingency, as our here and nows become the thens of yesterday.

So it is that the dead belong to us, and we to them, and a moral bond is established. We are physically engendered by those who went before us, and are in this sense a bodily projection of the past. Drawing on his Jewish roots, Benjamin gives voice to this sense that we are a projection of the past in these words: 'Every present must recognize a past that is meant in it.' In listening to the voices to which we lend our ears today, we need to listen especially hard for the echo of those voices which have been silenced. 'Been silenced', we should note, a wrong actively done. Benjamin writes of how our coming on Earth was expected, was hoped for.[4] We are, as he says, weak messiahs, those hoped for in the past who will in their future redeem the time, redeem the past presents of those now departed. This is so especially for peasants, the silent class, who are the class of survivors only by dint of the millions who did not survive, individual peasants who were a condition of the survival of the genus peasant. Those who left no trace.

How do we repay our debt to the past today, catch its actuality as it rises before us into brief existence? This past to which we only weakly belong, since it asks more questions of us than we of it, to echo Seamus Deane again (whose reflections on the Great Famine I quoted in the Prologue). Why ought we to remember peasants is my first question, but the one at issue now is the second one: how do we remember them? This involves considering what has happened to time itself, the time of the unrelenting present in which the past becomes 'heritage'.

The Reign of the Present

Something has happened to the past, as the twentieth century has merged into the twenty-first. This something is part of our changing experience of time: the idea of continuity between past and present and future has given way to that of their disruption. The twentieth century was the century that 'most invoked the future, the most constructed and massacred in its name'. To do this, it drew on a past that it hoped would be the driving force in a present that would bring the desired future about. This conception of the past could be brutal, but it could also be noble, for it was informed by the expectation not only that the future would be better than the present and the past, but also, decidedly, that much of that present then needed betterment, just as, decidedly, our present does now.

In this now-fading temporal dispensation, 'The present was considered to be inferior to the future, and time became an agent; not only was it palpably accelerating, but one must make it move faster still. The future lay in speed. Attempts were made to insert the future directly into the present.' These striking words are those of François Hartog, a historian of historical writing.[5] All of this fell apart well within living memory. Our present is not the same as this former one. Our present now engulfs us, is everywhere, and the future in the twenty-first century is no longer 'a bright horizon towards which we advance, but a line of shadow that we have drawn towards ourselves, while we seem to have come to a standstill in the present, pondering on a past that is not passing'.[6]

Hartog gives us one perspective, but there are many others who address the same phenomena as he.[7] In a different kind of formulation, that of Douglas Rushkoff, we have seen a shift from what fifty years ago was called 'future shock' to 'present shock'.[8] Because 'everything happens now', in the present, we have as a consequence no longer 'a history of the world but a map of the world'. As Rushkoff puts it, a story takes time to recount, whereas a picture or a map (in practice, a data visualization) exists in the static moment. We are technologically able to map the connections of people and things to an unprecedented degree, and these maps of the present are what we live by. The world of the present absorbs us, and it is this world we care for, not the world of the future nor of the past. What, in all this, is happening to the past? It has not gone away.

The omnipresent present would logically seem to lead to the obliteration of concern with the past. This is in part true, but far from completely so. Hartog writes of '[a] massive, overwhelming, omnipresent present, that has no horizon other than itself, daily creating the past and the future that, day after day, it needs'.[9] What has changed is that now it is the present that counts, so that we see time and the past from this vantage point alone. And this present seems to be in need of the past, but the past it needs is cast in the present's own image, the needs of which it serves. This is what is different, a perspective on time in which we no longer look forward to a future that time is moving towards, but now, from an isolated present, we look upon an uncertain future and a past that must serve our needs. Our present concerns have always shaped how we see the past, but how we see and what we see has radically changed.

Our present is, oddly, a time of memory addiction and of a perceived debt to the past, while also being a time 'of daily amnesia, uncertainty, and simulation'. (Simulation because ours is the age of the reproduction constantly reproduced, so that what is real and what is true are difficult to discern.)[10] We exist therefore in a state of in betweenness, caught as we are 'between amnesia and the desire to forget nothing'. If we are engulfed by the present, we are, it seems, engulfed by the past too. For the acceleration of technical change in our age also involves the multiplication of pasts. Not only does time seem to accelerate at a hitherto unseen velocity,[11] but the digitalization of information means that we now seem able to archive almost everything for posterity in a future that is now not just indeterminate, but threatening. Our goals for the future have vanished or are no longer worth striving for. Another historian of European memory writes of a 'squeezed present', where change is so fast that the past arrives more quickly than ever before, banks up in mounds, as it were, ones which overwhelm us. The acceleration of time is cumulative, so that, moving ever faster, things become 'history' sooner.[12]

Thus it is that our overwhelmed attention is now splintered into thousands of pasts that in their turn serve thousands of needs. Each woman and man, each group, each identity, seems as if isolated on its own island of the past, the past itself no longer capable of holding us together, as once it did in the old dispensation of time, under the temporal regimes of the nation state and society, with their various manifestations: 'the people', 'the republic', 'the proletariat', and so on.

What purpose does this thousand-fold past serve in our overwhelming present? Sometimes it is a diversion and release from the present, our need for diversion intensified by our obsession with a present that is experienced as a sort of tyranny – sometimes as a duty, sometimes as a right, sometimes as what is now called an identity. Ethnic identity is a particularly important element in identity in the present. 'To be Jewish is to remember that one is such', as François Hartog puts it. When it comes to identity, it is memory that counts. Pierre Bourdieu once remarked that what is learned by the body is not something that one has, but something that one is. Identity before contemporary identity emerged is similar, something one had, not something one was. Heritage is similar, once something one had, now something that defines who one is. Previously one's 'identity' was more fixed and known than now, carried in the body and less in the head, as is the case today. The expression of identity in the present of liberal societies is more about the individual who, in embracing an identity, expresses their freedom. Now identity is more suppressed and insecure than before, and so something that has to be searched for and, hopefully, found in the past.

Heritage has emerged as the form of the past that is in keeping with our presentism. 'Heritage' is so overused a word these days as to be next to meaningless. I discover I wear a shirt that for no reason

I can discern is described with the word 'heritage'. I eat 'heritage' tomatoes without any knowledge of what this means in relation to the red fruit that innocently waits before me. People are themselves held to be of this heritage and that heritage. What I mean by heritage clearly needs further elaboration. This elaboration can be done in conjunction with some clarification of presentism, so-called, heritage being the child of presentism.

Presentism is the social condition whereby present time is at once everything and nothing, an eternal now that manifests and disappears in the instant.[13] The instant is, in other terms, the *now*, and it is in the *now* that we increasingly live. The internet reflects and augments this 'nowness'. Time is accelerated, also compressed, so that things are over with, 'done with' quickly and one moves on to the next. The internet puts you 'There', as it has been said, privileging what is happening now, so that the value of depth is sacrificed to immediacy. This 'depthlessness' has frequently been remarked upon by observers, and it inheres in a popular culture which puts a premium on the immediacy of form and of content. The algorithmic and market principles of online life create an effect of randomness. A kind of mosaic memory results, the product of 'browsing', made up of information that is free-floating, bereft of context and already selected for us. As the world is connected, understanding is disconnected. This popular culture is also highly commercialized, the past itself becoming a commodity.

In this presentist time regime, space retreats before time, in that the sense of place gives way to the timeless time of the present. The political philosopher Agnes Heller describes this new mode of existence as 'the absolute present', where people feel at home not in a place but in a time, the timeless time of the present.[14] Once people went to places, now it is as if, Heller writes, places move to them. The effect seems to be that people are desensitized to time, as they are to anything which is not immediate and fast-moving. Past time thus becomes something akin to a void, something that either people have no time for or wish to flee to as respite from the nowness pressing in on them.

Into this void comes heritage and a heightened sensitivity to memory. And also what may be called 'pastness', the notion that the past is stable, knowable and simply a continuation of the present backwards, and the future a continuation of the present forwards. The past is simply the same old thing, and engaging with the past is making more of the same old thing. Heritage is the realization of pastness.

How might this state of affairs itself be historically explained? The 1970s seem to have marked a decisive break with the old-time dispensation. First, there is the momentous fact of the vast increase in world population since 1945, especially in the third quarter of the twentieth century, the time of the precipitous decline of the peasantry. In his 'Campo Santo', W. G. Sebald once mused on all of this, noting how those living now come to outnumber all those born in the whole span of human history. When the living outnumber the dead, the dead are forgotten, and we no longer dwell with them, do not know how to dwell with them, whereas our ancestors had this knowledge. It was a peasant village graveyard in Corsica that drew forth these musings from Sebald.[15] There is a massive sundering of past and present. In the decline of the world peasantry, we have seen perhaps the most important single expression of this sundering. As Eric Hobsbawm said, the death of the peasantry cuts us off from the past in the most radical way of all.

In western and central Europe, post-war economic growth stalled in the 1970s, and what the French call *Les Trente Glorieuses* ended, the Thirty Glorious Years that followed 1945 and the end of the war. The future began to look more and more threatening and unknown. The process was different in the East of Europe, though the pace of change from 1989 (and the fall of Communism) onwards was, if anything, even more striking than in the West. Across all of Europe, West and East, the idea of the planned society waned; the notion that the future could and should be planned. The future was to be left to the market, a development especially marked in Britain and the USA, and in eastern Europe later on.

The self-fashioned individual became paramount with the rise of the market. Time, in the sense of the importance of the past, was, in this new economic reality, meaningless, *Homo economicus* having no use for it (not that the past was not manipulated for political purposes). However, thereafter the value of what was 'modern' waned everywhere, so the past was reached for anew: in Britain, as one instance of this, the failures of the great, modernist surge of urban redevelopment and post-war mass rehousing were painfully apparent.

The French historian Pierre Nora argued in the 1980s that we were witnessing the waning, if not the end, of what he called social memory: a term denoting time that is part of 'lifeworlds' – time as experienced in families and other social groups where memory resides in these bodies rather than in institutions,[16] institutions such as the growing number of heritage bodies emerging from the 1970s onwards,[17] and also the vast number of museums that now populate the entire globe. The peasant view of time entailed one variant of social memory, but so too did the lifeworlds of manual workers, and it is remarkable that the end of the manual working class and that of the peasantry were near-simultaneous, whereas, in political theory, the worker was supposed to follow and supplant the peasant. Prior to the disintegration of the traditional, manual working class, social memory was locked up in urban industrial culture, in urban villages and small towns especially, as much as in peasant culture: although this involved not the circular time of peasants, but the unilinear, progressive time of a modernity which (from the 1970s onwards) fell apart before the workers' eyes. In Britain, one thinks of the catastrophic end of the once-mighty mining industry.

Now what is called the 'precariat' has emerged, a class where precariousness is central to their existence. By dint of brutal necessity, their experience of work will most probably fix their attention on the immediate present of just getting by, day by day. There is no future; one is unable to plan ahead. The old forward-looking career structure has simply disintegrated. One was once anchored in a trajectory of time, and there was a story, and like all stories a past, present and future, in that order. I grew up in this now old world.

The new consumption-driven service economy emerged, in a so-called globalized world. Rapid technical innovation and the pursuit of rapid returns involved the rapid obsolescence of goods and people. The ephemeral came to be highly prized, which is logical, given this kind of society. The world itself is consumed in the form of tourism.

There is a feeling that time is constantly disappearing, being constantly eaten up, just as time itself seems to eat people. So people search for an anchorage, for some sense of being rooted. The contemporary craze for genealogy is part of this, also the turn towards popular history, in the anodyne form of television history programmes, but also in the more serious forms of popular history found in 'public history', the growth of which has been striking.

The fading, if not the ending, of social memory saw what was in effect a closing down of its authority as the post-war decades unfolded into the present. This was represented in the breakdown of social trust. Trust had kept the old class society together, a double-edged trust in Britain, indeed, trust in the form of class solidarity, and trust in and deference to established authority, bordering at times on servility. The end of social trust saw the rise of what was called in the 1980s the 'risk society', in which instead of trust managing risk, institutional authority did. Ulrich Beck's *Risikogesellschaft* (*Risk Society*) was first published in 1986. Nineteen eighty-six was also the year of Chernobyl. The future began to shock us, as ecological disaster loomed closer. The management of risk coincided with the consolidation of what has been called an 'audit culture'. In this, all branches of life are monitored, measured and ranked, so that our 'performance' can be audited.[18] Again, trust went out of the window, trust being something which involves looking to the future in hope.

This pervasive mode of government, in turn, meant, in the first place, shaping reality in such a way that it would be auditable. The continuous surveillance of performance involved the production of a reality in which not only did trust go out of the door but so too did time, in that, past time had no place in the continuous present that made up a countable reality. Or rather, if real time went out of the door, time reconfigured as auditable stayed within it. 'Heritage' was among these auditable things. The problem, then, was the production and hence the authority of truth, and in the present century this problem has only accelerated, now appearing in the form of the post-truth society.

When it came to the authority of who governed time, time – like every other sphere of life – became institutionalized. This was and is realized nowhere more than in the form of the museum, and in the raw material the museum now came to work with, which was heritage. The museum has become perhaps the central institution of contemporary memory. Heritage was knowable and measurable, especially when put in museums. It could be marketed: indeed, that was a large part of the point. Also, governments can control time and the past through heritage.

Heritage is thus the form of the past for those who have neither the time nor the interest to ask questions of it, and who do not understand that the past asks more questions of us than we do of it. It is for those for whom the past is the same as them, who do not recognize its radical otherness, who do not hear its silences, who do not question. Do my words on heritage apply only to the heritage institutions, or to the people whom these institutions cater for? The answer is both, one feeding the other in a spiral of rising expectations. But the answer is also in neither, for institutions often struggle against the very heritage they must work within, and the consumer of institutional pasts asks questions and is not always satisfied. But it is an uphill task, this questioning.

Museumified: Experiencing the Past

If museums have become the central institutions of contemporary historical memory, it is necessary to dwell on them for a little while. When it comes to peasants, there is little doubt of the museum's importance, for where we will find their past today is above all in the museum, the ethnographic museum, in particular, and across Europe the ethnographic museum in the form of the 'open-air' museum, the *skansen*, as it is called in central and eastern Europe (following the example of the original open-air museum, Sweden's Skansen of 1891). This manifestation of the past is now a worldwide phenomenon.

Museums are institutions that authenticate the past, tell us what is 'true' about it. The manifestation of the omnipresent present in our time, and the resulting and paradoxical hungering for the past this brings about, have called into being new versions of the authentic. These in large part are to be found in the location of the past in *ourselves*. While the past is always so located, this location now takes a new form of the recent emergence of *experience* as the bedrock of the authentic. And this authenticity that lies in ourselves is to be found in 'ordinary' experience, the experience of the 'everyday', and of that which is 'living history'.[19] This is not unexpected, for if pastness is the same old thing, just recycled, namely the present's image of itself projected back in time, then it would seem natural that visitors to museums would want to see themselves mirrored in the past and the past mirrored in them, that their 'experience' would be the key that unlocked the past, something which curators increasingly saw to be the case. Thus the 'everyday' and 'ordinary' life ruled, and rules even more in our populist times.

Our experience has come to meet the experience of those in the past on equal terms, and in this way we believe the real past is found, despite the real past and truth being fugitive. The violence done to and by people in the past is simply spirited away. The same is true of how power worked and was resisted. The same with fear, hunger, dirty feet, chapped hands, lousy bodies, the Devil in our purses. The same indeed with the critical distance inseparable from historical writing. The time of events is flattened out into an unchanging landscape of the eternal past, the mirror image of the eternal present.

In France, as the historian Philippe Hoyau observed in the 1980s, 'the nation's greatness is seen as residing not so much in the magnificence of its Art as in the exquisite variety of its popular skills and the indestructible nature of its forms of social life, which have endured through so many social upheavals.'[20] The national past was not only real, but safe and reassuring. It is the same in Britain – the once reassuring 'stately home' is now being slowly eased out (but is still a 'big day out "experience"') by the equally reassuring vernacular, as shown in the slowly changing policies of the National Trust, itself founded in 1895. Almost a century later, in the 1980s, books began to be published in the UK with titles like *The Heritage Industry* and *On Living in an Old Country*. Heritage was a matter of debate, high or low, good or bad, as it was in France, which celebrated the bicentenary of the Revolution in 1989.[21]

It was then that the peasant memoir began, for a while, to sell in France in vast numbers. What fed the sense of an ending in France was complex: ranging from 'post-colonial nostalgia' for a France then vacating empire, to nostalgia for the vanishing condition, the latter represented in the fantasies of second-home owners, for whom the newly acquired peasant house was the material expression of the peasant soul. The former peasant house gave the urban bourgeois unmediated access to what in Britain came to be known as 'the good life', one lived like the peasants of yore, precisely those who had flocked to the cities in the 1950s and 60s to get away from the good life, and so left the empty houses behind them that created a bonanza for the property market. France was a 'world leader' in second-home ownership during the 1970s, the British flocking into the same property market thereafter, and with the same delusions as their French cousins.[22] The Briton's *gite* in the Dordogne became one symbol of this, 'Chiantishire' another. One could be a bourgeois, a chic one, and a peasant, all at the same time.

It was at this point that Bourdieu's scorn was directed to the peasant 'reserves' where the last of the peasants would be free 'to dance and sing their *bourrées* and gavottes' for the greater satisfaction of the urban tourists, 'so long as their existence is economically and symbolically profitable'. Profitability was, in the event, to be great.[23]

*

Anna Engelking makes the mordant observation that there is no monument to her people in Minsk, the capital of Belarus. No monument to suffering and endurance, that is. Instead, there are museums, two in particular that would naturally be expected to relate to the *kolkhozniks*, the Podlaskie Museum of Folk Culture in Białystok in eastern Poland, which concerns western Polesie, and just outside Minsk in Belarus there is the State Museum of Folk Architecture and Rural Lifestyle. Among the topics assiduously covered in Białystok and Minsk are: food and cooking; dress or what is called 'costume', rather than the real clothes peasants wore; landscape and ecology; and music, where 'folk bands' will sometimes play. You try the food, to eat or to cook, listen to the music, perhaps try on the costumes. You try your hand at building a wall, or a stockade, heedful of nature in doing so. You are taking part in real things, doing real things, experiencing them. (This is worldwide, and the similarity between examples is striking: between the US slave plantation museum and these examples, for instance, dishonour done to the slave and the serf alike.)

Sometimes, where there are any left, peasants will themselves be on hand, perhaps in these craft sessions. It is a welcome source of income for them in the East, and people are proud of their pasts being on show. Just like the people in Basilicata they 'precariously walk a line between the celebration of rurality and becoming a defunctionalized spectacle'.

I look at the websites of these museums and those of western as well as central and eastern Europe. Museums these days exist almost as much online as in reality, insofar as we are now able to tell the difference. In the museums themselves, you can bodily walk around while simultaneously consulting the virtual-reality version of the place you are walking in, and there are these days umpteen audiovisual displays within the 'walked' museum. It becomes difficult to know quite where to locate a museum in time and space. In one sense museums manifest themselves more in time than in space, as they can be accessed at any time from any place. Place again seems to retreat in importance, and the virtual replaces immediate reality.

This is ironic when it comes to peasant culture, one grounded so profoundly in the local and in concrete things.

Physically and emotionally near to my own experience there is the Connemara Heritage and History Centre outside Clifden in Galway, only established in the late 1980s. There one may try one's hand at turf cutting or visit Dan O'Hara's Cottage, which is in remarkably good repair given its original construction in pre-famine days. On the park's website, a man sits at the door of old Dan's place, welcoming the visitor, pint of stout in hand, cloth cap on. Also founded around this time, in my mother's county of Wexford, is the Johnstown Castle Irish Agricultural Museum, run now by the Irish Heritage Trust, itself founded in 2006, a latecomer to the heritage stakes. This offers a 'new and exciting visitor experience to benefit the wider community sustainably over the long term'. There are now, it is said, '19 different exhibitions – everything from tractors to country kitchens'. It is very heavy on the machines, for there is nothing like an old tractor to draw the crowds. The rural worker is as usual barely to the fore, mechanical parts and kitchen drawers having to speak for them.

When it comes to remembering peasants, institutionalized memory appropriately takes the form of the peasant house itself, and the other buildings that made up peasant villages. But something decidedly strange is going on in such places. The former peasant house is taken apart, transported and then reassembled in the form of villages of houses such as those in the Minsk State Museum of Folk Architecture and Rural Lifestyle. (In this version of the past, peasants have a 'lifestyle'.) Entire village settlements are taken and set down elsewhere, intact. If the originals cannot be installed, then painstaking reconstructions were, and are, made.

In these museums everything is present and correct, and this includes the stuffed models of peasants standing to attention that sometimes are on show, though this practice is now thankfully falling out of fashion. The houses are empty, as are the streets, except for us, the visitors. We receive the echo of the past that is summoned up by these now empty houses and streets, this strange silence in which we hope that the objects that surround us may somehow be made to speak. The echo we hear, however – unless we listen hard for the voices of objects – only seems to reinforce the silence. We wander as strangers into the empty streets and pristine houses.

It is a premise of the existence of the museum in these times that it be an institution of leisure. Museums are places that to thrive must be visited as often as possible, and the nationals of the country in question or the international travellers making these visits are very often tourists. Tourism is thus another distinguishing mark of museums, as well as leisure. They are part of what is now called the experience economy, which is the sale of the experience itself as a commodity. The more memorable the experience, the better the sales. The experience that is given in museums is for the visitor something that takes place in the immediate time of the visit and so is by its nature an immediate, living one, and this word 'living' is often used (as in 'living history' museum: the idea is that history lives when one's own experience is brought to it: then the past itself comes alive in the visitor's immediate experience and so 'lives').

The past lives, but solely through the visitor's life, by engaging their personal and immediate experience, so that what takes place in the present is more about the visitor's present than, in this case, the peasant's past. The event of the visit, in order to be successful, is, as it were, loaded down with the present, the immediate, the memorable: it is full of bodily stimuli and sensations.[24] It must by definition be about living now, much more than it is about those who lived then. Something to remember, in fact, an experience to be taken away as memorable and so worth repeating. The visitor to the museum does not in general want to see too much reality – starvation, death, exploitation – and least of all to 'experience' these things. All is clean, scrubbed, sanitized. In being more about us who live now, than those who lived then, the museum experience forecloses the sense that those in the past are different from us, not the same. The otherness of the past is lost sight of. Paradoxically, it is by seeking existences that are other than our own that we are most connected to the past.

I write so far about what I call the 'experience' museum. Museums have been with us now for several centuries. The great public museums came into their own in the nineteenth century. On the other hand, the museum explosion after the 1970s has been astonishing. Continuity and rapid change mean that museums are in practice mixtures of different curatorial traditions. In fact, museums are themselves historical artefacts, mixtures of institutional traditions reflecting different eras of collection, which in the present are all concentrated in the one place. They are places of fragments, contradictions, something unfinished and in motion that represents one view of how the past might be represented to another. The visitor is caught in the middle of these contradictions.

The regime of what we might call the didactic museum (as opposed to the new museum of experience) is marked by spectatorship, looking upon the object with what authority decrees is quiet, ordered and deferential contemplation (of things in glass cases with labels). One was there to learn, or rather, by hook or by crook, to be taught. Either take it or leave it, not to come and experience it. Both types are related to nation-building.

The only major national museum dedicated exclusively to peasants, at least in name, is the National Museum of the Romanian Peasant (Muzeul Național al Țăranului Român) in Bucharest.[25] Conceived in a country that was among the most peasant ones in Europe, it was dedicated to identifying the nation with the peasant, in a way, more directly than elsewhere in the continent. The history of the building itself is a lesson in Romanian, and eastern European, history: it was once a museum of the Communist Party, at other times a shrine to Ceaușescu himself, Ceaușescu the peasant, the son of a farmer with a minuscule holding of 3 hectares. (Nikita Khrushchev, the Russian leader, was also the son of poor peasants, born not far from the present Ukrainian border.)

The Bucharest museum is a 'national' one and the Belarus museum is a 'state museum'. As for the Białystok one, the Polish Ministry of

Culture and Heritage is in a state of constant war over attempts to deviate from the right nationalist line in all areas of culture, including museums. The grand panjandrum of remembrance is the Institute of National Remembrance, set up by the Polish Parliament in 2018, a sort of Ministry of Truth. Among the 'main tasks' of the Belarus Ministry of Culture is to 'pursue a state policy in the sphere of culture and to implement government control in this sphere; and to determine an overall strategy for the development of the sphere of culture'.[26]

As for the rest of Europe, things are not so directly nationalist, but essentially the same, which is to say the big collections are national, and the nation is the hidden script. This has been so from the birth of the museum long before the present day, but almost everywhere in the last half century or so, state bodies, 'non-governmental' and otherwise, have greatly multiplied and come to institutionalize the past as never before. This institutionalization of heritage still has strong national credentials.

However, the past is more than just a mirror of ourselves, and to know the past we need more than mirrors. Museums and curators have to accommodate to the 'heritage' tide, but fighting back the pressures to serve the community and get an audience is difficult. Curators, some of them, are well aware of the direction of change towards experience. At other times there is imaginative engagement with the new face of museums (the creativity of the Bucharest museum is striking). It is impossible not to be struck by the diligence and devotion of those who are responsible for ethno-museums, and museums almost everywhere. Such places are great centres of collection, and of learning, and this aspect continues in parallel with their public function, despite commercial and political pressures.

As for the writing of history itself, twenty years ago one of the leading American historians in this area, Lynn Hunt, acknowledged how history had itself come to adopt the mantle of presentism.[27] History had become, in her terms, an instrument to deal and come to terms with the present, a place where society's conflicts were worked out, where we recognize our present selves more clearly.

The recognition that those in the past were not simply versions of us was traditionally secured by the linear notion of time, the kind of time that made history possible, narrative time in which the assignation of causes and effects could be made. Time itself is seen as an irresistible agent of change, and nothing can escape its own transformation. Social reality is a historical stream where no two instances are comparable or reversible. Because of this, anachronism is discovered; things can be 'out of time'. Otherness and difference are rendered possible, and so we are helped to avoid sameness. On the other hand, in the experience museum, things are real now, simply because they were once 'experienced' then, a nice piece of temporal legerdemain which made history disappear in the process. One empathizes with one's temporal doppelgänger.

What does it mean to historicize when time's arrow is broken? When it is rightly broken, that is, for the idea of time's arrow is only one among many ways of understanding time, if a vastly productive and necessary one when it comes to academic history. The question becomes, then, that of how to hold on to otherness in the new temporal dispensation. To do this, more realistic and open-minded notions of time than solely linear time are needed.[28] How to empirically address these ideas about and experiences of time?

The three times of Saint Augustine in his *Confessions* come to mind:

> Perhaps it might be said rightly that there are three times: a time present of things past; a time present of things present; and a time present of things future. For these three do coexist somehow in the soul, for otherwise I could not see them. The time present of things past is memory; the time present of things present is direct experience; the time present of things future is expectation.[29]

Henri Bergson, 1,500 years after Augustine, saw the idea of time as *flow*, where the experience of music is invoked: we don't listen to a succession of notes, just as time is not a succession of singular instants, but to a whole ensemble of notes. The notes 'melt' into one another, the flow is not simply additive. (Bergson, the great admirer of Proust.) To put it more analytically, past and present are not things of separate being, but together collectively constitute a single field, sometimes of harmony, at others tension.

The image of time as a gathering is pregnant too, a constant process of regathering, in fact, rather like the harvest of the peasant in the cycle of nature. These views of time, if not circular like peasant time, seem nonetheless to have a kinship with it.[30] The present is put in the foreground, for there we experience time directly, but the past endures, accumulating in the present, where it becomes *now*. Far from never putting your foot in the same river twice, it is always the same river you put your foot in. Or in another articulation, 'the present is not actually what is happening right now, but rather the accumulation of all past times.' In other words, the 'past as it was is at all times the outcome of the gathering of previous pasts'. These and the following are the words of the archaeologist Laurent Olivier: 'If the past returns, it is because it has never really left; it was hidden motionless in the folds of the present, forgotten but in fact ready to spring forth.'[31] Walter Benjamin says something similar, namely, that history should not be told like the rosary is said, one bead at a time. Instead all time awaits its telling. It is ready to spring forth, but you have to go to meet it, to gather it in, like the peasant who gathers in the harvest. Otherwise it will be motionless and forgotten, the harvest lost.

A figure very different to Walter Benjamin, T. S. Eliot, put similar thoughts into different words, in the 'Little Gidding' section of the *Four Quartets* of 1943:

> See, they depart, and we go with them.
> We are born with the dead:
> See, they return, and bring us with them.
> The moment of the rose and the moment of the yew-tree
> Are of equal duration. A people without history
> Is not redeemed from time, for history is a pattern
> Of timeless moments.[32]

These thoughts and words help me ponder further on the things I have seen in museums, including the strange, empty streets of the open-air *skansens*, places in which I attempt to receive the echoes of pasts, the pasts that emanate from the objects that surround me. The echoes that reproduce the voice of objects.

The Voice of Objects

Traditionally museums are places where objects are kept, which is at once their limitation and their power. Objects are mute, yet they seem to radiate meaning. When it comes to objects, which are material things, the idea of accumulated time seems especially pertinent. Time accretes around material things, they are physically, literally, shaped by time, so that time is to all intents and purposes contained in them. The Rock of Ages is more than the title of a hymn. Time is present physically in the various sedimentary layers of the planet (sedimentation is another philosophical metaphor for time). Photographs themselves are, or at least were, objects too, and there is a kinship between them and what we usually take as objects, namely three-dimensional things. This is the kinship found in the poignant moments of realization when we apprehend the marriage of the contingencies of now and then, present and past. This marriage explains something of the magic and the mystery of objects, and with it the magic and mystery of time.

It is April 2022, Covid has abated, and I go in search of the museum object. I am in the Museum of English Rural Life in the town of Reading in the South of England.[33] 'Rural Life', it should be said, not folk, peasant or agricultural worker, so that the remit is wide. This has the effect of squeezing the human into the corner somewhat, surrounded by the history of all aspects of the rural; for instance, agricultural technology. Unlike with the Scots, Welsh and Irish, there is no national English museum of rural life and this modest version of the museum must suffice. The English are more interested in nature and the landscape than in those who peopled the landscape.[34] The museum's public is chiefly interested in four things, my enquiries tell me: transport, machines, animals and the 'personal' – the human stories behind the objects.

Objects: a deliberately large collection of these is presented to the visitors on entry, designed to appeal to as many tastes as possible. The sheer plenitude of objects as one walks through is overwhelming, even in a small museum, and the eye, and with it the mind, becomes clouded, and so, undiscerning. The attempt at comprehension falters, and in the end I give up. The will to display defeats itself, and one ends up seeing only one's own image in the glass cases rather than the past made manifest. The eyes grow weary, the legs too, the back also, from bending to read the many descriptive notices. The 'agricultural' sounds playing in the background do not improve the experience for me.

And then suddenly in the museum I turn a corner and see an item that fixes my attention powerfully. This is because there is something about it that does not seem to fit in, and more particularly fit in to the story which gives it its prescribed meaning. This story is that of the display theme it is set within, which is the advance of rural medicine and health, one of those seemingly self-evident stories, progress, by means of which we tell ourselves who we are. The object is unexpected, and seems to ask us questions. It is a simple, cheap mattress, catalogued as: MERL 61/242. This is the museum catalogue photo of it.

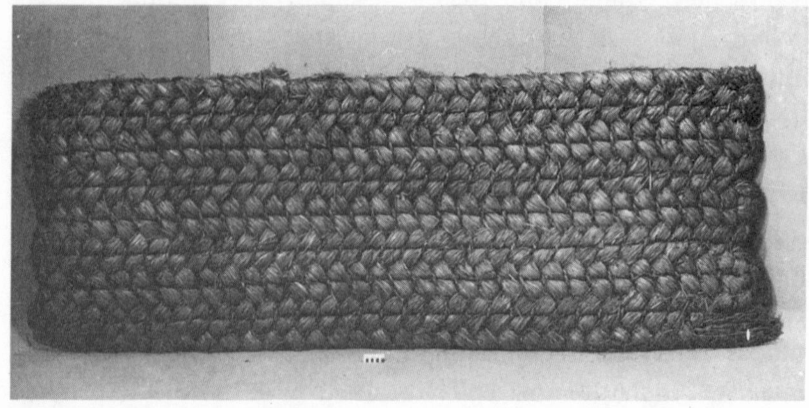

The mattress, for so it is called, is actually made of woven carex (sedge), rather than from wheat or barley straw. In the coils of the object time is itself coiled, ready to spring. It was found walled up in a house in Titchfield, Hampshire, and may date from the seventeenth century or earlier. Such mattresses were used either for laying out the dead before they were placed in the coffin, or for the use of a woman in childbirth, and after use would probably have been burned, so this mattress may not have ever been used for either purpose. Or else it was so used and has survived. Of course, it fits into the museum's story, that of progress from primitivism to the NHS.

But it also does not fit in either: it has too many potential meanings to be contained, for the object concerns the nature of life and death, both linked together in a sort of circle. It is also a mystery because this sort of thing was not supposed to survive, but this one did. It was designed to be destroyed, yet exists. 'The past speaks directly only in things that have not been handed down,' writes Walter Benjamin, *not* been handed down, so that the manifold silences of the past are opened up to our hearing by what is not bequeathed, the chance object, the detritus of the past included, like this mattress of the born and the dying.

The mattress eludes storying, eludes firm meanings, eludes our understandings but suggests much. Precisely because it seems to have meant so little in its time.[35] It sits in its own glass case, and I am again struck by the marked oddness of objects in museums, which are places radically set aside from the everyday world. This oddness consists of their being taken out of everyday use, and, this being so, they will and must never be used again. It is decidedly strange to think of a museum object being returned to circulation, a spade to dig a trench, say. The object is relocated somewhere else, and so taken out of real time into museum time, where it sits, potentially, to the end of days. It enters museum space too, alone in its purpose-built wood-and-glass case, so that it is chaste where once it might have been smeared with the bodily fluids of the dying and the newly born. You, the visitor, may not touch or smell it. It is precisely not what it was originally, but has been sacralized as a token of time. It is sacred and not mundane. You should not mess with it, for it has entered a collection. The collection is made up of items which are catalogued in long and elaborate forms, and these add to the otherness of the museum object and so its sacrality.

It is late spring verging on early summer and I visit the National Museum of Ireland's Museum of Irish Country Life, in Turlough Park, just outside Castlebar in Mayo, far from large centres of population. It is fitting that the museum is located in deep rural Ireland, in my own Mayo. But this means that it is not highly visited, with about 100,000 visitors a year (the National Gallery of Ireland in Dublin has about 800,000 visitors annually, the Natural History Museum in London over five million). I feel contrary things: good that it is here, but conscious that, because what it depicts is 'low' culture, then putting it out here in the sticks is thought a good idea, out among the culchies of whom it is all about. The lateness of the museum's founding is striking – it was only established in 2001 – so that compared to other European states this is a very poor showing. What this showing, or failure to show, indicates is the simple fact that the Irish authorities for well more than half a century looked back on their own past and saw nothing much worth preserving or exhibiting (except folklore).

At the museum I get into a discussion about how objects are valued by older people, those who have probably known want in their lives. Those, like myself, who grew up in post-war austerity Britain have these feelings about objects too. Things should not be thrown out without serious reflection, as you never knew when they would be useful, as times might turn to the bad again. This is make-do and mend, and has in many cultures in Europe been identified as characteristic of peasants, the arch-survivors who must always look to a potentially hazardous future to survive in the present. In the past, an object remained with people for a long time, and associations were built up around it, so that in a sense we have a different universe of meaning altogether when we consider this old connection to the object world. Most museums do not suggest this old human intimacy with the object, nor the extraordinary nature of peasant conceptions of objecthood, a world where a word might be a thing.

I have visited the museum several times over a long period of years, and when I visit my heart sinks, and I feel that for all the devotion of the curators and their best endeavours somehow it is all inadequate to what really went on in peasant life in the past. Perhaps museums must fail anyway, fail to convey the blistered lips, the chapped hands, the bitten fingernails, the worn body, the sufferings of 'The poor peasant talking to himself at a stable door', of whom Patrick Kavanagh writes in his poem 'The Great Hunger', writing indeed of himself, the Devil in his own pocket:

> Nobody will ever know how much tortured poetry the pulled
> Weeds on the ridge wrote
> Before they withered in the July sun.[36]

The visitor at Turlough Park encounters instead the old regime of the white plaster model of the human being, and before me are four members of a seemingly typical Aran Islands family, each togged out in costume (for so one is forced to conceive of the clothes). I wonder why we must start with the Aran Islands, the Bethlehem of the faux-spiritualized Irish peasant, when near the entrance, in a sobering display of photographs, we have just been warned against romancing the rural (the display includes the photograph of the impoverished young woman sitting by the dying fire, taken on Gorumna Island, in Connemara, which appears in Chapter 4).

The caption to the plaster islanders says the dress is not original, as the collectors of the 1930s aimed to show the skill of the makers, and not to bring out a personal and human story. I find myself in sympathy with the 1930s. This old way seems rather similar to the Japanese way of understanding the past, in fact, heritage lying in the process, not the origin. Where non-linear notions of time are still strong, as in Japan, the past is realized in terms of actualization, the actualization of the past in the present, like the temple made of wood that is painstakingly and expensively taken apart and then rebuilt every twenty years in the same form each time. Truth lies in the remaking, the bringing into actuality in a time that is not linear nor gone and out of mind. Therefore, objects are not precious, and do not need to be protected from the depredations of time.[37] Peasants share in this older sense of time.

In late June 2022, I manage at last to get to the Kraków Ethnographic Museum. The museum was founded in 1911, and converted into a public, state-owned institution in 1945. Since 1948 it has been housed in the former town hall of Kazimierz, in the heart of Kraków's historically Jewish quarter. The Kraków collection, the oldest and finest in Poland, survived the destruction wreaked by the Second World War, as did the city itself. There is a vast number of objects housed here, many more than in the Irish and English museums, almost three times more than the national Irish one. The new regime of the museum stretches back some fifteen years and aims to be non-elitist, democratic and 'post-scientific', which is to say, not didactic. The National Ethnographic Museum in Warsaw actually designs 'reflexivity' in, with a walk-in display of the museum archives called 'The Order of Things'. The emphasis in Kraków, as in Warsaw, is on what is called 'aesthetic experience', their website describing one gallery as a colourful 'total environment'.[38]

This is 'not the first-choice museum in Kraków', I am told by a curator. Ethnographic and rural-life museums everywhere are small beer. The National Museum in Warsaw has over half a million visitors annually, a figure itself dwarfed by the likes of the Louvre and the great London museums. The Auschwitz museum outside Kraków had 2.3 million visitors in 2019.

I enter the exhibitions and at first am confronted by a long gallery of what I can only call stuffed peasants. There they stand, costumed and motionless now for decades, in their long glass case, each with an empty face, each one labelled at their feet below.

Another corner is turned and one may enter specially constructed versions of peasant houses built into the museum after the Second World War. Each is totally authentic. One enters, it is dark, there is little signage. The houses are the equivalent of an open-air museum indoors, which increases the sense of unreality. It is difficult to dwell with the dead here.

But then I am told the story of how these houses were constructed after the devastation of the war, how they brought pride to peasants who visited them from an exhausted countryside, and how memories of the immediate aftermath of serfdom are recorded in the visitors' book. Time banks up on itself to overwhelming effect when one knows the story, and the old museum order is redeemed by the simple understanding that this was all new once.

The Warsaw ethnographic museum features the post-1945 history of Cepelia, the state-run organization that after the war fostered 'peasant art', so attempting to include the contemporary peasant as part of the political imaginary of the new Communist state (Cepelia once had a shop on Madison Avenue in New York City). That attempt came to naught in the end, but there is, it seems, a new taste for folk art, much of it ironically indebted to the work of the Communist state apparatus of yore.[39]

I go into the next room, and suddenly it is possible once again to dwell for a time with the dead. The old museum (not short of mysteries itself) gives way to the new, and the result is remarkable as I turn into two small rooms with only forty objects between them. Less is more. Objects here are made to speak by being connected to stories, but these objects carry not heartwarming human stories, but remind one of the absence of a person. This is because the objects, at least some of them, are stray, lost objects, which one would not expect to find in a museum. They are what has not been handed down, rather like the rush mattress in Reading, here a thimble, there a worn tin box, a roughly marked ceramic tile, and this, a prayer book made by a peasant who was almost certainly illiterate. The maker is known, a peasant called Jan Żądło, who lived between 1896 and 1982. He was born in the *shtetl* village of Spytkowice, 20 miles west of Kraków.

The prayer book absorbs me greatly. It reminds me of my mother's missal, another sacred object, a book she could read, but one where the book as object was as important as the words. Jan Żądło's book is of no artistic merit, being composed of numerous crudely drawn and coloured depictions of the Passion of Christ. On the opened pages, mysterious marks are made, one would guess as exercises in writing, although they bear limited relation to real letters, for the man who made it was illiterate. It would seem that to make it a proper holy book, writing had to be included. For, as we know, for Polish peasants, words were things. The sacrality of the object is precisely that of the peasant cosmologies we have already seen at work, where words are magical. The opened book on display opens this magic to us.

Of course, being in a museum the object is hallowed in another sense too, and another magic is at work, museum sorcery, that which translates the ordinary into what is curated, selected as being of significance. That which is indeed of the Elect, of what is to be saved. I have been sent photographs of the book: in these it is held almost reverently in the gloved hands of a curator, and one could be forgiven for thinking that the images are reminiscent of a priest holding up the Host at Mass.

The sight of the book when I came upon it propelled me into the flow of time, for in it time seems to be accumulated and this accumulation is as if released into the present by the book itself, by its not fitting in, by the questioning oddity of the marks themselves, more striking and mysterious as they are than the many illustrations. Perhaps, like with the humble mattress, a sudden epiphany is enabled, a moment that announces the essential nature of something; in this instance, the vanished cosmogony of peasants, suddenly, in the fleeting present, emerging into life again. Just like the photograph, objects can be epiphanic.

Then, when more information is disclosed about the object, other possible pasts spring forth. The curator Karolina Pachla-

Wojciechowska writes online that the author of the prayer book was deaf and mute: 'The presentation adorning the last page in the prayer book . . . shows the figure of a man playing a pipe, standing in a meadow where a flower and a tree are still blooming. If it is a self-portrait, it is peculiar, because it either presents the artist's dream of himself as a hearing person or denies that he was deaf. If we only knew more about their author.'[40]

There is also a juniper-root basket in the same small gallery, a mundane enough object, this one from the late nineteenth century. Again, it is words that release the past in the object, but the words have power only because the material object itself carries time within it. The several manifold times coiled in the basket are released only in part, because in museums one must not touch the exhibits. Some of these older juniper baskets, like this one, are so finely and tightly woven that they can hold water, just as this one holds the past. Across peasant Europe juniper was regarded as a protection against evil as well as against sickness.

The juniper basket evokes absence, the absence of the Lemko ethnic-minority population of southern Poland, a real historical absence. The object was donated to the museum in 1970 by the formerly Lemko village of Wisłoczek. The Lemkos there had been taken to Ukraine by the Soviet-installed Polish army in April 1946 and abandoned. Local Ukrainians were deported with them. Other local Lemkos and ethnic-minority Boyko people were forcibly taken westwards to the so-called Recovered Territories in the West, where Poles displaced Germans, just as Poles had displaced minorities in the East. Ethnic cleansing. Absence after absence.

'Operation Vistula' they called what happened in Wisłoczek and places like it, payback time for the ultra-nationalist Ukrainian slaughter of ethnic Poles in 1943–5, the 'Volyn tragedy' as it is known. In Volhynia and eastern Galicia thousands of Polish peasants were slaughtered, women and children in the main, perhaps as many as 100,000 in some estimates. The southern Polish village of Wisłoczek was burned down after the deportations, and largely abandoned. However, a state farm was set up there in the 1950s, which then went bust, everyone leaving once again. In 1969 members of a Pentecostal movement from Teschen Silesia settled there. The basket was donated by these villagers.

One of these hidden histories that wait in the Kraków Ethnographic Museum is that of the Jews, some of whom had hidden in the building when the Nazis rounded up the Jews in Kazimierz (by then many Jews had already been moved over the Vistula to the suburb of Podgórze, on the outskirts of which a transit camp was set up). The history of the museum is itself part of the history of a Polish nation that is Catholic and Slavic. There is little evidence in the exhibitions that Jews were part of that history. Liberal Poland ponders how to include Jews as part of 'Polish history': are they to be, as one source puts it, similarly different, or differently different, which is to say, treated like other national minorities under the banner of a renewed and liberal national-ethnographic charter, or is their historical fate such a radical one as to need separate treatment?[41] The latter often suits Jewish sensibilities more, recognition of unique status as this is, which of course also suits many nationalist Poles, who can then safely present the idea of the homogeneously ethnic Polish nation, unworried by difference. Prior to the new regime of 2011, the Kraków museum's curatorial approach was to frame Jews in terms of their role in peasant cosmologies, with Jewish experience and conflict edited out. The texts used for exhibits were also almost exclusively in Polish, and their content implied an audience that was Catholic, and presumed to be uncritical of the materials on display.

The walls of the museum I am in are covered with photographs of objects but also of peasant men, women and children. These are but the visible part of the enormous photographic collections that this museum and similar institutions hold. Are photographs objects? Photographs are apprehended in one visual act, absorbing image and object together, yet we forget the object part of them. We forget this even more these days, because now the image is digitalized and so rendered two-dimensional. Photographs have weight and depth and are displayed in various ways that accentuate these characteristics, in photo albums, say, with which their meaning and physicality are enmixed.

The image of Michał Rauszer's family portrait in Chapter 5, on page 122, shows this, the worn and frayed edges of the photo apparent. Such things are fingered by use, their backs written on, their corners torn. They in turn absorb the bodies of those who handled them, the smell of flesh, the finger's print. Being themselves used, like all objects, they shape what we do in the world in ways that would not have occurred if they did not exist. Objects are enmeshed in human action and not merely passive entities. They have a sort of agency in the world.[42]

Photographs

In what does the magical quality of the photo so often remarked upon reside? The quality of evanescent magic in photographs is paradoxically conveyed by the solidity of the photo as an object: the photograph shows what was real then, for, at that precise moment, the light fell that way, and imprinted itself on the substance which received it. Light was captured in its precise reality and transmitted potentially for all time in the mechanical contraption of the camera. What is timeful becomes timeless, but only by virtue of its being one precise moment in time that has been captured. The photo thus survives as an object carrying the time of then, of its taking, into the time of its being seen. Timelessness is made up of the juxtaposition of precise moments of time, the now of then meeting the now of now. We search photos for this spark of mutual contingency. Markéta Luskačová found this spark of contingency between herself and the peasants hitherto unfamiliar to her in Šumiac and Levoča; Josef Koudelka on the top of Croagh Patrick.

Susan Sontag writes that 'Photography is an elegiac art, a twilight art' – 'Most subjects photographed are, just by the virtue of being photographed, touched with pathos . . . To take a photograph is to participate in another person's (or thing's) mortality, vulnerability, mutability.'[43] The mutability which photographs reveal reminds us of our human fragility, of the relentless passing of time. Sontag writes further that the character of a mystery issues from each moment the photograph carries. She is thinking of how photographs produce their own kind of truth, truth which is different from the truth of history. Both truths are necessary. She reveals how the truth of photography is made up, for, clearly, it does not lie in the simple fact that the photo was taken, the simple idea that the camera cannot lie.

Photographs are a token of absence as well as presence, suggesting in this first guise a sense of the unattainable and the mysterious. The ultimate wisdom of the photographic image is to say, '[T]here it is, a surface, now think – or rather feel it, intuit it – what is beyond it. What the reality must be like if it looks this way.'[44] This accounts for our sense that some photographs are timeless, or outside of time, as with Josef Koudelka's work. Outside of time because time itself becomes the surface we are invited to feel, to intuit, the veil that might be parted. Paul Valéry's observation again comes to mind, '[P]hotography encourages us to stop trying to describe what can clearly describe itself.'[45]

Writing of the meaning of photography in the peasant world of Béarn, Pierre Bourdieu recognized that the photograph is for peasants something different from such conceptions, being a functional thing, appropriate to the great events of family and collective life, such as weddings. It affirms the unity, standing and boundaries of the groups involved. Lying outside everyday routine, photographs solemnize the image of itself that the group wishes to present. They are, in a wonderful sociological term he uses, sociograms, maps of the social links that bind. Or, better put, perhaps, links that are made to bind by the photograph itself – for photographs in this sense materialize the invisible. In this world, photos are not appreciated for themselves, and their aesthetic qualities (or at least what we would regard as aesthetic) are insignificant.[46]

In *Another Way of Telling*, by John Berger and Jean Mohr, we can see better how this is so. An old Savoyard hill farmer called Marcel, who lives much of the summer alone on the high pastures, does not want to be photographed in his work clothes, or at work. He combs his hair, puts on a clean shirt, and says with relief after the photo is taken, 'And now my great-grandchildren will know what sort of man I was.' Another man, a forest worker, wants to be photographed at work, but only the images that convey, not just any moment of work, but rather the climactic moment when the tree he fells comes crashing down and falls exactly where he wants. 'That's the photo I've dreamt off since I began cutting down trees,' he says.[47]

The ethnographic image is different again, but no less a token of absence than the rush mattress, the prayer book and the other objects I have dwelt on. Ethnographic images, at least the older ones, tended to identify 'types', types by locality, region, nation; by face ('physiognomy', as it was called, by August Sander, among others), by costume, by house construction and condition, typical peasants usually being posed at the door of their typical house. These types were then classified. Types and classes made up the science of the composition of nations, ethnicities, empires, of 'society' itself. And of race.

Michał Greim lived between 1828 and 1911. He was part of the early generation of artisan photographers who saw a chance for a career in running a photography shop for the public.[48] He became a printer in Warsaw, then worked as a typesetter in Lublin, eventually becoming manager of the Government Printing House in Kamieniec Podolski, which was in the far east of then Russian Poland, and is now the part of Ukraine neighbouring Moldova. He quit this job, possibly as a result of intensifying repression of Poles in the Russian Partition, then decided to set up independently, specializing in taking photographs of 'folk types' of Podolia and Bessarabia, in images of Jews (for *goyim* tastes) and also images of various craft trades and tradesmen. The photos are mostly posed in a studio.

What is unusual about Greim is that he seems to have concentrated not on the better-off but on rural people and the poor, and on Jews. What was a living (which must have been a precarious one) became a scientific interest too: he became a corresponding member of the Anthropological Committee of the Polish Academy of Arts and Sciences, regularly sending photographs to that body for almost three decades after 1875. It follows that his are among the very earliest photographic images of peasants. This is one example below, catalogued thus: 'Inv. no. III / 14342 / F sygn m III / 10621: Peasant 100 years old and more, Pudłowiec, Kamieniec county, 1870s–1880s, albumen print. Photograph by Michał Greim'.

The man is posed and presented as a type, but there he sits resolute in his distant, disengaged stare, his huge fists clenched. His mortality is revealed. The man, if resolute, does not seem at home.

He is present, but seems somehow to absent himself as well, for in these early days of photography perhaps he feels that this is not the way a peasant should be seen. The absence of colour enhances the effect of absence, so too in all the photos I present (this is the only one that has a sort of colour, the albumen tint often seen in early photography). John Berger writes that the painting invites what isn't there to become present. Visual art is a chase after the invisible. A black-and-white photograph shares in this chase because it 'reminds you of what can't be seen, of what's missing; never for one moment do they pretend to be complete, whereas colour photos do'.[49]

The following four photographs are different, though the intention with which the images were made is still ethnographic. They are from a large scrapbook of photos and postcards covering the county of Sieradz, just to the south-east of Łódź. Like the Greim portrait, I came upon the originals of these photographs in the Kraków museum by chance. The album was in all probability compiled by Stanisław Graeve, a large local landowner, and, like Greim, an enthusiastic amateur ethnographer.[50] The album covers the first decade of the twentieth century. In it peasants seem to break cover from their typification, and the object asserts itself as subject.

In the following two images, of a young woman and man who were a peasant couple from the village of Mnichów, the 'typicality' of their dress is being brought out, but with it comes the humanity of the two, her beauty and his beauty, one the equal of the other. (They pose together in another photo at the door of their house and are a married couple, it would seem.) The young woman looks out with complete confidence and pride. I do not know if the striking coils that make up her elaborate neckwear are made of coral. If not (some are very large) perhaps they are made as copies of coral. Peasants greatly prized coral, as did all classes, and such objects were handed down from generation to generation, one row being added to another, if possible, as here perhaps. Coral was believed to bring good health, and so good fortune.

Alongside, the man in the splendour of his swagger and self-confidence serves to belie so many thoughts about peasants as abject, or as stuffed costume dummies. He is alive in his body and in the pride with which he wears his splendid clothes. He is 'the dashing young blade', 'the roving young blade', of a thousand traditional songs across Europe. Nonetheless, the album description is 'Type, Mnichów, poviat [county] Sieradz'.

The richness of the dress in the photos is striking. This is regional dress, not national costume, and what the couple are wearing is the same as the other villagers wear. It is their best, deliberately far from their workday clothes, and an assertion of pride. Look at the cut of me, he seems to be saying, Jack the Lad. It is likely they were paid to pose, so they were keen to put on the full show. There is a debt to the military in the style, especially his greatcoat, and there is clearly a fair amount of borrowing going on as regards the style in general. Men such as he might have served in the army and the peasants' idea of grandeur is the soldierly style, including the long leather military boots.

This is another image from the album, of an old man from the same village known as 'Old Ciapy', which might be a surname or a nickname. Old Ciapy looks not towards but away from the camera. The child looks directly at it. He is the old blade, not the young one. The two figures sit on the stairs at the front of what I take to be his house, which is clearly a stout and substantial one. All the photos are so posed, with wood and thatch behind, as if to say, This is my place, my house. This is so in the last image too.

In the last one from the album, the Young Turks of the village are taking their ease, as confident as the man in the second of the four photos. The buttoned tunics, the fur collars, seem to say, We are as good as the landlord. Icicles hang from the unkempt thatch. It is winter and as in all such villages the house and its surrounds are a little drab, and in want of attention. The hats they wear are, again, military-looking, typical across the country as a whole. Such hats, the famous *Maciejówka*, became a symbol of the Polish peasant, and then of workers as well, even though the style was borrowed from Germany originally. Eventually it was taken up as a symbol of the Polish people by Piłsudski's national movement. Times were changing. Old Ciapy's day was almost done.

As for Baron Stanisław Graeve, his grandfather was a Prussian army officer who had fought alongside the Napoleonic armies. This grandfather married a Pole and considered himself Polish. Land came into the family and Stanisław's father bought the Biskupice estate in Sieradz in 1882, one comprising many peasant farms. It was here Stanisław Graeve took up residence as a manor lord, and here his extensive ethnographic enthusiasms were assiduously prosecuted, so much so that he may have paid with his life for them. His most serious work was his co-authored *Guide to the Kalisz Governorate*, published in Vienna in 1912. This included a level of cartographic detail which is said to have caught the attention of the Tsarist authorities. It seems that Graeve shot himself after learning

that he was accused of espionage for Austria. The shot was fired on the terrace of his neo-Renaissance mansion on a freezing November day in 1912.[51]

On the Saturday morning after I had looked at Baron Graeve's album, I left the Ethnographic Museum in Kraków at noon. Outside in the grand Kazimierz Square in which the former town hall is located a wall thermometer was reading 35 degrees centigrade. The week ahead was due to be hotter still. The planet was frying. Later that day I left for the East, for the extreme south-east corner of Poland, travelling into old Galicia.

10.

Time Accumulates

East

You travel east from Kraków and not so far away, only 160 miles, is the Ukrainian border, with Belarus to the north. Unlike the road to Belderrig, here the roads are wide and new. Progress is sedate, for the major roads, if new, are single-lane, and one is reminded that this is 'Poland B', a distinction for the slow-growing, rural and less densely populated portion of Poland. As you leave the city the level of traffic drops off considerably. I had not realized rural Poland, Poland B, east of the Vistula, would look so decidedly A class. The houses are large and many are newly built, or else appear to be recently renovated. They are surrounded by large and well-tended gardens. The long, linear villages are greatly unfamiliar to me, used to western Europe as I am, and they seem to go on for ages, the bigger ones especially. This is far from a ruined countryside: in fact, going on appearances, one could almost be in rural Germany or Austria.

I travel with Michał Rauszer in late June 2022, and, even in the ten years since he was last here, Michał is struck by the evident change. Membership of the European Union has been crucial, for the roads, the look of the towns, the houses. Just like Ireland, Portugal, Spain and other countries that preceded Poland into the EU. Further on, into Subcarpathia, the land begins to roll wonderfully, and the valleys are beautiful, none more lovely than the valley of the River San, not far from the borders with Slovakia and Ukraine. The number of holiday homes multiplies along the way, and the display of these marks them out from the houses of locals. Behind the latter stretch the well-tended strip fields which make up the extraordinary mosaic of the landscape.

I am puzzled by what I see: later on in the day I enquire of a young man who is a curator in the Sanok open-air *skansen* what is going on. He immediately announces that 'It is all a façade', a metaphorical one, which is also literal. Of the schoolmates of his year, fifteen or so in number, he is the only one who has got a job locally. All the others have emigrated to Poland A or further westwards. The prosperity is real enough, relatively speaking, but farms in Poland are still tiny, and can only support one family, and even then those who stay must often rely on other forms of employment as well as the farm.[1]

As I journey east there are the strangest of conjunctions: we travel for miles on quiet roads and then suddenly come to small towns which are dominated by a large steelworks, a chemical plant, or some other large factory enterprise of an older vintage than in western Europe. Most of these were set down among the fields in Communist times in the interests of developing Industrial Man. One drives quickly through these towns and then is immediately swallowed up in the all-encompassing countryside and the long empty stretches of road, then the linear villages, and always the small religious shrines along the way, marking the entrance and exit from the villages. From time to time I see people working in the fields, not many, because of the heat, and they do so with machinery. The machinery is old: old tractors, very old combine harvesters, which, despite their age, have changed everything.

I am old enough to remember the days before the 'combine' in Wexford, when, by the mid-to-late 1950s, the scythe had not so long before given way to the reaper–binder, drawn by the tractor, a now quaint-seeming form of mechanization. In the 50s, my mother's kin owned neither tractor nor binder, the big farmer locally supplying those. Two or three men working in a line together, the edges of the fields were cut by the scythe, in order that room be made for the binder to work on the field after the first cutting. The coordinated labour of large groups of men was still to be seen at the cutting, binding and stacking of the corn, and then its threshing, for it was the manual labour of the land that then still counted most. At the work of harvesting all knew what to do, all worked as one, then all assembled in the kitchen at midday to be fed, the women's labour from the early morning in preparing the food and the house as important as the men's. Reaper–binders were in wide use in Communist Poland long after the 1950s and 60s. However, farmers often could not operate them, due to shortages of twine and the lack of replacement parts. This was such a regular occurrence that baling twine remains a symbol of the dysfunction of the Communist economy in the cultural memory of Poland.

In Poland that June more fields of rye than of wheat and barley passed us as we travelled east. Outside the temperature consistently peaked at over 35 degrees centigrade. Until ten years ago, these temperatures were unheard of. Correspondingly, the winters now are far less harsh than they used to be, snow not so prevalent. On the way to Sanok we stop at Tarnów, which is only 45 miles east of Kraków, but already seems a universe away from the city. Tarnów was the epicentre of the 'Galician slaughter' of 1846. The town is spick and span in the brilliant sunlight. The central squares of these towns are huge, a legacy of the Austrian empire. In Communist days, the squares were full of trees: post-Communist modernity in Poland decreed that the trees be chopped down, so that there is no shade in the stifling heat. I am told the local people do not approve of this modernizing move.

In the square is the town hall, the building before which the peasants of 1846 brought the bodies of the landlords they had murdered. There is no mention whatsoever of this in the square, nor of the peasant rising. I can find no mention of it at all in the various town museums (museumification is rife here too). Instead, in the square there are placards saying how Poles helped Jews in the last war. I visit the town churchyard, and the memorial to the fifty-two people murdered by peasants who are buried there in the one mass grave. The inscription from Chapter 4 of Genesis is just about visible: 'And the Lord said, "What have you done? The voice of your brother's blood is crying to me from the ground" '. Only, in this case, those who did the killing were not the brothers of the slain, but the serfs who hated those putative brothers for what they had done to them in the long years of serfdom. The brotherhood on display here is that of the nation, the nation now, just as the nation was then in the nineteenth century. The town, Tarnów, is named after the great magnates, the Tarnowski family, who basically ran the place, as they did large parts of southern Poland. In some cases, as ministers and diplomats, they ran the whole country. The main town church within is a veritable monument to the Tarnowski family: power made visible to any who doubted.

On the way south-east from Tarnów we visit the ruined mansion of the Bogusz family, which is to be found, after much looking, up an unmarked dirt track. Here Jakub Szela led a band of peasants in the destruction of the house and family. There are now just scattered, decaying walls, themselves on the point of crumbling, and the 'property' is now on the market for sale. Perhaps as many as 3,000 people were killed in the 1846 uprising, but no Jews were harmed.[2] Before 1939, 25,000 Jews lived in Tarnów – 40 per cent of its population – hardly any of whom survived. The South is a place of absences, of silences, the absence of the old peasant world, and the most present of all absences, that of the Jews.

Sanok is 90 miles south-east of Tarnów. In the Sanok Museum of Folk Architecture one has to take the accompanied tour. If you want to explore on your own, this is not possible, as the buildings are kept locked. Only a few guides know English, and these are not in when we call, which is perhaps understandable, given the weather. There is hardly any signage in English or any other language but Polish. Few non-Poles venture this far south, and non-Polish visitors are rare. It is a long way to go, and one must be very interested in folk architecture to make the journey. The setting is exquisite, beside the River San, the sun brightly shining on the abundant greens of the valley. There is the continuous sound of humming bees throughout my visit. The visit is long, our guide wanting to tell us everything about everything, it seems. Then it is all translated back to me. I wilt in the heat. The guide has been doing her job since Communist times. Again, the museum itself, the building and its history, is the real museum. I ask her how things have changed. She is not particularly forthcoming. The *skansen* has got bigger, is all she says. Set up originally in 1957, in Communist days, everything is ethnographically authentic.

The museum is a strange experience: a mixture of the didactic, plus embalming. There is a little village square, toytown-like. Here one may see crafts being practised, and one may buy mementoes. There is a replica post office, in which a lone man sits all day behind a grille, to whom one may apply to send a telegram. I perambulate further. I see a large wooden synagogue as I go around. The sight is stunning. For this westerner, the past is suddenly opened up in this place of empty, locked and relocated houses. Part of this is the physical manifestation before me of a culture that is one of wood. For all the differences between them, wood unites the Jew and the peasant. I did not, however, know what to make of what confronted me when I exited the building, a Polish man dressed up as a Jew, authentic cap on, authentically long-bearded, chosen for his resemblance to someone's idea of a Jew. It is well-meant, I suppose.

The first empty houses I see attempt to magic back into presence the exiled minority of Boykos and Lemkos, cruelly treated as these groups were. There is little here about that treatment (nothing much is said about the numerous Sanok Jews either). But one learns, nonetheless: one lesson is simply how people and nature were connected in the houses themselves, for even though these houses have been severed from the earth they were once set in, one still gets a sense of how they grew out of that earth (they were made out of the surrounding trees, of course), but also out of the ground itself. If you wanted to renew the (surprisingly durable) earthen floor of a house or barn you went outside and got some more earth, but you needed it to be the right sort and to know where this sort was to be found. To build an oven, one also used the earth. This is how the Boykos lived. They carved the sun and the moon into the great central wooden beam that kept the house standing, the symbols of the man and the woman.

The weight of the massive wooden logs used in house construction has a certain profundity about it, as if, already lasting this long, the houses will last for ever. The understanding of how these things of the earth worked seems itself profound. The Lemko way of cutting roof slats of precisely the right size and shape from the whole tree trunk, for instance. The colours in which the houses are attired are made from pigments taken from the ground. There is one long-enduring wooden Lemko house from the late eighteenth century. It was lived in by an old man until the 1960s, one who, it was said, refused to move with the times, one of the few Lemkos who then remained.

The skill of peasant makers is evident in the large wooden church on the site, one shared in past times by the Uniates and the Orthodox, so that the interior is of consuming interest – so many signs and symbols of peasant faith being held up before the visitor's eyes. Inside the church, as inside the synagogue, I am moved as the past returns for the time of our brief visit. (One has only an allotted time for each building, and our guide is a severe timekeeper.) Within the spaces of churches and houses, and the tavern that is also here, one gets a sense of people's bodies, how small people were compared to people today, and how they lived in what we would call discomfort. Only by coming here does one learn the scale of worlds, although because you must not tarry, you have to work it out yourself, against the clock.

The splendours of the iconostasis are the product of specialist craftsmen, some from the villages, but mostly from the few largish towns in the region. Local peasants did some of the carving and painting within the church, the Uniate parts in particular. Inside the church, men stood to the fore of the nave, the women to the rear, or they occupied a side gallery. Women, after all, were seen as part of men's bodies, and the order of precedence is clear. Outside, on one side of the great wooden tower, there is painted a large clock: a symbol for the congregation that they were modern, in their day. The time on the clock is for ever nine o'clock.

We travel on to Przemyśl the next day. The town is on the rail line that leads east from Kraków to Lviv and on to Kiev. Here is where most of the massive exodus of Ukrainian refugees arrived earlier in the year. The railway station then was a scene of disorder and suffering. Now all is quiet. Around the city, Ukrainian is to be heard, but, just as in the small towns, things are quiet here too, for many have left Poland B, and the Ukrainians do not hang around either. These places are far from the hubs of European life. Go north or east and you will find no considerable population clusters for hundreds of miles, not until Białystok, Vilnius, Minsk. On the road earlier in the day we passed long lines of trucks waiting to cross the border into Ukraine. Sometimes a few large military vehicles are on the road. But, as they say, you would not know there was a war going on.

In the town, as in Sanok the night before and Zamość on the following night, I visited many churches. There are no churches in Europe as well restored as these, no country where Church and State are as hand in glove as here, one as right-wing as the other. Onwards from Przemyśl north into the great central plain the villages are bigger, and less prosperous. The road to Zamość leads near to the Bełżec death camp. Here, some 500,000 Jews were killed in an astonishingly short period of time between 1942 and 1943. Only two people are held to have survived, though there may have been a few (at most) more. Treblinka is 170 miles in a straight line to the north, Majdanek 80 miles and Sobibór only 73. This is the great killing corridor of the Holocaust, the overwhelmingly Jewish part of it, in fact, for the vast numbers of eastern Jews had not to travel far to their deaths. None of these eastern camps is much visited by westerners, and Bełżec least of all. It is less well known than Treblinka, Majdanek and even Sobibór. Auschwitz, Treblinka and Bełżec, in that order, are the camps in which most people were killed. From almost all the many small towns and villages we have passed through in Galicia so far in our journey, Jews were sent here to die. All roads, paved and rail, led here.

We visit the camp. Only there is no camp to visit, as the Germans levelled the whole camp well before the war's end. Surely this is a special place, the unknown camp, compared to the others, that is? The invisible camp as well as the unknown. There is only one survivor's account of camp life, and in the camp museum itself almost no evidence that a camp ever existed.[3] When we visit, there is only one small group there. They go, and it is only us two. The sense of absence is overwhelming. Also the weight of the historical silence, the real, very marked, physical silence around us on that day accentuating the historical kind. If time, and the pasts it carries, endure, accumulating in the present, then this does not mean that there are pasts that will never, can never, be known, such as those of the people who met their deaths here.

Only in 2004 was the present site in Bełżec constructed. It is very impressive. Before then, there was for a time a memorial of sorts, one also from the Communist period, but for a good deal of the time after 1943 there was simply nothing, barren ground; the camp that was, invisible.[4] On arrival one passes through a makeshift car park, which is full of cars. I had thought those in the cars were visitors to the site of the camp, but quickly learn that it serves the factory which is almost directly opposite the camp. The factory makes wooden furniture. The present village of Bełżec goes about its daily business, as it must. The village is big, and not so prosperous, and the factory gives necessary employment to those who work on the land.

The following evening we visit the Rotunda in Zamość. It is getting dark: frogs croak in great numbers and bats fly in and out of the interior of the circular construction, which was originally a fortress built in the early nineteenth century. In these borderlands, the lands of the Kresy, as they were known, the past accumulates as perhaps nowhere else on Earth. The interior of the Rotunda now houses a museum to the atrocities committed on this same site, where thousands were shot to death in the course of the Second World War, peasants and intellectuals both. From 1940 onwards, about 40,000 people were kept prisoner in the building and 8,000 were murdered there, most of whom were shot in the Rotunda's inner compound. The wall against which they were executed still stands. The remains of 45,482 people lie buried around the Rotunda. I go there to pay my respects, as I did in Bełżec. However, here, unlike there, the traces of the murdered are multiple. There is a monument to the Peasant Battalions of the Second World War, the *Bataliony Chłopskie.* This was created in 1940 by the agrarian-populist People's Party, which the summer of 1944 had 160,000 members: its first big action, in 1942, was in defence of the peasants of the Zamość region.

What follows is a picture of a young peasant girl, Czesława Kwoka, one of many Polish children from the region murdered in the camps. She was born in 1928 in the town of Wólka Złojecka, near Zamość, and her family village was displaced by the Germans in early December 1942. She and her mother were sent from UWZ Lager Zamość (the Rotunda), in the first transport from this so-called 'resettlement' camp on 13 December 1942, to Auschwitz. The girl was given the camp number 26947. Her mother was given the number 26946.[5] The photograph was taken by a Polish inmate of Auschwitz, who, once it was known he was a photographer, was ordered to take photos like these. The camp personnel, it seems, liked to send affecting images of their victims to family members in Germany. Perhaps this photograph should not be seen, so exploitative is it; but, by showing it, something of the nature of the depths of exploitation may be revealed.

I visited the Zamość City Museum the next day. It reproduces the structure of peasant society within the building itself: on the first floor, noble culture is displayed; at the top level, peasant culture, as near the attic as possible. I discover that Rosa Luxemburg, the 'La Pasionaria' of the early German left, was born in Zamość. In the January of 1919, at the age of forty-seven, she was assassinated in Berlin by the kind of people who led to the rise of the Third Reich. In 2018 a plaque commemorating her was ripped out from the wall on which it was mounted. Agents of the state-sponsored Institute of

National Remembrance were responsible. We go on to Lublin the next day, once the spiritual home of Polish Jewry. There is an enormous car park where the ghetto once was, and little signs on the pavement remind you where the ghetto started and stopped, if you look down, that is.

It is here that I saw striking carvings of the 'Pensive Christ'. This Christ, constantly evident over the centuries, is a marker of peasant society in Poland. This is the peasant God: it would not be blasphemous to say God as the peasant, or at least God the luckless demiurge, pensive in His lucklessness. This pensive Christ of the Passion enabled people to endure what had happened in Zamość, and the *Generalplan Ost* as a whole. Peasant resistance around Zamość meant that the Germans were losing control of the countryside as early as the spring of 1943.

We leave Lublin and then turn back towards Kraków in the West. Travelling south and then west, it is 95 miles to Tarnobrzeg. The town is another Tarnowski fiefdom, beside which is Dzików, Jan Słomka's village. I go to visit his grave and pay my respects there. This Tarnobrzeg church houses the greatly venerated image of Our Lady of Dzików. The Baroque interior is stunningly beautiful, painted in the most charmingly light greens and pinks, which sit beside the ample gold. Słomka is presented on a plaque as a bastion of Polish nationalism, a peasant patriot, in fact, also an exemplar of devotion to Catholicism and teetotalism.

His likeness is presented not only on his tombstone, but also in the form of a sculpted bench near the main square. One end of the bench is his bodily likeness in stone. One may sit down beside him. Dzików is now a maze of lanes, one of which bears his name. The old village itself seems not to exist. Most of the houses are new. The place is now inhabited by people from the local town of Tarnobrzeg.

In the town's main square, there is an imposing statue of a peasant who was an aide to Tadeusz Kościuszko, the leader of the 1794 rising, and a great symbol of liberal Poland. In November 1918 the Republic of Tarnobrzeg was declared. Its main founders were two socialist activists, one of whom was a Roman Catholic priest, Eugeniusz Okoń by name, the child of peasants.

The short-lived Republic of Tarnobrzeg had its roots in the mass demonstrations of peasants then taking place almost daily in the region. On 6 November 1918, after a demonstration of some 30,000 people in the town, local peasants seized power. Following the recent example of the Russian Revolution, they demanded the end of capitalist government and the introduction of land reform. They also formed a peasants' militia. Events culminated in 1919 with the suppression of the uprising by the newly founded Polish army. Father Okoń was arrested, soon released, and then promptly elected to the (also new) Polish Parliament.

There is no record whatsoever of these events in the main square, or indeed as far as I could find in the town as a whole. None in the Historical Museum of the City of Tarnobrzeg, for sure, which I visit. It is in effect a shrine to the Tarnowski family, not surprisingly as it is located in a family seat of the Tarnowskis, Dzików Castle. We enter the museum, which has had serious money spent on it. We are allotted a guided tour of a strictly enforced thirty minutes.

Peasants are the last thing on our guides' minds. We leave and return south and then westwards to Kraków.

Behind us we leave a bastion of electoral support for the increasingly autocratic, ultra-nationalistic Law and Justice Party. In the East, but also in other rural parts of the country, what has been called post-peasant populism advances because it gives both recognition and economic benefit to the erstwhile poor and excluded. The peasant past is alive in this post-peasantism: as a reality, because the remnants of peasanthood do still remain, but mostly as a dream, increasingly so as time goes on.[6] However, populism thrives on dreams.

South

In September 2022, the small, mountainous village of Aliano commemorated the one hundred and twentieth anniversary of Carlo Levi's birth. The village of Aliano is one of the two villages where Levi was exiled during 1935 to 1936, the place where he wrote that Christ had stopped, going no further, giving up on humankind. Aliano is Eboli, but the other village of exile, Grassano, informed Levi's account as well. Aliano is far up in the mountains and difficult to get to. Nonetheless, one benefit of the isolation and poverty of these mountain villages was that the Mafia thought them not worth bothering with.

If there was what Levi called 'a lively human feeling for the common fate of mankind' in the old times, there was also in Aliano a lively human feeling directed against Levi himself for a long time. The village much disliked his depiction of them, their backwardness, so-called. They did not think of themselves as immemorial. Levi also raised their hackles by naming names and getting things wrong. They would only have him back in the last few weeks of his life. In a short piece of writing which he shared with me called 'Memories of the Final Journey', Nicola Scaldaferri tells the story of the last days of Carlo Levi thus: 'Monday 9 December 1974 is a day that has remained ingrained in the memories of the inhabitants of San Costantino Albanese: it is the day that Carlo Levi was heartily welcomed by the population to what was then the premises of the Pro Loco, where he drew the faces of three young people wearing traditional *Arbëreshë* costumes on the wall.' The aim of the visit to San Costantino was one leg of an intense programme to present and promote the newly created lithographs of the villagers of Basilicata that Levi had produced.

On the day following the visit to San Costantino, Levi went to Aliano. This moment marked his delayed acceptance by the old community where he had spent his long months of confinement As Nicola writes: 'In the end, also thanks to the endeavours of the young mayor of Aliano, Maria Santomassimo (the first female mayor in Basilicata, of the Communist Party), a pathway was opened to their reconciliation which made the person and work of Levi a fundamental part of the local memory and identity.'

Within weeks, Levi fell into a diabetic coma and died. His body was taken back to Basilicata, to be buried in Aliano. Levi had no family, and his agent suggested he be buried there. As Nicola Scaldaferri reports, 'Almost as if to express this last will and testament, in the lithograph titled "The Cemetery" Levi had portrayed himself relaxing in the cool of a newly dug grave in the cemetery of Aliano, next to the undertaker and two boys grazing goats.'[7] The last painting Levi ever did is of San Costantino. In *Christ Stopped at Eboli*, written some four decades before his death, Levi wrote of the freshly dug grave he would regularly find in the cemetery of Aliano: 'I had made it my custom on these hot days when I came up here to lower myself into it and lie down. The earth was smooth and dry, and the sun had not burned it. I could see nothing but a rectangle of clear sky, crossed occasionally by a wandering white cloud; not a single sound reached my ears. In this freedom and solitude I spent many hours.'

West

In the far west of the West that is the Atlantic side of Galway and Mayo, as ever now it is the vividness of the many shades of green that strike me. Even more, it is the purity of the air, scoured as the sky is by the constant westerlies. Unlike in the Polish East, the sky constantly changes, rain and sun alternating, the former easily predominating. There is water everywhere: the heavy dews, the water flowing down the hills in narrow silver rivulets, the lakes and the ocean. One does not experience the purity of nature to this degree too often. I am out again, as so many times, far west, at the edge.

I drive the new roads, and, like in Poland, the houses are big, too big now as family size lessens. Rooms are not used, are expensive to heat, and in one house I visit there is a room as big as the whole house in which the owner's parents raised them only a handful of decades ago. I recall the Connemara of the 1970s and 80s, with its mobile homes, makeshift shacks, in effect, and a sign of poverty. People now are house-rich and land-rich, at least in the rural parts where people retain the old farms, but, as in Poland, this is somewhat misleading. Ironically, given the large houses that abound in the countryside, the country as a whole has a chronic housing shortage. It also has enormous levels of obesity, in a land once famous for its hunger.

Emigration from these Connaught parts has at last, and greatly, lessened, something that is in its own way momentous. The extraordinary tidiness of the villages strikes me again as I drive through them, compared to the shambling places of the 1950s and 1960s that I remember; then the long rows of tiny, huddled houses in the villages and small towns, the smell of turf smoke heavy in the air, the straggle of it all, and the unkemptness of things compared to the then civically conscious England from which I had journeyed. Nonetheless, it is the vivacity of these villages and towns that I recall, despite the enormous migration of the 1950s. The vivacity of market day in the town of New Ross in my mother's Wexford, when I entered the seemingly ancient, dark and – to the London child – mysterious shops, with their vivid shop signs outside in counterpoint to the darkness within. Many of the pubs contained small shops, such as Roche's Bar on the quay, where I helped deliver salmon caught by my uncles from the Barrow. Deliver, that is, with the mighty fish wrapped in hessian, strapped to the crossbar of an old black bicycle. The combined weight of this unsteady ensemble taxed the strength of the city boy.

P. J. Roche's is still there on the quay, over sixty years later. New Ross is now, like so many of the small rural towns of Ireland, near to hollowed-out ruin, overtaken by the new times of the car, the supermarket, the internet. If you are not on the tourist trail, times can be hard, for tourism has in large measure taken over from retail and the agriculture that sustained the place. The quay is quiet now, when in those earlier times it had a purpose, the ships calling, the place full of activity. Once New Ross had been a point of departure for America and Canada in the days after the Great Famine.

I left the quay that summer and drove west across Ireland to Joyce Country. A journey that once took all day by car now takes a little more than four hours. Again, as so often, I return to my father's townland of Kilbride. The farm is transformed, the place tended now by one of Paddy Kenny's twin sons. Paddy is the man with the powerful profile in Josef Koudelka's image of Ireland in 1972 in Chapter 1 (Paddy's profile once adorned several New York bars, I am told). His son Pádraíg, like many here, does not make much out of sheep and cattle, but is determined to continue. This determination takes the form of a desire to improve the old place, almost as if they are repaying a debt to the past by attending properly to it now that they have a bit of money to do so. Pádraíg has rebuilt the barn entirely, which is now a model of modern agricultural convenience. The house is spick and span. There is an old stone sheep pen up on Kilbride Mountain that once, many years ago, belonged to a family long since gone, one family of the throng of the invisible departed that once populated the hillside. Pádraíg has rebuilt the old pen perfectly. This for no purpose but to offer remembrance. He remembers his Uncle Seán in the new barn, the house accoutrements and tools of the old place now cleaned and displayed together, for the benefit of whichever few will ever see them.

In the summer of 2022 the houses and hotels in Joyce Country and around were full (even though the number of 'tourist beds' has sprung up considerably in recent years). The reason for this unusual occurrence was that the director Pat Collins was making a film of John McGahern's book *That They May Face the Rising Sun*. The film crew were shooting scenes here, so beds had to be found. I felt somewhat incommoded by this turn of events, but glad, if apprehensive, that the place would be shown to the world in celluloid. The director himself was staying in a house of a cousin of mine, from which he could look over the lake to Kilbride on the other side.

That They May Face the Rising Sun concerns the life of a small community. McGahern was himself raised on a small farm. There is a clear sense in his book that it too marks the ending of the old world. In the little universe McGahern depicts, the various resonances of the characters are revealed in their ways of speaking. On this journey west it is, as always, the language that connects me, the hearing of Irish but most of all the delight that Irish English still brings me after so many years. Delight is grounded within me, in the body, in the ordinary speech I inherited as a child, the speech of my parents which changed not one iota from that of their childhood despite decades spent in England. I was listening to the speech of an Ireland that was only a little bit away from that of the nineteenth century. Just as with the photograph, language is absolutely of the moment and yet carries within it multiple times. The past works its way silently through us in the present, shaping it and us in ways not immediate to the conscious mind.

In McGahern's novel, there is the figure of Johnny Murphy – the brother of the man at the heart of the book, Jamesie – a man deeply accomplished in the linguistic skill so characteristic of the Irish countryside. The author writes of the emigrant Johnny's room in London, looking down as it did on the Prince of Wales pub, beside the Edgware Road in the north-west of London. I know that pub and that road, the pub beside Kilburn High Road Station. Kilburn was the spiritual home of the London Irish immigrant. (I was married in the church that is the spiritual centre of this spiritual home.)

And I was raised beside another Prince of Wales, a mile or so down the road from McGahern's one.[8] I knew the lost men, the bachelor men, who made these pubs their homes. The pub has become the centre of Johnny's being in McGahern's book, the darts matches, the ritual pub conviviality the man depends on in his loneliness. His room is described, for he lives alone in 'digs', the spartan nature of which is revealed in the detail of the lone gas ring on which he cooks, and the tiny few items of furniture he lives with.

Without a woman his life is restricted. His existence is full of regret, which he tries to hide, for as it turned out he was one who did not have to leave, but nonetheless went and was rejected by the woman he left for. He fools himself and tries to fool his brother Jamesie and Jamesie's wife Mary: 'Once you get used to London, a place like the lake gets very backward. You are too far from everything. Jamesie and Mary, God bless them, came to see it that way as well, without a car it would have been hopeless. You'd be stuck there in front of the alders on Maroney's Hill facing.' In a magnificent line McGahern writes that, 'He was moving in his blindness, as if he was speaking for multitudes.'[9]

I remember the life of the first generation of emigrants everywhere, how they had it hardest of all, and I remember the debt that is owed. In this case to the first-generation immigrant Irish, among them my own family of fifteen aunts and uncles, so many of whom were forced to emigrate. (I would have had nineteen, but four died early, four of the fourteen children my Wexford grandmother gave birth to.) My father was another Johnny, this time one who had to leave, but one who married and had children, and so had the solace of these things. My emigrant parents were in the end no better off than those who stayed, indeed, in the end, they were worse off. Once they had gone they were forgotten by the Irish State they had left, neglect when at home and neglect when gone being their lot. When gone, they had the economic hardships of the time, including the 'No Irish Need Apply' signs of their adulthood.

Johnny and Kitty Joyce lie in St Mary's Cemetery in London's north-west, along with the multitudes of the Irish Catholic dead that surround them, going back to the time of the famine. In McGahern's book it is one Patrick Ryan who orders that Johnny's head must lie to the west in the local burial ground, 'so that when he wakes he may face the rising sun'.[10] Johnny and Kitty too face the rising sun in Kensal Green, awaiting the call of their Saviour.

In Ireland now, the Patricks, Josephs, Michaels and Martins of yore are gone, or at least in full retreat. So are the Marys, Brigids, Mollys, Maggies and Kittys. Both my grandfathers were Patrick, one grandmother Mary, another Brigid. I, Patrick Joseph, am Pat Johnny Pat. Patrick in the year 2018 was only Number 18 on the list of favoured names, the Pádraígs, Pats, Paddys, Páudís and Patsys of long ago fading fast. What's in a name? The astonishing transformation of Ireland since the 1970s is. Part of what names are is the history of the peasant family, the names binding the generations, making past and present one, the matronymics and patronymics stones set in a ground now scarcely visible any longer. Now it is Emilys, Sophies and Emmas, Jacks, Jameses and, more recently, I see that in 2021 Noah has made it to Number 2. Irish names are making a comeback of sorts, but poor Paddy and Mick have had their day. In the remaining Gaeltacht areas, and among the Irish-speaking middle classes, a determined resistance is led in favour of Irish first names, but nationally these are still second place to English ones, the favourites on the other side of the Irish Sea. Even in the Irish-speaking West, the kings, Pat and Mick, the queens, Brigid and Mary, have been dethroned.

I will leave the last word to the people of Ronald Blythe's *Akenfield*, natives of the other of my two countries, England. Akenfield is a made-up name, but the villages Blythe writes of are well known. They are in East Suffolk in England's rural East. In ways seldom recognized the two islands are one, and with the civilization of European peasant society as one also. In the 1960s Blythe put on record the voices of those who knew 'Akenfield' intimately:

> The old people think deeply. They are great observers. They will walk and see everything. They didn't move far so their eyes are trained to see the fine detail of a small place . . . The old men can describe exactly how the ploughing turns over in a particular field. They recognize a beauty and it is this which they really worship. Not with words – with their eyes.

And then another observer states, 'They are hard people. Their lives at the higher level – and make no mistake, there *is* a higher level: I have seen it, a fugitive glimpse into a country where I cannot belong . . . The old look inward at things we cannot see.'[11]

One of these old people is Billy. A man who knew him says to Blythe, 'Billy was one of the old people. The old people have gone and have taken a lot of truth out of the world with them. When Billy died, his wife walked down the garden and told the bees, and hung black crêpe on the hive. My grandfather did this, too. He said that if you didn't, the bees would die as well. Bees are dangerous to some folk and a gift to others. You'll get someone who'll get stung once and perish and another who'll get stung all over and get cured of all manner of things. There were a rare lot of bees in the village in those days.'[12]

Permissions

Copyright is given in italics.

p. 6. Seán Joyce.

p. 8. Josef Koudelka, 'Irlande 1972'. *Josef Koudelka / Magnum Photos.*

p. 27. Jean-François Millet, *Man with a Hoe. Artefact / Alamy Stock Photo.*

p. 60. Peasants marking the first sheaf of the harvest with a cross. *Paul Shau, Gliwice Museum, Poland.*

p. 61. Three women pulling a plough in France, taken sometime between 1917 and 1919. *Imago History Collection / Alamy Stock Photo.*

p. 68. Úna Breathnach of Maam Cross, County Galway. *Coimisiún Béaloideasa Éireann / Irish Folklore Commission.*

p. 72. Drawn plan of a house in Curragh, 1945. *National Museum of Ireland Collections – F: 2006.113.*

p. 73. The *izba biała* ('white room') with its bed. *Narodowe Archiwum Cyfrowe (National Digital Archive), Warsaw, Poland.*

p. 74. The Donegal house shows the adaptation to the Atlantic wind. *Coimisiún Béaloideasa Éireann / Irish Folklore Commission.*

p. 75. Polish peasant with axe, *c.*1918–39.

p. 78: A white Polish peasant stove. *Narodowe Archiwum Cyfrowe (National Digital Archive).*

p. 82. Two photographs, one man and one woman, Podlesie, Poland. *Narodowe Archiwum Cyfrowe (National Digital Archive).*

p. 83. Woman on Gorumna Island, Connemara, 1910. *Coimisiún Béaloideasa Éireann / Irish Folklore Commission.*

p. 84. A man and woman in the town of Gródek Jagielloński in Galicia, 1934. *Narodowe Archiwum Cyfrowe (National Digital Archive).*

p. 85. The interior of a better-off peasant's house, in the district of Łowicz, *c.*1921. *Popperfoto / Getty Images.*

p. 86. A peasant village in the Polish South. *Narodowe Archiwum Cyfrowe (National Digital Archive).*

p. 87. The settlement of An Chloch Bhreac (Cloghbrack). *Photograph by Robert French, held in the Lawrence Photograph Collection, National Library of Ireland.*

p. 94. Jan Słomka, 'mayor' of Dzików. *Narodowe Archiwum Cyfrowe (National Digital Archive).*

p. 120. Mícheál Breathnach sitting beside American folklorist Stith Thompson. *The Photographic Collection, M013.01.00006, National Folklore Collection, University College Dublin.*

p. 122. The Rauszer family from Poland's Upper Silesia.

p. 132. Seán Joyce (left), the author and his father, 1948 or 1949.

p. 151. Caterina of Nardó and Donato of Matino. *Ernesto de Martino,* The Land of Remorse, *1961.*

p. 153. A violin player in the *tarantismo* cult. *From Ernesto de Martino,* The Land of Remorse, *1961.*

p. 158. Procession from Košice, Levoča, Slovakia, 1968. *Markéta Luskačová,* Pilgrims, *1983.*

p. 159. Mr Ferenz singing, Obišovce, Slovakia, 1967. *Markéta Luskačová,* Pilgrims, *1983.*

p. 161. Women after communion, Levoča, Slovakia, 1965. *Markéta Luskačová,* Pilgrims, *1983.*

p. 162. The procession, Čirč, Slovakia, 1965. *Markéta Luskačová,* Pilgrims, *1983.*

p. 167. Three men with the cross, Easter procession, Kalwaria Zebrydowska, Poland, 1968. *Markéta Luskačová,* Pilgrims, *1983.*

p. 169. Men praying at the pilgrimage to Croagh Patrick Mountain, Ireland 1972. *Markéta Luskačová,* Pilgrims, *1983.*

p. 174. The author's mother's Mass and prayer missal, *The Treasury of the Sacred Heart.*

p. 176. A woman tending a grave in Polish Upper Silesia in the 1930s. *Gliwice Museum, Poland.*

p. 179. The blessing of the fields with holy water, Upper Silesia, 1931. *Gliwice Museum, Poland.*

p. 195. Peasants at work in a field reaping corn, Poland, 1942 or 1943. *Narodowe Archiwum Cyfrowe (National Digital Archive).*

p. 203. Patrick (Paudeen) Joyce on entering and on leaving prison. *National Library of Ireland.*

p. 213. Jakub Szela in the *Illustrirte Chronik* of 1848.

p. 215. Peasant insurrection in Galicia. *Ilustrowany Kuryer Codzienny*, 1848.

p. 230. People in the village of Chersk in 1910, in what was then Russian Poland. *FolkCostume&Embroidery blog.*

p. 289. Woven mattress found in Titchfield, Hampshire, which may date from the seventeenth century or earlier. *Museum of English Rural Life.*

p. 300. 'Peasant 100 years old and more', Pudłowiec, 1870s–1880s. Photograph by Michał Greim. *Muzeum Etnograficzne w Krakowie (Kraków Ethnographic Museum), Poland.*

p. 302 and p. 303. A peasant couple from the village of Mnichów. *Muzeum Etnograficzne w Krakowie (Kraków Ethnographic Museum).*

p. 304. 'Old Ciapy', Mnichów. *Muzeum Etnograficzne w Krakowie (Kraków Ethnographic Museum).*

p. 305. A group photograph in the Łódź area. *Muzeum Etnograficzne w Krakówie (Kraków Ethnographic Museum).*

p. 316. A young peasant girl, Czesława Kwoka, born in 1928. The photograph was taken in 1942 or 1943 in Auschwitz.

Acknowledgements

This book could not have been written without the unstinting help of Michał Rauszer of the University of Warsaw. He was my guide through a peasant Poland he knows intimately, knows in the blood. It is to him I owe the most. Wiktor Marzec helped me start the Polish part of the work, and Anna Engelking was generous with her time and in sharing her own work. Grażyna Kubica-Heller informed me about peasant Protestantism. Magdalena Zych was a wonderful guide at the Seweryn Udziela Ethnographic Museum in Kraków (MEK). Anna Sulich and Anna Sak of the same institution also guided me through the collections of this remarkable institution, and Ewa Rossal was very helpful. My thanks also to Aleksandra Bilewicz.

On the Irish side, Ailbhe Nic Giolla Chomhaill took me deep into aspects of Joyce Country I was not aware of, as did Martin O'Halloran. Ailbhe also helped me on matters to do with the Irish language. Lawrence Taylor advised me regarding Irish peasant religion. I benefited from talking about music with the great Irish fiddle player Martin Hayes. And from talking with the novelist Timothy O'Grady and the film-maker Pat Collins. Margaret Kelleher answered questions about Maamtrasna. I also thank Breandán Mac Suibhne, Tony Varley and Cormac Ó Gráda, the latter for reading earlier versions of several chapters.

Paul Ginsborg, my friend in the years before his untimely recent death, talked with me about Italian peasant politics and culture, and Nicola Scaldaferri was a great help on the peasants of the Italian South. My thanks too to Lorenzo Ferrarini. Keith Snell advised me on English 'peasants', Peter Gatrell on Russian peasants and William G. Pooley on French ones. I thank Tom Overton, biographer of John Berger, for the opportunity to talk about Berger and peasants. Terry Eagleton commented helpfully on my treatment of peasant religion. My thanks too are due to Patrick Wright, Markéta Luskačová and Marcus Colla. I thank the staff at the Museum of Irish Country Life in Turlough village, Castlebar, County Mayo, and the Museum of English Rural Life in Reading, in particular Liam Doherty in the former and Ollie Douglas in the latter. Mine is the responsibility for any mistakes in this book.

Chris Richards was a splendidly sensitive and judicious editor at Simon and Schuster as was Tom Penn at Penguin, where Eva Hodgkin also helped greatly with the photographs. My agent, John Ash, was a rock of support. My thanks also to Kasia Beresford for her translations from Polish to English. I hope some of these will see the light of publication before too long. Thanks also to my copy-editor, Louisa Watson. I thank a number of the above in the notes, as well as here and now, so that their contributions may be made more explicit than is possible here alone. One cannot give too much in the way of thanks for the generosity that has come my way in the writing of *Remembering Peasants*. The international fraternity of the academy continues onwards, the fellowship of knowledge resisting the marketization of the university.

Research for the book was supported by the award to me of a Leverhulme Trust Emeritus Fellowship. My wife of almost half a century, Rosaleen, was there beside me all the long way. Including the years of Covid, when my children Seán and Róisín also helped keep the show going.

Thanking each is, however, not thanking all: to those I have almost certainly forgotten, my thanks, and apologies.

Patrick Joyce, August 2023

Notes

Prologue

1 William I. Thomas and Florian Znaniecki, *The Polish Peasant in Europe and America* (Dover Press, 1958), vol. 1, Introduction, pp. 209–13, 220. The book was originally published in five volumes during the years 1918 to 1920.
2 Robert Bernen, 'The Thatched Byre' (essay),in his *Tales from the Blue Stacks* (Hamish Hamilton, 1978), p. 26.
3 John Berger, *Into Their Labours* (Granta Books, 1992), Introduction (to his three works on the rural–urban transformations of peasant life in the twentieth century).
4 Berger, *Into Their Labours*, pp. xiii and xxviii.
5 Eric Hobsbawm, *Age of Extremes: The Short Twentieth Century, 1914–1991* (Penguin Books, 1994), p. 289 and pp. 289–95.
6 Andro Linklater, *Owning the Earth: The Transforming History of Land Ownership* (Bloomsbury, 2014), p. 328. One of the essential books on peasants is Eric R. Wolf's pointedly titled *Europe and the People without History* (University of California Press, 1982).
7 Seamus Deane, 'Expunged', *Dublin Review of Books*, March 2018, reviewing Breandán Mac Suibhne, *The End of Outrage: Post-Famine Adjustment in Rural Ireland* (Oxford University Press, 2017).
8 Carlo Levi, *Christ Stopped at Eboli* (Penguin Books, 2000), first published in Italian in 1945 and hugely influential way beyond Italy; Larry WolFf, *The Idea of Galicia: History and Fantasy in Habsburg Political Culture* (Stanford University Press, 2010).
9 John Berger, 'The Vision of a Peasant', in Teodor Shanin (ed.), *Peasants and Peasant Societies* (Penguin Books, 1987), p. 278.

1. The Vanishing

1 John M. Synge, *Travels in Wicklow, West Kerry and Connemara* ([1911] Serif, 2005).

2 Jonathan Bell, 'A Contribution to the Study of Cultivation Ridges in Ireland', *Journal of the Royal Society of Antiquaries of Ireland*, vol. 114 (1984).

3 Seamus Heaney, *North* (Faber and Faber, 1975).

4 Patrick Joyce, *Going to My Father's House: A History of My Times* (Verso, 2021).

5 Joyce, *Going to My Father's House*, pp. 312–14.

6 William Trevor, *The Hill Bachelors* (Viking, 2000).

7 Tim Robinson (ed.), *Connemara after the Famine: Journal of a Survey of the Martin Estate by Thomas Colville Scott, 1853* (Lilliput Press, 1995), p. xvii.

8 World Bank figures, 2020. World Bank information is also available at statista.com. One may go directly to World Bank Open Data, at https://data.worldbank.org/, accessed 24 July 2023; Hobsbawm, *Age of Extremes*, pp. 289–95, gives the proportion of total population numbers working in agriculture. World Bank information is on both the total populations and the proportion of the workforce in agriculture.

9 S. H. Franklin, *The European Peasantry: The Final Phase* (Methuen, 1969), is an excellent guide, with some especially interesting photographs.

10 Craig Taylor, *Return to Akenfield: Portrait of an English Village in the 21st Century* (Granta Books, 2006).

11 In Pierre-Jakez Hélias' wonderful peasant memoir, *The Horse of Pride: Life in a Breton Village* (Yale University Press, 1978).

12 The following figures record the agriculture sector in general, which covers hunting, forestry and fishing, as well as agriculture. However, the vast majority of those recorded are solely in arable agriculture.

13 Figures from Stephen Broadberry and Kevin H. O'Rourke (eds.), *The Cambridge Economic History of Modern Europe*, vol. 2: *1870 to the Present* (Cambridge University Press, 2010), and World Bank figures. These may be supplemented by those of the UN Food and Agriculture

Organization (their *Statistical Yearbooks* are especially useful), also the statistics of the International Labour Organization.

14 For EU data, I have consulted the website Eurostat: Statistics Explained.

15 Our World in Data is representative of the blizzard of statistics that are online. See especially Max Roser, 'Employment in Agriculture', Our World in Data, at https://ourworldindata.org/employment-in-agriculture, accessed 24 July 2023.

16 B. R. Roberts, 'Peasants and Proletarians', *Annual Review of Sociology*, vol. 16 (1990).

17 Sally Sargeson, 'The Demise of China's Peasantry as a Class', *Asia-Pacific Journal*, vol. 14, issue 13, no. 1, 1 July 2016.

18 On 'agropoly' see, for instance, https://econexus.info/publication/agropoly-handful-corporations-control-world-food-production, accessed on 24 July 2023, and https://waronwant.org/profiting-hunger/3-corporate-capture-agriculture.

19 Katy Fox, *Peasants into European Farmers? EU Integration in the Carpathian Mountains of Romania*, Freiburg Studies in Social Anthropology (Lit Verlag, 2011).

20 F. H. A. Aalen, Kevin Whelan and Matthew Stout (eds.), *Atlas of the Irish Rural Landscape* (Cork University Press, 2011), pp. 120 and 156–7.

21 Pierre Bourdieu, *The Bachelors' Ball* (Polity Press, 2008), Introduction, especially pp. 3–5.

22 Bourdieu, *Bachelors' Ball*, Chapter 4, 'The Peasant and his Body'. See also Appendix 1: Bibliographical Notes.

2. *What Is a Peasant?*

1 Chayanov's major work was *Peasant Farm Organization* (originally published in Russian in 1925) and *On the Theory of Non-Capitalist Economic Systems* were first translated into English in 1966 (Chayanov was influential for John Berger and Teodor Shanin).

2 A historians' argument about the emergence of modernity and within it individualism arises from the disputed claim that England was not a peasant society in the first place. The *locus classicus* of the debate is

Alan Macfarlane, *The Origins of English Individualism: The Family, Property and Social Transition* (Blackwell Publishing, 1978).

3 Hamish Graham, 'Rural Society and Agricultural Revolution', in Stefan Berger (ed.), *A Companion to Nineteenth-Century Europe, 1789–1914* (Wiley-Blackwell, 2009), p. 31.

4 Anne O'Dowd, *Spalpeens and Tattie Hokers: History and Folklore of the Irish Migratory Agricultural Worker in Ireland and Britain* (Irish Academic Press, 1991). This fine book is a fitting monument to the *spailpíní*.

5 Émile Guillaumin, *The Life of a Simple Man*, ed. Eugen Weber, rev. trans. Margaret Crosland (University Press of New England, 2012). The book was first printed in England in 1923 in a limited edition of one hundred copies, with commissioned woodcut illustrations.

6 For these pejorative usages, see the *Oxford English Dictionary*.

7 James Agee and Walker Evans, *Let Us Now Praise Famous Men* (Penguin, 2006).

8 Zvi H. Lipschitz, *Midor Ledor* (Warsaw, 1901), quoted in Mordechai Zalkin, 'Can Jews Become Farmers?', *Rural History*, vol. 24, no. 2 (2013). (The answer is that, in some cases, they did.)

9 Gil Ribak, 'Drunkards Lying on the Floor: Jewish Contempt for Non-Jewish Lower Classes', *AJS, Perspectives*, Spring 2020; Gil Ribak, *Gentile New York: The Images of Non-Jews among Jewish Immigrants* (Rutgers University Press, 2012).

10 In Joseph Roth's deeply loving portrayal of the Eastern Jews, *The Wandering Jews*, the age-old relationship, peasant–Jew, is revealed as far from one of mutual contempt. This is also evident in his great novel *Job*.

11 There is an excellent discussion of the Communist versions of folklore in Joanna Kordjak (ed.), *Poland – A Country of Folklore?* (Zachęta – Warsaw National Gallery of Art, 2016).

12 Neil Murphy and Keith Hopper (eds.), *The Short Fiction of Flann O'Brien* (Dalkey Archive Press, 2013), p. 44.

13 Samuel Beckett, *First Love* (Calder & Boyars, 1999), pp. 30–31.

14 Alain Corbin, *A History of Silence: From the Renaissance to the Present Day* (Polity Press, 2018).

15 In Robert James Scally's fine book *The End of Hidden Ireland: Rebellion, Famine, and Emigration* (Oxford University Press, 1995).

16 This paragraph owes much to Pierre Bourdieu, *The Bachelors' Ball* (Polity Press, 2008), Postscript: 'A Class as Object'.

17 Fernand Braudel, *Civilization and Capitalism, 15th–18th Century*, vol. 1: *The Structures of Everyday Life* (University of California Press, 1992), p. 510.

18 Jim Handy, ' "Almost Idiotic Wretchedness": A Long History of Blaming Peasants', *Journal of Peasant Studies*, vol. 36, no. 2 (2009).

19 John Berger and Jean Mohr, *Another Way of Telling: A Possible Theory of Photography* (Granta Books, 1989), pp. 106–8.

20 For other observations on time and tradition, see the Introduction to John Berger's *Into Their Labours* (Granta Books, 1992) and his essay 'That Which Is Held', in Geoff Dyer (ed.), *John Berger: Selected Essays* (Bloomsbury Publishing, 2001).

3. The Church of the Peasants: Society

1 Ignazio Silone, *Fontamara: A Novel*, trans. Eric Mosbacher, rev. Darina Silone (Cluny Classics, 2019), pp. 5–6, first published in Italy in 1949. See Silone's Foreword of summer 1930. The work is the first part of the Abruzzo Trilogy. The book was first published in English in 1934.

2 Stanislao G. Pugliese, *Bitter Spring: A Life of Ignazio Silone* (Farrar, Straus & Giroux, 2009).

3 Teodor Shanin (ed.), *Peasants and Peasant Societies* (Penguin Books, 1987).

4 *The Journal of Peasant Studies*, which is subtitled 'Critical Perspectives on Rural Politics and Development, 1973–Present'. Europe now takes a back seat, and the perspective is a strongly political economy one.

5 Teodor Shanin was born in Vilnius in 1930, to wealthy and highly educated Jewish parents (they owned a galoshes factory). His father was arrested by Stalin and the family exiled to Siberia and then to Samarkand (travelling there by cattle train). He was an ardent and then disillusioned Zionist and fought for Israeli independence in

Palestine. See Karen Gold, 'Peasants' Professor', *Guardian*, 10 September 2002.

6 For Europe alone, there is the seventeen-volume Belgian publisher Brepols' series *Rural History in Europe*, whose general editor is Gérard Béaur. More focused is the Brepols series *Rural Economy and Society in North-Western Europe, 500–2000*. In this series I have found these volumes very useful: Eric Vanhaute et al. (eds.), *Making a Living: Family, Income and Labour* (Brepols, 2012), and Bas J. P. van Bavel and Richard W. Hoyle (eds.), *Social Relations: Property and Power* (Brepols, 2010). However, the emphasis on peasant culture is limited in all these volumes.

7 The following is very useful: Marc Edelman, 'What is a Peasant? What are Peasantries? A Briefing Paper on Issues of Definition Prepared for the First Session of the Intergovernmental Working Group on a United Nations Declaration on the Rights of Peasants and Other People Working in Rural Areas', Geneva, 15–19 July 2013. The tendency in social definitions in recent years has been towards the inclusive, e.g., Jan Douwe van der Ploeg, *The New Peasantries: Struggles for Autonomy and Sustainability in an Era of Empire and Globalization* (Routledge, 2009).

8 B. R. Roberts, 'Peasants and Proletarians', *Annual Review of Sociology*, vol. 16 (August 1990).

9 This section is based on the work of the late Paul Ginsborg, a truly great historian of modern Italy, from whom I have in conversation learned much about peasant culture. Paul Ginsborg, *A History of Contemporary Italy: Society and Politics 1943–1980* (Penguin, 1990).

10 Carlo Levi, *Christ Stopped at Eboli* (Penguin, 2000), p. 12.

11 Ginsborg, *History of Contemporary Italy*, pp. 32–3.

12 F. G. Friedmann, 'The World of "La Miseria"', *Partisan Review*, vol. 20, no. 2 (1953).

13 Edward C. Banfield, *The Moral Basis of a Backward Society* (Free Press, 1958).

14 Friedmann, 'The World of "La Miseria"', quoted in Frank Cancian, 'The Southern Italian Peasant: World View and Political Behavior', *Anthropological Quarterly*, vol. 34, no. 1 (1961), p. 10.

15 Frank Cancian, *Un paese del Mezzogiorno italiano: Lacedonia (1957)*, ed. Francesco Faeta (Postcart, 2020).

16 On Basilicata, see also John Davis, *Land and Family in Pisticci* (Athlone Press, 1973).

17 Cancian, 'Southern Italian Peasant', p. 8.

18 Jerome Blum, *The End of the Old Order in Rural Europe* (Princeton University Press, 1978), Chapter 5 and especially p. 98. Blum's book is the classic in the field of serfdom studies, but suffers from the not unusual (and always irritating) espousal of the idea of the 'backward' peasant.

19 In this section, as well as the works in note 6 above, I have drawn on Werner Rösener, *The Peasantry of Europe* (Blackwell, 1994), and Tom Scott (ed.), *The Peasantries of Europe: From the Fourteenth to the Eighteenth Centuries* (Longman, 1998), including Scott's Introduction. There is an excellent critique of this volume in *The Journal of Peasant Studies*. There is also Henry Bernstein et al., 'Forum: Fifty Years of Debate on Peasantries, 1966–2016', *Journal of Peasant Studies*, vol. 45, no. 4 (2018). The essays in Stefan Berger (ed.), *A Companion to Nineteenth-Century Europe, 1789–1914* (Wiley-Blackwell, 2009) are very useful, as are those in Peter H. Wilson (ed.), *A Companion to Eighteenth-Century Europe* (Wiley-Blackwell, 2013).

20 Martine Segalen, *Fifteen Generations of Bretons: Kinship and Society in Lower Brittany, 1720–1980* (Cambridge University Press, 1991).

21 See table in Blum, *The End of the Old Order*, p. 437.

22 Richard Heath, *The English Peasant* ([1893] Cambridge University Press, 2011), another condemnation of the condition of the labourer; Joan Thirsk, *English Peasant Farming: The Agrarian History of Lincolnshire from Tudor to Recent Times* (Routledge, 1957). The reviews of this work at the time took 'peasant' to be a natural usage, none remarking at the word's use.

23 John-Paul Himka, 'Serfdom in Galicia', *Journal of Ukrainian Studies*, vol. 9, no. 2 (Winter 1984), p. 14, citing a work of Vasilii Kelsiev published in St Petersburg, 1868.

24 James R. Lehning, *Peasant and French: Cultural Contact in Rural France during the Nineteenth Century* (Cambridge University Press, 1995), p. 5.

25 Norman Davies, *God's Playground: A History of Poland*, vol. II: *1795 to the Present* (Oxford University Press, 2005), pp. 137–44.

26 As in the long memoir that forms the third volume of William I. Thomas and Florian Znaniecki, *The Polish Peasant in Europe and America* (Gorham Press, 1919), *Life Record of an Immigrant*.

27 For other perspectives on land in Poland, see Jan Kajfosz, *Magic in Popular Narratives* (Peter Lang, 2021), and Tomasz Rakowski, *Hunters, Gatherers, and Practitioners of Powerlessness: An Ethnography of the Degraded in Postsocialist Poland* (Berghahn, 2016).

28 Marcin Brocki, 'Landscapes of Memory – Narratives of Past Places', in Eva Näripea, Virve Sarapik and Jaak Tomberg (eds.), *Kohtja Paik/Place and Location VI* (Research Estonian Academy of Arts, 2008), pp. 221–2.

29 Pierre Bourdieu, *The Bachelors' Ball* (Polity Press, 2008), pp. 36–7.

30 It was taken in Gliwice County, and the photographer is Paul Schau. It is now in the collections of the Gliwice Museum.

31 Émile Guillaumin, *The Life of a Simple Man*, ed. Eugen Weber, rev. trans. Margaret Crosland (University Press of New England, 2012), Chapter VIII.

32 Sula Benet, *Song, Dance, and Customs of Peasant Poland*, with a Preface by Margaret Mead (Dennis Dobson, 1951).

33 As remarked in William I. Thomas and Florian Znaniecki's Introduction to *The Polish Peasant in Europe and America* (Dover Publications, 1958), vol. 1, p. 000.

34 George M. Foster, 'Peasant Society and the Image of Limited Good', *American Anthropologist*, vol. 67, no. 2 (April 1965), pp. 293–315.

35 John Berger, *Into Their Labours* (Granta Books, 1992), pp. xiv–xv.

36 Thomas and Znaniecki, *The Polish Peasant*.

37 Conrad M. Arensberg and Solon T. Kimball, *Family and Community in Ireland* ([first edition Harvard University Press, 1940], 3rd edn, CLASP Press, 2001). See the excellent long Introduction to the later edition by Anne Byrne, Ricca Edmondson and Tony Varley, 'Arensberg and Kimball and Anthropological Research in Ireland: Introduction to the Third Edition'. My thanks to Tony Varley for his help. The thoughtful and sympathetic review of Timothy W. Guinnane is worth seeing, and is free online at *Field Day Review*, itself a truly remarkable journal: Timothy W. Guinnane, 'Returns, Regrets and Reprints', *Field Day Review*, vol. 3 (2007).

4. *Lives: The House*

1 Robert Pogue Harrison, *The Dominion of the Dead* (University of Chicago Press, 2003). For a discussion of these themes, see also Patrick Joyce, *Going to My Father's House: A History of My Times* (Verso, 2021), pp. 260–61.

2 Luigi Pirandello, 'Requiem Aeternam Dona Eis, Domine!' The story is in vol. 3 of Pirandello's fifteen-volume series of short stories *Novelle per un Anno*, and was first published in his collection *La trappola* (*The Trap*) (Treves, 1915).

3 There is much information online these days about Irish farms and farm buildings, in particular at www.heritagecouncil.ie.

4 *The Spirit Level* (Faber, 1996).

5 Henry Glassie, *Passing the Time in Ballymenone*: *Culture and History of an Ulster Community* (O'Brien Press, 1982), Chapter 13.

6 There is a film about Henry Glassie called *Henry Glassie: Field Work*, directed by Pat Collins. There is also the foundational work of Emyr Estyn Evans, among many works, *Irish Folk Ways* ([1957] Routledge and Kegan Paul, 1969).

7 Glassie, *Passing the Time*, p. 338.

8 Joyce, *Going to My Father's House*, Chapter 2.

9 House plans are given by Glassie, *Passing the Time*, pp. 345–50.

10 Glassie, *Passing the Time*, p. 365.

11 There is a vast compendium of Polish house interiors (and some exteriors) photographed in the 1970s and 80s by Zofia Rydet: see Krzysztof Pijarski (ed.), *Object Lessons: Zofia Rydet's Sociological Record* (Warsaw Museum of Modern Art, 2017).

12 Regina Schulte, *The Village in Court: Arson, Infanticide, and Poaching in the Court Records of Upper Bavaria, 1848–1910* (Cambridge University Press, 1994).

13 Seán Ó Tuama and Thomas Kinsella (eds.), *An Duanaire, 1600–1900: Poems of the Dispossessed* (Foras na Gaeilge, 1981), p. 351.

14 This image is from the Polish National Digital Archive (Narodowe Archivum Cyfrowe), and has the merit of being free to use as the viewer wants, unlike the commodification of the image that now governs so many historical photographs.

15 Ignazio Silone, *Fontamara: A Novel*, trans. Eric Mosbacher, rev. Darina Silone (Cluny Classics, 2019), Introduction.

16 I draw heavily in this section on the English-language sources of William I. Thomas and Florian Znaniecki, *The Polish Peasant in Europe and America* (Dover Publications, 1958), discussed in the previous chapter, and on Sula Benet, *Song, Dance, and Customs of Peasant Poland*, with a preface by Margaret Mead (Dennis Dobson, 1951), 'The Home Circle' section. Benet wrote of the Poland she knew in the 1940s and 50s. She was a great admirer of Znaniecki. Also, Yvonne Kleinmann et al. (eds.), *Imaginations and Configurations of Polish Society* (Wallstein Verlag, 2017). There are also diverse English-language publications with material on peasants which I have consulted, especially *Eastern European Countryside*, and the *Acta Poloniae Historica* of the Institute of History, Polish Academy of Sciences.

17 Christine D. Worobec, *Peasant Russia: Family and Community in the Post-Emancipation Period* (Princeton University Press, 1991), see Chapter 15 on the subject. Sula Benet also edited and translated the very interesting *The Village of Viriatino: An Ethnographic Study of a Russian Village from before the Revolution to the Present* (Doubleday, 1970), first published in Moscow in 1953.

18 Stanley Brandes, 'Fascism and Social Anthropology: The Case of Spain under Franco', *Anthropological Quarterly*, vol. 88, no. 3 (2015). There was an affinity, if not direct connection or collusion, between Spanish anthropology and Fascism. I quote from Brandes: 'The culture concept, which linked particular territories to particular customs and ways of life, was in complete accord with the fascist division of society into named geographic entities, each with its own folklore, speech patterns, and popular forms of ritual and religion.' Class was neglected.

19 Among many stories in many books, there are, for example, David D. Gilmore, *The People of the Plain: Class and Community in Lower Andalusia* (Columbia University Press, 1980); Julian Pitt-Rivers (ed.), *Mediterranean Countrymen: Essays in the Social Anthropology of the Mediterranean* (Mouton, 1963); also his great *The People of the Sierra*, Introduction by E. E. Evans-Pritchard (Criterion Books, 1954); Joseph B. Aceves and

William A. Douglass (eds.), *The Changing Faces of Rural Spain* (John Wiley, 1976); Susan Tax Freeman, *Neighbors: The Social Contract in a Castilian Hamlet* (University of Chicago Press, 1970); Ruth Behar, *The Presence of the Past in a Spanish Village* (Princeton University Press, 1991). Comparison, and similarity, across Europe is especially rewarding in the case of João de Pina-Cabral, *Sons of Adam, Daughters of Eve: The Peasant World View of the Alto Minho* (Oxford University Press, 1986).

20 Tomasz Wiślicz, *Love in the Fields: Relationships and Marriage in Rural Poland in the Early Modern Age: Social Imagery and Personal Experience* (Tadeusz Manteuffel Institute of History, Polish Academy of Sciences, 2018) and his essay 'Dialectics of virginity: Controlling the Morals of Youth in the Early Modern Polish Countryside', in Satu Lidman et al. (eds.), *Framing Premodern Desires: Sexual, Attitudes Ideas, and Practices in Europe* (Amsterdam University Press, 2017).

21 James R. Lehning, *Peasant and French: Cultural Contact in Rural France during the Nineteenth Century* (Cambridge University Press, 1995), Chapter 5, on gender.

22 Martine Segalen, *Love and Power in the Peasant Family: Rural France in the Nineteenth Century* (University of Chicago Press, 1983). The book argued long ago against the stereotype of male dominance.

23 Rudolph M. Bell, *Fate, Honor, Family and Village: Demographic and Cultural Change in Rural Italy since 1800* (University of Chicago Press, 1979).

24 Émile Guillaumin, *The Life of a Simple Man*, ed. Eugen Weber, rev. trans. Margaret Crosland (University Press of New England, 2012).

25 [Jan Słomka], *From Serfdom to Self-Government: Memoirs of a Polish Village Mayor, 1842–1927*, trans. William John Rose (Minerva Publishing Co., 1941), from Chapter 1, 'Youth and Marriage'. Additional chapters were added in 1929. Parts of the book were reprinted in Alfred J. Bannan and Achilles Edelenyi (eds.), *Documentary History of Eastern Europe* (Twayne Publishers, 1970) and are available online.

26 [Słomka], *From Serfdom to Self-Government*, from Chapter 4, 'Arts and Crafts'.

27 I draw on the Introduction to Giovanni da Col and Andrew Shryock (eds.), *From Hospitality to Grace: A Julian Pitt-Rivers Omnibus* (HAU Books, 2017).

28 [Giovanni da Col and Andrew Shryock (eds.)], *From Hospitality to Grace.*

29 Benet, *Song, Dance, and Customs of Peasant Poland.* See note 16 above for information on Benet.

30 The information in this and immediate paragraphs is from Benet, *Song, Dance, and Customs of Peasant Poland*, pp. 207–28, in the section called 'The Child Grows Up'.

31 Ailbhe Nic Giolla Chomhaill, '"The Gifts of the Little People": The Ethos of the Gift in Traditional Irish Narratives of Fairies' (2016), copy provided by the author.

32 John Berger, 'The Eaters and the Eaten', in Geoff Dyer (ed.), *John Berger: Selected Essays* (Bloomsbury Publishing, 2001).

33 Berger, 'The Eaters and the Eaten', p. 371, 372–3.

34 A flood of light is thrown on the peasant body, if only for a small slice of peasant Europe, in William G. Pooley, *Body and Tradition in Nineteenth-Century France: Félix Arnaudin and the Moorlands of Gascony, 1870–1914* (Oxford University Press, 2019). I have benefited from discussions with Will Pooley. David Le Breton, *Sensing the World: An Anthropology of the Senses* (Bloomsbury Publishing, 2017) is invaluable.

35 And, after him, Bakhtin: see Mikhail Bakhtin, *Rabelais and His World* (Indiana University Press, 1984).

36 There is a fine contemporary description of the place of the bridal wagon in marriage ceremonies in Chapter 3 of Schulte, *Village in Court.*

37 Benet, *Song, Dance, and Customs of Peasant Poland*, p. 151.

38 Benet, *Song, Dance, and Customs of Peasant Poland*, pp. 145–79.

39 Benet, *Song, Dance, and Customs of Peasant Poland*, for this point and much information on old age, 'Declining Years', pp. 228–47.

5. The World: The Lark that Sees into Heaven

1 William I. Thomas and Florian Znaniecki, *The Polish Peasant in Europe and America* (Dover Press, 1958), vol. 1, pp. 205–206, 220, 221. For the

account which follows I draw on the book-length Introduction written by Znaniecki, in particular the section on religious and magical belief, pp. 205–88. The remarkable account of another peasant 'world view' to the Polish one, that of peasants in Portugal, can be compared with the account that follows here, even though it is of a later date. The fundamental similarities are great (the *casa*, the village/commune, religion and the spirits, envy, coping with evil): João de Pina-Cabral, *Sons of Adam, Daughters of Eve: The Peasant World View of the Alto Minho* (Oxford University Press, 1986).

2 Thomas and Znaniecki, *The Polish Peasant*, pp. 205–303. The work is a product of its time: it views world, spirit, God, as developmental, one emerging out of the other in a forward march, rather than, in practice, as constantly overlapping (though, in fact, the authors constantly, and fruitfully, contradict themselves in recognizing the very frequent co-presence of the three spheres). They identify a fourth sphere as well: mysticism, the tendency towards self-perfection and salvation. This involves a personal relation with the divinity, and often fights free of organized Christianity. The authors' demotion of mysticism makes little sense, however. For a modern corrective, there is Magdalena Zowczak, *The Folk Bible of Central-Eastern Europe* (Peter Lang, 2019), Chapter 1.

3 Thomas and Znaniecki, *The Polish Peasant*, Introduction, p. 226.

4 [Jan Słomka], *From Serfdom to Self-Government: Memoirs of a Polish Village Mayor, 1842–1927*, trans. William John Rose (Minerva Publishing Co., 1941), pp. 132–3, see also p. 225. There is much material on Polish peasant culture in Władysław Reymont's *The Peasants*, published originally between 1904 and 1909. It won Reymont the Nobel Prize for literature. When writing my book I only had access to the English translation of 1924, which I found so dated as to be unreadable. There is now a much better modern translation published by Penguin in 2022. There is also an animated film of the book, which I watched in a cinema in Stalin's Palace of Culture in Warsaw in late 2023, a fantastical representation of peasants being enacted within the confines of another fantasy, a palace dedicated to making peasants into workers.

5 [Słomka], *From Serfdom to Self-Government*, pp. 134 and 135–7.

6 Thomas and Znaniecki, *The Polish Peasant*, pp. 206, 215, 216.

7 Jan Kajfosz, *Magic in Popular Narratives* (Peter Lang, 2021), on the theory of magic, on order and chaos, and on peasant beliefs in Teschen Silesia.

8 Seamus Heaney, 'The Poet as a Christian', *The Furrow*, vol. 29, no. 10 (October 1978).

9 Kevin Williams, 'Can Religious Sceptics Celebrate Christmas?', *Irish Times*, 22 December 2018.

10 Heaney, 'The Poet as a Christian'.

11 William G. Pooley, *Body and Tradition in Nineteenth-Century France: Félix Arnaudin and the Moorlands of Gascony, 1870–1914* (Oxford University Press, 2019), pp. 6–7, on anger, and *passim* on the body; Laura Stark, *The Magical Self: Body, Society and the Supernatural in Early Modern Rural Finland* (Finnish Academy of Science and Letters, 2006); Eugen Weber, *Peasants into Frenchmen: The Modernization of Rural France, 1870–1914* (Stanford University Press, 1976), pp. 54–7.

12 Michel Foucault, *The History of Sexuality* (first volume, 1976), four volumes in various published forms, also *Discipline and Punish* (1975). Foucault also edited a remarkable book on peasants, *I, Pierre Rivière, Having Slaughtered My Mother, My Sister, and My Brother . . .: A Case of Parricide in the 19th Century* ([1973] University of Nebraska Press, 1982).

13 Berger, *Into Their Labours*, Introduction.

14 In Stith Thompson, 'Folktale Collecting in Ireland', *Southern Folklore Quarterly*, vol. 2, no. 2 (1938).

15 Ailbhe Nic Giolla Chomhaill, Sabhal Mòr Ostaig Spring Seminar Series 2021, 'Digital Folklore Archives as "Thick Corpuses": A Case Study of Text and Context in the Folklore of Maam Village, Co. Galway'. Paper sent me by Ailbhe, and there is also her account of the folklore collected at the Seanadh Farracháin National School by the Irish Folklore Commission in 1937–8, *An Chaora Ghlas* (An Cheád Eagran, 2016). Ailbhe writes mostly in Irish.

16 In email communication, June 2022.

17 It has a correspondingly grand title, in English translation, *The People: Their Customs, Way of Life, Language, Folk tales, Proverbs, Rites, Witchcraft, Games, Songs, Music and Dances*. For a completely exhaustive and authoritative account of Kolberg and his work there is the important

and highly active Oskar Kolberg Institute in Poznań. This has a considerable online presence. Kolberg's complete works are now available online in Polish. Kolberg is almost completely untranslated.

18 Kolberg was scrupulous in writing down what he heard, though he edited a good deal of it for publication. He also exemplified the prurience of his day about sexual matters. For a recent work on Kolberg, there is Elżbieta Millerowa and Agata Skrukwa, 'Oskar Kolberg (1814–1890)', in *Dzieje folklorystyki polskiej 1864–1918*, ed. Helena Kapełuś and Julian Krzyżanowski (Państwowe Wydawnictwo Naukowe, 1982).

19 There is an interesting interview about Kolberg, and a good deal else, online: for the interview, see Filip Wróblewski, 'A Hidden Treasure: Interview about Oskar Kolberg', *New Eastern Europe*, no. 4, 2014.

20 Henry Glassie, *Passing the Time in Ballymenone: Culture and History of an Ulster Community* (O'Brien Press, 1982), p. 576.

21 Glassie, *Passing the Time*, Chapter 2, 'Silence, Speech, Story'; Ray Cashman, *Packy Jim: Folklore and Worldview on the Irish Border* (University of Wisconsin Press, 2016), and also his *Storytelling on the Northern Irish Border: Characters and Community* (Indiana University Press, 2008).

22 Guy Beiner, *Remembering the Year of the French: Irish Folk History and Social Memory* (University of Wisconsin Press, 2007), p. 81, and his *Forgetful Remembrance: Social Forgetting and Vernacular Historiography of a Rebellion in Ulster* (Oxford University Press, 2018).

23 'Disenchantment' was discussed by Weber in his essay of 1919, 'Science as a Vocation', republished in *From Max Weber: Essays in Sociology* (International Library of Sociology), various editions.

24 Angela Bourke, *The Burning of Bridget Cleary: A True Story* (Pimlico Books, 1999), p. 000.

25 Angela Bourke, 'Inside History: Storyteller Éamon a Búrc and the "Little Famine" of 1879–1880', in Joep Leerssen (ed.), *Parnell and His Times* (Oxford University Press, 2021), p. 122.

26 Bourke, 'Inside History', p. 122.

27 Thomas and Znaniecki, *The Polish Peasant*, pp. 295–302.

28 John Berger, 'The Storyteller', in Geoff Dyer (ed.), *John Berger: Selected Essays* (Bloomsbury Publishing, 2001), pp. 365–9.

29 John Berger, 'The Storyteller', p. 369.

30 William G. Pooley, *Body and Tradition in Nineteenth-Century France: Félix Arnaudin and the Moorlands of Gascony, 1870–1914* (Oxford University Press, 2019), Chapter 4, 'Body Talk'.

31 Anna Engelking, *The Curse: On Folk Magic of the Word*, trans. Anna Gutowska (Institute of Slavic Studies, Polish Academy of Sciences, 2017). Engelking draws on the work of Joanna Tokarska-Bakir, which I employ in the next chapter, on religion.

32 See www.duchas.ie for the Irish Folklore Commission collection online. The reader can search for the plentiful examples under the heading 'stray sod'.

33 Nic Giolla Chomhaill, 'Digital Folklore Archives as "Thick Corpuses"'.

34 Seán Mac Giollarnáth was someone who collected from Mícheál Breathnach. His manuscript collection now forms part of Cartlann Ghaeltacht Chonamara (Connemara Gaeltacht Archives, at cartlann.ie). As a full- and part-time collector, Mac Giollarnáth collected a vast quantity of folklore in Joyce Country and the surrounding localities in counties Galway and Mayo. Proinnsias de Búrca, a schoolteacher from Tír an Fhia, Corr na Móna, in Joyce Country, also amassed an enormous local collection, upwards of 30,000 manuscript pages and a large body of tape recordings, which all form part of the National Folklore Commission collections. In an account entitled *Lucht Múinte an Sgéalaidhe* – 'The People Who Taught the Storyteller' – Mícheál Breathnach tells of the storytellers from whom he learned his trade as a young man.

35 Bourke, *The Burning of Bridget Cleary*; Diarmuid Ó Giolláin, *Locating Irish Folklore: Tradition, Modernity, Identity* (Cork University Press, 2000), and 'The Fairy Belief and Official Religion in Ireland', in Peter Narváez (ed.), *The Good People: New Fairylore Essays* (University Press of Kentucky, 1997). Also Diarmuid Ó Giolláin (ed.), *Irish Ethnologies* (University of Notre Dame Press, 2017).

36 Glassie, *Passing the Time*, p. 577, also pp. 602–3 and 664–5.

37 See http://irishhedgerows.weebly.com, accessed 31 July 2023.

38 The recordings were made in September 2018. These are catalogued at www.folklore.ie. There is also Diarmuid Ó Muirithe and Deirdre

Nuttall's *Folklore of County Wexford* (Four Courts Press, 1999), for earlier times.

39 Mártan John Mhailic Sheáin Leachlainn/Martin O'Halloran, *The Lost Gaeltacht* (Homefarm Publishing, 2020). Martin has also shared with me his vast genealogical work called 'Band of Cousins', based on the histories of local families in Cloghbrack and surrounding townlands. It is complete with the 'American cousins'. He and I seem to be related to a considerable portion of the population of the United States and Great Britain.

40 Leachlainn/O'Halloran, *The Lost Gaeltacht*, p. 41.

6. *God: I Have Created the Vermin and the Birds for People to Prosper*

1 This is from Appendix 1, on peasant religious piety, in Oskar Kolberg, *The Complete Works*, vol. 48: *Tarnów and Rzeszów Regions*.

2 Ernesto de Martino, *Magic: A Theory from the South*, trans. Dorothy Louise Zinn ([1959] Hau Books, 2015), p. 120.

3 [Jan Słomka], *From Serfdom to Self-Government: Memoirs of a Polish Village Mayor, 1842–1927*, trans. William John Rose (Minerva Publishing Co., 1941), p. 103.

4 Mircea Eliade, *The Sacred and the Profane: The Nature of Religion* (Harper Torchbooks, 1961), trans. Willard R. Trask, p. 164, and see also his *Images and Symbols: Studies in Religious Symbolism*, trans. Philip Mairet (Princeton University Press, 1991).

5 Klaus E. Müller, 'Concepts of Time in Traditional Cultures', in Jörn Rüsen (ed.), *Time and History: The Variety of Cultures* (Berghahn, 2007).

6 Mircea Eliade, 'Normality of Suffering', in his *The Myth of the Eternal Return: Cosmos and History* (Princeton University Press, 1971), trans. Willard R. Trask, pp. 95–102, at p. 98.

7 Ernesto de Martino, *The Land of Remorse: A Study of Southern Italian Tarantism*, trans. Dorothy Louise Zinn (Free Association Books, 2005), p. 136 (image at p. 137); originally published 1961. On de Martino's thought, there is Flavio A. Geisshueslero, *The Life and Work of*

Ernesto de Martino: Italian Perspectives on Apocalypse and Rebirth in the Modern Study of Religion (Brill, 2021).

8 De Martino's work spawned a great number of films, sound recordings and photographs of the local peasant religion and the culture it was embedded in. Contributions in the wake of de Martino, by, among others, Gianfranco Mingozzi, Diego Carpitella and Cecilia Mangini can be watched on YouTube, a remarkable turn of historical events indeed, though congruent I suppose with 'showing'. I discuss this further in Chapter 8.

9 Susan Sontag, *On Photography* (Penguin, 1979), p. 23.

10 Michaela Schäuble, 'Images of Ecstasy and Affliction: The Camera as Instrument for Researching and Reproducing Choreographies of Deviance in a Southern Italian Spider Possession Cult', *Anthrovision*, vol. 4, no. 2 (2016); de Martino, *The Land of Remorse*, p. 11, on the 'knot of contradictions' the photos present.

11 De Martino, *Magic*. Diarmuid Ó Giolláin makes productive use of de Martino in relation to Ireland: 'The Fairy Belief and Official Religion in Ireland', in Peter Narváez (ed.), *The Good People: New Fairylore Essays* (University Press of Kentucky, 1997).

12 De Martino, *Magic*, p. 123. For more on 'Lucanian' magic and southern Italian Catholicism, see de Martino, *Magic*, pp. 120–28. The difference between magic and religion is one of the 'continuity of moments', it is a scalar question. '[N]o matter how "high" religions are . . . they always contain a mythic-ritual nucleus.' The distinction between 'magic as a ritual "constraint" conducted by the magician, and religion as "submission" to a higher reality and a moral relationship with divinity, is in itself schematic and superficial, since even in the lowest ranks of magic ritual words and gestures draw their efficacy from the repetition of an exemplary myth'. Even the most elementary magic 'entails . . . a reintegration into values, otherwise it would be existential crisis and illness'.

13 Michael P. Carroll, 'Rethinking Popular Catholicism in Pre-Famine Ireland', *Journal for the Scientific Study of Religion*, vol. 34, no. 3 (September 1995).

14 Carlo Levi, *Christ Stopped at Eboli* (Penguin, 2000), quotations at pp. 11, 79. Levi was not able to leave his village of exile and so there are inevitable limitations to his reporting. There is also, on Sicily, Levi's *Words are Stones: Impressions of Sicily* (Modern Voices, 2005), originally published 1955.

15 Levi, *Christ Stopped at Eboli*, p. 79.

16 Markéta Luskačová, *Pilgrims* (Victoria and Albert Museum, 1983). This is now a collectors' item and hugely expensive.

17 My warm thanks to Markéta Luskačová for the chance to discuss her work with her personally.

18 Luskačová, *Pilgrims*.

19 [Słomka], *From Serfdom to Self-Government*, pp. 144–6.

20 Marysia Galbraith, 'On the Road to Częstochowa: Rhetoric and Experience on a Polish Pilgrimage', *Anthropological Quarterly*, vol. 73, no. 2 (April 2000).

21 Seamus Heaney, *Station Island* (Faber and Faber, 1984), p. 144.

22 Lawrence J. Taylor, *Occasions of Faith: An Anthropology of Irish Catholics* (University of Pennsylvania Press, 1995). I am grateful to Lawrence for our discussions on Irish religious faith.

23 Harry Hughes, *Croagh Patrick: Ireland's Holy Mountain* (Croagh Patrick Archaeological Committee, 2005). *Cruach* in Irish is a stacked-up hill.

24 Norman Davies, *God's Playground: A History of Poland*, vol. II: *1795 to the Present* (Oxford University Press, 2005).

25 Peter Brown, 'A Dark-Age Crisis', *English Historical Review*, vol. 88, no. 346 (January 1973), cited in Marina Warner, *Alone of All Her Sex: The Myth and Cult of the Virgin Mary* (Oxford University Press, 1976), an indispensable book. See also Peter Brown, *Treasure in Heaven: The Holy Poor in Early Christianity* (University of Virginia Press, 2005).

26 Anna Niedźwiedź, *The Image and the Figure: Our Lady of Częstochowa in Polish Culture and Popular Religion* (Jagiellonian University Press, 2010), and Cathelijne de Busser and Anna Niedźwiedź, 'Mary in Poland: A Polish Master Symbol', in Anna-Karina Hermkens et al. (eds.), *Moved by Mary: The Power of Pilgrimage in the Modern World* (Ashgate, 2009).

27 I draw in this section on Joanna Tokarska-Bakir, 'Why is the Holy Image "True"? The Ontological Concept of Truth as a Principle of Self-Authentication of Folk Devotional Effigies in the 18th and 19th Century', *Numen*, vol. 49, no. 3 (2002); Tomasz Wiślicz, *Earning Heavenly Salvation: Peasant Religion in Lesser Poland. Mid-Sixteenth to Eighteenth Centuries*, trans. Tristan Korecki (Peter Lang, 2020); also on Wiślicz's articles in *Acta Poloniae Historica*. The essays in John-Paul Himka and Andriy Zayarnyuk (eds.), *Letters from Heaven: Popular Religion in Russia and Ukraine* (University of Toronto Press, 2006) are very helpful.

28 From Oskar Kolberg, *The Complete Works*, vol. 48: *The Tarnów and Rzeszów Regions*. The volume was first published in 1910, after Kolberg's death, and a further, fuller edition by the Kolberg Institute in 1969. The section on religion was translated for me by Kasia Beresford, 2021.

29 On peasant religion I have drawn on parts of the classic work of Stefan Zygmunt Czarnowski (1879–1937), translated for me by Kasia M. Beresford.

30 Władysław Piwowarski, 'Continuity and Change of Ritual in Polish Folk Piety', *Social Compass*, vol. 29, nos. 2–3 (1982).

31 James Obelkevich, *Religion and Rural Society: South Lindsey, 1825–1875* (Clarendon Press, 1976); James Obelkevich et al. (ed.), *Disciplines of Faith: Studies in Religion, Politics and Patriarchy* (Routledge, 1987).

32 K. D. M. Snell, *Spirits of Community: English Senses of Belonging and Loss, 1750–2000* (Bloomsbury Publishing, 2016), and *Parish and Belonging: Community, Identity and Welfare in England and Wales, 1700–1950* (Cambridge University Press, 2006). My thanks to Keith Snell for our discussions on religion and peasants.

33 Marion Bowman, 'Vernacular Religion and Nature: The "Bible of the Folk" Tradition in Newfoundland', *Folklore*, vol. 114, no. 3 (December 2003).

34 Magdalena Zowczak, *The Folk Bible of Central-Eastern Europe* (Peter Lang, 2019).

35 Zowczak, *The Folk Bible*, pp. 15–17, 60–61 and 64, from the section 'Luckless Demiurge'.

36 Seamus Heaney, 'Weighing In', in his *The Spirit Level* (London: Faber and Faber, 1996).

7. Suffering and Its Redress: The Devil in Our Purses

1 Pierre-Jakez Hélias, *The Horse of Pride: Life in a Breton Village* (Yale University Press, 1978), pp. 17–19. The book was made into a film by Claude Chabrol.

2 Hélias, *The Horse of Pride*, p. 18, and Chapter 1 as a whole, on poverty.

3 Hugh Dorian, *The Outer Edge of Ulster: A Memoir of Social Life in Nineteenth-Century Donegal*, ed. Breandán Mac Suibhne and David Dickson (Lilliput Press, in association with Donegal County Council, 2000), p. 247. On people's fear of rent day, pp. 179–80, 24, 85, 192. There is a long and very fine Introduction by the editors. As always, I thank Breandán Mac Suibhne for his help.

4 '1892 Report of the Congested Districts Board for Joyce Country'. See UK Parliament, *Hansard*.

5 [Jan Słomka], *From Serfdom to Self-Government: memoirs of a Polish Village Mayor, 1842–1927*, trans. William John Rose (Minerva Publishing Co., 1941), pp. 45–7.

6 The story of the lost child is 'The Stranger', *An Strainséara*, in Máirtín Ó Cadhain, *The Quick and the Dead: Selected Stories*, edited and introduced by Louis de Paor (Yale University Press, 2021). The stories are translated from the Irish. Ó Cadhain is esteemed by many to be the greatest twentieth-century writer of Irish prose. His masterpiece is *Cré na Cille*, variously translated as *The Dirty Dust* and *Churchyard Clay*.

7 Christine D. Worobec, 'Death Ritual among Russian and Ukrainian Peasants: Linkages between the Living and the Dead', in John-Paul Himka and Andriy Zayarnyuk (eds.), *Letters from Heaven: Popular Religion in Russia and Ukraine* (University of Toronto Press, 2006).

8 On Heaney, see Sean Williams and Lillis Ó Laoire, *Bright Star of the West: Joe Heaney, Irish Song Man* (Oxford University Press, 2011).

9 Alexander Watson, *The Fortress: The Great Siege of Przemysl* (Penguin Books, 2020).

10 Ignazio Silone, *Fontamara: A Novel*, trans. Eric Mosbacher, rev. Darina Silone (Cluny Classics, 2019).

11 Rudolph M. Bell, *Fate, Honor, Family and Village: Demographic and Cultural Change in Rural Italy sine 1800* (University of Chicago Press, 1979).

12 Antonio Gramsci, *Selections from Political Writings, 1921–1926*, ed. and trans. Quintin Hoare (Lawrence and Wishart, 1978). Alastair Davidson, 'Gramsci, the Peasantry and Popular Culture', *Journal of Peasant Studies*, vol. 11, no. 4 (1984).

13 Bell, *Fate, Honor, Family and Village*, p. 33.

14 For the human suffering involved, see Yang Jisheng, *Tombstone: The Untold Story of Mao's Great Famine: 1958–1962* (Penguin, 2013).

15 See https://ourworldindata.org/famines.

16 Tim Robinson (ed.), *Connemara after the Famine: Journal of a Survey of the Martin Estate by Thomas Colville Scott, 1853* (Lilliput Press, 1995).

17 Robinson (ed.), *Connemara after the Famine*, p. xix.

18 James H. Tuke, *A Visit to Connaught in the Autumn of 1847*, 2nd edn (Charles Gilpin and John L. Linney, 1848), pp. 18–26.

19 Dorian, *Outer Edge of Ulster*, p. 238.

20 Robinson (ed.), *Connemara after the Famine*, p. 41. In the 1870s three members of the Joyce family of Cullaghmore, in Leenaun, owned 1,179 acres. In June 1927 the *Tuam Herald* reported that the Land Commission had taken over the estates of Thomas Walter Joyce and Theobald Paul Joyce, amounting to approximately 2,700 acres in the barony of Ross, my father's barony. A good deal of this land, it should be said, was mountain and bog.

21 Robert James Scally, *The End of Hidden Ireland: Rebellion, Famine and Emigration* (Oxford University Press, 1995), especially on the 'Defendants' as go-betweens and leaders.

22 I consider the case at more length in my *Going to My Father's House*, including James's responses.

23 Jarlath Waldron, *Maamtrasna: The Murders and the Mystery* (Edmund Burke, 1992).

24 A. P. W. Malcolmson, *Virtues of a Wicked Earl: The Life and Legend of William Sydney Clements, 3rd Earl of Leitrim (1806–78)* (Four Courts Press, 2008). This work is largely an apologia for Leitrim. Which is fair enough, but Leitrim's virtues were greatly outweighed by his vices, vices which were rooted in the assumption that the power over others that wealth brought was his by the right of Nature and of God. Imperialism is at bottom this assumption that one person has by right possession of another person's soul.

25 Dorian, *Outer Edge of Ulster*, p. 256.

26 The *locus classicus* of the moral economy idea is E. P. Thompson, 'The Moral Economy of the English Crowd in the Eighteenth Century', *Past and Present*, vol. 50, no. 1 (February 1971). However, Thompson writes of the 'crowd', which includes diverse social elements, and not just rural people in general or peasants in particular.

27 James C. Scott, *Weapons of the Weak: Everyday Forms of Peasant Resistance* (Yale University Press, 1985), on South-east Asian peasants.

28 Alain Corbin, *The Village of Cannibals: Rage and Murder in France, 1870*, trans. Arthur Goldhammer (Harvard University Press, 1992).

29 Corbin, *The Village of Cannibals*, p. 119.

30 Patrick Joyce, 'The Journey West', *Field Day Review*, vol. 10 (2014).

31 George Bolton, *A Short Account of the Discovery and Conviction of the 'Invincibles'* (Hodges, Figgis and Co., 1887). Pamphlet available online at http://opac.oireachtas.ie/Data/Library3/Library3/DCT131005.pdf.

32 E. J. Hobsbawm, *Primitive Rebels: Studies in Archaic Forms of Social Movement in the 19th and 20th Centuries*. This was first published, by Manchester University Press, in 1959.

33 Information in this section from *The Clements Papers: The Papers of the Rosshill Estate* at the Clements Archive in the Irish Manuscripts Commission, http://www.irishmanuscripts.ie. Also http://www.landedestates.ie, the University of Galway's website: A Database of Landed Estates and Historic Houses in Connacht and Munster, *c.*1700–1914. A. P. W. Malcomson (ed.), *The Clements Archive* is invaluable, at https://www.irishmanuscripts.ie/product/the-clements-archive/?attachment_id=6186&download_file=t03za61culqce. Also Mártan John Mhailic Sheáin Leachlainn/Martin O'Halloran, *The Lost Gaeltacht* (Homefarm

Publishing, 2020); J. F. Quinn, *History of Mayo* (Breandan Quinn, 1993; in five volumes) and William Edward Vaughan, *Landlords and Tenants in Ireland, 1848–1904* (Dundalgan Press, 1984).

34 Philip Gabriel Eidelberg, *The Great Rumanian Peasant Revolt of 1907: Origins of a Modern Jacquerie* (E. J. Brill, 1974), wording from the front cover.

35 'Na panskii roboti [On corvée labour]', in *Khodyly opryshky*, p. 45 (Pechatnia V. Golovina, 1868).

36 From John-Paul Himka, 'Serfdom in Galicia', *Journal of Ukrainian Studies*, vol. 9, no. 2 (Winter 1984); also by John-Paul Himka, *Galician Villagers and the Ukrainian National Movement in the Nineteenth Century* (Macmillan Press, 1988), p. 58.

37 Woodcut, probably by Henryk Dmochowski.

38 Michał Rauszer, *Bękarty pańszczyzny: Historia buntów chłopskich* (Wydawnictwo RM, 2020). Michał has generously shared his work on 1846 with me, translating many passages into English. My translator Kasia Beresford also worked on these passages. The English translation of the title of Michał's book is given as *Bastards of Serfdom*. There is also Tomasz Szubert, *Jakób Szela* (Wydawnictwo DiG, 2014); Wojciech Stanislawski, 'Szela, the Black Horse of Revolution', *Aspen Review*, 15 March 2017; Ewa Danowska, 'The Peasant Slaughter of 1846 in the Accounts of Father Jan Popławski of Niegowić', *Folia Historica Cracoviensia*, vol. 19 (2013); and Keely Stauter-Halsted, *The Nation in the Village: The Genesis of Peasant National Identity in Austrian Poland, 1848–1914* (Cornell University Press, 2015).

39 All quotations are from Rauszer, *Bękarty pańszczyzny.*

40 John Ball, sermon at Blackheath (12 June 1381), quoted in John Stow, *Annales, or, A Generall Chronicle of England* (1631).

41 Rauszer, *Bękarty pańszczyzny.*

42 See https://www.it.tarnow.pl/en/worth-seeing/other-interesting-places-in-tarnow-region/smarzowa-home-town-of-jakub-szela/, accessed 27 July 2023.

43 For an account of better-off Jews, including Jewish landowners, there is, in English, Joseph Margoshes, *A World Apart: A Memoir of Jewish Life*

in Nineteenth Century Galicia (Academic Studies Press, 2008). It shows how badly peasants were treated, worse than Jews, in the aftermath of the 1846 rising.

44 Stauter-Halsted, *The Nation in the Village.*

45 The most important peasant leader was Wincenty Witos, whose memoirs are not translated. He was three times prime minister of Poland. In English there is W. J. Rose, 'Wincenty Witos', *Slavonic and East European Review*, vol. 25, no. 64 (November 1946), also a good deal online.

46 Timothy Snyder, *Bloodlands: Europe between Hitler and Stalin* (Vintage, 2011), p. 29.

47 Snyder, *Bloodlands*, p. 181.

8. They Remember

1 See the ninth item in the list at https://www.unep.org/news-and-stories/story/10-things-you-should-know-about-industrial-farming, accessed 27 July 2023.

2 Anna Engelking, *Kołchoźnicy* (Mikołaja Kopernika University, 2012). The book is available free online on open access at https://wydawnictwo.umk.pl/pl/products/2552/kolchoznicy-antropologiczne-studium-tozsamosci-wsi-bialoruskiej-przelomu-xx-i-xxi-wieku. There is a long English-language résumé of the book within the body of the text, and all quotations are from that. I have benefited greatly from the help of Anna Engelking, also from some of her other works: 'The Myth of the Tower of Babel and Its Consequences', *Český lid*, vol. 102, no. 1 (2015); 'Between the Lord and the Jew: Some Remarks on the Identity Structure of Belarusian *Kolkhozniks* in the Late Twentieth and Early Twenty-First Centuries', *Acta Poloniae Historica*, vol. 109 (2014); 'Simple Hardworking Christian Folks, or the Self-Image of Contemporary Belarusian *Kolkhozniks*: An Anthropologist's Assessment of a Two-Decade Research Study', *East European Politics & Societies*, vol. 27, no. 2 (January 2013).

3 Anna Engelking is also the author of *The Curse: On Folk Magic of the Word*, trans. Anna Gutowska (Institute of Slavic Studies, Polish Academy of Sciences, 2017). Magdalena Zowczak, *The Folk Bible of Central-Eastern Europe* (Peter Lang, 2019) is apposite here too.

4 Engelking, *Kołchoźnicy.*

5 'One Costume, Three Countries', see FolkCostume&Embroidery blog, at http://folkcostume.blogspot.com/2011/03/one-costume-three-countries-nadbuzhansk.html?m=1, accessed 28 July 2023.

6 There are now umpteen books on social or collective memory. The founding father of the idea is Maurice Halbwachs: see his *On Collective Memory*, ed. and trans. Lewis A. Coser (University of Chicago Press, 1992).

7 John Berger, *Into Their Labours* (Granta Books, 1992), pp. xxi, xx.

8 Engelking, *Kołchoźnicy.*

9 The quotations are from the King James Bible, Chapter 3 of the Book of Genesis, on the Fall.

10 Engelking, *Kołchoźnicy.*

11 Anna Engelking, 'Die Kollektivierung als Gründungstrauma. Über die Identitätserzählung der belarussischen Kolchosbauern aus Sicht ethnographischer Feldforschung', in Magdalena Marszałek et al. (eds.), *Über Land. Aktuelle literatur- und kulturwissenschaftliche Perspektiven auf Dorf und Ländlichkeit* (transcript Verlag, 2017).

12 Especially in her remarkable '"Our Own Traitor".

13 Breandán Mac Suibhne, 'It Is 1970, and Two "Yanks" Have Moved to Donegal's Blue Stack Mountains', *Irish Times*, 17 April 2022.

14 Robert Bernen, *Tales from the Blue Stacks* (Penguin Books, 1978), and *The Hills: More Tales from the Blue Stacks* (Penguin Books, 1983).

15 John Berger, 'The Value of Money', in his *Pig Earth* (Writers and Readers, 1979).

16 Bernen, 'Sacrament of the Sick' (essay), in his *The Hills: More Tales*, p. 60.

17 Wiesław Myśliwski, *Stone upon Stone*, trans. Bill Johnston (Archipelago Books, 2010), p. 69.

18 Bernen, *The Hills: More Tales*, pp. 141–3.

19 Ibid., pp. 144–7.

20 Bernen, 'Two Lives' (essay), in his *The Hills: More Tales*, pp. 133–4.

21 David Le Breton, *Sensing the World: An Anthropology of the Senses*, trans. Carmen Ruschiensky (Routledge, 2017).

22 Ciaran Carson, *Last Night's Fun: A Book About Traditional Irish Music* (Jonathan Cape, 1996), pp. 82–3.

23 Carson, *Last Night's Fun*, p. 83.

24 The recording can be heard on YouTube, at the time of writing this, at https://www.youtube.com/watch?v=Sc619_aGOsgits, accessed 28 July 2023.

25 Carson, *Last Night's Fun*, p. 11.

26 Martin Hayes, *Shared Notes: A Musical Journey* (Penguin Books, 2022).

27 Timothy O'Grady and Steven Pyke, *I Could Read the Sky* (Harvill Press, 1997). My thanks to Tim O'Grady for our talks about these matters.

28 O'Grady and Pyke, *I Could Read the Sky*, pp. 68–9. Martin Hayes and Iarla Ó Lionáird, the great *sean nós* singer, have provided musical accompaniment to readings of O'Grady's book, as well as playing on the soundtrack of the film of the book. The pedigrees of all those involved in the old tradition are densely interwoven: Elizabeth ('Bess') Cronin, a renowned Cork *sean nós* singer whose singing was recorded by Alan Lomax, was Ó Lionáird's great-aunt. Ó Lionáird sang 'Casadh an tSugain' ('The Twisting of the Rope') in the 2015 film *Brooklyn*, based on Colm Tóibín's novel. Ó Lionáird has worked with Tony McMahon, another great accordionist. It was McMahon who recorded Joe Cooley's playing in 1973.

29 Angela Bourke, 'Singing at the Centre of a Life', *Journal of Music* (2023), at https://journalofmusic.com/focus/singing-centre-life, accessed 28 July 2023. She is reviewing a book on Heaney in Irish by Liam Mac Con Iomaire, *Seosamh Ó hÉanaí: Nár fhágha mé bás choíche* (Cló Iar-Chonnachta, 2007). The book includes a CD of Heaney singing. The quotation is from Liam Clancy, in *Seosamh Ó hÉanaí*, p. 229 .

30 Zbigniew Jerzy Przerembski, 'The *Muzykant* as a Product of Nature and Culture', *Interdisciplinary Studies in Musicology*, no. 8 (2009).

Professor Przerembski is the author of a large number of erudite books in Polish, including *Bagpipes: The History of the Instrument in Old Polish Culture* (2006).

31 Andrzej Bieńkowski is generally regarded as the leading Polish authority on peasant music, and is the author of *Ostatni Wiejscy Muzykanci: Odkrywanie Tradycji Mazowsza* (*The Last Country Musicians: Discovering the Tradition of Mazowsze*), 2nd edn (Muzyka Odnaleziona, 2012), with CD accompanying. Bieńkowski has many publications, all in Polish. As usual, there is a good deal free to listen to online.

32 Caroline Bithell and Juniper Hill (eds.), *The Oxford Handbook of Music Revival* (Oxford University Press, 2016). I am grateful to Caroline Bithell for the chance to discuss music revivals and Corsican peasant music with her. Catherine Bithell, *Transported by Song: Corsican Voices from Oral Tradition to World Stage* (Scarecrow Press, 2007). There is also the illuminating 'Traditional Music of Poland – Recorded in situ 1945–50', https://www.womex.com/virtual/folkers/various_artists/traditional_music_of_poland. For a traditional Polish singer, see 'Malec Anna: Music of Roztocze' on muzykaroztocza.pl, a repository of regional material, accessed on 31 July 2023.

33 At archive.culturalequity.org.

34 The recordings are available at the Lomax Digital Archive, https://archive.culturalequity.org/radio-shows/folk-music-italy-bbc.

35 Ruth Behar, *The Presence of the Past in a Spanish Village: Santa María del Monte* ([1986] Princeton University Press, 1991).

36 See above, Chapter 4, note 19, for references to complementary works on the peasants of Spain.

37 Behar, *Presence of the Past*, pp. 11–12, 39–40.

38 William A. Christian, Jr, *Person and God in a Spanish Valley* (Princeton University Press, revised edn, 1989); also Susan Tax Freeman, *Neighbors: The Social Contract in a Castilian Hamlet* (University of Chicago Press, 1970).

39 Behar, *Presence of the Past*, pp. 286–304.

40 Text translated from https://santamariadelcondado.com/urb-montesol/, accessed 31 July 2023.

41 Lorenzo Ferrarini and Nicola Scaldaferri, *Sonic Anthropology: Identity, Heritage and Creative Research Practice in Basilicata, Southern Italy* (Manchester University Press, 2020), pp. 6–7. Also there is Dorothy Louise Zinn, *Raccomandazione: Clientelism and Connections in Italy* (Bergahn, 2019). Zinn is also the translator and editor of de Martino.

42 Ferrarini and Scaldaferri, *Sonic Anthropology*, pp. 12, 174–5. For de Martino's original work on Colobraro, see Ernesto de Martino, *Magic: A Theory from the South*, trans. Dorothy Louise Zinn (HAU Books, 2015).

43 Ferrarini and Scaldaferri, *Sonic Anthropology*, pp. 64–5.

44 Ibid., p. 125.

45 'Human Suffering in Italy's Agricultural Value Chain', Oxfam Case Study, June 2018. Available at https://oxfamlibrary.openrepository.com/.

46 COLDIRETTI (Confederazione Nazionale Coltivatori Diretti–National Confederation of Direct Cultivators), https://www.coldiretti.it/.

47 Ella McSweeney and Holly Young, 'The Invisible Migrant Workers Propping Up Ireland's €4bn Meat Industry', *Guardian*, 28 September 2021.

9. *We Remember*

1 Walter Benjamin, 'A Small History of Photography', in *One-Way Street and Other Writings* (New Left Books, 1979), pp. 242–3, with Benjamin quoting a poem by Stefan George.

2 Walter Benjamin, 'Theses on the Philosophy of History', in *Illuminations* (Fontana, 1973), p. 000. The essay was written in early 1940, shortly before Benjamin's suicide as he fled Vichy France.

3 Benjamin, 'A Small History of Photography', p. 243.

4 Walter Benjamin, Thesis 2 of 'Theses on the Philosophy of History'.

5 I draw in this section as a whole on François Hartog, *Regimes of Historicity: Presentism and Experiences of Time* (Columbia University Press, 2017); François Hartog, 'Time and Heritage', *Museum International*,

vol. 57, no. 3 (2005). Hartog is in essence a historian of historical writing, not of time, related as the two are, however. The social history of contemporary time is not yet written. My comments on the subject are only a sketch.

6 Hartog, 'Time and Heritage', p. 16.

7 There is an excellent review of some of this new literature in Marcus Colla, 'The Spectre of the Present: Time, Presentism and the Writing of Contemporary History', *Contemporary European History*, vol. 30, no. 1 (February 2021).

8 Alvin Toffler, *Future Shock* (Bantam Books, 1970); Douglas Rushkoff, *Present Shock: When Everything Happens Now* (Penguin, 2013).

9 Hartog, 'Time and Heritage', p. 14.

10 Jean Baudrillard, *Simulacra and Simulation*, trans. Sheila Faria Glaser ([1981] University of Michigan Press, 1994), p. 000.

11 Hartmut Rosa, *Social Acceleration: A New Theory of Modernity*, trans. Jonathan Trejo-Mathys (Columbia University Press, 2013).

12 Sharon Macdonald, *Memorylands: Heritage and Identity in Europe Today* (Routledge, 2013).

13 I have in previous work written about this tyranny of the instant, relating it to the British sense of the past, British self-identity and the sense of being at home: Patrick Joyce, *Going to My Father's House: A History of My Times* (Verso, 2021), Chapter 11, 'Home'.

14 Agnes Heller, 'Where are We at Home?', *Thesis Eleven*, vol. 41, no. 1 May 1995.

15 W. G. Sebald, 'Campo Santo', in *Campo Santo* (Penguin Books, 2006), pp. 34–5.

16 Pierre Nora and Lawrence D. Kritzman (eds.), *Realms of Memory: Rethinking the French Past*, 3 vols. (Columbia University Press, 1996–8); Pierre Nora and David P. Jordan (eds.), *Rethinking France: Les Lieux de Mémoire*, 4 vols. (University of Chicago Press, 2001–10); Pierre Nora, 'Between Memory and History: *Les Lieux de Mémoire*', *Representations*, no. 26, 'Special Issue: Memory and Counter-Memory' (Spring 1989).

17 The UN established the Convention Concerning the Protection of the World Cultural and Natural Heritage in 1972. In the UK, the

organizations English Heritage and Historic England were established in 1983. In France similar bodies were set up in the 1970s and 1980s.

18 The subject is valuably considered in Nikolas Rose, *Powers of Freedom: Reframing Political Thought* (Cambridge University Press, 1999), and the large associated literature in the Foucauldian vein of 'governmentality'. I have written historical work partly in this vein.

19 John H. Falk and Lynn D. Dierking, *The Museum Experience* (Whalesback Books, 1992), introduced the 'interactive experience model' of learning into museum studies.

20 Philippe Hoyau, 'Heritage and "the Conserver Society": The French Case', trans. Chris Turner, in Robert Lumley (ed.), *The Museum Time-Machine: Putting Cultures on Display* (Routledge, 1988). In the same volume, see also Tony Bennett, 'Museums and "The People"'.

21 Robert Hewison, *The Heritage Industry: Britain in a Climate of Decline* (Routledge, 1987); Patrick Wright, *On Living in an Old Country: The National Past in Contemporary Britain* ([1985] Oxford University Press, 2009). My thanks to Patrick Wright for the chance to discuss this subject with him.

22 Sarah Farmer, *Rural Inventions: The French Countryside after 1945* (Oxford University Press, 2020).

23 Pierre Bourdieu, *The Bachelor's Ball* (Polity Press, 2008), p. 199.

24 I have drawn on the following, among other works: Andreas Huyssen, 'The Metamorphosis of the Museal: From Exhibitionary to Experiential Complex and Beyond', also Martin Hall, 'The Reappearance of the Authentic', both in Ayşe Gül Altınay, María José Contreras et al. (eds.), *Women Mobilizing Memory* (Duke University Press, 2019). See also Tony Bennett, *The Birth of the Museum: History, Theory, Politics* (Routledge, 1995); Tony Bennett and Patrick Joyce (eds.), *Material Powers: Cultural Studies, History and the Material Turn* (Routledge, 2010); Ivan Karp, Corinne A. Kratz et al. (eds.), *Museum Frictions: Public Cultures/Global Transformations* (Duke University Press, 2006). The Pitt-Rivers Museum's 2006 'Relational Museum' project combined the postcolonial and reflexive trends in museum creation. For the Pitt-Rivers Relational Museum project, see https://history.prm.ox.ac.uk/. See also

the Material World (https://materialworldblog.com/2009/01/the-relational-museum/) for the Pitt-Rivers initiative, 16 January 2006.

25 Gabriela Nicolescu, 'Art, Politics and the Museum: Tales of Continuity and Rupture in Modern Romania', PhD thesis, Goldsmiths College, University of London, 2015. The museum has a very lively journal called *Martor*, which covers much more ground than peasants alone.

26 See the Ministry of Culture website at https://president.gov.by/en/statebodies/the-ministry-of-culture, accessed 31 July 2023.

27 Lynn Hunt, 'Against Presentism', *Perspectives on History*, 1 May 2002.

28 Hartog's grim and pessimistic outlook is one I find congenial, but in other views the new configurations of time and of past and present take more optimistic forms, as in the influential Aleida Assmann, *Is Time Out of Joint? On the Rise and Fall of the Modern Time Regime*, trans. Sarah Clift (Cornell University Press, 2020).

29 St Augustine, *Confessions*, Book 11, Chapter 20, Heading 2.

30 It should be noted that 'peasant time' is also made up of linear dimensions, e.g., the life course of the person.

31 Laurent Olivier, 'The Business of Archaeology is the Present', in *Reclaiming Archaeology* (Routledge, 2013), p. 124; Laurent Olivier, *The Dark Abyss of Time: Archaeology and Memory*, trans. Arthur Greenspan (Rowman and Littlefield, 2015). The reader may want to pursue the new literature on time, and the following are illuminating: Marek Tamm and Laurent Olivier (eds.), *Rethinking Historical Time: New Approaches to Presentism* (Bloomsbury Publishing, 2019); Dan Edelstein, Stefanos Geroulanos and Natasha Wheatley (eds.), *Power and Time: Temporalities in Conflict and the Making of History* (University of Chicago Press, 2020). The literature on 'historical memory' is now vast. There are now eighty-two titles in the Palgrave Macmillan Memory Studies series alone.

32 T. S. Eliot, *Four Quartets* (Faber & Faber, 1944).

33 My thanks to Kate Arnold-Foster, Ollie Douglas and Isabel Hughes at the Museum of English Rural Life (MERL), Reading.

34 On English country life and the priority of nature over man, there are the rural 'classics': W. H. Hudson, *A Shepherd's Life* ([1910] Little Toller

Books, 2010); Adrian Bell, *Men and the Fields* ([1939] Little Toller Books, 2009) – the 2009 edition has a Foreword by Ronald Blythe; George Ewart Evans, *The Pattern under the Plough* ([1966] Little Toller Books, 2013).

35 Item MERL 61/242 is in fact discussed in an academic work of history: Hannah Newton, *Misery to Mirth: Recovery from Illness in Early Modern England* (Oxford University Press, 2018).

36 Patrick Kavanagh, *Collected Poems*, ed. Antoinette Quinn (Penguin, 2005).

37 Mark Teeuwen and John Breen, *A Social History of the Ise Shrines: Divine Capital* (Bloomsbury Publishing, 2018), and Hartog, 'Time and Heritage'.

38 My thanks for their help, and for their curatorial flair, to Anna Sak, Anna Sulich and Magdalena Zych at the Kraków Ethnographic Museum.

39 The story of post-war folk art is fascinating: see Joanna Kordjak (ed.), *Poland: A Country of Folklore?* (Zachęta – National Gallery of Art, 2016), for an account. Also the work of Ewa Klekot: for example, 'The Seventh Life of Polish Folk Art and Craft', *Etnološka tribina*, vol. 40, no. 33 (2010).

40 Karolina Pachla-Wojciechowska's online account of the book and its maker is at https://etnomuzeum.eu/zbiory/modlitewnik.

41 Erica Lehrer and Monika Murzyn-Kupisz, 'Making Space for Jewish Culture in Polish Folk and Ethnographic Museums: Curating Social Diversity after Ethnic Cleansing', *Museum Worlds*, vol. 7, no. 1 (July 2019).

42 Elizabeth Edwards and Janice Hart (eds.), *Photographs Objects Histories: On the Materiality of Images* (Routledge, 2004).

43 Susan Sontag, *On Photography* (Penguin, 1979), p. 15.

44 Sontag, *On Photography*, p. 23.

45 Markéta Luskačová, *Pilgrims* (Victoria and Albert Museum, 1983).

46 Pierre Bourdieu, *The Bachelors' Ball* (Polity Press, 2008).

47 John Berger and Jean Mohr, *Another Way of Telling* (Granta Books, 1989), pp. 37, 67.

48 On Greim at the Kraków Ethnographic Museum, see https://etnomuzeum.eu/kolekcje/fotografie-michala-greima.

49 John Berger, 'Understanding a Photograph', in his *Understanding a Photograph*, ed. Geoff Dyer (Penguin, 2013).

50 The photo album 'Sieradz and Surroundings' is available online at the website of the Ethnographic Museum in Kraków, see https://etnomuzeum.eu/zbiory/album-fotograficzny-sieradz-i-okolice, accessed 31 July 2023.

51 The most extensive introduction to Graeve is on the website of the Kalisz museum, www.info.kalisz.pl/biograf/graeve.html, accessed 31 July 2023. See also the website of the Regional Museum of Sieradz, https://www.poland.travel/en/museum/regional-museum-and-ethnographic-park-in-sieradz.

10. *Time Accumulates*

1 See Csaba Csaki and Zvi Lerman, 'Land and Farm Structure in Poland', Department of Agricultural Economics and Management, Center for Agricultural Economic Research, Discussion Paper no. 10.01, 2001, Hebrew University of Jerusalem, for the situation in Poland. *Teagasc National Farm Survey 2021: Preliminary Results*, at https://www.teagasc.ie/publications/2022/teagasc-national-farm-survey-2021.php, accessed 31 July 2023, for the Irish situation.

2 There is now an acclaimed novel on 1846, in Polish: Radek Rak, *Baśń o wężowym sercu albo wtóre słowo o Jakóbie Szeli* (*A Tale of a Serpent's Heart or a Second Word about Jakób Szela*) (Powergraph, 2019), and a film is mooted.

3 Rudolf Reder, *Bełżec* (Fundacja Judaica: Państwowe Muzeum Oświęcim-Brzezinka, 1999).

4 Robert Kuwałek, *Death Camp in Bełżec* (Państwowe Muzeum na Majdanku, 2016).

5 See https://polishhistory.pl/my-name-was-czeslawa-kwoka/. The site is an offshoot of the Polish History Museum, which is an offshoot of the Ministry for Culture and National Heritage. The message of the museum is heavily nationalist. The museum runs an educational programme called 'Patriots of Tomorrow'. One must, it seems, appreciate

the state's version of freedom to be a patriot, 'Freedom' and 'Poland' being synonymous in this version of reality. There is, however, no reason to doubt the story of Czesława Kwoka, and of thousands like her.

6 Juraj Buzalka, *Nation and Religion: The Politics of Commemoration in South-East Poland* (Lit Verlag, 2007).

7 Nicola Scaldaferri, 'Memories of the Final Journey', in *Carlo Levi a San Costantino Albanese*, Archivi della Basilicata, vol. 2 (Humboldt Books, 2020), pp. 55–71. My thanks to Nicola Scaldaferri for supplying me with an English-language version.

8 Patrick Joyce, 'Returning to London I', Verso Blog, at https://www.versobooks.com/en-gb/blogs/news/5260-returning-to-london-i, accessed 31 July 2023.

9 John McGahern, *That They May Face the Rising Sun* (Faber & Faber, 2009), p. 259.

10 McGahern, *That They May Face the Rising Sun*, p. 282.

11 Ronald Blythe, *Akenfield: Portrait of an English Village* (Allen Lane, 1969), from the account of the Teacher in the book.

12 Blythe, *Akenfield*, from the account of Sammy Whitelaw in the book.

Index